Islam and the State in Myanmar

Islam and the State in Myanmar
*Muslim–Buddhist Relations and
the Politics of Belonging*

edited by
Melissa Crouch

OXFORD
UNIVERSITY PRESS

OXFORD
UNIVERSITY PRESS

Oxford University Press is a department of the University of Oxford.
It furthers the University's objective of excellence in research, scholarship,
and education by publishing worldwide. Oxford is a registered trademark of
Oxford University Press in the UK and in certain other countries

Published in India by
Oxford University Press
YMCA Library Building, 1 Jai Singh Road, New Delhi 110 001, India

© Oxford University Press 2016

The moral rights of the authors have been asserted

First Edition published in 2016

ISBN-13: 978-0-19-946120-2
ISBN-10: 0-19-946120-1

Typeset in ScalaPro 10/13
by Tranistics Data Technologies, New Delhi 110 044
Printed in India by Rakmo Press, New Delhi 110 020

Contents

Foreword

It gives me great pleasure to write this foreword for a fascinating book edited by Melissa Crouch, which is the result of a workshop held in January 2014 on 'Islam, Law and the State in Myanmar', at the Faculty of Law, the National University of Singapore. I would like to congratulate her for publishing this timely book based on the research papers presented at the workshop. Her book will be remembered as a pioneering work in view of the current lack of reliable sources and empirical research on this subject.

One important aspect that this volume bears testimony to is the history of Islam in Myanmar. It is well-known that Islam has existed as one of the religions of the communities in Myanmar since as early as 800 AD. The Kings of the ancient kingdoms of Myanmar not only recognized Islam as a religion, but also appointed Muslims in the royal service and in special units of the army due to their loyalty in service. There are historical records that Myanmar Kings even appointed top Muslim scholars as chief Muftis (religious decision-makers) to decide disputes between Muslim subjects according to Islamic Law (*Shari'ah*).

This volume also captures the consolidation of Islamic Law through state institutions in Myanmar. During the colonial era, the British authorities, as was the practice in other Southeast Asian colonies, allowed the people of Myanmar to practice their own religious or customary laws in personal matters. Personal laws were officially recognized by the British colonial authorities through the Burma Laws Act 1898, section 13(1), which provides for

'Muhammadan law'.[1] I have argued, however, that the terms 'Muhammadan' and 'Muhammadan law' were mainly used by Anglo-Indian writers and also the British colonial government, and that the Burma Laws Act should be revised to replace the term 'Muhammadan law' with 'Islamic law' and 'Muhammadans' with 'Muslims'.

The Burma Laws Act is the authority for the legal existence of personal laws in Myanmar. In so far as Islamic law is concerned, the two main sources for the Myanmar courts to apply are legislation and case law. According to the common law tradition, Myanmar courts normally follow previous judicial decisions, and the courts in Myanmar have applied Islamic law to decide personal law disputes if the parties are Muslims. Islamic law can be found in the contents of every publication of Burma (Myanmar) Law Reports. However, it is noteworthy that if one of the parties is a Buddhist woman, the Buddhist Women's Special Marriage and Succession Act 1954 and the Buddhist Women's Special Marriage Act 50/2015 prevails over any contrary law.

Despite the restrictions and limitations felt by Muslims under the current government, Islamic law has long been recognized by the state as the personal law for Muslims in Myanmar during the colonial time, after independence, and even under the military regime. Today, Islam is one of the religions officially recognized in the 2008 Constitution of the Republic of the Union of Myanmar.[2] However, due to recent widespread violence against Muslims in Myanmar, as captured in several of the chapters in this volume, there are serious concerns that Muslims will not be able to practise their own religion freely or apply their own personal law any more. It is hoped that the Government of Myanmar will continue to

---

[1] For Muslims, these terms may be considered misnomers and derogatory because they never call themselves as Muhammadans. The Holy *Qur'an* clearly prescribes the name of the religion as 'Islam' and the people who profess Islam as 'Muslims'. See *Al-Qur'an*, 2: 128, 2: 132, 5: 3. See Khin Maung Sein, *The Islamic Law as Applied in Myanmar*, third ed., Yangon: Ywet Sain Sarpay, 2014, 2–4.

[2] The Constitution of the Republic of the Union of Myanmar, 2008, Article 362.

practise the tradition of allowing Muslims in the country to freely practise their religion and recognize Islamic law to be applicable in courts if the parties are Muslims.

This book is a significant and timely contribution to our understanding of Muslim communities in Myanmar, and it will provide a solid foundation for future research in this area.

Abdul Ghafur Hamid (U Khin Maung Sein)
International Islamic University Malaysia
Kuala Lumpur
February 2015

Preface

Note on Terminology

In 1988, the name of the country was officially changed by the military junta from 'Burma' to 'Myanmar'. In this volume, the country is generally referred to as 'Burma' when referring to pre-1988, and 'Myanmar' for the period since 1988. This also applies to the names of states and towns, such as Rangoon/Yangon, that were officially renamed in 1988.

In terms of personal names, the Burmese do not usually have a family name but honorific titles are commonly used. In this volume, terms that appear include *Daw* (aunt) for an older woman, and *U* (uncle) for someone older. It must be noted that it is very common for Burmese Muslims to have two names—a Burmese name (or one common to an ethnic nationality of Myanmar) and a Muslim name. In this text, Burmese Muslims who are discussed are usually introduced by both names, and then the most common name they are known by is used after that.

A particular challenge this volume confronts is consistency in terminology used by Burmese Muslims. There is no standard spelling for Islamic words and phrases in Myanmar, for example *Musalin* or *Mutsalin*, *Mohamedin* or *Muhatmadan* may be used. This volume has sought to use the most common spelling of these terms wherever possible, while acknowledging other common spellings where necessary.

The currency in Myanmar is the kyat (K). The official exchange rate at the time of publication was approximately 970 kyat to US$1.

In citing Burmese-language sources, this volume follows the Romanisation system based on the BGN/PCGN 1970 agreement. The names of well-known government institutions (such as the Pyidaungsu Hluttaw) and Burmese places and towns have been cited according to the most commonly accepted English spelling (which may not necessarily be consistent with the Romanization system). Where Burmese-language sources are cited, the translation of the title is indicated in brackets. Occasionally, some Burmese language sources have both an English and Burmese title; in these cases the original English title has been retained and is not included in brackets.

A note on the compilation of this volume: the introductory chapter provides an overview and starting point on the topic. Yet the book is not necessarily designed to be read from cover-to-cover, and so each individual chapter contains some reference to the history and context relevant to their topic.

Abdul Ghafur Hamid (U Khin Maung Sein)
International Islamic University Malaysia
Kuala Lumpur
February 2015

Acknowledgements

The idea for this publication emerged in 2007 when I was preparing for a talk on the resettlement of the Burmese Muslim refugees to Melbourne to be presented at a conference organized by the National Centre of Excellence for the Study of Islam, at the University of Melbourne, Australia. As I began to research the practices and history of the Burmese Muslim community, I was struck by the basic lack of empirical resources and scholarly publications available. Over the following years, through my involvement with organizations that supported the refugee community from Myanmar (including Burmese Muslims) in Melbourne, I resolved that one day I would find a group of scholars to begin a new field of research in this area.

That opportunity finally came seven years later in 2014. In January 2014, I organized a workshop on *Islam, Law and the State in Myanmar*, which was hosted at the Centre for Asian Legal Studies, Law Faculty, the National University of Singapore. The participants included Burmese scholars as well as experts from academic institutions in America, Europe, Southeast Asia, and Australia. The workshop was interdisciplinary and included perspectives from anthropology, history, political science, international relations, law, religious studies, and Islamic studies. In addition, the workshop was attended by a diverse group of Muslims from Myanmar living in Singapore, including Kaman Muslims, Karen Muslims, Shan Muslims, Chinese Muslims, Burmese Muslims, and Rohingya, thanks to the enthusiasm of Saw Clo Say. Their contribution greatly enriched the workshop, and I would like to thank them for making it a truly unique and memorable experience.

The workshop and this edited volume would not have been possible without significant institutional support. I am extremely grateful to Professor Andrew Harding, Director of the Centre of Asian Legal Studies at the Law Faculty, the National University of Singapore, for his generous support and enthusiasm for this project. Thank you for allowing me to indulge in an interdisciplinary project, despite the fact that there was less 'law' in the final volume than I had originally hoped. I would like to thank Regana Mydin, event organizer extraordinaire, and her team for the incredible work they put into the organization and administration of the conference.

I am grateful to the speakers and authors for their invaluable contributions, and for taking the risk to present them at such a conference, despite security concerns and the sensitive nature of the subject matter at this particular time in Myanmar's political history.

I would like to express my appreciation to the two anonymous reviewers who generously provided extensive comments and suggestions on the draft manuscript. I am also grateful to Oxford University Press for taking on this project, and for their wonderful assistance and professional support in the publishing process.

As always, the intellectual debt that I owe to my former PhD supervisors, Professor Tim Lindsey and Dr Amanda Whiting, continues to linger on. I would like to thank them both for opening my eyes to a lifetime of research on Southeast Asia, and for introducing me to the art of academic editing through the *Australian Journal of Asian Law*. I still recall the heated discussions over whether a comma should go after 'and'. Although I do not recall who won the debate, I am left with the impression of the importance and challenge of good editing.

It is difficult to find a way to express my thanks to the many friends I have made along the way. I would like to thank Ma Maw Maw and Ma Sandar for their help in Myanmar. I am also grateful to Clark Lombardi for his contribution to the workshop and for his incisive comments at the conclusion of the workshop that captured the deep emotion and fragility of the situation at the time.

I must also express my personal thanks to the Burmese Muslim community in Melbourne and to the leaders of the Burmese Muslim Community Association in particular, who are the reason I embarked on this project in the first place. I hope that you will be able to visit your village in Karen State again one day and find the acceptance in your country that you long for. I am also grateful to the Burmese Muslims I have come to know, who live in Singapore, Thailand, and Myanmar, for their generous hospitality and friendship. Thank you for trusting me with this information, which I hope will be of benefit in promoting understanding about your community, its rich past and its future welfare.

This volume aims to pioneer research from what is largely a blank slate, and so it is inevitably limited in the scope of what it can achieve. I hope that it will provide a basis from which a whole range of other research projects, including historical, empirical, and ethnographic studies, can expand in the future. May this be the beginning of new scholarly perspectives on the Muslim communities of Myanmar, which can illuminate both academic and policy approaches on Islam and the State in the region.

Abbreviations

AAPP	Assistance Association of Political Prisoners
ABMC	All Burma Muslim Congress
ABSDF	All Burma Student Democratic Front
ABYMA	All Burma Young Monks Association (*Yahanphyu Aphwe*)
AFPFL	Anti-Fascist People's Freedom League
AIPMC	ASEAN Inter-Parliamentary Myanmar Caucus
AMIRO	All Myanmar Islamic Relief Organisation
ARIF	Arakan Rohingya Islamic Front
BBS	Bodu Bala Sena
BLR	*Burma Law Reports*
BLT	*Burma Law Times*
BMA	Burmese Muslim Association
BMCA	Burmese Muslim Community Association
BMSA	Burma Muslim Student Association
BSPP	Burma Socialist Programme Party
CMRTF	Cholia Muslim Religious Trust Fund
CMU	Ceylon Moor's Union
CoI	Commission of Inquiry
CPB	Communist Party of Burma
CPC	Criminal Procedure Code
DHRP	Democracy and Human Rights Party
DIAC	Department of Immigration and Citizenship
ECHO	European Commission's Humanitarian aid and Civil Protection department, formerly European Community Humanitarian Aid Office

FBO	Faith-Based Organizations
FRC	Foreign Registration Certificate
GCC	Gulf Cooperation Council
GPM	Global Peace Mission Malaysia
IGLP	Institute for Global Law and Policy
INGO	International Non-Government Organizations
IOR	India Office Library and Records
IRAC	Islamic Religious Affairs Council
IRW	Islamic Relief Worldwide
JeI	Jamaat-e-Islami
JHU	Jathika Hela Urumaya (National [Sinhala] Heritage Party)
JIMMA	*Journal of the Institute of Muslim Minority Affairs*
KNDP	Kaman National Development Party
KNLD	Kaman National League for Democracy (later renamed KNPP)
KNPP	Kaman National Progressive Party (earlier known as KNLD)
KNU	Karen National Union
LBR	Lower Burma Rulings
LRC	Law Reporting Committee
LTTE	Liberation Tigers of Tamil Eelam
MA	Muslim Aid
MRF	Myanmar Resources Foundation
MLR	*Myanmar Law Reports*
MSF	Médecins Sans Frontières, also known as Doctors Without Borders
NAML	North Arakan Muslim League
MMES	Myanmar Muslim Educational Society
NLD	National League for Democracy
NDPD	National Democratic Party for Development
NMA	National Minorities Alliance
NUS	National University of Singapore
OIC	Organization of Islamic Conference
PAM	Patriotic Association of Myanmar (*Amyo Ba-tha Tha-tha-na Ka-kwaè-saung-shauk-ye Apwè*, abbreviated *Ma-Ba-Tha*)
PAS	Pan-Malaysian Islamic Party (Partai Islam Se-Malaysia)

PJS	People's Judicial System
PKS	Prosperous Justice Party (Partai Keadilan Sejahtera, Indonesia)
PMI	Indonesian Red Cross (Palang Merah Indonesia)
PWD	Public Works Department
RDT	Rangoon Development Trust
RNDP	Rakhine Nationalities Development Party
RPF	Rohingya Patriotic Front
RSD	Refugee Status Determination
RSO	Rohingya Solidarity Organization
SLMC	Sri Lanka Muslim Congress
SRIC	State Religion Inquiry Committee
TBBC	Thailand Burma Border Consortium
UBR	Upper Burma Rulings
UN	United Nations
UNCP	United National Congress Party
UNHCR	United Nations High Commission for Refugees
UNOCHA	UN Office for the Coordination of Humanitarian Affairs
USDA	Union Solidarity and Development Association
YCDC	Yangon City Development Council
YMA	Young Monks Association (*Thathana Mamaka*)
YMMA	Young Men Memon Association
YMJ	Yangon Memon Jamaat

Introduction

Islam and the State in Myanmar
MELISSA CROUCH

This edited volume explores the relation between Islam and the state in Myanmar from both an empirical and comparative perspective. It provides an informed and scholarly response to contemporary issues facing the Muslim communities of Myanmar by furthering knowledge of the dynamics and the interaction between state institutions, government policies and Muslim communities. This volume addresses the lacuna of informed and contemporary scholarship in this area. This is important because recent events demonstrate a profound lack of understanding about Muslims and Islam in Myanmar. For example, a gap between local discourse and international rhetoric has surfaced in debates over the anti-Muslim violence that began in Rakhine State in 2012 but spread to most major towns across Myanmar. This is most evident in comments directed at Daw Aung San Suu Kyi, member of parliament and of the National League for Democracy (NLD), and her response to the situation. From the side of the Myanmar government, there have been repeated attempts to discredit her because of her alleged links to and sympathy for Muslims in Myanmar. On the other hand, the international community has expressed profound disappointment, and at times, outrage, concerning Daw Suu's perceived failure to speak out in support of Muslims and the Rohingya in particular. I give this example not as a reflection on Aung San Suu Kyi or the policies of the NLD, but as an example that illustrates both the gulf in local and international perceptions about Muslims, as well as a misunderstanding of the Muslim community in Myanmar.

In order to build a new body of scholarship on the Muslims of Myanmar, this volume is broadly oriented around a series of questions about the politics of belonging and how Muslims interact with, or distance themselves from, the state in a Buddhist-majority society. It explores how Muslims understand their own identity and their position in relation to the state, how we can conceptualize the relation between Muslim communities and the state in Myanmar, and what function and position religious institutions have in Muslim communities in Myanmar. This volume also examines how government policies affect the status and freedom of Muslims, and the agency and influence that Muslims have in this period of transition in Myanmar.

Further, this volume investigates the way the state has regulated the Muslim community, and the implications of state policies for Muslims. This relates to a wide range of issues such as marriage, divorce, and inheritance; Islamic education; places of worship; the role of religious leaders; as well as broader social issues such as the rapid growth in communications technology, and access to employment opportunities. The chapters in this volume consider how the state regulates the practice and expression of Islam, and how this has varied during different political and military regimes in Myanmar. It considers how the state has legitimized its policies and the extent to which it has enforced these regulations and laws. This leads to broader questions about whether the approach of the state towards Muslims is similar to or different from the way in which it regulates other minority groups or the way in which other countries in the region deal with minority Muslim communities.

This volume aims to reinvigorate scholarship on Islam in Myanmar, to explore the diversity within the Muslim community, and to bring a scholarly perspective and insight into complex issues raised by the position of Muslims where they form a minority in states across Asia. It brings together a range of scholars from Burma Studies to Islamic studies, from a diverse array of disciplines—religious studies, international relations, political science, history, Islamic studies, law, and anthropology. Importantly, it also features a number of chapters by Muslim scholars from Myanmar, some based in Myanmar while others are based abroad, and who represent a diverse range of ethnic backgrounds.

This book has been preceded by a preface from Professor Abdul Ghafur Hamid, who is the leading Burmese professor on Islamic law. Previously a lecturer at the law departments of the University of Yangon, East Yangon University and Mandalay University, he is currently a professor at the International Islamic University, Malaysia. He is the author of a book on Islamic law (in Burmese), which was revised and republished in 2014 by the Islamic Religious Affairs Council in Myanmar.

The volume begins in Chapter 1 with an overview of the literature on Islam and Muslims in Myanmar that is designed to orient readers to this emerging area of research. Crouch identifies four key areas for inquiry, illustrating the importance of these areas with profiles from her own field research. She challenges scholars to participate in and contribute to this new area of inquiry in a way that is both conscious to avoid stereotypes of Islam and Buddhism, while also ensuring that the Muslims of Myanmar are not studied in isolation but are incorporated into global discussions about the past and present dynamics between Islam and the state.

Colonialism and the Law

Part I reconsiders past histories of Muslims and their interactions with the colonial state, in order to understand and provide a deeper reflection on the present. In his presentation at the workshop for this volume, Keck noted a striking comparative example: a historian would not be taken seriously today if he wrote a history of the United States that excluded the Jews or the African American community. He used this example to criticise existing histories of Burma, which have been written with little or no reference to the Muslim community, effectively writing Muslims out of the history of Burma. Keck's work seeks to redress this bias. Building on his thesis of Muslims as an invisible minority (Keck 2009), in his chapter on 'Reconstructing Trajectories of Islam in British Burma', Keck argues that British colonial discourse on Muslims effectively separated 'Burmese' from 'Islam'. Keck considers the ways in which the Muslim communities—specifically the Panthay of China and Indian Muslims—provided a critical link to Burma's two most important neighbours, China and India. Keck explains British interest in the Panthay in economic terms as an expression of British desire at the time for a new trade route and the expansion of economic opportunities for Burma. In turning to Indian Muslims, he considers the profiles of several Indian Muslim elites in order to highlight the contribution they made to society during the colonial period. His chapter suggests that only by considering the connection between China, India and Islam as part of the history of Myanmar can we begin to reimagine the multicultural foundations of modern Myanmar.

The subsequent chapter by Crouch on 'Personal Law and Colonial Legacy' studies the practise of Islamic personal law as a site of interaction between Muslims and the state legal system. She traces the origins and development of Islamic personal law in Myanmar, and considers it in the light of constitutional changes on religious freedom. In contrast to the scholarship of Hooker and Yegar, she argues that while Islamic personal law in Myanmar may once have been 'artificial', this is no longer necessarily the case. Instead, she suggests that we need to reorient our inquiry to consider how and why Muslims seek to access Islamic personal law through the general courts in Myanmar. She also demonstrates that Islamic personal law is in many ways a reflection of broader trends in legal system in Myanmar, which was largely cut and pasted from British India.

Everyday Experiences

Part II contains three chapters and each offer a wealth of new empirical data on the lived, local experiences of Muslim communities in Myanmar. These chapters provide rich insights into the everyday politics of belonging. Farrelly focuses on 'Muslim Political Activity in Transitional Myanmar', which offers the first analysis of the dynamics of Muslim engagement in the political arena in recent decades. Coming at a critical time in Myanmar's electoral history, Farrelly deftly captures the nature and extent of Muslim political participation and the particular geographical concentration in Rakhine State. He recognizes that the handful of political parties that primarily rely on a Muslim supporter base are active in northern Rakhine State, and that even non-Muslim political parties such as the military-backed Union Solidarity and Development Party (USDP), have several Rohingya members of parliament. This is consistent with the broader trend in Myanmar politics whereby political parties affiliate along ethnic, rather than religious, lines. His chapter clearly demonstrates that Muslim political participation in Myanmar has nothing to do with 'Islamist' politics, in terms of an agenda to introduce Islamic law, as it is understood in other parts of Southeast Asia. That is, when compared to regional neighbours such as Malaysia's Pan-Malaysian Islamic Party (Partai Islam Se-Malaysia, PAS) or Indonesia's Prosperous Justice Party (Partai Keadilan Sejahtera, PKS), the Muslim-based political parties in Myanmar do not share a similar Islamic ideology. At most, these parties in Myanmar may be brave enough to publicly advocate for equal rights for all citizens, and perhaps even for Muslims in particular, but there is no evidence at all to suggest they seek to further state policies on Islam.

Farrelly highlights that Muslims have been significantly worse off in terms of political representation post 2011, due to the barrier created by campaigns of anti-Muslim sentiment. Through a focus on three political parties, he captures the tensions among them in the 2010 elections, where several seats for the Rakhine State Hluttaw were closely contested. This led to lodging of complaints against the USDP to the Union Election Commission, although not surprisingly these were later dismissed. His chapter also points to the complicity of the government in the marginalization of Muslims from public life and government policies, and how it has only fostered deeper resentment against Muslim communities in Myanmar. For example, the Election Commission has enforced discriminatory policies by rejecting the use of the term 'Rohingya'. Further, the fact that the situation for the Rohingya is so politically sensitive that Muslim representatives of the USDP have not attended parliamentary sessions since 2012 is a dire indication of the informal methods of exclusion of Muslims from public participation and debate.

The chapter by Beyer, 'Houses of Islam: Muslims, Property Rights, and the State in Myanmar', focuses on the particular story of one Shiite Muslim family from the Kalai Memon community, in order to illustrate broader trends and challenges in urban property regulation in Myanmar. She highlights the essential social services that this tight-knit community provides for its members, as well as its focus on helping the poor. Her anthropological approach to the complex challenges of property regulation demonstrates the issues facing many

Muslim communities based in downtown Yangon today. Housing prices have risen dramatically, yet communities wish to remain living in proximity to the mosque and community buildings, given the difficulties of gaining permission to build a new mosque.

The third chapter in this section by Phyu Phyu Oo, 'Muslim Women's Education in Myanmar', provides a series of original insights based on both field research and her personal experience as a woman growing up in the Indian Muslim community in urban Myanmar. Phyu Phyu Oo charts the ways in which social, cultural, and religious norms in Myanmar inhibit the potential of Muslim women in terms of their educational and career prospects. She provides an important contribution to our understanding of Muslim women in Myanmar. She is careful to note the general divide between Indian Muslim communities and Burmese Muslim communities in their attitudes towards women and their role in society. Her chapter also highlights the problems inherent in the current system of state education as well as the lack of access to quality education, which is clearly not only experienced by Muslim women in Myanmar. The fact, for example, that women are often required to obtain a higher score than men for certain university degrees highlights the systemic discrimination that exists in the current government education system. Yet Phyu Phyu Oo aptly captures the particular barriers to accessing education which Muslim women face, while emphasising the potentially positive role that Islamic religious leaders, parents, and the government could play in reversing this situation in order to empower Muslim women.

Uncertainty, Security, and Violence

In Part III, this volume turns to the darker side of the everyday lived experiences of Muslims to consider the very real humanitarian, security, and safety concerns. Nyi Nyi Kyaw, in 'Islamophobia in Buddhist Myanmar: The 969 Movement and Anti-Muslim Violence', offers an incisive account of the foundations and motivations of the radical 969 Buddhist movement, which espouses an anti-Muslim agenda. The chapter reminds us that we cannot study Muslims in isolation, but must consider their relations with non-Muslims in Myanmar, specifically Buddhists. Nyi Nyi Kyaw seeks to go beyond populist discussions and explanations for the violence that has occurred against Muslims since 2012, and the 969 Movement in particular. He highlights the paradox that, while it is generally accepted in Myanmar that monks must not be involved in politics officially, the reality is that due to their high social position, they have often influenced national politics throughout Myanmar's history. He demonstrates that the motivations and inspiration for the 969 Movement are not new, and that strong anti-Indian and anti-Muslim sentiment is clearly evident since colonial times. He explains the power behind 969 as a symbol that appeals to Burmese Buddhist sensibilities and builds on existing practices. He also shows the way in which monks affiliated with the 969 Movement have defined the 969 symbol in direct contrast to Islam and the 786 symbol, often used on Muslim shops and signs in Myanmar. This demonstrates how previously benign and internal religious symbols can be used for anti-religious propaganda, and raises questions about how a purely internal religious symbol becomes a rallying point for 'anti-religious' sentiment.

The second chapter in this section by Schissler, 'New Technologies, Established Practices: Developing Narratives of Muslim Threat in Myanmar', takes a critical approach to the study of information technology and its contribution to religious violence, taking the July 2014 conflict between Muslims and Buddhists in Mandalay as a starting point. He uses the example of Buddhist perceptions of Muslims to explore both past practices of communication under the military regime, and the future potential of the expansion of internet access, mobile phone usage and social media platforms such as Facebook. He demonstrates the distrust which official media channels are usually met with—as typified in the *New Light of Myanmar*, which still evinces a heavily censored government agenda—and how this has amplified the role that trusted friends and family members play in validating information and rumours. His chapter highlights the ways in which new forms of technology that are now becoming accessible across Myanmar may, at times, exacerbate existing anti-Muslim sentiment and stereotypes, while also holding the potential to reinforce a more inclusive and peaceful democratization process.

The third chapter in this section by Schonthal, 'Making the Muslim Other in Myanmar and Sri Lanka', advances a convincing argument as to why Sri Lanka is a crucial point of comparison for Myanmar, through an analysis of the 969 movement and Sri Lanka's most active Buddhist nationalist group, the *Bodu Bala Sena* (Army of Buddhist

Power). At a broader level, both countries provide for the recognition of Buddhism in the Constitution. Both have an ethnically diverse Muslim community who have experienced growing tensions and opposition from militant Buddhist groups. Schonthal considers the ways in which identity may be imposed on Muslim communities or asserted by Muslim communities. He notes the overlap between religion and ethnicity, where in Sri Lanka today to be Muslim is both a reference to one's ethnicity and religion, in a similar way that to be Muslim in Myanmar often assumes that one cannot be Burman. Schonthal considers the way in which legal discourse has structured and restricted what Islam and being Muslim means in Myanmar. His chapter highlights the importance for scholars to think both comparatively and regionally in order to enhance understanding of Muslims of Myanmar and those who would oppose them.

In a separate chapter, 'The Global and Regional Dynamics of Humanitarian Aid in Rakhine State', Cook considers the response of aid organizations, particularly faith-based organizations, to the humanitarian crisis of displacement in Rakhine State. His point of departure is the Myanmar government's decision in early 2014 to expel international NGOs from Rakhine State after concerns of bias, in particular accusations against MSF, which it has rigorously and publicly denied. Cook acknowledges the different approaches or kinds of Muslim-based aid organizations, and the challenges that all aid organizations, regardless of religious affiliation, face in Rakhine State. While the challenges for the Rohingya community are not new, the response to displacement since 2012 has seen an increase in the involvement of Muslim countries and Muslim INGOs, which often operate with respect for traditional sovereignty norms of non-interference in domestic affairs. In his examination of the present dynamics between Myanmar and Bangladesh in terms of aid, Cook demonstrates that any solution will clearly require cooperation between Muslims and Buddhists and therefore will be a test of Muslim–Buddhist relations in the region.

The volume concludes with a reflection from Clark B. Lombardi, based on his insightful comments made at the workshop held in January 2014. I am under no illusion that this volume represents a small beginning on a large and complex task that lies ahead. It is my hope that others may respond to this challenge of rethinking Islam–state relations from the perspective of Myanmar.

1 Myanmar's Muslim Mosaic and the Politics of Belonging

MELISSA CROUCH

The purpose of this chapter is to provide an introduction to the study of Islam and Muslim communities in Myanmar.[1] I use the 2014 census as a lens through which to open up the politics of belonging in Myanmar. I then provide an overview of what I call Myanmar's 'Muslim mosaic', that is, its diverse Muslim communities. I suggest that we need to move away from rigid ethnic-based assumptions of Muslims in Myanmar and reframe our understanding along a continuum of relations with the state, in terms of those who identify first or equally as 'Burmese' at one end, and those who identify primarily as 'Muslim' at the other.

[1] This research builds on my previous experience since 2007, working with various non-government organizations that supported the settlement of the Burmese refugee community in Southeast Melbourne. It is informed by field trips to the refugee camps on the border of Thailand and Myanmar, where approximately 10 per cent of the refugee population are Burmese Muslim (Thailand Burma Border Consortium 2010). It is also based on field research and interviews with a range of Muslim religious leaders, community leaders, lawyers and youth in Shan State, Mandalay, Naypyidaw and Yangon, Myanmar; and also in Singapore. In order to ensure anonymity, some names mentioned in this chapter have been changed. I am grateful to Nick Farrelly and Kerstin Steiner for their comments on an earlier version of this chapter. All errors in this chapter are my own.

I then identify important areas for research, while acknowledging both the contribution and the limits of the existing literature. The chapter is structured around four key themes: the history of the Muslim community; Muslim political engagement; Muslims in times of crisis; and the practice of Islam. My argument in this chapter is that, in order to reconceptualize our understanding of the politics of belonging, and expand our understanding of Muslims and the state in Myanmar, we need to make two movements. First, we need to move away from characterizing Islam in Myanmar as violent, hostile, and strange. To place Islam on an equal footing with other religions in Myanmar will inevitably require displacing Buddhism from its privileged position as a supposedly 'non-violent' religion.[2] Second, the study of Islam in Myanmar needs to be acknowledged and welcomed into wider academic discussions on Islam and the state. That is, rather than studying Muslims in Myanmar as an isolated anomaly, in this era of transnational Islam we need to reposition the study of Muslims in Myanmar as an important 'Islamic crossroads' between Central, South, and Southeast Asia.

The Politics of Belonging

There is no data available on the number of Muslims in Myanmar today. It is estimated that between four to ten per cent are Muslim, and that the Muslims of Myanmar are a diverse group both ethnically and geographically. Even if the conservative government estimate of four per cent of the population is correct, this means that Myanmar has a higher percentage of Muslims in comparison to both Thailand and the Philippines (Selth 2004), two other minority Muslim contexts in the region. Yet in comparison to scholarship on the Muslim communities of Thailand[3]

---

[2] The literature by Jerryson and Juergensmeyer (2010), Jerryson (2011), and Elverskog (2013), emphasizes the reality of and capacity for violence in Buddhism, although this approach has not yet informed inquiry in the context of Myanmar.

[3] On Muslims of Thailand, see for example Leyland 2009; Funston 2010; McCargo 2012; Jerryson 2011; Liow 2009; Brown 2013.

and the Philippines.[4] we have only a fraction of the research available on Muslims in Myanmar.

In March 2014, a national census was held in Myanmar in cooperation with the United Nations Population Fund. Provisional results did not reveal religious affiliation, but the population was found to be 50 million (far short of previous government figure of 60 million). An estimated 1.2 million (including many in Rakhine State) were not included in the 2014 census (Republic of the Union of Myanmar 2014). The census provides one lens through which to understand the politics of belonging for Muslims in Myanmar, particularly because of its connection to the project of nation-building and nationalism in this time of political transition.

In the lead up to the census, the international commentary primarily focused on the categories the state would use to identify a person's religion and ethnicity, and specifically whether the government would allow a person to list their ethnicity as 'Rohingya'. But there was little coverage of Muslim responses to the census. This is despite the fact that, in the lead up to the census, there was fierce discussion and debate *within* Muslim communities about what categories they wanted to use to define their religious and ethnic status in the census. Representatives of the Muslim community were summoned to Naypyidaw for 'consultations' with government officials in regards to the census. Yet in these meetings they were often told how the census would work and what categories would be used, rather than invited to give their opinion on what categories would be most appropriate.[5]

Prior to the census, the debates within Muslim communities varied on what they should list in the ethnicity column. Many in the Burmese Muslim community were confused: they did not want to list their ethnicity as 'Burman', even if they were part Burman, because they felt that the ethnic category 'Burman' may be conflated by the government with 'Buddhists'. That is, to be Burman in Myanmar is to be Buddhist. Many who identify themselves as 'Burmese Muslims'

---

[4] On the Muslims of the Philippines, the only major anthropological work is Kiefer 1972; on the politics of daily resistance see McKenna 1978; and on Islamic law in the Philippines see Hooker 1984: 231–45; Stephens 2011; Chiarella 2012.

[5] Interview with Muslim community leaders, Yangon, 13 November 2013.

felt that this may allow the numbers of Buddhists in the country to be overestimated. On the other hand, as Muslims who take pride in their 'Burmeseness'—from the use of Burmese language, to Burmese clothing and culture, and ancestry—they wanted recognition that they belong to Myanmar too. As a compromise, some leaders from the Burmese Muslim community were advocating for the use of the term 'Pathi' Muslim. This is a term that was used during the period of the kings. There have been attempts to revive the term in the past, such as in the 1960s, in order to carve out specific recognition for this group (Yegar 1972: 7, 80; 2002: 20). The term Pathi is today used in a broad sense to encompass Muslims of many different ethnic backgrounds in Myanmar, but particularly those with part-Burman ancestry (or ancestry of another recognized race in Myanmar).

From another perspective, some religious leaders from the Indian Muslim community issued a fatwa (Islamic legal opinion) to their community members to instruct and guide them on how to list their identity in the census. Part of their emphasis was simply that Muslims should not be afraid or hesitant to list their religious identity on the census. Some Indian Muslim leaders informed their followers that it was haram (forbidden) for a Muslim to fail to list his or her true religion on the census. Different debates again were held within the minority Shiite community, with some Islamic religious leaders from Yangon advising that all Shiites should list themselves as 'Mogul Shia' on the census, although some Muslim Shiite leaders from Mandalay disagreed. Like the Burmese Muslim resurrection of the term 'Pathi', the use of 'Mogul Shia' was also an attempt to revert back to past categories—in this case the reference to Muslims who had migrated from the Mogul empire—in order to recreate and redefine their future as a community in Myanmar. There were also some Muslim organizations, such as the Kaman National Development Party, that announced they would conduct an independent census of their community (in this case, Kaman Muslims) to ensure they were not undercounted by the Burmese government and to combat any concerns that foreigners had obtained Burmese identity cards Kaman ethnic nationality by bribing officials (Narinjara 2013). This short insight into broader debates surrounding the 2014 census points to the more complex debates at the heart of how the state identifies and limits the public identity of Muslims, and the importance of equally considering how Muslims want to be identified by the state.

Myanmar's Muslim Mosaic

The anti-Muslim violence since 2012 has both exposed the limits of our understanding of Muslims from Myanmar, and the politics inherent in the categories used to define them. While Muslims in Myanmar have generally been categorized along ethnic lines (see, for example, Selth 2003; 2004), I argue that we can also consider Muslims in terms of their degree of affiliation or the manner in which they engage with the state.

Accommodating the State

On one end of the spectrum there are those who identify first as 'Burmese', and it is a sense of 'Burmeseness'—in terms of their language, dress, and customs—that pervades and shapes their practise of Islam and their relations with the state. This includes the Zerbadi/ Zerbadee,[6] that is, those who are of mixed descent, whose grandparents were usually of an Arab, Persian, or Indian father and Burman mother. They may also refer to themselves as simply 'Burmese Muslims' or 'Pathi' (explained above). The term 'Zerbadi'[7] was used during the colonial era and appears in court documents and census data. For example, in 1911 there were 59,729 'Zerbadis' recorded, and by 1931, this number rose to 122,705 (Mahajani 1960: 29), although the categories that the British used for Muslims in the various census conducted were inconsistent. Even in the 1930s, however, the Burmese Muslims had lobbied the government not to use the term 'Zerbadi' but instead to use the term 'Burmese Muslim' in the census, because Zerbadi had negative connotations, and is widely perceived to be a derogatory term (Yegar 1972: 64). They felt that the term

---

[6] Burmese Muslims generally dislike this term because it is derogatory and has negative connotations. In 1891, a population census taken by the British used the term 'Zerbadee' for Burmese Muslims. In 1941, the use of the term 'Zerbadee' was replaced with the term 'Burmese Muslim': Myo Win 2011.

[7] For the most comprehensive discussion of the possible origins of the term Zerbadi, see Yegar 1972: 33–4. Thant Myint U (2007: 51) claims that the word Zerbadi is derived from Persian word 'zir-bad', meaning 'below the winds', a reference to Southeast Asia.

'Burmese Muslim' also allowed them to identify with, and emphasize their connection to, the country of Burma and the movement for
independence (Mahajani 1960: 23). At times, Burmese Muslims have
been referred to by the demeaning term '*kala*'.[8] This term has even
been used by some political leaders, such as General Ne Win during
the socialist era[9], and more recently by some local media when referring to the Rakhine conflict of 2012–13.

In terms of status and occupation, many Burmese Muslims were
well-known as public intellectuals, prominent members of government, civil servants, and business persons (Chakravarti 1971: 125). Yet
most of our knowledge of Burmese Muslims only reaches up until
the 1960s, before the full effects of Ne Win's socialist regime, and
the post-1988 rule of the military junta. In contrast to the pre-1962
era, over the last few decades very few Muslims have entered the civil
service, and those that have managed to get in have often remained
in low positions, due to the difficulties of obtaining a promotion. In
Myanmar today, it is common for Muslims to work as small-scale
traders in private business, although there are some prominent
businessmen who own construction companies, hotels and other
businesses.

In terms of their customs, Burmese Muslims are notable for their
insistence and emphasis on Burmese culture, at times over Islamic traditions and teachings, and this has been a cause of tension with other
Muslim communities (Yegar 1972: 57–67). Since independence, some
Muslims have worked hard to create a 'Burmese Muslim' identity by,
for example, supporting Muslim women wearing traditional Burmese
dress and leaving their head uncovered. These efforts are reflected
in signs in some community buildings that specifically emphasize
their 'Burmeseness'. For example, the Islamic Centre of Myanmar,
an organization known for its comparatively tolerant outlook, has a
centre in downtown Yangon where a sign visible inside the entrance

---

[8] Yegar (1972: 6–7) provides the most useful review of the term *kala/kula*.
Many others have also tried to define its precise origins, yet it may have come
from multiple sources, such as the Sanskrit word *kula* (caste man), the term
kala (black man): Chakravarti 1971: 11.

[9] Noted by Huxley, 1990: 250, quoting Address to the Central Committee
of the Burma Socialist Programme Party (BSPP) Forward, 8 October 1982.

to the main room states that one of the key aims of the centre is to educate the Muslim community about the teachings of Islam in a way that is consistent with Burmese culture. It adds that this is to be done 'without gender discrimination', which is presumably a reference to the fact that the Burmese Muslim community insists that its women can and should wear Burmese clothing. This is considered to be contrary to what is permissible for Muslim women to wear according to traditional Islamic teachings.

The most prominent supporter of the 'Burmese Muslim' identity is the Islamic Religious Affairs Council (IRAC). The IRAC began in 1954, founded by U Khin Maung Lat, a politician and religious leader. It has 'consultative status' with the Ministry of Religious Affairs,[10] alongside four other national Islamic organizations.

Of all Muslims in Myanmar it is Burmese Muslims who generally have the closest affiliation with state actors, institutions, and local culture, and identify themselves as 'Burmese' (although not necessarily ethnically 'Burman'). Aside from Burmese Muslims, there are Muslims who identify ethnically as one (or often more than one) national race of Myanmar and therefore as part of the Myanmar state. The Kaman Muslims are one group recognized by the government,[11] and most speak Arakanese. The history of the Kaman has been traced to the period of the Burmese kings when the Kaman served as archers (Yegar 2002: 24). One Kaman Muslim who attained a prominent position in the independence period was U Si Bu, a judge who sat on the trial of the assassination of General Aung San, among other cases. There is no scholarship on the Kaman to date, although the Kaman have risen to public consciousness due to the fact that the serious

[10] The Ministry of Religious Affairs in Myanmar was formed in 1989 (Matthews 1995). It is a poorly funded ministry in contrast to other departments (and in contrast to the Ministry of Religion in Indonesia, which is one of the most well-funded departments). Further, unlike in Sri Lanka, the Ministry of Religious Affairs in Myanmar only represents Buddhism and does not have a separate representative for Muslims, although it provides a nominal amount of funding to five Islamic organisations.

[11] There are several other ethnic groups that are Muslim, such as the Myedu, who claim that they used to be recognized on the government list of ethnic groups, but have since been taken off the list.

violence in Rakhine State in 2012 and 2013 also affected the Kaman community there.

Challenging the State

At the other end of the spectrum of Islam–State relations are Muslims who identify either with an ethnic group other than a recognized race of Myanmar, or who would perceive their identity as 'Muslims' of greater importance than, or at least equal to, their ethnic identity (as non-Burmese). The primary example here is the Indian Muslim community. The Indian Muslim communities in Myanmar today are much smaller than they were at the height of the colonial period. Between 1963 and 1967 alone, an estimated 300,000 Indians (most Muslim) were forced to flee Burma (Yegar 2002: 52), with little but the clothes on their back and a nominal amount of cash. Often Indians in Burma have been studied as a 'problem' and as a people group 'foreign' to Burma (for example, Khin Maung Kyi 1993; 2006). The status of Indian Muslims, particularly in terms of their role in the colonial economy, has been frequently discussed, although usually in the context of Indians generally and not Muslims specifically (Adas 1974; Chakravarti 1971; Taylor, 1993; Tin Maung Maung Than 1993; Mya Than 1993; Mahajani 1960; Egreteau 2011). There is a need to go beyond the negative stereotype of Indians and to consider the contemporary dynamics of the Indian Muslim community. The chapter by Phyu Phyu Oo (this volume) begins to take scholarly inquiry in new directions as she considers the position of Indian Muslim women and attitudes towards education for women.

A second group whose identity is perceived as a challenge by the state are the Rohingya,[12] who are referred to by some non-Muslims in Myanmar as 'Bengalis'. While the Rohingya insist that they should be recognized as a national race of Myanmar, the government has

---

[12] For research on the Rohingya, see Yegar 2002: 19–72; Yegar 1972: 95–105; Selth 2004: 111–14; Fealy and Hooker 2006: 269–71. I acknowledge that the term Rohingya is contested, and that many in northern Rakhine State may not necessarily identify themselves as such. Yet in the absence of an alternative, and in recognition of the fact that many do identify themselves as Rohingya, I continue to use the term here.

consistently failed to include them in its infamous list of 135 national races. The human rights situation for the Rohingya, who primarily live in northern Rakhine State where they form a majority in at least two townships near the border of Bangladesh, has been of particular concern to both scholars and advocacy groups over the past few decades (see for example Yegar 2002; Islam 2007; Selth 2003). The history of Muslims who today identify themselves as Rohingya in what is now known as Rakhine State dates back to the ninth century, and there are records from at least the thirteenth century onwards demonstrating their presence in the region (Yegar 1972: 1–17; 2002: 19–20). The situation of the Rohingya has raised acute concerns of statelessness, humanitarian aid, irregular migration and citizenship (discussed further below).

Muslims in Myanmar may also identify with a range of other ethnic groups and fall somewhere in the middle of the continuum of Islam–State relations. There are a small number of Panthay[13] or Chinese Muslims, who mainly live in north east Burma (Yegar 1966), although many moved to resource-rich areas, major towns and centres of trade including across parts of Shan State, Mandalay, Yangon, Moulmein, Myitkyina, among other areas (Forbes 1986). Some Muslims from Myanmar have also settled in China (see Egreteau 2012). Sometimes religious identity is defined geographically. For example, some Muslims living in Shan State may also be referred to, or refer to themselves, as 'Shan Muslims'. In 2013 it was reported that 'Shan Muslims' were also targeted when violence broke out in parts of Shan State.

In addition to Burmese Muslims, the Rohingya, the Kaman, the Panthay and Indian Muslims, there are a small number of Pashu or Malay Muslims.[14] While I have inevitably charted the various communities along ethnic lines, these should not be considered mutually exclusive and it is true to say that most Muslims in Myanmar identify with more than one ethnic group. Many Muslims in Myanmar today have multiple backgrounds, and this is further complicated by the

---

[13] While the origins of the term 'Panthay' are unclear, Forbes (1986) suggests that the term 'Panthay' was derived from the term '*pathi*' (Muslim) and that its use emerged in the late 1800s.

[14] See Fealy and Hooker 2006: 25; Selth 2004: 108.

artificial identities assigned to them on their national identity card. For example, Muslims may have up to four categories listed on their national identity card such as 'Burmese-Muslim-Shan' (indicating that one parent was Burmese Muslim and the other was Shan), or 'Indian-Muslim' or 'Burmese-Mon-Muslim'.

I have reconceptualized the identity of Muslims of Myanmar as existing along a spectrum that at one end strives to accommodate the state through a 'Burmese Muslim' identity, and at the other end are Muslims who retain their (non-Burman) ethnic identity and are therefore perceived as a challenge to the image of the Burman-Buddhist state. From the individual identities of Muslims, I now turn to offer a new perspective on Islam–State relations in Myanmar.

Reconsidering Islam and the State in Myanmar

Before we can begin to take scholarship further, it is important to consider how the Muslims of Myanmar have been studied and represented in academic scholarship. In this section, I draw together insights from the existing literature to map out current scholarly knowledge on the Muslims of Myanmar. It needs to be kept in mind that empirical research, on Islam and the Muslim communities in Myanmar is thin and has suffered the same fate as Burma/Myanmar Studies generally, due to the challenges raised by an extended period of military rule for both local and foreign researchers (Crouch 2014b). I chart several areas: the history of Islam in Myanmar; Muslim engagement in national politics; Muslims in times of crisis; and the practice of Islam among Muslim communities. In doing so, I demonstrate the gaps that need to be filled, the biases that need to be addressed, and therefore a future agenda for the study of the Muslims of Myanmar.

The History of Islam in Myanmar

Historical accounts of Islam in Myanmar can be divided into three major phrases: Muslims during the time of the Burmese kings (pre-1885); Muslims under colonial rule in Burma (1885–1947); and Muslims during the period of parliamentary democracy (1948–62). In terms of the first timeframe, Muslims played an important role during the era of the Burmese kings, yet we only catch glimpses of this in scholarly literature. Yegar provides an important analysis and detailed description of the arrival and establishment of Muslim communities in Burma (1972). His work is perhaps the most extensive analysis to date that recognizes the role and contribution of Muslims during the period of the Burmese kings, including in the army (Yegar 2002: 19–20). Some scholars have referred in passing to Muslim traders and Muslim soldiers under the kings (see for example Liebermann 1984: 26, 29, 226). Other scholarly accounts have recognized the presence and contribution of Muslims during the period of the kings, such as the 'sizeable Islamic community' during the Ava period (Thant Myint U 2007: 11) and the favours that King Mindon did for the Muslim community during his reign, such as building a mosque in Mandalay (2007: 136). This particular act of recognition by King Mindon is often raised by Muslims when discussing the history of relations between Muslims and the State today, in an attempt to affirm a sense of history of their community and belonging to the nation.

Events such as the construction of mosques are also occasionally noted in scholarship, such as the construction of the first mosque in Pegu by Muslim merchants in the 1550s (Liebermann 1984: 28), or the construction of a mosque at Mrohaung in the 1400s (Harvey 1925: 139). While some mosques and grave sites remain as potential reminders and relics of the past history of Muslims in Myanmar, these are also often sites of contest and violence. For example, in early 2014 it was reported in Burmese media that old grave stones of some famous Muslims were demolished by the Mandalay City Development Council. Two significant tomb stones had been demolished, but two still remain although they are in terrible condition, and have been heavily vandalized. One of these is the tombstone of U Nu, who was the intelligence chief for King Badoun during the Konbaung Dynasty (1752–1885). The Shiite mosque in the same compound still stands, although it also remains in a dilapidated condition. Not far from the site of these tombstones is the famous U Pain bridge, a wooden bridge that is an iconic tourist travel site in Mandalay. Less well-known is that U Pain, the man who built the bridge, was a Muslim. In 2014, there were news reports in the *New Light of Myanmar* (the government-sponsored mouth-piece) that attempted to cast doubt on the legacy of U Pain, suggesting he was of bad character and spreading lies about his behaviour. These allegations were used to suggest that the bridge should be renamed, which, alongside the demolition of the tombstones, would further wipe away these physical traces of Muslim history in the region. In a similar way to these physical acts of destruction, some scholarly accounts promote a history of Burma as a history of Burmans, and almost make no mention of Muslims in the history of Myanmar (for example Aung-Thwin and Aung-Thwin 2012); this needs to be challenged and reconsidered.

Following on from the period of the kings, other scholarly accounts have focused on the colonial period and British colonial responses to Muslims in Myanmar. Keck (2009) provides a searing inquiry into, and rereading of, how colonial sources portrayed Muslims in Burma. He examines how colonial references from the period 1885–1914 took a particular view of the Muslim community, and more often than not were relatively silent regarding Islam in Burma. He identifies a number of common perceptions among colonial authorities, including that Muslims did not really 'belong' to Burma; that Islam was 'transitory' and 'alien' to Burma; that Muslims were somehow regarded as 'non-Burmese', despite the fact that Islam in Burma long preceded the arrival of the British; and that Islam was seen as a potential threat that may contribute to the end of the Burmese race. By uncovering these prejudices and common assumptions, Keck unmasks the reasons why Muslims were not the subject of a great deal of colonial writing in Burma. His genealogy of British colonial discourse shows that they contributed to the creation of this invisible minority. Keck's work provides a starting point for historians, and he builds on this in his chapter in this volume.

Muslim Political Engagement

The second important theme is the involvement of Muslims in the political life of Myanmar. Some Muslims in Myanmar have been active in the political arena and have made a vital contribution to national politics, both in the immediate post-independence period, and during the military period. These stories need to be recovered and emphasized in order to build a more positive discourse on the role of Muslims in public life and State building, rather than as a threat to the State.

Leading up to and during the period of parliamentary democracy there were several famous leaders and politicians who were Muslim.

This time was marked by the activism of leaders from organizations such as the Burma Muslim Congress, which was affiliated with the Anti-Fascist People's Freedom League (AFPFL) (although the Burma Muslim Congress was forced to close in 1956); the Muslim Free Hospital, Yangon; and the Burma Muslim Student Association, based at the University of Yangon. In the lead-up to independence, there were also key figures such as Sultan Mahmood (1897–1958), an Indian Muslim who was a member of the Legislative Council in 1936, and was later Member of Parliament for Buthidaung North (People's Literature Committee 1961: 83); U Pe Kin was a Burmese Muslim who attended the Pinlon conference of 1947; and U Aung Thin, who in 1939 went to London as a representative of Muslims at the Round Table Committee discussion on whether Burma should be separated from India. U Razak (also known as Abdul Razak) was Cabinet Minister in the interim government, Minister of Education and National Planning, and Chairperson of the Burma Muslim Congress. On 19 July 1947, he was assassinated alongside Aung San and other cabinet members, and is commemorated annually on Martyr's Day (Razak 2007).

Through the lives of these individuals, we catch a glimpse of the diversity and debate between Burmese Muslims and Indian Muslims. This was evident in the political participation of two prominent individuals, U Raschid and U Khin Maung Lat.[15] U Khin Maung Lat was a Burmese Muslim who had been active in the students' organizations of Yangon University and had taken part in the students' strike of 1936. He worked as secretary for U Razak before the latter was assassinated. He held positions as the General Secretary of the All Burma Muslim Congress (1945); member of the Constituent Assembly (1947); Minister for Judicial Affairs (1950–8); and Chairperson of the Islamic Religious Affairs Council (Yegar 1972: 76; People's Literature Committee 1961: 74). When the AFPFL split in two, U Khin Maung Lat sided with the Stable Faction.

---

[15] Although profiles of these two individuals and their contributions are discussed in Yegar 1972, his book was focused on 'The Muslims of Burma'. There is no general history of Burma or its politics that spends significant time on Muslim leaders such as these men.

The views of U Khin Maung Lat were at times opposed by U Raschid, an Indian Muslim. He was the leader of the 1936 student boycott, and in 1939 he was an Executive Committee member of the Rangoon University Students Union. He became a prominent businessperson and in 1947 he participated in the Constituent Assembly. In the 1950s he held various ministerial positions, including Minister for Housing and Labour (1952–3), Minister for Trade Development and Labour (1954–5), Minister for Mines (1956), and Minister of Commerce and Industry (1960) (Trager 1966; People's Literature Committee 1961: 138). In 1958, he was the Vice President of the Trade Union Council of Burma. It has been said that he was 'intellectually and technically one of the most qualified persons in Burmese political life' of his time (Butwell 1963: 153). Yet there were some voices of dissent against U Raschid and other Muslim leaders, simply because they were perceived to be 'Indian' and/or Muslim.

This is reflected in some profiles we have that are coloured by prejudice, such as a profile of U Raschid by Dr Maung Maung (2008), who became one of the most influential legal figures during the socialist regime. Although U Raschid was considered to be next in line when the first president of the Rangoon University Students Union resigned, Maung Maung (2008: 232) notes that there were concerns raised because Raschid was a '*kalah*'. Maung Maung tries to suggest that attitudes changed as the student movement grew and he depicts the university as a place 'where *kalah* meets Bamah' (2008: 237) a phrase which he claims was intended in a 'spirit of unity'. The All Burma Students Union was formed after the 1936 strikes with Raschid as president, as well as president of the Rangoon University Students Union, which Maung Maung suggests was evidence that a shift in mindset had taken place. Yet Maung Maung evinces the common perception that Muslims were not 'liberal'. For example, he expressed surprise that Raschid and his wife 'though Muslim and devout ones too, had liberal views' (2008: 239). When Raschid was appointed as Minister of Labour under U Nu, Maung Maung observes that '... now and then, he came up against criticism that being a "kalah" he favoured the "kalah" or simply that being a "kalah" he should not be in cabinet' (2008: 241). Maung Maung suggests that U Nu ignored these criticisms, although he admits that U Nu unsuccessfully attempted to force Raschid to adopt a 'Burmese name' as part of his project of

Burmanization. Maung Maung appears to try and advocate for the involvement of Muslims in politics: 'In the Union cabinet today there are people of "kalah" blood...and sad would be the day which sees Burma's affairs handled only by the narrow and limited circle of "pure Burman"' (2008: 241). Yet these words ring hollow given that Maung Maung was a key part of the legal and political system under the socialist regime during which Muslims faced severe impediments and disincentives to serving in government office.

Aside from Muslims in the parliamentary period, there is little that has been written on the role of Muslims in public life since the 1960s, although this may partly be because of the significant restrictions Muslims face in seeking employment or gaining promotion in the public service since then. However, Muslims were politically active in key moments of Myanmar's history since the 1960s. After the end of the socialist period in 1988 and the re-emergence of political parties, several Muslim-based political parties such as the Rohingya-based National Democratic Party for Development (NDPD) ran in the 1990 elections and several Rohingya candidates were successful, although they were never allowed to take office. Further, in 1988, the Muslim community in Mandalay was active in voicing its disagreement with the socialist regime and organized collective demonstrations and protests on behalf of the Muslim community. Yegar even suggests that the government response to Muslims who were involved in the 1988 democracy demonstrations was particularly harsh (Yegar 2002: 63).

There were Muslims in the All Burma Student Democratic Front (ABSDF) that formed in Thailand, and Muslims members of the National League for Democracy (NLD). One example is Ayub Khan, a Burmese Muslim who grew up in Yangon.[16] In addition to his Burmese name, he also has a Muslim name, like most Burmese Muslims do. His grandfather was from Pakistan, his grandmother was from Mon State. He was sixteen years old at the time of the democracy uprising. In 1990, he was put in prison for his involvement in the democracy protests and ongoing political activities in the late 1980s, which became known as '8888', which refers to 8 August 1988. He was in prison for three years until 1993, then spent several years as

[16] Interview with Ayub Khan (not his real name), Melbourne, 14 January 2011.

a bodyguard for Daw Aung San Suu Kyi. From 1996 until late 2002, he was put in prison again for his political activities, this time for another seven years. After being released from prison for the second time, he got married, and Daw Aung San Suu Kyi attended as the special guest of honour. In 2004, facing further risks for their political involvement, he and his wife fled to Thailand. He was involved with the Assistance Association of Political Prisoners (AAPP) based in Mae Sot, Thailand. In 2008, Ayub Khan and his family came to Australia as part of the humanitarian settlement program. Ayub Khan travels back to the Thai-Burma border frequently to support friends there and continue his work with the AAPP. In Melbourne, he is actively involved in the Australia Burma Society, an inclusive community organization that supports the arrival of refugees and organizes annual community festivals. He has also established his own Burmese grocery store with the support of the local council. In November 2013, he again acted as a bodyguard for Daw Aung San Suu Kyi when she made her first visit to Melbourne; a Muslim protecting the voice of democracy in Myanmar.

Muslim political engagement has continued to evolve rapidly in the new political environment. Since 2008, new parties have been formed and in the 2010 elections there were several Muslim-based political parties, as well as several Rohingya who ran as members of the Union Solidarity and Development Party (USDP) in constituencies in Rakhine State. Since 2011, several other Muslim-based political parties have emerged. This includes the United National Congress Party (UNCP), formed by those who identify themselves as 'Pathi' Muslims, and the Kaman National Development Party (KNDP) (Narinjara 2013). This discussion of Muslim engagement in politics is taken further in the chapter in this volume by Farrelly.

Aside from formal political party affiliation, Muslims have engaged in the new political process in other ways, sometimes voluntarily and at other times involuntarily. For example, in August 2012, after the conflict occurred in Rakhine State, the President established a National Investigation Commission[17] and four of its 27 members were Muslim religious leaders, although none of the members were Rohingya. Some of the Burmese Muslims on the Rakhine Investigation Commission

---

[17] Presidential Notification 58/2012 on the establishment of the Rakhine Investigation Commission.

later stepped down from the Commission due to disagreements, and therefore did not contribute to the final report.[18] Another example is the constitutional amendment process. In November 2013, some Muslim lawyers submitted recommendations to the Constitutional Review Committee, and in their submission they emphasized the need for the right to freedom from discrimination and equal citizenship rights in the Constitution.[19] There is also need to consider whether and how Muslims have engaged with other independent bodies such as the Myanmar National Human Rights Commission (see generally Crouch 2013a). For example, one of the members of the National Human Rights Commission was appointed as a member to the Rakhine Investigation Committee; but the Commission failed to initiate its own investigation.

Finally, there is a need for research on the responsiveness of non-Muslim Members of Parliament to minority groups, and the risks inherent in speaking out in support of Muslims. One such incident related to the 2013 visit by the UN Special Envoy to Meiktila, who was threatened when a mob attacked his car. The Member of Parliament for Meiktila Township, U Win Htein, (of the NLD) admitted to the local press that the UN Special Envoy had been attacked while visiting the area and condemned the attack. In response, he was accused of favouring Muslims and was threatened. Public sentiment in Meiktila against his action is such that he may be unlikely to be re-elected from the seat if he runs in the 2015 elections. The chapter by Farrelly in this volume begins the task of analysing Muslim engagement in politics in the contemporary period.

Muslims Beyond the State

A third critical theme is the study of Muslims beyond the state; that is, those who have been displaced due to conflict or who have fled to neighbouring countries, or sought asylum in third countries. I highlight the story of Burmese Muslims in Karen State here to emphasize the global realities of these issues and the regional and international implications of the denial of belonging.

---

[18] Interview with Muslim members of the Rakhine Investigation Commission, Yangon, January 2013.

[19] Submission is on file with the author.

There has been significant irregular migration of Muslims to parts of South Asia—including Bangladesh, Pakistan, India, and even as far as the Middle East, such as Saudi Arabia—and Southeast Asia, including Malaysia, Thailand, and Indonesia. Some have made their way as asylum seekers, or as recognized refugees through the United Nations High Commission for Refugees (UNHCR), to Western countries, including the United States, New Zealand, and Australia. Over the past decade, large numbers of refugees living in camps along the Thai-Burma border have been resettled in third countries.

In 2004, the Australian government significantly increased the number of refugees that it accepted through its Humanitarian Resettlement Program who were from Myanmar and living in the refugee camps on the border of Thailand and Myanmar. From 2004 to 2007, Myanmar has featured in the top ten countries from which people were granted offshore protection visas to Australia. Since 2007, Myanmar has consistently featured amongst the top two nationalities within the offshore Humanitarian Program (the other country consistently in the top two being Iraq) (DIAC 2013). While these refugees from Myanmar are scattered across Australia, many have settled in Melbourne. A significant percentage of Burmese refugees who settled in Southeast Melbourne are Burmese Muslims. The area in which they settled was already home to a handful of Anglo-Burman families, who fled Burma in the 1960s and 1970s; 8888 generation activists and their families who came to Australia for further studies in the 1990s; and since 2013, Rohingya asylum seekers who were usually detained at one of Australia's offshore processing centres until their claims for asylum were found to be legitimate

The majority of Burmese Muslims in Melbourne are from villages in Karen State. Their journey is illustrated in the lives of Hassan and Salemar, a Burmese Muslim couple.[20] They come from Kyaikdon, a small village in what used to be a 'black' area[21] of Karen State, formerly

[20] Interview with Hassan and Salemar (not their real names), Melbourne, 4 January 2011.

[21] From the 1960s, the military labelled certain areas of the country 'black', where conflict with insurgents remained; 'brown' for areas that were under dispute; and 'white' for areas that were uncontested and without conflict. For example, the liberated part of Karen State was labelled a 'black' area. For more on this strategy see Smith 1999: 259–60.

under the control of the Karen National Union (KNU). In the 1990s, their village was repeatedly targeted and attacked by the military. As they lived in a KNU controlled area, some of the men fought with the KNU.[22] The military eventually swept through their village, burning houses and mosques, and forcing them, along with an estimated 4,000 other Muslims from surrounding villages, to flee.[23] They made the journey to Thailand along with their relatives and neighbours, and were among the first refugees to establish the camps in that area of the border of Thailand–Burma. They later settled in a camp that is today known as Nu Po, located a day's drive along 'death highway' (known for its dangerous bends), which winds its way to the border town of Mae Sot.[24] They lived in Section 11 of the camp, which is referred to by some non-Muslim camp residents as the 'Indian' section, although most of the people who lived there identified themselves as 'Bama Muslim', not Indian.

Like many displaced families from Karen State, the camps became their reality and home for over ten years, while other family members lived there for fifteen or twenty years, and still others had their claims for asylum rejected as they were unable to pass the medical check, which meant that the camp was effectively their permanent home. During this time, Hassan was a camp medic and Salemar raised their three boys. Their two older sons attended school, where classes were taught in Karen language, although their first language was Burmese; they also learnt to recite the Qur'an at the mosque and adjacent *madrasa* in their section of the camp. Since 1997, over 10,000 Muslims have sought refuge in the camps in Thailand. Many did not have citizenship cards, although most at this time were able to register with the UNHCR. In 2007, Hassan and Salemar and their

---

[22] Yegar claims that a small Muslim armed group operated in Karen State in 1983, but there is no evidence to suggest this was the same community (2002: 60).

[23] See Images Asia and Burma Network, 1997; TBBC, 2010: 12, citing Supamart Kasem (1997) 'Cleric Says Mosques and Schools Torched: forced relocation of villagers reported' *The Bangkok Post*, 10 March 1997. This is briefly mentioned in Fink 2009a: 239–40.

[24] In 2009, it was estimated that approximately 10 per cent of the refugee population on the border of Thailand and Burma were Burmese Muslim (TBBC 2010).

children were accepted as refugees to resettle in Australia as part of the government's humanitarian resettlement program.

As well as helping many families and friends, who arrived after them, to settle in Australia, Hassan and Salemar are involved with the Burmese Muslim Community Association (BMCA) and assist in the organization of annual festivals and religious events, including *Eid-ul-Fitr* and *Eid-ul-Adha*.[25] They have travelled back to the Thai-Myanmar border to support family and friends still living there, and they have sponsored some of their relatives to come to Australia. In 2012, they became Australian citizens, a fact they recount with obvious pride, as this is the first time they have ever been recognized as citizens of a country. Since 2013, they have also helped newly-arrived Rohingya asylum seekers in the area, despite the differences between Burmese Muslims and Rohingyas in terms of language and culture. With the support of a local council programme and a community organization, Hassan and Salemar have founded a café serving Burmese food in Melbourne. In 2013, they were able to see Daw Aung San Suu Kyi on tour when she visited Australia for the first time. They long to visit Myanmar one day, yet like many Burmese Muslims in Melbourne, they feel that they are unable to return under present circumstances, particularly given that some of their relatives and contacts inside Myanmar have fled to countries such as Thailand and Malaysia.

This profile suggests that the scholarly gaze must not only look at urban populations, but extend to rural Muslim communities often beyond the reach of the state, such as the Muslims of Karen State, including those in the liberated areas and on the Thai-Myanmar border. Our line of vision must not just consider Muslims within the territorial boundaries of Myanmar, but those on its borders as well as those scattered across the globe. The challenges of finding a place to belong for the Muslims of Myanmar implicate a range of countries in the region and in the West, and therefore should be of concern to them.

The one issue that has captured the attention of the West is the predicament of the Muslims of northern Rakhine State, generally referred to as the Rohingya. Displacement has been a major issue

---

[25] *Eid* is the breaking of the fast after the end of Ramadan; *Eid Ul-Adha* is the celebration that marks the commemoration of Abraham's willingness to sacrifice his son Ishmael.

for the Rohingya, even prior to independence. Due to the war in the 1940s, there were said to be 13,000 Rohingya in refugee camps in India and what was then Pakistan (present day Bangladesh) (Yegar 2002: 39). In 1962, many Rohingya Muslims were required to accept foreign registration cards, although some chose not to take these. The targeted campaigns of the government against the Rohingya were particularly fierce in the 1970s through Operation Naga (Yegar 2002: 55) and again in the 1990s, and both times this led to mass exodus to Bangladesh. While there were previous issues over citizenship, the introduction of the 1982 Citizenship Law is widely regarded as having effectively deprived the Rohingya of their citizenship, and remains a source of grievance today. The violence in the beginning of 2012 has been the most recent cause of displacement, and marked a critical low in Western humanitarian engagement in Myanmar after the Myanmar government forced all that were providing basic health care to displaced persons to leave the region. This has raised questions of international law, citizenship, irregular migration, and statelessness, and human rights advocacy organizations have shown concern for these issues.[26] In this volume, Cook captures the situation of the Rohingya and the regional dimensions of the crisis in more detail in his chapter on humanitarian aid in Myanmar.

One excellent example of sustained field research on displaced Rohingya communities, which stands out from other studies both for its methodological rigour and its originality, is Anwar's research on Rohingya migrants in Pakistan (Anwar 2013; 2014). I highlight Anwar's research here because it provides a crucial example of the kind of academic research that is needed, in contrast to top-down human rights analysis, or surface assessments of Myanmar's failure to adhere to international law. Anwar's sophisticated research·project involved a significant period of field research in Pakistan and required critical language skills and cultural knowledge. She focuses on the Rohingya community in Pakistan, which grew particularly after the 1960s when many fled Burma after Ne Win's military coup. She

---

[26] There have been numerous reports by international organisations on the issue: see for example Human Rights Watch (2002, 2012, 2013b); International Crisis Group (2013); Physicians for Human Rights (2013a); and the Islamic Human Rights Commission (2005).

explores why the Rohingya made the decision to leave Burma and head to Pakistan, as well as why they had decided not to return to Burma. She highlights the longing for citizenship and the illusion of Pakistan as an imagined 'Islamic homeland'. Anwar uses the migrants' own narratives of fleeing Burma for Pakistan to explore ideas of belonging and return. She discusses the wide range of problems that the Rohingya community, as migrants, face when settling in Pakistan, and the lack of recognition they experience there. She demonstrates how they are marginalized economically and socially, and generally work for low wages or in the informal labour sector; a far cry from their dreams of belonging to an Islamic homeland.

Aside from the issue of irregular migration, another reason that the Rohingya have been the focus of study is because of the concern of links between these communities and the broader global issue of terrorism. Our knowledge of armed Islamic groups in Myanmar is thin, and this is a reflection of the fact that there is little evidence of such groups. There was a mujahideen rebellion after independence in 1948, which was in armed conflict against the government (Yegar 2002: 39). It was only a small group of approximately 500 men, and did not have the support of all Rohingyas (Yegar 2002: 40). At that time, many Rohingyas, and other Muslims in Yangon in fact attempted to lobby the government to find a way to stop the mujahidin. While there were terrorist connections in the 1970s, these groups were again small in number and never a real threat to the government (Selth 2003; 2004), and there is no evidence of such groups today.

The Practise of Islam

The final theme I highlight here that needs attention is the practise of Islam by the Muslims of Myanmar. Most Muslims in Myanmar are Sunni Muslims of the Hanafi school of law,[27] although some follow the Shafi school of law, and there is also a smaller community of Shiites. Muslims therefore have more in common, at a doctrinal level, with Muslim communities in South Asia, compared to Muslim

[27] The Hanafi school is one of four schools of law and is prevalent across approximately one third of the Muslim world, including India, Pakistan, Afghanistan, Syria, Jordan, and Lebanon: Kamali 2008: 73.

communities in Southeast Asia, as most of the latter follow the Shafi school of law. There are almost no studies to date on the beliefs and practises of these Muslim groups.

One argument that has been raised by activists, journalists, and scholars in relation to the challenges to the practise of Islam in Myanmar is the attempt by the majority-Burman elite to 'Burmanise' the Muslims of Myanmar (Berlie 2008). The term 'Burmanisation' is used to refer to the aggressive and coercive promotion of Burman culture and Buddhist religion to the exclusion and suppression of Islam as a religion and culture. In this light, it is even more important that studies of the practise of Islam are undertaken.

Islamic education is one area of research that remains open to new inquiries and would benefit from comparative inquiry.[28] There are two main types of Islamic education in Myanmar, *madrasa* and *jameahs* (college or university), also known as *maulvi*[29] schools or *hafiz* schools, as well as *metthab* (place of writing or learning), which are for young children. At each level, the standard of education in both is not comparable to the quality of similarly named education institutions in other countries (see Nyi Nyi Kyaw, n.d). The *hafiz* course is at least three years, while the *maulvi* programme may run up to 10 years (Nyi Nyi Kyaw, n.d). The style and content of teaching in *madrasas* across Myanmar are generally similar to those in South Asia (Sulaiman 2008; Berlie 2008: 79–94). There is a common path to become a religious leader, with boys who can recite the *Qur'an* receiving the title of *hafiz*, then undertaking further study to become a *maulvi*, and often going to countries such as Pakistan, India, or Malaysia for further study. The controversial 2013 report of the Rakhine Investigation Commission recommended state intervention in mosques and schools in Rakhine State, though there is no evidence to support the claim that Islamic education institutions were one of the causes of the violence. Scholarship is needed in this area to promote understanding of the role and function that Islamic education

---

[28] For an overview of Islamic legal education in Southeast Asia, see Hefner and Zaman 2007; and Noor et al. 2008.

[29] There are several terms that are generally used interchangeably in Myanmar to describe an Islamic scholar who has received education beyond the level of a *hafiz*, including *mauvli*, *mawlawi*, and *mawlana*.

institutions play in Myanmar, particularly given the dire state of the government education system.

Many *madrasas* in Myanmar are located in mosques, yet most research to date has only documented the number of mosques that can be found in major towns and cities in Myanmar (Berlie 2008), rather than exploring deeper questions about the function and significance of mosques for Muslim communities. Mosques are highly visible symbols and given that many of them were built during the colonial era, they remain signs of the vibrant Muslim community during the colonial period. One particular feature of mosques in Myanmar is that women are not permitted to enter (according to Hanafi practice). The exception is Shiite mosques and less than a handful of Sunni mosques take a more open view and have a separate demarcated space for women within the mosque. Mosques can therefore be sites of exclusion for minorities (such as women) within Islamic communities, and research needs to be sensitive to sources of such internal barriers to belonging.

There is perhaps only one major city in Myanmar without a mosque—the new capital Naypyidaw. While most of the commentary on the move to Naypyidaw has speculated on motivations in terms of security, historical patterns of political leaders and superstition (Seekins 2011), one cannot help but contrast Naypyidaw to Yangon or Mandalay. The purposeful removal of the capital from Yangon has also led to the establishment of a capital with no overt traces of a Muslim population, nor of the influence of Indian traders on the economy and business. Muslim businessmen have also reported that they have not been allowed to purchase land in Naypyidaw, either for commercial or religious purposes.[30] The fact that Naypyidaw is under the direct control of the President according to the Constitution[31] implicates the executive and the government in this design and omission.

Neither *madrasas* nor mosques are regulated through national laws, although a system of Islamic personal law was introduced in Myanmar during the period of British colonialism. Based on the Anglo-Muhammadan law of British India, access to the courts to resolve disputes concerning family law according to Islamic law

---

[30] Interview with Muslim businessmen, Yangon, 17 November 2013.

[31] See 2008 Constitution art 50, 284–7.

is still practised today. This is an area in which Myanmar is both similar to and different from the rest of Southeast Asia. Although most countries in Southeast Asia do also recognize some form of Islamic personal law, Myanmar is the only country where cases concerning Islamic personal law are heard and determined by the general courts, rather than by a separate institution of Islamic Courts. The jurisprudence developed by the courts is based on classic Anglo-Muhammadan textbooks in English (Hooker 1984: 42–84), although we know little about the case law since the 1960s. The chapter by Crouch in this volume begins to fill a gap in this area.

The practise of Islam has been the subject of an important study of the refugee population on the border of Thailand and Burma, an estimated ten to twenty per cent of whom are Muslims and fled Burma in the 1990s (Thailand Burma Border Consortium (TBBC) 2010). TBBC (2010) provides a thorough and informed account of the life and customs of Burmese Muslim refugees, reflecting on the life of these villagers more broadly. TBBC identifies a high degree of collectivism within the Muslim community; a strict adherence to conservative moral and religious codes; highly defined gender roles; the patriarchal nature of the community; and, the challenges Muslims face in the context of refugee camps dominated by Buddhist leaders. It demonstrates that up until this time, INGOs were unable to respond to the needs of the Muslim community because of a lack of basic awareness about Islam. For example, the fish paste supplied by (mostly Western and some Christian) INGOs was considered to be *haram* according to Muslims and was therefore not consumed. This contributed to the higher levels of malnutrition among Muslims in the camps, compared to non-Muslims. The challenges of humanitarian aid and the more recent development of aid provision by organizations from Islamic countries have posed new concerns, as discussed by Cook in this volume.

✳ ✳ ✳

The Muslims of Myanmar clearly constitute an understudied area of research. I conclude my review of the literature by suggesting that future scholarship in this area must do two things in particular. First, we need to overcome the stereotype of Islam as violent or unusual in the context of Myanmar. To do this we need to displace the myth of Buddhism as an inherently peaceful religion. While I cannot survey the vast literature on Buddhism in Myanmar here,[32] one reason that the study of Islam in Myanmar has been absent from scholarship is because of the disconnect between Western views of Islam and Buddhism. Buddhism has been studied in isolation and shielded from scholarly criticism for too long. I am not suggesting that Buddhism is not an important part of the study of Myanmar. On the contrary, just as Islam is critical to understanding the Indonesian local context, or Catholicism is vital to the study of the Philippines, Buddhism is clearly a central part of the study of Myanmar. Yet what this volume suggests is that we must be willing to reject both the rose-tinted glasses with which the West often views Buddhism, and the perception of Islam as a violent religion. Future scholarship must combat the stereotype that Islam is 'radical, bad and violent' and that in contrast Buddhism is 'peaceful, non-violent, and good' (Elverskog 2013). We must recognize that the tendency for violence can and does arise in any religion, including those who identify with Buddhism or who seek to use religion as a rallying point, and the evidence we have suggests that it is Buddhists (rather than Muslims) who are the main cause of violence and conflict in Myanmar.

The second aspect of my argument is related more broadly to the study of Islam in Asia. Muslims in Myanmar have been overlooked and forgotten in discussions and debates on Islam in Central, South and Southeast Asia. We need to go beyond the assumption that Islam in Myanmar is peripheral and irrelevant, or the residue of a colonial past. Rather, we must begin to see the potential for the study of Muslim communities in Myanmar to offer fresh insights as a 'crossroads' for Islam between Central, South, and Southeast Asia.

I conclude this chapter with a call for a new generation of scholars to interrogate the politics of belonging for the Muslim communities of Myanmar. There is a need for historians who are open to new perspectives on existing historical sources and, where possible, discovering and analysing new sources of historical evidence related

---

[32] For an extensive review of the literature on Burmese Buddhist law, which highlights the contributions of the late Professor Andrew Huxley and Dr Christian Lammerts in particular, see Crouch (2014b). Some of the most well-known monographs on Buddhism in contemporary Myanmar include Sarkisyanz (1965); Schober (2010); Spiro (1967; 1977; 1982).

to Muslim communities. There is a need for ethnographers and anthropologists to spend time in the field, to get to know these Muslim communities in a close and personal way in order to construct rich ethnographies of contemporary community dynamics. There is a need for religious studies and Islamic studies scholars to take the study of Islam in Myanmar seriously, and to use the linguistic and literary skills they have to open up this field to a deeper level of analysis. The chapters that follow in this volume constitute a small beginning that will hopefully be built on, clarified and extended in the future in order to enhance our understanding of and appreciation for Myanmar's Muslim mosaic.

I

Colonialism and the Law

2 Reconstructing Trajectories of Islam in British Burma

STEPHEN KECK

The persecution of Muslims in Myanmar makes the study of Islam under the British a priority because many key developments that occurred under colonial rule continued to shape the nation long after independence. Understanding the status of Muslims in 'British Burma' provides the possibility of generating a more complete and nuanced understanding of the contemporary situation in Myanmar. This subject has received less attention than it merits, but it is clear from the work that has been done that Islam in Burma was complex and multifaceted. Despite the fact that Muslims may make up 13 per cent of the population of Myanmar, they have been understudied—until recently (Khin Maung Yin 2005). In fact, it is notable that a recent and engaging interpretation of the country's history is strangely—but possibly predictably—almost silent about Islam in Myanmar (Aung-Thwin and Aung-Thwin 2012).

This chapter builds upon my earlier work 'The Making of An Invisible Minority: Muslims in Colonial Burma' by tracing the fates of two different Islamic communities in greater detail and, in so doing, supporting the overall argument that British discourses had the effect of differentiating Islam from things Burmese. In 'The Making of An Invisible Minority', I argued that the British tended to represent Islam as something that was not a natural feature of life in Burma. Instead, the ethnographic knowledge that the British assembled about the country's many ethnic groups ensured that Burma came to be understood as a place with 'one dominant population and many minor ethnic groups' (Keck 2009). All of this had the unintended effect of making Muslims, a minority defined by religious identification and practice, invisible as a minority in colonial Burma. Disregarding religion as the basis for identifying minorities produced a legacy which meant that the essential default condition for independent Myanmar was to conceptualize it as a country dominated by Burmans and governed in conjunction with other ethnic minorities.

Moving beyond 'The Making of an Invisible Minority', this chapter develops from the assumption that de-Indianization—by which Burma became independent from the Indian Empire of which it was a part until 1937—made an absolute difference to Islam in Burma. This process was painful and ugly: it resulted not only in the expulsion of the vast majority of Indians from the country, but put into place dynamics that almost certainly left distrust and antipathy in Myanmar towards many things that might be connected with India—especially British India. Separation from India required legal, political, social, cultural, economic, and educational transformation. It would also produce a determined historiographic agenda to support many of these changes. As Mary Callahan has also deftly demonstrated, it required the building of a non-Indian army, a challenge which occurred under trying circumstances (Callahan 2004). Therefore, both the process and result reshaped Myanmar at the outset of its development as a nation.

Tracing the relationships between Islam in Burma and British colonization is a complicated process and cannot be addressed satisfactorily in one chapter. The current situation in Myanmar virtually guarantees that addressing the complex term 'Rohingya' and its conceptual history remains an ongoing task. This discussion, instead, will briefly trace the ways in which British writers understood the presence of Islam in British Burma. It will then focus primarily on two relatively neglected facets of the British encounter with Islam in Myanmar. The first major theme of this chapter will be to trace—however briefly—the British perceptions of the Panthays in order to build on many of the features of the 'invisible minority' argument. The second theme is very different: the chapter tries to leave an incomplete portrait of the Indian Muslim elite who flourished in a number of (mostly urban) places in Burma in the early twentieth century. This second theme is introduced in order to exhibit not only the complexity of the subject, but to enable us to better imagine the many faces of Islam in Burma under the British. More important, these two groups of Muslims experienced both British Burma and independent Myanmar quite differently. One was a recently arrived diaspora population, while the other was part of a much larger pattern of immigration and economic development. The fate of the Panthays as immigrants from China and Muslims from India (which might well include the Rohingya) suggests that the latter suffered from both de-Indianization and its subsequent echoes. The argument here, however, is that in British Burma both were increasingly understood as external to the country, but useful and welcome in varying degrees in colonial society. Taken together, the chapter aims to suggest that their trajectories remain of interest for those who might study British Burma, but they are also critical for comprehending the fate of Muslims in independent Myanmar—long after the colonizers had left.

The Development of British Attitudes Towards Islam in Burma

It should be remembered that the British were aware that Islam had been present in Burma long before their own encounters with the area. British writers do not appear to have been interested in charting the arrival or development of Islam in Burma, but they did note its presence. In looking at a brief sample of British and colonial discourse, it becomes clear that Muslims were regarded as largely external to Burma, but easily adapted to it—especially as Burma's identity developed as part of the Indian Empire.

To cite one early example, Henry Gouger, who wrote incisively about Burma prior to the First Anglo-Burman War in 1825, recorded an incident which may well have been apocryphal, but it suggests something of the position of Muslims in the Kingdom of Ava. The monarch—'the old King, grandfather of the present one'—sought to find out about other religions. Learning that Muslims would rather 'die than pollute themselves' with pork he decided to put some Muslims to the test:

Now there were many Mahomedans residing in Ava, some of them foreigners, others native-born subjects of the King. Of these he commanded several of the most considerable to assemble at his Palace, where, to their consternation, the flesh of the hated animal was placed ready-cooked before them, and they were commanded, without further ceremony, to fall-to at once. What a study for Lavater! What a study for Leetch! I feel it is wrong to make tyranny, in its most detestable form, an occasion for amusement; but who can control the imagination in such a case.... The look of despair—the ill-concealed rage—the mutual, recognizing glances of the chief actors, as much to say, 'We are all in the same boat—don't tell of me, and I won't tell of you.' The scene must have been unique of its kind.... Sad to say they did all partake of the abominable pig and his Majesty's doubt remained unsatisfied (Gouger 1860: 97–8).

While this passage aptly points to a number of facets of Muslims in Burma prior to the arrival of the British,[1] it also says something of Gouger who did not trust Muslims. He admitted that 'the Indian Mahomedan is proverbially unfriendly to the Englishman' (Gouger 1860). Nonetheless, if Gouger's account has any veracity then it is clear that Islam was well-known at the Court of Ava: some Muslims in Ava were foreigners, but some others were 'native–born'. To put this a bit differently, Muslims were a 'visible minority'—partly 'foreign', partly Burmese—which meant that Islam, as such, was not new, but it was at the margins of Burmese life and society.

---

[1] Gouger explained that he had four Muslim servants who helped him obtain beef and veal without any issue, despite the fact that 'by some strange process of casuistry, these pious Buddhists appeared to weigh the enormity of the crime by the size of the animal that suffers, ...Among my servants were four Mahomedans, willing agents in obtaining beef and veal. We used to slaughter them at night in an out-building, but though all secrecy was used, it was impossible to say whether accidental discovery might not entail unpleasant consequences. We were living in a quarter of town under the Prince's immediate jurisdiction; complaints would therefore go to him. This facilitated matters wonderfully, as my compliments always went to His Royal Highness, with a quarter of an animal which "had unfortunately died in my yard last night." We perfectly understood each other, and the Prince being particeps criminis, we could eat our beef without fear of consequences' (Gouger 1860: 54–5).

A second example comes from the work of Albert Fytche, whose work *Burma: Past and Present*, comprehended the status of Muslims in Burma by perceiving them as a kind of offshoot to either the politics of the Mogul empire or that their presence in the country was best explained through a series of conquests—the most notable of which was that of Genghis Khan. Fytche, who was the second Commissioner of British Burma (1867–71) wrote the first historically oriented work entitled *Burma Past and Present* (1878), which was dedicated to his cousin Alfred Tennyson. The two-volume history did document some genuine scholarly passion for Burma's past; nonetheless it might just as easily be remembered as an icon of orientalist prejudices. To be sure, Fytche did attempt to draw upon both non-Burmese and indigenous sources in order to narrate the country's past. However, his curiosity had its limit, some of which might be deemed as characteristic of colonial biases. For instance, Fytche claimed that: 'the later history of Burma is the same old story of usurpations, commotions, rebellions and massacres' (Fytche 1878: 66).

With respect to Islam in Burma, Fytche understood the presence of Muslims in Burma as a direct consequence of the Mogul empire and its decline. In fact, he claimed that the history of Burma 'resembles, somewhat the history of a Mahommedan invasion' (Fytche 1878). He also chronicled the involvement of Arakan with Mogul politics. Fytche explained that in the politics that attended the succession of emperors involved in Arakan, there 'were some Mahommedans in the Kingdom of Arakan. They had either sought refuge in Arakan, or had been enslaved by the Portuguese in their kidnapping expeditions' (Fytche 1878). Fytche could hardly be considered a professional or rigorous historian, but what is useful here is that in his narrations, Muslims did not really belong to Burma. They might well live or have lived in the areas which became Burma, but they were essentially foreign to it. More important, perhaps, is the fact that these passages from *Burma Past and Present* might be said to represent the articulation of the connection between Islam and India.

A third example, Taw Sein Ko, who was a Chinese Burman and a leading figure in the country between 1890–1920, did not seem to regard Muslims differently from the rest of the population. Taw Sein Ko was an Asian modernizer who understood the country in terms of its future, which he believed to be tied to both India (of which it was already a part) and China. More important, he believed that Burma would be a place defined by its cosmopolitan realities, in which many different ethnic communities would be present. To some extent, this reflected what might be called a 'Rangoon worldview', because it would not have applied universally to British Burma. Many British observers preferred to believe that it was a static society with minimal social tension. However, by the early days of the new century these safe and reassuring assumptions were increasingly under siege. V.C. Scott O'Connor admitted as much in his elegiac, two volume, *The Silken East* (1904). An even more seasoned observer, Taw Sein Ko noted that ethnic and religious divisions were significant. In 1913, he observed that communitarian tensions existed in Burma. He believed that they were actually worse than in India. He explained:

> A Burman is seldom admitted into a mosque or a Hindu temple, and much less to an Indian religious function, while all pagodas and Buddhist religious functions are open to all the nationalities of the world. Praiseworthy efforts have been made in India to bridge the gulf of separation between different sections of Hindus, and between Mahomedans and the Hindus, and, so far, they have been attended with success. It now rests with the leaders of the Burmese, Hindu, and Mahomedan communities to initiate and organise similar efforts in Burma, so that the ties of friendship and brotherhood, as fellow-citizens of a common Empire, may be drawn closer and tighter to the advantage of all the communities concerned, as well as in the interest of the Indian Empire. (Taw Sein Ko 1913: 316–17)

This passage illustrates that empire intellectuals in Burma were cognizant of a set of communitarian tensions that might have actually been more complicated than those in India. Taw Sein Ko believed that Burma could be successfully modernized by becoming more 'Burmese' and emphasising national heritage and culture, but that it might do so in an inclusive way.

These examples suggest that the British saw Islam in Burma as relatively unimportant because it was unthreatening to the colonial social order. Accordingly, efforts to recover British documents about the subject are probably hindered—possibly fatally—by the lack of administrative interest in delineating the many facets of Islam in Burma. Nonetheless, it should still be clear that the British tended to see Islam in Burma as stemming from mainly external and diverse sources. First, some Muslims were believed to be descended from Arab traders who settled and became 'Burman'. Second, another group would be the migrants from Islamic communities in China, especially the 'Panthays' after 1855. Third, the migration of South Asians into Burma, which occurred with British colonization, produced a large population of Muslims. Fourth, British writers also identified those who were indigenous to Western parts of the country and might be regarded as forerunners to the 'Rohingya' Muslim minority.

Assessing the Panthays

Fytche is even more useful because in *Burma Past and Present* he addressed the Panthays, whom he understood to be a particular type of Chinese Muslims. John Anderson, who was part of the expedition to Momien, indicated that the term 'Panthay' was applied to them by the Burmese and 'adopted by the English'; it 'simply means Mahomedan' (Anderson 1871: 147). Fytche believed that the Panthays, who had formed the Dali Sultanate, could be useful for Burma's future. With the relationship between British Burma and China foremost in mind, Fytche provided a memorandum (in the shape of an index 'Panthays or the Mahommedan Population of Yunnan') to the second volume of *Burma Past and Present*. This document reflects Fytche's perception that the Panthay state, which had emerged in the wake of the rebellion against China, was much more durable than it proved to be. His interest in the subject was not primarily intellectual; instead, Fytche complained that with the rise of the Sultanate all of the caravan trade between Yunnan and Burma had disappeared. Fytche reported:

> Considerable difficulties exist in procuring correct intelligence of the Panthays, or Mahommedan population of Yunnan....they are not inclined to be communicative; but rather assume a studied ignorance of their own affairs:--Secondly, communication can only be held with them through Chinese Merchants and Brokers, residents of Burma Proper, who speak the Burmese language; and who, in addition to their own private and self-interested motives, for preventing free intercourse, with traders from Yunnan, are moreover in the pay, or subject to the influence of the King of Burma (Fytche 1878: 296).

What was at stake was actually more than the restoration of the caravan trade. The Panthays had the potential to be cultural intermediaries in that they could help British commercial interests build relationships with China. That is, because the Panthays were Muslims, it would be much easier for Indian Muslims to do business with them. Fytche explained that the basis for his knowledge was based on just two sources: Colonel Sladen and some Panthays that he had met in 1861, when they came to Moulmain as part of a Shan caravan. In 1866 Sladen had been commissioned by Fytche to go to Yunnan to head a mission to try to reopen the caravan trade. Fytche proved that like many who have written about the past, he was not particularly skilled at seeing what lay ahead. He explained that the Manchu dynasty had developed problems with 'the Mahommedan population of China, which may probably...end disastrously to that dynasty.' Fytche speculated further:

> How long it will take for the Chinese Government to disintegrate and re-appear under a new form; what effect such a change would have on the independent Mahommedan population of the Western Provinces; and will change be brought about by them, are questions which may probably affect a future generation. (Fytche 1878: 302–3)

To anticipate, Fytche's assessment of the Panthays underestimated the Qing empire's ability to recover from a series of sustained challenges—some of which were associated with Islam. He did distinguish the Panthays from the Dungans, but it might be noted that the latter group also revolted against the Qing by the time *Burma Past and Present* was published. The term 'Dungans' (or Tungans) was used to describe Chinese-speaking Muslims in Xinjiang (Kim 2004). The Dungans revolted in 1864 and they would be followed by Turkic Muslims making the 1864 rebellion a 'Muslim rebellion' (Kim 2004). The Dungan Revolt, also known as the 'Hui Minorities War' (a term which can also be deployed for the Panthay rebellion) was largely located in Shaanxi, Gansu, and Ningxia provinces. The Dungans would not be able to establish a lasting state despite the efforts of Yaqub Beg. In 1877, the Dungans were forced to flee China for Central Asia when the Qing armies crushed 'the Muslim Rebellion'. For our purposes, Fytche recognized that the Panthay lineage was different, but he also drew upon these developments to wrongly conclude that they would be able to successfully resist the Qing.

Commercial considerations may well have been at the basis for the ways in which the British came to understand and make sense of the Panthays. More broadly, Fytche's efforts might be understood as part of the larger attempt by the British to exploit the possibilities of trading with an 'open China' that the Opium Wars had established. By the 1860s it had become clear that there were commercial interests in India, especially Calcutta, which also sought Chinese trade by creating a direct route from India and bypassing Rangoon and Burma altogether. In 1870, Sladen toured British business establishments in order to refute the idea that the trade through Burma to China was not feasible. He identified Arthur Cotton (1803–99) as an advocate of a Calcutta-China route, which disregarded the significance of Rangoon. Cotton, who had actually served in the First Anglo-Burman War, had established a very impressive reputation as an engineer in India. In 1867, Sladen read a paper at the Royal Geographical Society in which he argued that the route from Rangoon (through Burma) to China would be fraught with difficulties (Sladen 1870). Yet, the story is actually much older: British interests in India had long sought to find a land route to China, which they believed would bring massive financial rewards. Those who supported such a vision tended to believe that a route through Burma to Yunnan would be the most feasible. British interest in Yunnan hardly followed the Opium War, but originated in South Asian or India Ocean interests.

Panthays in Yunnan

It is important to note that when Fytche analysed the Panthay communities, he was referring to a state and society that lay far from his idea of Burma. He located Panthays in a different historical trajectory arguing that they were a 'remnant' of 'the great wave of Mahommedan aggression' (Fytche 1878: 298). This wave included conquerors such as Mahomed of Ghuznee, Mahomed Ghuri and Genghis Khan, the last of whom Fytche believed was important for 'introducing a considerable Mahomedan population into China' (Fytche 1878: 298). Just as he had regarded Islam in Arakan (and Burma) as foreign, so too, he emphasized the non-Chinese origins of the Panthays, but it might be noted that he recognised them, like the Dungans, as an ethnic and religious minority in China.

Scholars have not been fully able to establish the exact origins of the Panthays, but it has been assumed that they were not essentially indigenous to Yunnan. The Panthays had lived in Yunnan since the Mongol invasions and appeared to have come with the Mongols to help govern China. It should be pointed out that Chinese sources are not clear as to whether they are a separate non-Han group or one of many of the non-Han groups that happen to be Muslim. Fytche was probably not aware that in settling into Yunnan, the Panthays had actually moved into an area that might be regarded as a perennial borderland or frontier for China. In fact, it had been referred to as 'South of the clouds' (Atwill 2005: 11) and the region has also been associated with disease, primarily malaria and bubonic plague (Atwill 2005). Looking at the region from China, Yunnan had many non-Han peoples (many of whom were regarded in relation to particular places and environments), and it would begin to get Han colonisers in the eighteenth century. In fact, the migration of the Han settlers into Yunnan produced the equivalent of a demographic revolution, which would have been evident in the nineteenth century (Atwill 2005). The surge in Han population would be one of the underlying factors that produced the 'Panthay Rebellion', which resulted in temporary autonomy.

It is instructive to recognize that the view north from Rangoon (or from Assam in the West) could easily produce a similar conclusion—even without taking Yunnan into account, because the areas associated with northern Burma were also classic border lands in their own right. They were, and are, populated by groups such as the Kachins, the Shan, the Burmese and a number of peoples whom colonial authorities often referred to as 'hill tribes'. The ethnographies of this area that bordered Yunnan were complex to say the least. Furthermore, the terrain makes many of these areas remote and inaccessible—even to this day. Travelling to Yunnan through Burma proved to be a difficult task. William C. McCleod, a British captain who served in India, appears to be the first Westerner to try to make this journey, which he attempted in 1837. He departed from Moulmein, journeyed to Chiang Mai and subsequently went to Keng Hung (now Yunjinghong), where he was not allowed to proceed further without the proper permissions (Stockwell 2003). Nonetheless, the prospect of creating a trade route which would link

India and China was a priority or even obsession for many business leaders in Rangoon. It is well known that the 'Burma Road', which was built during the World War II, was constructed against great odds and later much of the region remained defiant against the newly independent Myanmar state, which not surprisingly had difficulty enforcing its writ.

The Panthays, then, were part of a region which had been borderland for much of China's history and which itself was bounded by another borderland in what is now northern Myanmar. To put this differently, the Panthays were not only far from Rangoon, but resided in an area which had yet to develop firm or precise borders. Nonetheless, its inhabitants recognized many mutable boundaries, but it would be hard to claim that borders, in the full legal sense of the term, existed. Yet, the significations of difference were readily available: different languages, religious practices and customs abounded. Sumptuary laws were not in existence, but they might as well have been, as many of these groups relied upon their appearance to signify identities. These points of differentiation would be amply displayed when the Sladen Exhibition left Bhamo and travelled to Momien in order to seek an agreement with the Panthays and the restoration of the caravan trade.

The Sladen Expedition

Sladen's expedition remains an understudied subject, but one that is readily accessible because of the narratives it furnished. Fytche was careful to make sure that this mission (which would not take place until 1868) would be characterized as non-political (Yegar 1966). This required something of a balancing act between the needs of the mission to Talifoo (the capital of the Sultanate) and the Chinese government. It would be a number of years before the British would follow up and attempt to reopen the caravan trade (Yegar 1966). Three detailed accounts of the journey were published: John Anderson's *A Report on the Expedition to Western Yunan via Bhamo* (1871); Colonel Sladen's more modest account: *Trade Through Burma to China: An Address to the Glasgow Chamber of Commerce* (1870); and finally, Captain Bowers' *Report on the Practicability of Re-Opening the Trade Route, Between Burma and Western China* (1869). For our purpose, the separate accounts aptly document not only the huge difficulties poised by such a venture, but they also open the borderlands of both Burma and Yunnan (to a lesser extent) to view. In addition, they are a reminder that the British discourses about what they encountered could be variable. Sladen's narrative is actually valuable because it reveals the extent to which commercial interests shaped British initiatives. Bowers' aims were reflected in his remark that 'everything should be subservient' to finding ways to increase commerce. He disregarded the Burman state because it was made up of 'semi savages' who owe an equivocal allegiance to a despot, whose only policy is the amassing of riches, the propagation of abominable idolatrous superstitions, and the gratification of selfish and sensual indulgences' (Bowers 1869: 3). In contrast, Anderson's narrative exhibits a Victorian obsession with description and detail, and not surprisingly he came to his expedition with a much more open mind than did Bowers. Furthermore, *A Report on the Expedition to Western Yunan via Bhamo* also points to a very useful reference for how the British tried to manage their encounters with peoples and places that needed to deliberate on unintentional means of differentiation. Anderson's appendices alone provide a wealth of information about a number of topics (some of seemingly little relevance) including words and phrases for the primary border groups. Anderson rarely used the word 'border', but his narrative records the forms of life of the many peoples who were interacting with each other in the area that later became the border between Burma and China. *A Report on the Expedition to Western Yunan via Bhamo* amounts to a vivid account of a complex border region, where at that time the Panthays were a dominant borderland force as they were able to guarantee safe passage of the expedition through an area in which criminal gangs flourished.

The objectives of 'the Expedition' were primarily commercial, but they might also be regarded as scientific and political. The British were seeking to build a relationship with what they believed to be a future Panthay state because they anticipated that it might be able to guarantee the lucrative caravan trade, which had ceased in the 1850s. They assumed that it had successfully (and permanently) thrown off the weak Qing state and would soon become an independent nation—one that would control Yunnan and with it, the trade with Western China. That is, they believed that a Panthay state would emerge to dominate the borderlands of Yunnan and they sought to build a relationship with it, while trying not to antagonize the Chinese.

Seeking to go through Burma to Yunnan itself was ambitious: the obstacles were environmental, natural, criminal, economic, and political. More important, perhaps, was that the Expedition also had to traverse the cultural obstacles that came with going through these areas on a 'peaceful mission'. Anderson's narrative reveals that this seemingly easy task involved convincing peoples that their attentions were neither insurrectionary nor criminal. To state the obvious, they represented a tempting target to those in the borderlands whose activities were not in any way shaped by the rule of law.

Even before the expedition reached Yunnan, it was evident that the Panthays were a powerful force in the region. Anderson's account establishes that it was Panthay protection that was critical for their safe passage. It seemed clear to the British that the Dali Sultanate was developing into a credible state, which Fytche realized produced a diplomatic problem as to whether it should be recognized and what the Chinese reaction would be if recognition was afforded to the new state.

The Dali Sultanate had come into being in the wake of the 'Panthay Rebellion' as it has been remembered, which was an event that broke out about the same time that the British were facing the 'Indian Uprising' in the late 1850s. David Atwill's groundbreaking work on Yunnan—*The Chinese Sultanate: Islam, Ethnicity, and the Panthay Rebellion in Southwest China, 1856–1873* (2005)—challenges the frequently cited narrative of Muslims rebelling against a corrupt or indifferent Qing state. Instead, using a range of Chinese sources, Atwill showed that the violence of the 1850s was rooted in both demographic developments in Yunnan and in their possible results. Yunnan had been something of a frontier area for Chinese expansion. To be specific, from the late eighteenth century, Han (Chinese) settlers had increasingly populated Yunnan. This development may well have caused the striking incidents of violence that Atwill demonstrates, which preceded the 'Panthay Rebellion' (Atwill 2005). Atwill does not use the phrase 'ethnic cleansing', but it would be an apposite characterization for the mass killings of Panthays that defined these events.

However, David Atwill has demonstrated that this event needs to be understood by what preceded it: namely, nothing less than an attempt by the Qing to conduct organized violence against the Hui peoples in Yunnan. This development, which might be witnessed in the Baoshan Massacre (1845) and the Kunming Massacre (1856), is worthy of study in its own right because it serves to remind us that although 'ethnic cleansing' may be a twentieth century concept, it would be easily applicable here. French missionaries reported a high level of violence: 'Yunnan is consumed by turmoil and confusion. The Muslims want to kill the officials. The Chinese want to kill the Muslims, the officials want to kill the Muslims and the Chinese' (Atwill 2005). Again, one missionary recorded:

> That which is certain is that under the directions of a low-ranking military official and sworn enemy of the Muslims several thousand Chinese profited from the celebrations of Chinese New Year to organize a vast plot against the 'pilgrims of Mecca' (Atwill 2005).

By the beginning of the 1860s, the collapse of Qing power in Yunnan had left the Panthays as the veritable ruler of much of the area.

Fytche's inclusion of an appendix in *Burma Past and Present* suggests, accordingly, that he regarded the rise of Panthay power as significant for Burma. With the impulse of an amateur scholar, Fytche explored the term 'Panthay' and summarized the myths concerning their origin: both the Panthay version and its Chinese counterpart. He also reported on their customs, which might be regarded as a fusion of Arab and Chinese. He noted that the Panthays were 'Soonee' (Suni) Muslims and 'pride themselves on their Arab descent' (Fytche 1878: 301). In addition, many could take pride in the fact that they could converse in Arabic and 'their prayers are all in this language' (Fytche 1878: 301). Fytche highlighted the Panthay commitment to Islam—'They have Mosques or Musjids, of the true Moslem type and are fanatical and strict in their religious performances' (Fytche 1878: 301). However, Fytche regarded the Panthays as Chinese. After all, the Panthays dressed in accordance with 'Chinese habit', even though many cut their hair to a certain length and 'allow it to fall back on the nape of the neck' (Fytche 1878: 301). Fytche went further, noting that they also 'wear in many instances, a distinctive turban, of more ample form than in use amongst the Chinese' (Fytche 1878: 302). It is clear that he was impressed by the Panthays who he described as 'fair, tall, and strongly built men' who come from an 'interesting race' and after twelve years of 'absolute government in Yunnan, it is not improbable to suppose that their future independence is secure', he wrote (Fytche 1878: 302).

Fytche's analysis reflected the collective wisdom of the Sladen expedition, which took place at an interesting moment in the history of Yunnan. In September 1856, Dali fell to the rebellion and it became the seat of the state which soon emerged thereafter. Under the leadership of the rebel commander Du Wenxiu, who was proclaimed at once Generalissimo, 'Leader of all the Muslims' and Sultan, the 'Dali Sultanate' soon came into existence (Atwill 2005). This state would be the dominant polity in the region (especially western Yunnan) and there is evidence to suggest that its reach was much larger. The Dali Sultanate would be Islamic, but also multi-ethnic, drawing support from non-Hui, non-Han and Han alike. It is worth noting that it regarded itself as both Islamic and Chinese; Du Wenxiu's seal would contain both Arabic and Chinese characters. While it did open *madrasas*, it had not made any sustained effort to impose *shari'a* law. It might then be said that the expedition encountered the Dali Sultanate and with it the Panthays in their full glory. Captain Bower's description paints a vivid picture of a prosperous and stable society:

The wealthy city of Momien was occupied by the Panthays some 7 or 8 years ago, and they are still spreading. At the time we were residing at Momien the immense city of Yunnan fell into their hands, and the Proclamation (some eight feet in length) was placarded on one of the principal thoroughfares of the town. We believe that it will be difficult to stop the progress of this people. Unlike the Taepings, these Panthays try to restore peace and give confidence to trade wherever they conquer. This Panthay movement arose in the west of China about the same time as that of the Taepings in the south, but seems a higher and more enduring character, for they have consolidated themselves into a government, and created for themselves a name, which is feared throughout China. Their Government is purely a military one, and all that can bear arms are soldiers. They have a close resemblance to the Chinese in appearance, and imitate them in many things. Their manners and customs shew their Chinese origin; like the Chinese in their Government and dispensation of justice, unlike the Chinese, in the mildness of their government and the mercy which tempers their justice; like the Chinese in their local administration, and domestic institutions, but unlike them in the moderation of their assessments on the inhabitants, and in the comfort and contentment that seems to reign in their households; like the Chinese they are dignified and cautious, unlike them in the total absence of that arrogant and assuming bearing, that characterized the Chinese officials of former years of the eastern coast, in their intercourse with foreigners; like the eastern Chinese they are suspicious and cautious, but unlike them their suspicions are dispelled by a frank and open manner courteously accepting explanation, and expressing themselves satisfied when they see reason to be so: like the eastern Chinese in many respects, but differing from them in other [sic] this extraordinary people present a marked and favorable contrast to those Chinese with whom we have hitherto come into close contact. Their religion is Mahomedan without the fierce bigotry that we were led to expect, and which is one of the characteristics of this faith throughout India and Arabia. The city of Momien has only one Mosque and that built in shape and form to a Chinese temple without the idols. Some the Mahomedans eat pork and drink Samshoo, although this is not common among them, they neither smoke tobacco nor opium, but chew a great deal of betel-nut, of this they are very fond. They are not very strict in their religious observances as far as we could learn. They are particular in their marriages, marrying their daughters only to those of their own faith. All their religious services are conducted in Arabic, their priests having a knowledge of this language. Arabic characters and mottos are plastered over and hung up on the wall of their houses on strips of red or gilt paper alongside of characters and mottoes in Chinese. They do not keep their women concealed as is one of the rules of this faith, but permit them to go about as other people. The women have small feet and are invariably well dressed (Bowers 1869: 27–8).

The Panthays, then, would make perfect intermediaries to both Chinese and Islamic cultures. In fact, Anderson recorded incidents that suggested Islam could be the very basis of future partnerships. Upon leaving Momien they were accompanied for a mile by two Panthay officials whose affections became obvious:

when we came to part with them, they burst into tears, and after we had gone a long way, and turned round to take our last look at Momien, we saw the two figures standing on the spot where we had left them, gazing wistfully after us. One of them had spent the last two days with our men, refusing to go to his own home, and I believe, that his strong liking to the society of our guard arose from sympathy of feeling in matters of religion. There cannot be a doubt that a great part of the success of the Expedition is due to the presence of the Mahomedan element in our guard. The Panthays at once fraternized with them, and our *khyoung* {dwelling place} from the first day we arrived in Mo-mien was the constant resort of all the most respectable Mahomedans (Anderson 1871: 341).

Furthermore, it seemed obvious to the expedition that the Panthays ran much of Yunnan and their influence extended well into the bor-derlands of northern Burma. Atwill documents that they were toler-ant, drawing support not only from the Islamic population, but also from local hills people and some groups of Han Chinese. It is possible that the Burmese were interested in working with the Panthays, some of whom had come to Mandalay in the 1860s. Mindon Min provided some land in order to establish a mosque.[2]

In any event, the British were clearly impressed by what they regarded as an emerging polity. Bowers, for instance, reported that the Panthays were a 'warlike people, but anxious for peace' (Bowers 1869: 30) and even though the region was rife with crime he antici-pated that they would be able to secure it. He predicted that the 'Panthay Government will soon be able to afford all needful security to the people, and when that is the case, population will again flock to these regions as was shewn in Eastern China when the Taepings were subdued' (Bowers 1869: 31). Anderson's descriptions were quite positive and Sladen argued strongly that they might make useful part-ners. It was evident that they commanded a wide range of support in Yunnan and were well respected in the areas to the south. The whole purpose of Sladen's mission was an exchange of letters with the Panthays in order to reopen the caravan trade and offer the pos-sibility of gaining even greater trade between Yunnan and South Asia.

All of this would become evident when Colonel Sladen subsequently made the case for opening up the India–China trade. Speaking before the Chamber of Commerce in Glasgow, Sladen advocated for direct trade from India to China through Burma. His remarks (including the published supplemental materials) were extensive as he sought to refute General Cotton while speaking of the centrality of Rangoon. He explained to his audience that not only was a Rangoon route viable, but the trade with the Panthays might be restored. To this end, he quoted from his own diary from the expedition:

---

[2] I am indebted to Nyi Nyi Kyaw for pointing out Mindon Min's grant.

> Unlike other rebellions in China, the present Mohammedan occupa-
> tion of Yunan has proved itself durable in character; and my own ex-
> periences at Momein, as a guest for six weeks of the Mohammedan
> Governor of the place, gave proof of an intention, on the part of the new
> rulers, to act with moderation, and a desire to conciliate, rather than
> appear oppressive to their Chinese subjects...the 'Panthays' were more
> than hospitable. They shewed themselves to be alive to the interests of
> trade; and so far aided the efforts of the expedition to open up commu-
> nication, or to enter into commercial relations with their country, as to
> take up arms, and shed their blood in our cause, in ridding the country
> of armed opposition (Sladen 1870: 29).

He explained that the commercial problem did not stem from the
Panthays, whom he obviously liked, but from the diplomatic complexity inherent in deciding upon recognizing a state created by a rebellion. Sladen may well have remembered that a similar situation had
recently applied to the American South in the U.S. Civil War as he
explained:

> The real obstacle in the way of direct or recognized intercourse with
> the Panthay Government, lies in their present hostile relations to the
> Chinese, and the political difficulty of entering into friendly engage-
> ments with a race who are accounted rebels against a Government in
> treaty alliance with ourselves (Sladen 1870: 29).

From Sladen's point of view, the Panthays, who he clearly believed to
have created a powerful and stable Sultanate, offered an important
commercial opportunity for British business interests. Given General
Cotton's polemic, Sladen was actually saying that the Panthays held
one of the keys to the future economic development of Burma.

A Panthay Diaspora in Burma

What neither Sladen nor those who were part of the Bhamo Expedition
could foresee was that the Panthays would be crushed so effectively
that they would indeed be of little interest to the Kingdom of Burma
and British Burma. The defeat of the Panthays in 1873 would be total:
by one estimate the population of Western Yunnan was cut in half.
Atwill cites Imperial records that suggest that the Panthays were deliberately and systematically massacred: 'the road....was ankle deep in
blood...Neither man, woman nor child who was Muslim was spared.'

Survivors, especially women and children, were sold to Imperial officials and soldiers (Atwill 2005). One French traveller in Kunming later reported seeing soldiers 'followed by women and children who they sell here' (Atwill 2005: 187). That is, many of the Panthay women and children survived the massacres but found themselves enslaved in Kunming and elsewhere in Yunnan.

The more fortunate found ways and means to escape to Burma and Siam where they experienced a range of fates. Most immediately obvious, some joined criminal gangs which roved the Shan Hills on the road between Yunnan and Bhamo, while others went to the Irrawaddy Valley (Yegar 1966). Their number (and activities) appears to have been sufficient enough to produce a diplomatic concern for both Burma and China. Eventually, the King of Burma at the time announced that all captured Panthay criminals would be returned to the Chinese government (Yegar 1966). Others would be resettled in Burma, going to towns with pre-existing Panthay communities in the Shan Hills (such as Bhamo) and to Moguk, where they found work in the ruby mining industry—especially as mule drivers (Yegar 1966). Again, what would be clear is that this particular type of Muslims would be foreign and alien to Burma—even if they were valued for their economic activity.

Moshe Yegar's 'The Panthay (Chinese Muslims) of Burma and Yunnan', which appeared in the *Journal of Southeast Asian History* in 1966, carried this little known story further. Yegar noted that VC Scott O'Connor had portrayed the Panthay in favourable terms in *The Silken East*. O'Connor had been impressed by both their adaptations to Moguk (where many had settled) and modernity (Yegar 1966). He might have added that they were represented as content subjects of the British Empire. Yegar also drew upon Charles Crosthwaite's *The Pacification of Burma* (1912) to show further the positive light in which the British had come to regard the Panthays. Typically, perhaps, there were some Panthays who resisted colonial rule, while others were employed by the British to facilitate transportation operations (Yegar 1966).

Yegar argues that some British officials thought the Panthays (along with other people) might be brought to be resettled in Northern Burma. It is unclear whether this idea was ever acted upon or even thoroughly discussed. Unfortunately, Yegar appears to be relying only on Crosthwaite for this piece of information. Nevertheless, it might well be consistent with British thinking that a Chinese-Muslim minority might well provide additional stability to a region in which they were finding 'pacification' to be a challenge. Furthermore, the utility of the Panthays might be more appealing with the success which the Qing ultimately had with the event known as the 'Muslim Rebellion'. In addition, it is evident that Burma's loose borders and frontier areas were a priority for colonial policy makers. The attention devoted to the northern parts of Burma might be gleaned from the eventual hardening of the border towards the end of the nineteenth century (Tagliacozzo 2004). Taken together, then, the accounts from O'Connor and Crosthwaite illustrate that the Panthays had become a useful minority.[3] They were not a part of the land, were clearly external to Burma and were economically productive. In addition, even in Burma they could still work as the kind of cultural intermediaries which might make commerce between China and British India possible. The fact that they appeared to be loyal subjects of the empire would not have hurt either.

A Forgotten Elite: Indian Muslims

This chapter takes the position that the South Asian contribution to the making of modern Myanmar has been understated. In fact, it might not be too much to claim that Indians have been virtually written out of the history of modern Myanmar. Yet they were a critical—perhaps the most vivid embodiment—of British colonization. It might be worthwhile to add that most of the British soldiers who came to Burma were Indian and that inclusion into the empire meant governance from India. Furthermore, Burma represented a huge economic opportunity for Indians and so British expansion into the country was supported and populated by Indians. That said, the exodus of Indians out of Burma remains one of the most poignant events in the last two centuries of the country's history (Bayly and Harper 2005). It is commonly accepted that as many as 400,000 people perished in this event (Aung-Thwin and Aung-Thwin 2012).

---

[3] Yegar followed this community into the twentieth century as he sought to find places where they were still visible and vibrant. For more on the Panthays in the twentieth century see Yegar, 1966: 81–5.

However, this gruesome exodus—which might be usefully compared with some of the events associated with the 'Armenian Genocide'—has barely been investigated by historians and, accordingly, remains a neglected episode. Therefore, while some scholarship does exist on Indians in Burma, it remains an understudied subject.

Accordingly, the Indian Muslim community that existed in Burma has not been the subject of sustained academic scrutiny. Probably the best and most recent treatment of the subject is Nalini Chakravarti's *The Indian Minority in Burma: The Rise and Decline of an Immigrant Community* (1971), which is now more than a generation old, but provides a detailed look at South Asians in the country. In this study, Chakravarti relied on the census data that the British collected in Burma. While he acknowledged that this data was problematic in many ways, the conclusion that Chakravarti reached was that Indians in Burma were probably not as numerous as many believed. One reason for this misunderstanding was that many Indians in Burma were there on a temporary or even only a seasonal basis. In fact, he concluded that the Indian population constituted about 5 to 6 percent of the total population in Burma, but his study also documents that they were probably dominant in some areas (particularly Rangoon) and held a significant amount of wealth (Chakravarti 1971).

Yet, Chakravarti's analysis reflected the general experience of prejudice that was directed against 'Indians', which he recognized to be a feature of inter-war Burma. One of his tasks was to chart the rise of discrimination against Indians (which accompanied the growth of Burmese nationalism) and its impact upon a political process that promoted their expulsion from the country. More generally, this pattern of defining Indians as a unified community in Burma may well have been the way that they were perceived, but in fact, the Indian community in Burma was a dynamic and multifaceted entity. Nonetheless, it will be useful to draw upon Chakravarti to get a better view of Indian Muslims in order to improve our perspective on the status of both Indians and Islam, in Burma. Of possibly even wider significance, this subject has merit in its own right, and its character, achievement, and fate will shed light not only on the history of British Burma and the Indian Ocean, but also on the status of Muslims in contemporary Myanmar.

In order to briefly examine this community, this discussion will also draw upon *Who's Who in Burma* (Butler 1927). This book makes a useful primary source for historians because it contains a large number of mini biographies of key figures in British Burma. There are a number of obvious methodological limitations that caution against reliance upon this volume. Its accuracy cannot always be guaranteed and the process by which its informational base was assembled cannot be meaningfully reconstructed. Nonetheless, while this volume was not written with an eye for future historians, it almost certainly contains a wealth of information which might not be found elsewhere. At the same time, this volume can be utilized with the idea that it will be suggestive and not exhaustive; the value of the material may well be to spark the curiosity of scholars to probe other sources, in order to learn more about the colonial elite who ran Burma in the early part of the twentieth century.

Taking the biographical sketch from five Indian Muslims who flourished in Burma during the early decades of the twentieth century should provide something of an incomplete composite picture of a colonial elite. This means that the material from *Who's Who in Burma* can help to yield a picture of the Indian Muslim elite who flourished in the country from the last decades of the nineteenth century until the World War II. To that end, it should prove useful to examine the biographies of Ebrahim Ahmed, Alijah Mahomed Albhai, Mahmoud Auzam, Hajoe Mahmood Esoof Bhymeah, and Babu Ibrahim. These figures hardly exhaust the numbers of significant Indian Muslims that are contained within the pages of *Who's Who in Burma*.

Ebrahim Ahmed

Ebrahim Ahmed came from an Indian Ocean family. He was born in Mergui in 1869, but his grandfather hailed from Penang. He also had a Burmese name (Be Shew Myo), as did his brothers. He was the first member of Mergui to sit in the Legislative Council, but his real clout came from his commercial success. He owned a rice mill, tin mines and was substantially involved in pearling. He had significant business connections in 'London, Bombay, Calcutta, Penang and Singapore.' *Who's Who* mentioned that 'through sheer industry and hard work....he has raised his brothers also to their present positions by urging them on in his footsteps' (Butler 1927: 3). His business was (at the time *Who's Who* was written) managed by his son, A.E. Ahmed. He was active in charities, supporting the Red Cross and other activities. The entry added that he 'has built a huge Mosque, to which is added a Madrassa, Rest Houses, etc'. Finally, these achievements hardly went unnoticed as he was awarded 'the M.B.E. by the King Emperor on 1st Jan. 1919, awarded a Sanad by the Viceroy on the 26th of June, 1918 and awarded the badge for Voluntary War Work in India "1914–1919" in March 1919' (Butler 1927: 3).

Alijah Mahomed Albhai

A very different biography was that of Alijah Mahomed Albhai, who was identified as a 'Landlord and successful businessman of Burma'. He was born in 1884 in Rajkot, Kathiawar and came to Burma at age eight, going first to Mandalay and later to Rangoon. *Who's Who* would place him as a 'well known member of the Khoja community'. For his efforts the Aga Khan conferred on him the title of Alijah in 1914. When the Aga Khan visited Rangoon in 1922–3, Mr A.B. Mahomed was the most important member of the reception committee. The Aga Khan nominated him as leader and 'Chief Member of the Shia Immani Ismailia Khoja Council'. The entry concluded by noting that he was active in 'several important clubs in Burma' and he 'never refuses to give his support in any cause relating to the good of his community. Nowhere can be found a more powerful personality, a philanthropist and an able reformer of his community whose interest and welfare he has at heart' (Butler 1927: 7).

Mahmoud Auzam

Mahmoud Auzam was born in Port Blair in 1880, and his parents later moved to Burma. He studied at Rangoon College and then went to England to study law. He joined the Middle Temple and was called to the Bar in 1907. Returning to Burma, he practised law as an Advocate of the Chief Court of Lower Burma. He would prove to be a strong supporter of the war effort. *Who's Who* elaborated: 'He took part in every kind of collection.... He was instrumental in getting two motor ambulances and arranging Xmas dinners for several years for the Territorials.' At the same time, Auzam 'is recognized as one of the leaders of the Muslim Community in Burma.' He would be known as the sole proprietor of the *Rangoon Daily News*, which was the 'leading Indian daily in the province. The paper had the largest circulation of all English dailies in Burma and is popular with all communities.' Auzam owned significant property and was a senior member of the Rangoon Bar and possessed a large law firm. He cut a dynamic profile as well. *Who's Who* added that he 'owns race horses' (Butler 1927: 12).

Hajoe Mahmood Esoof Bhymeah

Bhymeah, whose house was displayed in *Who's Who in Burma*, was born in Rangoon in 1892, in a family with significant commercial connections. His father had been a merchant in Calcutta and a generation earlier the family had been located in Surat. His father came to Burma, marrying the daughter of well-known merchant and ship-owner Noor-ud-Naikwara, whose family had settled in the country before the First Anglo-Burman War. Hajoe Mahmood Esoof Bhymeah was educated at St. Paul's High School in Rangoon, and later was sent by his father to India to study Oriental languages. He graduated with Urdu and Gujarati and then went into Import and Export. He speculated in minerals and rubber and owned a mining concern in Palaw Township (Mergui District). However, *Who's Who* made clear that his impact was in two areas: education and community development.

To begin with, in 1906 he founded the Bhymeah Vernacular Free School (later the Bhymean High School). He would also found the Fatima Bibi Bhymeah Girls' School in honour of his mother. *Who's Who* put these efforts into perspective: 'The Bhymeah High School now affords education to about 500 boys of all nationalities, and one of the features of the school is that it possesses a Boarding Hostel, specially to suite the convenience of Muslim boys.' In addition, the school 'has improved very rapidly and the buildings now forming the school are valued at 3½ lakhs. There is a mosque attached to the school' (Butler 1927: 21).

It was pointed out that Bhymeah went beyond Muslim education as he 'figured very prominently in Educational affairs and has done many things in the interest of the Education for the country' including organizing between forty and fifty schools of all denominations

(Butler 1927: 21). In addition, in 1916 he presided over the All-Burma Muslim Educational Conference held at Meiktila and was active in supporting education in both Burma and India. He was a Trustee to the Nadvatul Ulma (an Islamic school which opened in Lucknow in 1894) and was a leader of the Burma Education Conference. What is more interesting, perhaps, is that in 1924 he made an extensive tour to Europe 'with a view of studying the various means and methods of teaching in Western Schools and Colleges....He has introduced many systems of Western teachings in his school with much advantage' (Butler 1927: 21).

Babu Ibrahim

Babu Ibrahim was born in 1890 in Gurudaspur in Punjab. He came to Burma in 1905 and began to work as a Contractor in the Public Works Department (PWD) and Burma Railways. His career benefitted from the advice and influence of his brother Khan Sahib Ali Mohamed, who was a well-known contractor (and the subject of another interesting entry in *Who's Who*) and with this connection he was able to achieve significant construction work on several major rail lines. These included (1) the Henzada-Bassein line; (2) the Henzada-Kyaungin line; (3) doubling the line from Rangoon to Pegu; (4) the Moulmein line; and (5) the Nyaunglebin-Madok line. His knowledge of the rail lines was evidently useful as he became quite wealthy. He came to own 'several Quarries which are supplying stone in huge quantities in different districts'. In addition, Ibrahim 'owns several palatial buildings in Rangoon and other districts'. *Who's Who* added that he lived a very simple life but was active in charities and helped 'very deserving case' (Butler 1927: 253).

Taken together, these five portraits provide a brief sketch of the Indian Muslim elite who flourished in colonial Burma in the early decades of the twentieth century. It should be pointed out that the vast majority of Indians were quite poor, with some living in desperate conditions. Chakravarti's study, however, traces Indian wealth in Burma because it helps to better contextualize the biographies drawn from *Who's Who*. The picture that Chakravarti left was a complicated one, but it might be useful to highlight a few basic points. To begin with, Indian wealth in Burma was diffuse as the Indians worked in many economic sectors. The most infamous were the Chettyars, or the moneylenders, who came from the Chettinand district of Madras and held the loans which many Burmans came to find oppressive (Chakravarti 1971). These moneylenders made easy targets for nationalist politicians. Moreover, Indians owned many factories in Burma and significant wealth in urban areas. For example, at one point Indians held 60 per cent of the real estate in Rangoon and by 1939 they owned roughly one third of all of the factories in Burma. More generally, Chakravarti argued that it was Indian finance capital that had built Rangoon (and other parts of Burma) and made much of the economic growth that defined some of the country's key trajectories in the early twentieth century.

Chakravarti explained that the expulsion of Indians from Burma could not be understood by the rise of ethnic nationalism alone. Instead, he faulted Indians for failing to make greater efforts to fit into Burman life. This could be seen in many ways including schools based upon communitarian interests (in some institutions the language of instruction was never Burmese but often Hindi and Urdu). In addition, many Indians lived under Hindu legal codes or 'Moslem Law'. Furthermore, many Indians were largely indifferent to the development of Burmese institutions; in other words, they remained 'Indians first and Burmans last' (Chakravarti 1971).

The figures cited from *Who's Who* fit this general profile: they were wealthy, connected to India and they were Muslims. Unlike the Panthays who were regarded as external and 'other' by the British, these Indian Muslims were well integrated into colonial Burma. They might, in fact, be regarded as 'insiders' or as part of a community which served to buttress British administration. They were powerful and active in virtually every aspect of Burman society. Their efforts did not go unnoticed as some were ultimately knighted and all of them had some sort of club presence (though it does not appear that they were accepted into the most elite and exclusive clubs) where they lived. These mini biographies also illustrate that Indian Muslims had diverse origins and a variety of trajectories once they had immigrated into Burma. At the same time, they were not heralded as some type of 'model minority'; that is, they would not have been regarded by the British in any way like the 'loyal Karens of Burma'. Instead, *Who's Who* represents them alongside Burmans, Hindus, Chinese, British, and other groups as being part of the leadership of a dynamic and cosmopolitan province in the Indian Empire.

More generally, if the Panthays might be remembered for making contributions to the caravan trade and the transportation operations of the British army, then this group of Indian Muslims actually shaped a much wider area of social life. That is, this particular set of individuals shaped the economic, social and cultural development of Burma—particularly in its rapidly growing cities. They had to live through the process of de-Indianization without recognizing that separation would eventually take place. They were interested in India, partly because Burma was a part of India until 1937. Hence, even if Chakravarti was critical of their reluctance to engage Burma, their indifference has to be understood at least in part by Burma's position as a province of British India. It is worth citing the example of Maulana Mohammed Ali, a prominent Muslim leader in India who came to Burma in 1929 to solicit funds for the Muslim National University in Delhi (Chakravarti 1971). The exodus of Indians was hard to foresee before 1930 and the impulses of this community (and the antagonisms against it) need to be understood in the context of the success of Indian business interests in Burma as well as de-Indianization. To understand the status of Muslims in British Burma, it is most important to realize that separation from India would not have seemed inevitable and possibly not even desirable for most of the population. Though the subsequent nationalist narratives largely wrote Indian populations out of Myanmar, the ground realities between 1852 and 1942 would have been very different.

* * *

In some ways this is an old story: the comprehension of things in Burma was significantly impacted by developments in both India and China. Furthermore, British comprehension of the Panthays was motivated first by its commercial appetites and then by an expedition of Yunnan. By the time Crosthwaite wrote, the Panthays were probably little more than an interesting footnote—a series of small Chinese Muslim communities. Even if they lived in Burma and served British interests, they were essentially foreign and alien to Burma. O'Connor's vivid descriptions notwithstanding, the Panthays belonged to Yunnan and might be regarded as a living monument to Manchu incompetence.

The contrast between the Panthays and the Indian Muslim community could not be more complete: the latter was much larger, urban, diverse, with a range of contacts spread across the Indian Ocean. More important, perhaps, was the fact that the Indian community was well known by the British and was interwoven with other groups of South Asians. British documents do mark religious differentiations, but they do not regard these Indians as a 'minority'. Instead, they are understood to be part of a cosmopolitan society which existed in Burma—a society which Taw Sein Ko would find exciting and would draw criticism from John Furnivall.

The treatment that these two different communities received reflects not only their different histories, but significant historical transformations. Since the Panthays had descended into Burma from China, they did not carry any of the baggage of being part of India. Their lineage, including their connection with the Mongols, did not threaten Burmese society or the self-esteem of its leaders. As a diaspora population it did not present significant problems for either the British, the Burmese or the other peoples in Burma. Indian Muslims, on the other hand, faced the perception that they were part of the wave of British colonization. Burmese nationalists worked to separate themselves from India and this meant more than detaching Burma as a province from the Indian Empire. In practice Burmese nationalism meant the rejection of many things Indian, even if trade between the two countries continued unabated. It bears repeating that the Rohingyas are associated in the minds of many in Myanmar with Bengal (and more generally British India). The fear that the Rohingyas represent another assault on things Burmese stems from the assumption that they are alien to Myanmar (Zan and Chan 2005). Indeed, it might not be too much to argue that the fear of 'Islamization' represents something of a hangover from the battle that many Burmese felt compelled to fight not only against British colonial institutions, but the Indian influences which had accompanied it.

The de-Indianization of Burma would take a number of forms: the political, administrative, and legal changes that began under British rule and the demographic transformation which soon followed. Most of this massive Indian community would either by pushed out of Burma or would flee in fear when British power was decisively challenged by the Japanese. The problematic status of Islam in contemporary Myanmar has many roots and one of them was the exodus of the South Asians from the country. Had they remained in Burma, they would have in all probability furnished Muslims with a broad base of economic, political, legal and educational support, which might have enabled them to flourish better in the new Myanmar. To be sure, Islamic life and practice in Myanmar was never likely to develop into a monolithic entity, but having a strong Indian community might well have made it less likely that Muslims in Myanmar would be persecuted on the basis of their religion. The removal of this community probably had the effect of making Islam in Burma even more marginal than it was external.

In addition, it is worth noting that the unintentional results of British discourse was to render Muslims an 'invisible minority' during the colonial period. The British were interested in understanding, describing and cataloguing ethnic minorities which appeared to belong to the country. Any serious student of British letters would recognize that this in itself was a gargantuan task and the great efforts made to understand the country's ethnic minorities had an unforeseen effect on Burma's Muslims. With the possible exception of the Panthays, British discourses rendered Muslims as an underidentified entity; as a consequence, Muslims were neither recognized as a distinctive community nor were they understood as intrinsically Burmese. Even if they spoke Burmese as a first language (and many did) and regarded themselves as Burmans, they were unintentionally cut off from any kind of Burmese identity. Furthermore, the emergence of an independent Burma in 1948 would produce a state where Indians would be a tiny and still resented minority. Like so many other new nations, it would also demand its own history—one in which the dominant themes would include the struggles for independence and then the post-colonial conflicts which would pit the dominant state against a number of well-armed ethnic minorities. The coup in 1962 led to sustained military rule in a country that was decidedly inward-looking. It was under these conditions that the legal status of Muslims in Myanmar underwent significant transformation. The passing of the 1982 Myanmar Citizenship Law had the effect of denying full citizenship to non-Burmans who came to the country after 1824. For the most part, this has been understood to be directed at Muslims located in Arakan (Berlie 2008). For our purposes, it might also be seen as an instance of the continuing process of de-Indianization. In all of this, another possibility for modernity—one which had been grasped by figures such as Taw Sein Ko and John Furnivall—was conveniently forgotten: namely, that Burma might develop into a cosmopolitan country which would look outside to build upon its many contacts beyond its borders and across the Indian Ocean. De-Indianization, then, proved to be the flip side of modern Myanmar nationalism, and removing or marginalizing influences perceived to be external and different proved to be one of the key strategies of nation-building. Finally, the larger narrative of de-Indianization would play out elsewhere: the Partition, the experience of Indians in a number of newly-independent African states come to mind, as for the growing restrictions on Indian presence in a number of emerging nations. Therefore, to better understand the situation of the Muslim community in Myanmar is to trace it first from within the country and then to look for echoes that might be found, listening to the rumblings contained in 'Indian Ocean history'. Coming to terms with this history—both inside and outside of Myanmar—is a necessary step in helping to understand and address the persecution of the country's Muslim minority.

3 Personal Law and Colonial Legacy
State–Religion Relations and Islamic Law in Myanmar*
MELISSA CROUCH

During British colonial rule, the customs and traditions of religious communities in colonies across the world were subject to a process of codification in matters of personal law, and for Muslim communities this often resulted in the codification of Islamic personal law. Burma was no exception, and a few years after the final stage of annexation by the British in 1885, a system of personal law for Muslims was introduced. As part of British India up until 1937, the law that was recognised and imported was largely identical in substance to 'Mahomedan law' (also known as Anglo-Muhammedan Law), as constructed by colonial authorities in British India.

For many, it may come as a surprise that the state of Myanmar recognizes any form of Islamic law at all, particularly given the anti-Muslim violence since 2012. Even those who studied Muslims in Myanmar, such as Yegar (1972; 2002), have paid little attention to the practise of

* The research for this chapter was funded by a grant from the Institute for Global Law & Policy at Harvard Law School, and an earlier version of this work was presented at the IGLP workshop. I would like to thank Jerusa Ali and Nurfadzilah Yahaya for their comments on an earlier version of this chapter. I am also grateful to Ma Maw Maw for her excellent research assistance on this project.

Islamic personal law as recognized by the state. The only work that has been published to date is Hooker's (1984) broad comparative overview of Islamic law in Southeast Asia, which includes a chapter on Burma. There is a large body of scholarship on the construction of Anglo-Muhammedan law in the context of India,[1] but this was never the case for Myanmar. There is no current academic work on how the secular courts of Myanmar have recognized and decided cases concerning Islamic law, or whether the approach of the courts has shifted over time in light of social and political developments.

For those who are familiar with Islamic personal law systems in other post-colonial contexts, the line of inquiry in this chapter is distinctive for several reasons. First, there have never been efforts to codify Islamic personal law in Myanmar, beyond the brief mention in the Burma Laws Act 1898. Second, there have never been efforts to expand the system of Islamic personal law with the creation of Islamic courts; these matters have always been heard and determined by the general courts instead. This means that the adjudication of Islamic personal law in Myanmar is distinct in comparison with other countries in Southeast Asia, where a special system of Sharia courts usually has the task of deciding cases of Islamic personal law. Third, there have also never been efforts to completely abolish the right to Islamic personal law in Myanmar, although some legislative efforts that purport to protect the rights of Buddhist women had the effect of reducing the scope of Islamic personal law in cases of inter-religious marriage.

In this chapter, I seek to situate the development of Islamic personal law post-independence, in the broader context of the shifting relations between religion and the state in Myanmar. I consider how and why Islamic law exists in Myanmar today. I do this by exploring two avenues of inquiry: the origins and development of Islamic personal law in Myanmar, and the subsequent persistence of Islamic law during the socialist and military regimes. I demonstrate that although the Islamic personal law imposed on Muslims in Burma

---

[1] For example, Strawson (1999) examines the construction of Islamic personal law in India through the compilation of volumes such as *The Hedaya* by Charles Hamilton in 1791 and Sir Williams Jones' translation of a text on the law of inheritance, *Al Sirajiyyah*, 1792.

by the British may have been 'artificial' at the time it was introduced (as Hooker claims), we now need to consider the ways in which it has evolved and developed over time. This includes how it is used by the courts today, and what Islamic personal law means to Muslims in Myanmar today.

For those who have been aware of the existence of Islamic personal law in Myanmar, it has generally been assumed that 'the law of Burma's Muslims was, in substance and content, the Anglo-Muhammadan law of India' (Hooker 1984: 47). This chapter seeks to address and deconstruct this claim. While it may have been the case that the courts primarily referred to British Indian jurisprudence prior to independence, I suggest that we need to reconsider the development of Islamic personal law since independence, in order to understand how its meaning and practise have changed over time. I consider the extent to which the courts have developed a distinctive line of jurisprudence on matters of Islamic law, and how state policies towards religion have influenced its development. This goes to the question of authority: what is the source of the courts' authority, what legal texts do they rely on, and to what extent and why this has changed over time? It also raises questions about why Muslims use the secular courts to resolve disputes in a Buddhist-majority state. I argue that the secular courts are one point of interaction between Muslims and the state, which provides insight into how disputes that arise between members of religious communities are resolved. It also reflects some the layered history of the legal system in Myanmar, that has been influenced by colonial rule, parliamentary democracy, socialist rule, and military regime.

The Foundations of Islamic Law in Myanmar

Islamic law in Myanmar can be understood as having been imposed on Burma through a process of 'double colonization'. The first act of colonization was that Islamic law was constructed by authorities of British India prior to the annexation of Burma. The second act of colonization was the transfer of this same body of law into Burma without any regard for local Islamic practise. This included the adoption of all laws that applied to Muslims in British India up until 1935. Based on this double act of imposition, Islamic personal law in Burma developed in three stages. Prior to independence, colonial judges drew on the jurisprudence of Anglo-Muhammadan law from British India and Islamic personal law primarily applied to Indian Muslims, who compromised the wealthiest section of the Muslim population in Burma at the time. But in the post-independence period, due to the growing political uncertainty and the violence directed against Indians and Muslims, many fled Burma. This second phase, from 1948 to early 1960s, was also characterized by the courts' increasing reliance on precedent as developed by courts in Burma. This led to the third stage, from the late 1960s to the present, in which Islamic personal law was primarily accessed by Burmese Muslims and was administered by judges who were primarily non-Muslim and who had no training in Islamic law.

The Origins of Islamic Personal Law

There are several factors that led to the recognition of Islamic personal law by the colonial state in Burma. The first was the broader fate of Burma's subjugation by British India after the final stage of annexation in 1885. The second was the introduction of British Indian legislation for Muslims in Myanmar. The third was the gradual control and limitations placed on Islamic personal law through laws passed by the legislature, mostly copied from British India.

The development and origin of Islamic law as it was adopted in Burma is intimately related to its colonial history as a former part of British India. The source of colonial personal laws in British India can be traced back to 1765, when the East India Company was given the right to collect revenue in three areas—Bengal, Bihar, and Orissa (Sen 2010: 131; Hardy 1973). This led to a separation between religious and secular laws, which was formalized in 1772. The Governor General, Warren Hastings, issued a directive that the Qur'an was to be used to resolve disputes concerning inheritance and marriage for Muslims (Sen 2010: 132), and there was also to be separate personal law for the Hindus. In order to overcome the judges' lack of expertise on either Islamic law or Hindu law, the courts were supported by local experts in Hindu and Islamic law (Lau 2010: 381). This system by which judges relied on local religious authorities to provide guidance in matters of religion remained in place for over 90 years. In 1864, this practice finally came to an end because colonial authorities deemed that local religious experts were no longer needed to assist judges due to the body of case law that had accumulated and the publication of English language compilations of religious laws (Anderson 1996; 1990). In their view, Islamic law had been defined and determined, and judges could now make decisions without need for assistance from local religious authorities.

Unlike in India, there appears to be no evidence that any research or inquiry was conducted into local practices of Islamic communities in Myanmar, despite the shortcomings of this process. Consistent with Keck's argument that Muslims were an invisible minority during the colonial period (Keck 2009), Islamic religious leaders were never relied upon to advise the courts on the law that applied in Burma when it was part of British India. This suggests an assumption or ignorance on the part of the British about the existence of Muslim communities in Burma at the time it was colonized. It also indicates that in Burma colonial authorities assumed that the law of British India was relevant because most Muslims were thought to be Indian, due to the mass migration of Indians to Burma during the colonial period (Chakravarti 1971). Similarly, the colonial legislature incorporated the same laws in Burma as were being passed for Muslims in British India, as I discuss next.

Legislative Borrowing

By 1890, not long after the end of the third Anglo-Burman War and the annexation of Burma to British India, the Indian Codes were applied to Burma as a province of British India. Staple bodies of law, from criminal law to property to contracts, were copied wholesale from India. Several laws were passed to establish a hierarchy of courts and administrative control, although different approaches were taken to the governance of Upper Burma and Lower Burma. In 1897, a Legislative Council was established in Rangoon and the role of its members was to assist the Lieutenant General in drafting legislation for Burma. In reality, it took most of the laws from British India, with no innovation. Up until 1922, the two courts from which official law reports were produced were the Chief Court of Rangoon, which published the Lower Burma Rulings, and the Court of the Judicial

Commissioner in Mandalay, which published the Upper Burma Rulings (see Cheesman 2014: 78).[2]

The final stage of the annexation of Burma to British India occurred in 1885, over twenty years after the end of the reliance on Islamic religious authorities in Indian courts. Thirteen years later, in 1898, the courts were granted jurisdiction over customary law through the introduction of the Burma Laws Act 1898.[3] This Act remains valid today, and at the time of its introduction achieved two goals. First, Upper Burma came under the umbrella of British India as the final stage of annexation. In terms of the ethnic nationalities in Upper Burma, some came under separate judicial and administrative systems under British rule. For example, customary law applied in Shan State provided that punishments were 'in conformity with the spirit of the law in force in the rest of British India'.[4]

The second effect of the Burma Laws Act 1898 was that it allowed for the recognition of customary law in matters of family personal law. The most important provision is Section 13:

> Where in any suit or other proceeding in the Union of Burma it is necessary for the Court to decide any question regarding succession, inheritance, marriage or caste, or any religious usage or institution: (a) the Buddhist law in cases where the parties are Buddhists; (b) the Muhammadan law in cases where the parties are Mohammedans; and (c) the Hindu law in cases where the parties are Hindus, shall from the rule of decision, except in so far as such law has by enactment been altered or abolished, or is opposed to any custom having the force of law.

The field of customary law, however, was only preserved in the confined areas such as marriage, inheritance and divorce. This was granted as a concession on the basis that it did not interfere with the 'aims of empire and entrenchment of colonial rule' (Huxley 2014). This included customary law for the adherents of three world

---

[2] For a list of all Burma law reports, see Crouch and Cheesman (2014).

[3] The Burma Laws Act (India Act XIII, 1898) (4 November 1898). Prior to this, Hooker suggests that it was the Burma Courts Act XVII/1875 that provided the earliest source of colonial authority for application of Islamic personal law in Burma. There only appears to be one reported case prior to 1898.

[4] Burma Laws Act 1898, s 11.

religions: Muslims, Hindus, and Buddhists.[5] This raises the question: what was this customary law for Muslims, and how did it develop? To answer this, British authorities turned to the case law of British India, as they did in most other areas of legal practice.

In addition, there were several other laws introduced by the British that only applied to Muslims, yet all came ready-made from British India. The Kazis Act 1880 allowed the government to appoint a *kazis* (that is, qadi or judge) to preside at a marriage or other ceremony, although it appears that this law was never implemented (Yegar 1972: 78). There were also two laws governing *wakf*, that is, the dedication of property for a charitable purpose. The Mussalman Wakf Validating Act 1913 provided for the creation of *wakf* either for the purpose of supporting children or descendants, or for the person's own benefit, or for payment of debts. The Mussalman Wakf Act 1924 provided for the supervision and accountability of *wakf*. These laws were copied from British India and were intended to protect the interests of landholders (Kozlowski 1985).

The practice of adopting legislation from British India ended in 1937, when the Government of Burma Act 1935 came into force. This law established Burma as a separate colony with its own Legislative Council. The effect of this change in administration meant that all legislative amendments, additions, and changes to Islamic personal law in India after this date were not adopted as a matter of presumption in Burma.[6]

The Operation of the Burma Laws Act 1898

At the same time that the colonial legislature cemented a form of Islamic law by legislation in Myanmar, the courts were drawing on British Indian precedent from 1898 up to the 1940s to develop a body of law on matters of marriage, inheritance, divorce, child custody, and succession for Muslims. Given the little scholarly attention this development received, I first turn to Hooker's work and demonstrate the its limitations. I then show how the courts were attuned to the needs

---

[5] Burma Laws Act 1898, s 13(1).

[6] For example, the Shariat Act 1937 of British India was not introduced in Myanmar.

of Muslim staff and how English-language Anglo-Muhammedan texts became a staple reference for the courts.

Hooker on the Burma Laws Act 1898

For Hooker, Islamic law was an anomaly that did not really belong in Burma. Professor Hooker has written prolifically on the legal systems, customs and traditions of Southeast Asia.[7] His work in Malaysia and Indonesia in particular is based on extensive experience there, and focuses on how legal texts are actually understood and applied in local practice. His work on legal history in Southeast Asia includes some discussion of the Burmese legal system in the context of broader trends and patterns in law and legal institutions in Southeast Asia.[8] He conducted a review of case law from 1898 up until the 1960s, and he focuses on two basic questions: Who is a Muslim? And, what is Muslim law in Burma? Yet in addressing these questions, his work on Burma appears to have been limited to English-language legal sources, and was unlikely to have been based on any field research due to the restrictions on foreigners visiting the country at that time (see Crouch 2014). He also appears to assume that Islamic personal law was a new arrival for Indian Muslim migrants, and does not recognize that Muslims existed in Myanmar long before the introduction of colonization.

Hooker opens his work with the claim that 'Islam in Burma had an artificial character to an outstanding degree'[9] (Hooker 1984: 44) and follows this in a footnote with the statement that '[t]he past tense is used to emphasize that Islam in Burma is now largely a matter of history'. This chapter refutes this statement and demonstrates that Islamic law in Burma must not be relegated to history, but acknowledged in the present. Hooker erroneously adopts a 'frozen in time' approach, and so his work, which constitutes the only detailed

---

[7] See, for example, Hooker 1975; 1978; 1984. For a comprehensive review of the life and work of MB Hooker.

[8] On Islamic law in Burma see Hooker 1984: 44–84; on Burmese law texts see Hooker 1978: 17–25, 143–7; and Hooker 1975: 85–94.

[9] Writing 20 years later, Yegar (2002: 29) also uses the term 'artificial' in describing Islamic personal law in Myanmar, but it appears that his claim that it came to an end is also based on Hooker's factually incorrect claims.

scholarship in English on Islamic law jurisprudence in Burma, should be treated with caution.

Further, his sole focus on the courts, rather than also looking to other forms of dispute resolution, goes against the philosophy of legal pluralism; that is, the need to recognize the existence of legal norms beyond state law. This is rather ironic given that legal pluralism is an idea which he pioneered (see for example, Hooker 1975), although it is understandably more difficult to access such sources. Despite the fact that Hooker focused considerably on *fatawa* (Islamic legal opinions) in contexts such as Indonesia (Hooker 2003), he appears to have overlooked the existence of *fatawa* in Burma and the role it may play in resolving personal law disputes.

Despite these shortcomings, Hooker's work nevertheless provides a starting point for the analysis of Islamic personal law as it was practised during the colonial period, and can be contrasted with current practice. Hooker's commentary is primarily doctrinal and focuses on the extent to which colonial courts, and later post-colonial courts in Burma relied on Indian case law for disputes involving Islamic personal law. He conducts a detailed review of case law issues of the validity of gift, questions of guardianship, marriage and divorce, inheritance and succession, apostasy and conversion, and also crime. He demonstrates that in most instances, established precedent from Indian courts prevailed. He does highlight one area that was distinct, which were cases concerning Zerbadi (Burmese Muslims), where the court was often asked to consider whether Burmese Buddhist law or Muhammedan law applied. He demonstrates that the courts refused to accept the argument that 'Buddhist law should apply to Zerbadis, as they had not necessarily consented to Buddhist law prior to colonialism.'

There are many ways in which Hooker's thesis of the artificiality of Islamic law in Burma could be challenged. One example of a more ingrained approach was the recognition given in the rules of the court itself to the Islamic practices of its staff.

Recognition of Islamic Practise in the Court Rules

In a similar approach to the way the legislature that copied laws from British India, the courts' policies and manuals were also adapted from British India. These rules demonstrated an awareness of, and accommodation for, the practise of Islam. One example of court policies that mirrored colonial practice in British India is the Court Manual. The High Court Manual was a compilation of the rules and regulations of the court, first published in Burma in 1930.[10] The Court Manual stipulated two key areas in which Islam needed to be respected by the court administration. First, it required judges to be aware of 'Mahomedans Sacred days' by ensuring that no court cases were heard on days of significance for Muslims. This included five particular days of the year: Muharram, the ninth and tenth days of the first month of the Islamic calendar;[11] the birth anniversary of the prophet Muhammad, known in Myanmar as *Fatiha-i-duwazhdaham*; *Eid-ul-Fitr*, the celebration to mark the end of the month of fasting; and *Eid-ul-Adha*, the Feast of Sacrifice, to commemorate Abraham's willingness to sacrifice his son Ismail. Second, the Court Manual went on in the same section 19 to state that:

> All Mohamedan employees of the Court who may ask for it should be granted leave for a sufficient time not exceeding two hours to say their juma prayers at such time as may be locally desired on Fridays, provided that, if necessary, the time is made up by extra work during some part of the day.

In 1958, the Court Manual was revised and updated to reflect the changes to the court system and practices after independence. The High Court also gave orders to similar effect concerning religious festivals, that were printed in the *Upper Burma Reports*. For example, the court issued a memorandum to determine the 'Muhammadan festival' dates.[12] However, by late 1913, the courts ceased the practice of determining the festival dates, and judges were instead instructed to 'obtain the necessary information by making enquiries each year locally beforehand'.[13] The courts' memorandum gives no reason for its decision to end this practice.

[10] See the *High Court Office Manual 1930*.

[11] This is when Sunni Muslims remember Moses leading the Israelites out of Egypt; Shia Muslims commemorate this day as the Day of Ashura, to remember the death of Husayn ibn Ali, the third Shia Imam and the grandson of Muhammad.

[12] Circular Memorandum No. 5 of 1910, in *Upper Burma Rulings* (UBR) (1910–13, Vol. 1), p. 197.

[13] Circular of Memorandum No. 15 of 1913, in *UBR* (1910–13, Vol. 1), p. 254.

In 1913, the courts issued a memorandum affirming that Muslim employees were to be permitted by the court to obtain permission for two hours leave to say prayers on Fridays, although employees were required to make up for those hours.[14] When the Courts Manual was updated in 1959, this was reduced by half an hour and the time of day was specified:

> All Mahomedan employees of the Court who may ask for it should be granted leave from 12 noon to 1:30pm on Fridays to enable them to say their Jumma prayers, provided that, if necessary, the time is made up by extra work during some part of the day.[15]

Although this was likely taken from British India, this can also be seen as one indication that there indeed were Muslim court staff in Burma at the time. This is not surprising, given that Indians were brought into Burma for their skills and familiarity with the British colonial complex, and it was Indians who staffed a large part of the colonial civil service in Myanmar. Traces of this can also be found, for example, in photos on the walls of the Union Supreme Court building in Naypyidaw today. One photo hanging in the upstairs library depicts judges during the colonial period surrounded by staff who, by appearance and dress, were clearly from India and some of whom were likely to be Muslim.

Aside from the court administration and regulations, the more substantive body of Islamic law was developed through hearing court cases and the application of Anglo-Muhammedan texts, as I discuss next.

Anglo-Muhammedan Law as a Basis for Case Law

The development of the courts' approach to the application of Islamic law in Myanmar started with case law and precedents established in British India. In terms of Islamic personal law, during the first fifty years of the application of Muhammedan law—from 1890 up until independence in the late 1940s—there were over 60 reported court cases on appeal at the Supreme Court or High Court. The *Burma Law Reports* (BLR) provide an important source of historical evidence not only of the existence of Muslims and their use of the secular courts in Myanmar, but also of

---

[14] Circular Memorandum No. 13 of 1913, in *UBR* (1910–13, Vol. 1), p. 254.
[15] *High Court Office Manual 1959*, s 30(1).

the practise of Islamic law as mediated by state authorities. Up until 1948, many different sources of Islamic law were referred to with little consistency, and judges only demonstrated knowledge of legal sources from British India, written in English (Hooker 1984). A significant proportion of disputes during this period raised issues of Islamic law related to inter-religious marriage (Ikeya 2013), and the question before the court was often which law (Burmese Buddhist law, or Muslim law) would apply. This began to change after independence.

There were a range of sources and guides that courts came to rely upon for the interpretation and application of section 13 of the Burma Law Act 1898, when cases of Islamic personal law arose in the courts. One primary textbook that came into popular use by lawyers and judges during the parliamentary period was *Mulla's Principles of Mahomedan Law*. This volume was first published in 1906 by Sir Dinshaw Faridunji Mulla and remains an authoritative casebook of precedents on Islamic personal law from British India, based on the Hanafi school of law.[16] While this book is now in its twentieth edition, most legal practitioners in Myanmar rely on a 1970s or 1980s edition of this volume. The book does include legislative developments on Islamic personal law in India, but these are not relevant to the context of Myanmar. While other English-language texts such as Ameer Ali's *Mahommedan Law* (1912), Wilson's *Digest of Anglo-Muhammadan Law*, and other such volumes were used in the early 1900s in Burma, by the 1940s and the 1950s it appears that *Mulla's* became one of the standard references for courts and the legal profession, in addition to already established case law. It is not surprising that an English textbook became the most popular reference, as up until the 1960s English was the primary language of the courts in Burma.

A brief review of *Mulla's* with reference to some court cases in Burma provides insight into how the courts developed Islamic personal law. *Mulla's* essentially addresses five main areas of law: inheritance, *wakf*, marriage, divorce, and guardianship. As a preliminary matter, it addresses the issue of conversion to Islam and how a court determines if a person is a Muslim. The general position is that courts do not have

---

[16] The Hanafi school is one of four schools of law and is prevalent across approximately one-third of the Muslim world, including India, Pakistan, Afghanistan, Syria, Jordan, and Lebanon: Kamali, 2008: 73.

authority to 'test' a person's belief, but rather accept as sufficient the testimony of a person who 'accepts the unity of God and the prophetic character of Mahomed' (Mulla 2013: 20). This was often a highly controversial issue in Burma, and the courts in the early 1900s were generally inclined to the view that Burmese women had usually 'stimulated conversion to Islam' to marry Muslim men,[17] and so should not be bound by Islamic law. This has recently re-emerged as an issue in Myanmar, with a law regulating conversion passed in 2015.

Having determined that the parties are Muslim, the second preliminary matter addressed in *Mulla's* is that the courts are to presume that a Muslim who comes before the court is a Sunni Muslim, unless proof is offered that they are Shia (Mulla 2013: 28). For example, in the case of *Shahar Banoo* the court had to consider who was the rightful trustee of the will of a deceased Shia Muslim man.[18] Even within Sunni Islam, there were cases where the courts were required to decide which of the four schools of law applied to the case at hand. For example, there were cases brought before the courts where one of the parties to the case was of the Shafi school of law, and the other party to the case was of the Hanafi school, and in such a case, the court had to decide which of these schools of law would apply to the applicants.[19]

Aside from this distinction the parties were generally referred to by the court as 'Mahomedans', although at times the court was more specific in terms of ethnicity. Occasionally, the court would note that the parties were Chulia,[20] or 'Zerbadis'.[21] One case even refers to the Zerbadis as 'native Mussulmans',[22] which appears to acknowledge the long history of some Muslim communities and suggests that there was recognition at the time that not all Muslims were recent migrants. As *Mulla's* was written as a textbook for British India, and later amended for post-independence India, it does not mention issues of identity that were specific to Burma.

---

[17] *Ali Asghar v Mi Kra Hla U* [1916] Lower Burma Rulings (LBR) 461.

[18] *Shahar Banoo v Aga Mahomed Jaffer Bindaneem and others* [1904] LBR 66.

[19] *Rahima Bi alias Ma Ta v Mahomed Saleh* [1914] LBR 54.

[20] *Mohamed Khan v Damayanthi Parekh and two others* [1952] Burma Law Reports (BLR) (HC) 356.

[21] See for example *Ma Pwe v Ma Hla Win* [1894] UBR 536.

[22] *Ahmed and another v Ma Pwa* [1895] UBR 529.

Aside from the identity of the applicant, *Mulla's* lays out the laws of inheritance according to the Hanafi school of law, which is based on the authoritative works of *Al Sirajiyyah* (by Shaikh Sirajuddin) and *Al Sharifiyyah*, a commentary on the former by Sayyad Shariff (Mulla 2013: 64). These sources are frequently relied upon by the Islamic Religious Affairs Council of Myanmar in the *fatwas* it issues, but they are not cited by the courts. *Mulla's* also sets out the particular principles in relation to wills, relying on the *Hedaya*, a Hanafi text first composed by Shaikh Burhan ud Din Ali in the twelfth century, and later translated into English by Charles Hamilton on the command of the Governor General of India, Warren Hastings (Mulla 2013: 132).

A second key focus of *Mulla's* is the principles surrounding *wakf*, that is, the dedication of property for a religious or charitable cause, which implies the end of the owner's rights and 'detention in the implied ownership of God' (Mulla 2013: 197). A *wakf* may be created either orally or in writing and is managed by a person known as the *mutawalli*. Disputes over *wakf* arise if a *mutawalli* is perceived to be unfit to continue his duties of administering the *wakf*, or if misuse of the trust property is suspected. Cases may also be brought to ensure that endowments are appropriated for the purposes to which they had been originally dedicated. For example, concerns may arise if the *mutawalli* is using the *wakf* as his own private property. These cases revealed the deep rifts within the Muslim community, such as the dispute over the administration of a mosque in Rangoon, between the Randheria and the Surati Muslim communities in the early 1900s.[23]

The final two themes dealt with by *Mulla's* are marriage and divorce, and guardianship. The section on marriage considers how to determine when a marriage has taken place, and stresses the necessity of the proposal and acceptance. It outlines what counts as *mahr* (dower), that is, money or other property that the wife is entitled to from the husband in consideration for the marriage (Mulla 2013: 371). It also details the three types of divorce: *talak* by the husband; *khula*, 'by consent', which is often considered to be the right of the wife to seek divorce (although *Mulla's* does not use these terms); and *mubara'at*,

---

[23] *Mahomed Ismail Ariff and others v Hajee Hamed Moolla Dawood and another; Mahomed Ismail Ariff and others v Mahomed Suleiman Ismail Jee and others* [1916] Burma Law Times 141.

by contract (Mulla 2013: 307). Finally, on guardianship, *Mulla's* refers extensively to the Guardianship and Wards Act 1890, which was also adopted in Burma from British India, and which prevails over Islamic personal law in cases of conflict (Mulla 2013: 431).

Islamic personal law in Myanmar was therefore modelled closely on the English language Anglo-Muhammedan texts that were produced in British India. Mulla's provides one example of the core principles that were applied, and this was a volume that gained particular currency in Myanmar, and remains in use in the courts today.

Independence and the Development of Islamic Personal Law

Personal law existed prior to the constitutional right to religion and therefore has operated in Burma largely independent of it. All constitutions in Myanmar have emphasized that past laws continue to operate unless specifically repealed. Further, constitutional provisions on religion have not affected the status and practise of Islamic personal law, and this explains why Islamic law has endured through socialist and military rule.

Law, Religion, and Islam in Myanmar

The main debate concerning law and religion that arose during the parliamentary period, after independence in 1948, was what place religion, particularly Buddhism, should be given in the Constitution. The transition to independence and subsequent period of parliamentary democracy was turbulent and chaotic. The new government under U Nu had to deal not only with the armed struggle launched by the Community Party of Burma (see generally Linter 1990), but also ethnic insurgency due to the breakdown of political agreement (Smith 1999). The army therefore had reason to consolidate its role in politics and administration. In terms of the judiciary, while the courts were restructured, it remained based on its common law colonial heritage. The Constitution guaranteed independence for judges, who were now Burmese, not foreigners, although all of the eleven judges on the Supreme and High Court in 1948 had studied overseas (Zan 2004). With independence in 1948, and up until 1962, the judgments of the Supreme and High Court of Burma, the two apex courts under the 1947 Constitution of the Union of Burma, were compiled in a series then called the Burma Law Reports. The Law Reports were mainly in English, with some cases reported in Burmese. From 1948 to the 1960s, 20 cases on Islamic personal law were reported. Yet these cases only represented those that were heard in the High Court or Supreme Court on appeal, and so the likely number of cases brought to the court at first instance remains unknown.

In 1953, the Burma Muslim Dissolution of Marriages Act 1953 was introduced to modify and limit the system of personal laws by allowing women the right to divorce (Huxley 1990: 248). Although the law stated that it does not affect the 'original Islam code of law', this was with the exception of a woman's rights to divorce. As per the law, granting of divorce depended on reasons including unknown whereabouts of the husband, his failure to live with the wife for one year, his abusive nature, or 'any other ground of divorce by Muslim Law given as a reason for divorce'(s 1(c)). The law also clearly stated in section 6 'that the divorce is affected if the married Muslim woman changes her religion', therefore allowing apostasy to affect the validity of a marriage.

The major debate on religion during the parliamentary period was the constitutional position of Buddhism. The 1947 Constitution initially did not identify Buddhism as the religion of the state. Prior to independence, during the drafting of the Constitution, there were some members who proposed the constitutional recognition of Buddhism; however, General Aung San was said to have been opposed to this proposal (Smith 1965: 230).

Yet Aung San was assassinated half way through the Constituent Assembly debates in 1947, and after his death the debate shifted. U Nu proposed to include a provision that recognized the special position of Buddhism, after being inspired by the provision in the Irish Constitution that preserved a 'special position' for Catholicism.[24]

The 1947 Constitution, as it was introduced, recognized that Buddhism had a special position as the religion of the majority of

---

[24] Constitution of Ireland 1937, s 44(1).

the population (s 21(1)), but it also provided for equality before the law regardless of 'religion, sex or race' and prohibited discrimination based on religion (s 13, 21(3)). It went on to provide that '[a]ll persons are equally entitled to freedom of conscience and the right freely to profess and practise religion subject to public order, morality or health and to the other provisions of this Chapter' (s 20). The explanation to this provision noted that it did not extend to 'any economic, financial, political or other secular activities that may be associated with religious practice'. The Constitution also specifically noted four other religions or beliefs that were followed at the time—Islam, Hinduism, Christianity, and Animism (s 21(2)). U Nu stressed that the government would work to 'faithfully implement' the provisions on religious freedom in the Constitution (U Nu 1951: 73). Since there were no reported court cases that concerned section 20 during the period of parliamentary democracy, it remains unclear how s 21(1) on the special position of Buddhism was to be reconciled with s 21(2) on the recognition of other religions. No laws were ever challenged in the courts on the basis of their constitutional validity in relation to the provisions on religion.

This uneasy and ambiguous balance between the special position of Buddhism and the recognition of other religions changed when the 1947 Constitution was amended in the early 1960s. This was highly controversial and indicated that the idea of a secular state in Burma was fragile and open to compromise. The impetus for this constitutional amendment came as early as 1956, when U Nu, leader of the faction of the AFPFL which was renamed as the Union Party, declared that he would work to make Buddhism the state religion (Maung Maung 1963: 117). Following the caretaker government, U Nu successfully contested the elections of February 1960, in part because of his promise to make Buddhism the state religion. A State Religion Inquiry Committee (SRIC) was subsequently appointed to consider the proposal to make Buddhism the state religion (Maung Maung 1963: 119). The proposal was opposed by groups such as the National Minorities Alliance (NMA), a coalition of Muslim, Christian, and other minority religious leaders, led by Burmese Muslim and well-known lawyer U Than Tun. When the Committee, led by former Chief Justice U Thein Maung, toured parts of the country, it faced significant opposition. For example, when the Committee members travelled to Myitkyina by train, they were pelted with stones, and so a curfew was declared under section 144 of the Criminal Procedure Code (CPC) to restore order in Myitkyina, Kachin State.[25]

Despite the opposition to this proposal, on 26 August 1961, it received the approval of two-thirds of representatives in both chambers and so the Constitution was amended to make Buddhism the state religion.[26] A provision was also inserted to compel the Union Government to allocate 5 per cent of its 'annual current expenditure for matters connected with religion'. This concerned religious minorities such as the Kachin (who are mostly Christian), who perceived this amendment as having the effect of imposing Buddhism on minorities (Farrelly 2014).

Further provisions were also added to protect and promote the teachings of Buddhism, to require the state to support the restoration of pagodas, and for the provision of hospitals specifically for members of the Sangha (ss 21, 43). The religion of Buddhism was mentioned as occupying a 'special position' as the religion of the majority of the population (s 21(1)). Though the amendment maintained a list mentioning Islam, Christianity, Hinduism and Animism, this list does not appear to be exclusive but rather identifies the four main belief systems at the time (s 21(2)). Further, the amendment inserted a prohibition on the abuse of religion for political purposes'. In addition to the Constitution, a national law known as the State Religion Promotion Act 1961 was also passed, which required all schools to teach the Buddhist Scriptures to Buddhist students, and to prisoners in prison.

The establishment of Buddhism as the state religion by constitutional amendment was a significant cause for concern for religious minorities, including Burmese Muslims.[27] A second amendment was passed in response to backlash from minorities. The amendment

[25] News article on file with author: 'Train Bringing State Religion Commission Stoned, Turned Back' 20 December 1960. I have argued elsewhere that s 144 of the Criminal Procedure Code has created an 'everyday emergency' in Myanmar: see Crouch forthcoming.

[26] The Constitution (Third Amendment) Act 1961, s 21, and The State Religion Promotion Act 1961 in Smith (1965: 329–35).

[27] For historical analysis of the dynamics between Buddhism, politics and the state more generally, see for example Smith (1965); Mendelson (1975); Spiro (1982); and Brohm (1957).

inserted s 21(6), and amended s 20 to include the word 'teach'. This was intended to reaffirm the teaching of religion in schools, and the right of parents to ensure that their children were taught about their religion. Yet this failed to ease the tensions, and the military coup of 1962 was also the end of Buddhism's short-lived status as the state religion. There was little time for the government to implement the proposal, and the courts never had the opportunity to consider the implications of this constitutional amendment. The shift from a secular state to a religious state, and then to a socialist regime post-1962, had a profoundly negative effect on relations between religious minorities and the state.

Socialism, the Military, and the Marginalization of Islam

The socialist period, followed by the period of military rule, effectively relegated religion to the private sphere. The effect of the changes made to the legal system during the period 1962–2010 was to undermine the system of public law, and with it, the right to constitutional review. I would suggest that it was civil law, including Islamic personal law cases, that were the least affected by these changes.

On 3 March 1962, General Ne Win declared that the military had taken over by forming the Revolutionary Council. The political and judicial landscape underwent radical reform. The Revolutionary Council began by abolishing the Parliament in March 1962, and later that same month, doing away with the existing structure of the judiciary by closing the Supreme Court and the High Courts, establishing the Chief Courts in their place (Myint Zan 2000: 31). The Special Criminal Courts and Appeals Court were then established, with three members drawn from the Revolutionary Council and Revolutionary Government (Cheesman 2009).

The socialist period had an effect on Islamic personal law in two ways. Before I address these, I need to emphasize that Hooker's claim, that the last reported case on Islamic personal law took place in 1960, is factually incorrect (Hooker 1984: 54). Hooker's research on Islamic law in Burma wrongly states that 'no reliable data on Muhammadan law have emerged from Burma since 1964' (Hooker 1984: 76). His research was published in 1984, although it appears that he had not had the opportunity to read Abdul Ghafur's

authoritative book on Islamic Law (in Burmese), which was first published in 1984 (and recently republished in 2014). Further, Hooker
presumably did not speak to any Burmese lawyers. If he had, they
could have pointed him to the court decisions that were published
in the Burmese language, as it is the custom of all Burmese lawyers
to keep their own personal libraries of the Burma Law Reports (see
Crouch and Cheesman 2014). Rather, Hooker's work is perhaps
an indication of the reality that it was in 1963 that the last case on
Islamic personal law was reported in English (Myint Zan 2000).
After this period, all Islamic personal law cases up to the present
have been in the Burmese language.

After 1962 it became increasingly difficult for Muslims to enter
the civil service, including the judiciary. In 1972, significant structural changes were made to the judiciary with the introduction of the
People's Judicial System (PJS). This was preceded by the removal of
all professional judges from the bench and their replacement with
members of the Burma Socialist Programme Party (BSPP), the
majority of whom had no legal qualification (Myint Zan 2000: 36).
Some of the former judges were reappointed to the position of 'court
advisor', although this was purely an advisory role. The courts initially
heard only criminal cases until June 1973, when civil cases began to
be heard.

One consequence of the restructuring of the courts and the replacement of all judges with 'people's judges' is that few Muslims were
able to enter the judiciary after this time. This is in contrast to the
parliamentary period, when there were several prominent Muslim
judges and politicians. One example was U Si Bu, a Kaman Muslim
who was one of three judges on the trial of Aung San's assassin.[28]
After the military coup, Muslims generally faced greater difficulties
seeking employment in the civil service, or getting promoted. One
consequence of this is that there are few Muslim judges in the courts
today. This led to the ironic situation in which Muslims who use the
courts and rely on Islamic personal law have their cases heard by
judges who are non-Muslim and who generally have no training in
Islamic law.

---

[28] See Maung Maung 1962. His son, Major Maung Aung, was the Deputy
Minister of Immigration Major Maung Aung.

At the constitutional level, while the 1974 Constitution included provisions for equality before the law regardless of religion and provisions on freedom of religion (ss 22, 147), these were subject to wide limitations that justified state interference in these freedoms. For example, the national races could exercise religious freedom, along with other cultural rights, on the broad condition that 'the enjoyment of any such freedom does not offend the laws or the public interest' (s 21(b)). This right was further subject to the limitation that it was not 'to the detriment of national solidarity and the socialist social order' (s 153(b)). The socialist order therefore came first, and religion was secondary to this. The right to have a religion was also mentioned along with the right to freedom of thought and conscience, although it was made clear that religion and politics should not mix (s 156(a)–(c)).

The socialist period brought the country to ruin economically, and there was growing unrest including the democracy protests of 1988, leading to the demise of the socialist regime in 1988 after the takeover of the military. This led to a period, from 1988 until 2010, during which time there was no Constitution. Although the Supreme Court was re-established in 1988, there is evidence of on-going interference in the judiciary by the executive, and the courts are a far cry from their former independent status during the parliamentary period. One of the main changes in state-religion relations in the 1990s was that religious affairs were given their own ministry, and the Sangha was further controlled by law.[29] Both measures were a way of bringing religious organizations under state control.

From 1993 to 2007, a National Convention was hosted by the military for the purpose of drafting a new constitution. The proposal in terms of religion was to include a provision almost identical to that which appeared in the 1947 Constitution. The resulting 2008 Constitution therefore returned almost word-for-word to the statement on religion under the 1947 Constitution. The main provision granting the right to religious freedom is s 34:

> Every citizen is equally entitled to freedom of conscience and the right to freely profess and practise religion subject to public order, morality or health and to the other provisions of this Constitution.

[29] The Law Relating to the Sangha Organization No. 20/90. See Matthews 1995.

The limitations on this right, 'public order, morality or health', are in line with general limitations by international standards. It is further limited by s 360(a), which states that the right excludes 'any economic, financial, political or other secular activities that may be associated with religious practice'. The 2008 Constitution goes on to explicitly recognize 'Islam' alongside Christianity, Hinduism, and Animism, and the special status of Buddhism (ss 361–2), similar to the 1947 Constitution. These provisions have yet to be interpreted or applied in court, and it is unclear whether this list is exclusive. For example, it is unclear whether the Buddhist Women's Special Marriage Law 2015 (see Nyi Nyi Kyaw, this volume) would be interpreted as upholding the 'special position' of Buddhism, or whether it could actually be interpreted and struck down for restricting the freedom of followers of a 'recognized' religion such as Islam.

The Constitution also prohibits the manipulation of religion for political gain, and contains the same ban on inciting hatred or conflict between religious communities (s 364). There is an additional provision that was not in the 1947 Constitution, which gives sweeping powers to the Union to 'assist and protect the religions it recognizes' (s 363)—presumably those mentioned above—at its absolute discretion. There have not yet been any court cases in relation to these provisions.

The 2008 Constitution also provides for protection from discrimination on the basis of religion (s 348). Mention of the right to have a religion is also made along with a list of cultural and linguistic rights, subject again to similar limitations of 'Union security, prevalence of law and order, community peace and tranquillity or public order and morality' (s 354(d)). The Constitution also contains some peculiar restrictions, such as the statement that members of religious orders are ineligible to vote in elections (s 392(a)), which presumably affects several hundred thousand Buddhist monks in the country (Lidauer and Saphy 2014). One feature of the political environment post-2011 is that there has been little reference to the constitutional provisions on religion, despite the potential for it to be a source of authority in resolving present tensions.

The Development of Case Law on Islamic Personal Law

While Islamic personal law in theory was still available and applications could be made on matters of marriage, inheritance, divorce, and child custody, in reality the number of overall cases reported in the Burma Law Reports declined after the 1960s. Most of the cases on Islamic personal law that reached the Supreme Court after the 1960s concerned matters of inheritance[30] or *wakf*.[31] This is consistent with the reality that wealth is often tied up in property due to the dysfunction of the banking system in Myanmar, and so disputes over property in relation to inheritance claims happen to be the disputes that more often go on appeal to the Supreme Court (Nardi and Kyaw Lwin 2014).

One development after the 1960s was the publication of some Burmese-language texts on Islamic personal law. These took on the role of summarizing, and at times substituting, Anglo-Muhammadan English textbooks, given that the courts no longer operated in English and the levels of English comprehension of judges declined dramatically. The primary book on Islamic Law (in Burmese) which is still referred to today is by Professor Abdul Ghafur (first published 1984, revised 2014), copies of which can be found in the library at Yangon University Law Department. There is also a volume on Mohamedan law by U Win Kyi (1984). More recently, U Khin Maung, who was the former Deputy Director of the High Court from 1984 to 1985, has also written on Islamic law. The common characteristics among these volumes are that they address the narrow matters of Islamic personal law such as marriage, inheritance and divorce; they are generally consistent with Anglo-Muhammadan law and therefore the Hanafi school of law as articulated in volumes such as *Mulla's Principles*; and they primarily cite from these volumes as well as from established case law from India and Burma.

It is difficult to make a general assessment of who accessed the court, because there have been so few reported court decisions; and the decisions that are reported rarely mention the applicant's identity

---

[30] See for example *Mahmut Yakut Mansa hnin Ayut Itsamel Atiya* (1973) BLR Chief Court (CC) 15–17; *Daw Rahema hnin Daw Thi pa hnit* (1975) BLR Central Court (CeC) 79–83; *U Bo Gyi hnin U Ko Gyi* (1985) BLR (CeC) 6–8; *Daw Than Myin hnin Daw Tin Myin (ka) Daw Cho Tu* (1993) MLR 66–72; *Ma Ôn Than ba ku-hnit-se hnin Ma Hla Hla Than pa le* (2001) Myanmar Law Report (MLR) Civil Index (CI) 493–504.

[31] *Saya Chè hnin Daw Tin Tin pa shi* (1994) MLR 45–55; *U Chit Pe v Daw Mya May* (1966) BLR 710; *U Ahmed Ebrahem Madar v M Chella Sarmi Swar bir & 10 others* (1966) BLR 15.

in terms of ethnicity or socio-economic status. However, appeal cases would suggest that the courts are generally accessed by well-off, urban Muslims, and in situations where the applicants were unable to obtain their desired resolution through religious leaders.

The Myanmar legal system today still recognizes Islamic law for Muslims in matters of personal law such as marriage, inheritance, divorce, *wakf* (charitable trust), *zakat* (alms), and child maintenance. These matters are usually heard at first instance by the Township Courts,[32] but these cases are not reported. The only cases now reported in the Myanmar Law Reports are cases heard in the Supreme Court, which in matters of personal law are likely to be appeal cases. The Myanmar Law Reports are also a highly restricted publication and only about 20 cases are published per year in an annual volume (Crouch and Cheesman 2014). As such, there have only been a handful of reported cases on Islamic personal law in the Supreme Court in the past decade.[33] I select two of these cases for discussion to illustrate the kinds of appeal cases on Islamic personal law that come before the Supreme Court and how the court deals with these cases. The Burma Laws Act still remains the primary legal touchstone of authority for the courts.

In the case of *Daw Ma La & 5 others v Daw Myin Myin Kain*, the question before the court was whether a Buddhist daughter could inherit from her deceased Muslim mother. In 2000, the inheritance claim was heard at the first instance in the Yangon Division High Court. The case was originally brought by the daughter, Daw Khin Myin, who was Buddhist. Her deceased mother Daw Thein Shin had been married three times. Her mother's first husband had been Muslim and they had three children who were said to be Muslim. Her second husband, who was the father of Daw Khin Myin, was 'Hindu Buddhist' and her mother was also said to practise Buddhism for sixty years. But one year before her death, the mother was alleged to have converted back to Islam. After her mother's death, Daw Khin Myin

---

[32] This depends on the nature of the matter and the amount of money involved, and cases may be appealed to the District Court, High Court and Supreme Court.

[33] It should be noted, however, that this may be consistent with the more general trend of the Law Reporting Committee, which has only reported a very small number of cases per year since 1972.

sought her share of the inheritance. By the time the case reached the Supreme Court on appeal, the original applicant had passed away and her five sons and daughters (the grandsons and granddaughters of the deceased) continued to pursue the claim. The original appeal was unsuccessful, then in 2005 the applicants applied for the case to be heard under the Supreme Court's revisional jurisdiction. The inheritance claim included property in Yangon, gold, and gems.

The court had to consider both the religion of the deceased at the time of death, and the original religion of the daughter at the time of birth. Both parties agreed that Daw Thein Shin died as a Muslim, and the court held that the distribution of the inheritance must be according to Islamic law under s 13 of the Burma Laws Act 1898, citing the case of *Daw Pu v Amat Issasi Maesimar*.[34] The court also cited precedent for the principle that the estate of a deceased person who had converted from Buddhism to Islam before her death cannot be inherited by Buddhists.[35]

In considering the religion of the applicant, it was argued that the Caste Disabilities Removal Act 1850 had the effect of preserving a person's right to inheritance, even if they had converted to another religion. The Caste Disabilities Removal Act 1850 is another law that was derived from British India along with six other laws, which were originally designed to address the issue of inheritance for Hindus. It was previously held under Hindu law that persons who converted out of Hinduism to another religion lost their rights of inheritance, but the Caste Disabilities Removal Act 1850 overturned this. The Supreme Court of Myanmar, in interpreting this law, held that this law only intended to preserve the right of inheritance of the person's original religion (presumably the religion at birth) in the event that they changed religion, but it did not aim to remove all limitations on inheritance due to differences in religion. In this case, the Supreme Court held that the applicant, Daw Khin Myin, was 'born' Buddhist and was not Muslim. On this basis, the court held that she did not have any right to inherit the property and the case was dismissed.[36] Interestingly, the court noted that if the applicant had been born 'Muslim' and later converted to Buddhism, she would still have been entitled to part of the inheritance.

[34] (1955) BLR (HC) 21.
[35] *Asha Bibi v Ma Kyaw Yin and others* (1920) BLT 217.
[36] *Daw Ma La pa nga hnin Daw Myin Myin Kain pa le* (2005) MLR (CI) 1–12.

The separate case of *U Ba Min v Daw Mya Mya & two others* was heard in 2007. The case was brought by three siblings after a breakdown of an agreement concerning the inheritance of property from their parents. The deceased parents, and their children (the plaintiff and respondent) were all Sunni Muslims. After the parents' death in 2002, the land they had owned was divided equally among the three of them, but not in accordance with Islamic Law. The agreement was signed in front of the chairperson of the Ward Peace and Development Council and several other witnesses were present. Later, one of the siblings disagreed and took the case to court, seeking a settlement according to Islamic law, which would mean that he and his brother would receive more than their sister. While the original agreement was not disputed, the applicant claimed that he had been coerced into signing the agreement. The case was first heard in the Mandalay Division High Court, but was dismissed as the court found no evidence of coercion. In 2007, the applicant appealed to the Supreme Court. The Supreme Court held that the siblings had initially agreed to divide the property equally, and this agreement was witnessed by authorities from their ward. The Supreme Court also cited precedent to the effect that a person could not make a complaint about the distribution of an estate three years after an agreement had already been made.[37] The Supreme Court noted that if the case had been brought to the court soon after the deceased's death, then it would have been obliged to decide the case according to Islamic law. But in the circumstances of the agreement made and the time that had passed, it held that it would not interfere in this matter to re-decide the distribution of the inheritance according to Islamic law. The Court dismissed the applicant's challenge.[38]

In both the 2005 and 2007 cases, the court referred to past precedent from the parliamentary and socialist period. Case law was cited both in relation to evidential and procedural elements of the case, as well as in relation to substantive aspects of Islamic personal law. This suggests that the use of precedent has remained unaffected by the various political periods in Myanmar, at least in matters of personal law,. It also suggests that courts prefer to cite established case law from Myanmar, where available, rather than legal commentaries or comparative case law. No religious authorities gave evidence in court in these cases.

---

37 *U Aung Nyun hnin Maung Ohn Myin* (1981) MLR (CI) 121.
38 *U Ba Min hnin Daw Mya Myapa hnit* (2007) MLR (CI) 75–89.

* * *

Given the wide time frame that this chapter has sought to cover, from 1898 to the present, it has only been able to provide a broad review of law and religion in Myanmar and the place of Islamic personal law within this system. This study is clearly limited in several ways. Most people in Myanmar do not have access to the law, and even if cases are brought to the courts, most cases do not go on appeal. Even if appeals are made to the Supreme Court, case reporting today is highly selective. Of all the reform efforts taking place and areas of law in need of research, legal scholars may wonder why I have chosen to focus on what may seem to be an obscure area of law. I have argued in this chapter that Islamic personal law provides a unique window into the courts as a site of interaction between the state and Muslim communities. It is a reflection of the code-like application of law by the courts and also the role that courts play in resolving civil disputes. In addition, the case study of Islamic personal law is one example that can further our understanding of the origins of Myanmar's legal system as a colonial construct, and as a form of double colonization, with strong ties to the legal system of the former British India.

I have argued that Hooker's understanding of Islamic personal law in Myanmar is limited to a useful explanation of the pre-1960s period. While the incorporation of Islamic personal law into state law was initially cut-and-pasted from India, I have demonstrated that we need to appreciate how Islamic personal law has been sustained and developed since then. Islamic personal law in Myanmar has demonstrated resilience, having weathered socialist rule and the military regime. This is partly because the socialist and military periods affected public law most heavily, while the practise of private law was affected to a lesser extent. While we can identify the initial roots of the courts' authority on matters of Islamic personal law in the Burma Laws Act 1898, the case law that has subsequently developed has generally followed similar lines as Anglo-Muhammadan jurisdiction, typified in volumes such as *Mulla's Principles,* with the exception of the issue of inter-religious marriage. There is therefore little room for judicial interpretation, reference to *fiqh,* or to Islamic *fatawa.*

II

Everyday
Experiences

4 Muslim Political Activity in Transitional Myanmar

Nicholas Farrelly

This chapter explores the historical, cultural, and spatial conditions related to Muslim political activity in Myanmar. The catalyst for recent change in political activity by Muslims in Myanmar has coincided with the implementation of the former military government's 2008 Constitution, and also with the 2010 general elections. These important changes to the national political climate, which were followed by the more free and fair 2012 by-election and 2015 general election, are a frame through which it is possible to observe the role of Muslims in Myanmar politics during its nascent transition from five decades of military rule. Until recently, Muslims, like many others in Myanmar, were limited in their ability to actively and publicly engage with political processes, especially through formal political parties. While there was still political activity by Muslims, such efforts were peripheral to the national story of entrenched military government. One of the most significant changes since the 2010 general election is that certain types of politics related to the Muslim population have vaulted to the centre stage. Yet, many Muslims are still greatly constrained in their political work, which was rarely given attention beyond a narrow slice of terrain in northern Rakhine State, where the dense concentration of the Muslim population makes them an important part of the political calculus.

The general expansion of spaces for political activity, as experienced by Myanmar's peoples, has been accompanied by the growth of more assertive Muslim politics, including at the party level. At the same time, resurgent attacks on Muslims by Buddhist political interests, and the potential for this to remain a destabilizing influence, add extra urgency to the need for understanding how the various pressures relevant to the current political moment, at both national and local levels, are re-shaping Muslim political activities. Among the different sources of anguish for Myanmar's Muslims, there is the often-remarked tension between acceptance in personal encounters—where Muslims and Buddhists have co-existed for generations—and the politicization of virulent anti-Muslim currents, with an emphasis on enforcing segregation of the two religious communities. Muslim responses to these new opportunities and pressures require careful consideration.

During the decades of military rule that commenced with the coup of 2 March 1962, the scope for Muslims to be active in politics was dramatically reduced by the need to adjust to the priorities of majoritarianism in its martial and dictatorial form. As Yegar explains, '[t]he military regime of General Ne Win stepped up its suppression of autonomy seeking minorities, including the Muslims' (Yegar 2002: 55). Muslims continued to play their roles in society, often working closely with other diverse populations of urban Myanmar. When opportunities were made available, Muslim leaders would present themselves for senior roles. However, the deficit of Muslims in the armed forces and in senior bureaucratic positions meant that the ordinary pathways to greater influence, enjoyed by many Buddhists and even by some Christians, were unavailable. Local political roles, especially for the small Muslim elite in parts of Rakhine State, required complicity with the military government. Since the promulgation of the 2008 Constitution, a number of politicians who are Muslim have gained prominence, with three political parties comprising majority Muslim memberships looking to gain votes. There were also a small number of Muslim politicians who were members of the ruling Union Solidarity and Development Party until 2015. In Naypyidaw, Yangon and Sittwe, they tended to fit uneasily into the categories of political affiliation expected by the transitional authorities who controlled the country until the 2015 general election.

This chapter explains the variety of political experiences in formal political parties of Muslims in Myanmar, during the recent tentative post-authoritarian transition. First, the social and cultural orientation of Myanmar's Muslims is explained with reference to their politics. The status of Muslims in Myanmar society remains heavily contested. Among the 135 'national race' categories used by the government to order the country's cultural and linguistic diversity, there is only one group that is explicitly defined by its Muslim faith—the Kaman of Rakhine State. Second, the chapter analyses the history of Muslim political engagement in Myanmar. This discussion clarifies the enmeshment of Muslims in a society where their 'foreign' or mixed origins have marked them as targets for discrimination and violence. In northern Rakhine State, antagonism between Buddhist and Muslim groups has led to regular episodes of conflict. Yet Muslim politics in Myanmar has other layers, especially in recent years when a degree of electoral competition has emerged. Third, in this context, Muslim politicians and political parties have sought to campaign for inclusion while encountering obstacles at the local and national levels. Consternation from Myanmar's Buddhists about the disputed category of 'Rohingya' Muslims has become a preoccupation. Such dispute tests Myanmar's capacity for tolerance, while also highlighting the regional differences relevant to Muslim politics. For now, those Muslims in Myanmar who are officially welcome are most commonly categorized, in a generic sense, as 'Bama – Islam'. The chapter concludes by analyzing the integration of Muslims in the political process and their persistent estrangement from the Burman Buddhist majority.

Categories of Myanmar Muslims

In any discussion of Muslim politics in Myanmar, it is necessary to clarify the extent to which such faith-based categorization is a meaningful analytical starting point. When scholars turn their attention to minority-majority political relations in Myanmar, the long-term habit has been to lead with ethnic categories. The topic of Muslim politics has been discussed only in the broadest terms by scholars, partly as a consequence of the military's dominance of national life from the 1962 coup up to the general elections of 2010.[1] Though there were brief periods when democratic politics sprang to prominence during those decades, the politics of Muslim minorities remained under-appreciated. In one of the rare overviews of the topic, Lambrecht indicates that 'Muslims in Burma are dispersed geographically and are highly diverse in ethnicity, religious practice, socio-economic background, and social and political integration' (2006: 23). He goes on to offer a breakdown of six groups of Muslims: the Rohingya in Rakhine State; Panthay, also known as Chinese Muslims; Malays, also called Pashu; immigrants from Bangladesh, India and Pakistan (further broken down as Tamil, Bengali, Telugu, Punjabi and Chittagongian); the 'Burmese Muslims' who are often called Zerbadee, and the Kaman, a 'national race' category from Rakhine State (2006: 23, 25). Under such complex conditions it is difficult to be too confident about the overall character of Myanmar's Muslim populations, precisely because the long-term research required has not been undertaken. For political reasons, even the basic enumeration of these different groups has proved impossible. It is alleged the 1983 census 'deliberately' under-counted the Muslim population (Carroll 2014). Then, with no quantification during the intervening thirty years, in 2014 an independent assessment of the most recent census acknowledged that efforts to count the Rohingya population in northern Rakhine State were a 'complete failure' (McLaughlin 2014).

This is crucial to how the various categories of Muslims are understood in Myanmar, especially with respect to their diverse political standing. While Myanmar officially recognizes a Muslim minority comprising 4.2 per cent of the population, based on the 1983 census, others suggest that the number is significantly higher. Zainuddin claimed that Muslims make up around 15 per cent of the

---

[1] The difficulties faced by researchers during these earlier periods of Myanmar's political history were profound. It was not conceivable to undertake long-term research on sensitive political subjects in areas controlled by the military government. Some researchers were successful in studying more historical (such as Callahan 2004) or anthropological (see Skidmore 2004) topics. Yet a topic like Muslim politics during the decades of military rule tended to be ignored in favour of studies of ethnic minority issues, especially in those parts of the country that were more accessible from Thailand, India, or China (for examples see Farrelly 2008; 2009).

population—roughly seven million people (2000: 50).[2] In 2006, the United States government published a report that noted 'Muslim leaders claim that there are approximately 7 to 10 million Muslims in the country, which is about 14 to 20 per cent of the population—although it is impossible to verify this number' (State Department 2006). If Buddhist assertions that the Muslim population is growing quickly are true, then there are reasons to imagine that the current figure could be around ten per cent. That would mean approximately six million Muslims, in a population of roughly 60 million. This would make the Muslims the largest group that does not receive 'national race' endorsement as one of the 135 ethnic and cultural groups considered 'indigenous' to Myanmar.[3] If the population of Chinese people is roughly 2.5 million, then the two groups taken together are a very large contributor to the national count. There are some hopes that the 2014 census will help to clarify such vital demographic details. However, the political sensitivities around the Muslim population may mean that future governments would be likely to remain wary of releasing exact figures about the various Muslim categories that were or were not counted in the census.

Such problems are products of the diverse experiences of Myanmar's Muslims, who jostle along with Hindus, Chinese, Burmans and so many others, in the bumping, dusty world of Myanmar's trading towns and commercial neighbourhoods. As traders, peddlers, artisans and intellectuals, Muslims are noticeable in almost all large population centres, including in the Shan and Kachin States, far from the coastal zones most readily associated with their presence. In some rural areas, especially in the northern Rakhine State, Muslims are also farmers or work in the various trades supporting agricultural livelihoods. Rohingya identity politics, a major issue since violence in the northern Rakhine State was catapulted to attention in 2012, has become a prism through which discussions

---

[2] For a useful but hesitant summary on historical data about the number of Muslims in Myanmar see Yegar 2002: 385–6.

[3] The exception to this exclusion from 'national race' status are the Kaman, also spelled Kamein, who are the descendants of Muslim soldiers living, in what is now known as Rakhine State, since the seventeenth century. They likely number fewer than 10,000, although there are no up-to-date statistics on the Kaman population.

on Muslim politics are generally judged (see Coates 2013; 2014). The claim that the Rohingya are illegal migrants recently arrived from Bangladesh has been widely contested in Myanmar and international circles.[4] Yet the fact that the stigmatization of Muslim identity has been inflamed, ensures that any effort to deal with the ambiguities of such categorization is deeply political. Anxiety among Myanmar's non-Muslim majority has generated widespread efforts to delegiti-mize the presence of any Muslims, including the Kaman, a 'national race'. It is not an exaggeration to say that many of Myanmar's people have embraced reactive 'Islamaphobia' (as discussed by Egreteau 2011; Green 2013; see Nyi Nyi Kyaw, this volume). The violence that has accompanied recent tension along the Buddhist-Muslim fault-line suggests that communities of different faiths are struggling to live together, even in historically peaceful places such as Mandalay (Fuller and Wai Moe 2014).

Muslims on the Margins of Myanmar Politics

Muslims have lived for centuries in what is now known as Myanmar, as they have in adjacent areas of South and Southeast Asia, and it is on that basis that many continue to claim indigenous status (see Keck 2009).[5] Taylor has recounted that in 'the Islamic quarter of pre-colonial Mandalay...Muslim troops loyal to the Buddhist kings of the Konbaung dynasty resided' (2005: 266). Those troops constitute one of the many groups of Muslims, from China, from the Indian sub-continent, and from elsewhere in Southeast Asia, who have made long-term homes in Myanmar. During this earlier period, Yegar suggests:

> ...the Burmese had no interest in Muslim internal organization or reli-gious life, nor did they try to convert Muslims to Buddhism. Mosques (as well as churches) were constructed without prejudice wherever there was a foreign community (2002: 22).

---

[4] For a discussion of the context from the Bangladesh side of the border see Farrelly and Hossain 2014.

[5] The usage of the terms 'Myanmar' and 'Burma' in this style of histori-cal discussion is inevitably problematic. I have sought to quarantine the use of 'Myanmar' to the period after 1989, when it was introduced as the official English language designation for the country.

Yet such prejudice has grown over time, proving a catalyst for tumultuous interaction, with sporadic efforts to purge Muslims from their established neighbourhoods. The situation was aggravated by the British administration in the nineteenth and twentieth centuries, which brought large numbers of Muslims from the sub-continent to help secure its colonial footing (see Keck, this volume). Nowadays the most obvious concentrations of Muslims, particularly those with origins in what are now India, Bangladesh and Pakistan, are in central Yangon, particularly in the Pabedan and Mingalar Taung Nyunt townships.

They are the descendants of waves of migrants who had sought opportunities in Burma for hundreds of years. In the early twentieth century, as Taylor (2005: 276) explains:

> ...the Bamar Muslim Aphwe, or General Council of Burmese Muslim Associations...was founded to distinguish Muslims who had been living in Myanmar before the arrival of the British from the thousands of Islamic immigrants who arrived after 1826. Throughout the twentieth century, Bamar Muslims have organized politically to emphasize their Bamar-ness and hence their indigenous standing. Their lack of links with the politically powerful Buddhist monkhood, however, undermined their political power, except in the late 1940s and early 1950s, when a broad coalition of nationalist political forces was constructed under the umbrella of the Anti-Fascist People's Freedom League...

Other political interests, most often drawn from the majority Burman Buddhist population, contested their status in Burma. Egreteau offers an indication that '[r]enewed waves of anti-Indian pogroms were reported between July and September 1938, but with this time clear anti-Muslim overtones' (2011: 38). Such violent campaigns are a deeply rooted aspect of Myanmar society. Egreteau (2011: 52) goes on to explain that today's:

> ...hostile Burmese perceptions of the 'Kalas' [South Asians] developed through old colonial-rooted resentment [although they] now tend to be more and more articulated around anti-Muslim sentiments, as most of the Burmese Muslims—including the Rohingya minority—happened to share the same Indian origins. Beside an almost folkloristic 'indo-phobia' (or 'Kala-phobia') still noticeable in day-to-day attitudes or language idioms, a growing 'Islamophobia' has been observed in the past two decades.

The notion that the *entire* Muslim population is a product of colonial meddling persists. It is true that large numbers of people from the Indian sub-continent, including Muslims, were transported to British-ruled Burma to support the colonial enterprise. As soldiers, administrators, police, and labourers, they kept the imperial machine working. They were not much liked by the local, Burman population, who would often seek out ways to undermine their perceived high status. When the local nationalist resistance to British rule emerged, some of its primary targets were the Indian administrators and traders who helped to keep the imperial machine working.

After the Second World War—during the years when the Indian sub-continent was being divided into Muslim and Hindu portions, and when Burma gained independence—many Muslims fled for the newly independent countries of India and Pakistan. Later, after General Ne Win's 1962 coup, further great waves of Indian emigration occurred. These saw the country's Muslim population drop precipitously. Those who remained, enjoyed lesser positions in a system where their diminished political and economic standing were tied to a cultural fault-line. For many of the country's Buddhist-nationalists, the history of Muslims has been defined by exploitation and inequality. According to Egreteau, '[t]hese attitudes now have taken the form of a dormant 'Islamophobia', for most of the Burmese Indians resisting full assimilation to Burmanization trends are mainly of Muslim confession, especially of the Rohingya minority' (2011: 35). It is this minority in western Myanmar for whom the history of settlement is the most heavily contested.

Such fierce battles about the appropriate telling of history are beyond the scope of this chapter; however, the political implications of different historical experiences cannot be ignored. During the decades of military rule from 1962 to 2010, there were few opportunities for Muslims to take on senior positions in society. Some of this exclusion was founded in deliberate discrimination by part of the Burman majority. At the same time, it is fair to judge that during this period very few of the other minority peoples enjoyed consistent opportunities for involvement in national life. Many of the country's ethnic minorities, most notably the Mon, Kayin, Shan and Kachin, violently resisted the central government. Until 1989, the Communist Party of Burma was also a significant fighting force harnessed to anti-government resentments. In this context, Muslim armed groups were only ever a small fraction of the national whole. Pudjiastuti points to socio-cultural identity and economic discrimination as drivers of Muslim separatism in the case of Myanmar (2000). Matthews offered a similar analysis by suggesting that 'the Rakhine Muslims are culturally impenetrable as far as any prospect of 'Burmanization' is concerned' (1995: 287). Rebellions that claimed to gather in the name of Islam in western Myanmar were first spearheaded by what were usually called 'Mujahedeen' groups, and then, in the 1970s and the 80s, by outfits such as the Rohingya Patriotic Front (RPF), Rohingya Solidarity Organization (RSO), and Arakan Rohingya Islamic Front (ARIF). They sought to create networks with sympathetic individuals and organizations abroad, particularly in the Muslim world. Bangladesh's Jamaat-e-Islami, a proscribed extremist political group, is often described as a key backer for the Islamist ideology that motivates some Rohingya political activism.[6]

There are other factors, particularly some of the notorious anti-Rohingya campaigns, that have generated enthusiasm for resistance among Myanmar Muslims. Two government campaigns, in 1978 and 1992, which were called *Nagamin* ('Dragon King') and *Pyithaya* ('Clean and Beautiful Nation') in Burmese, helped to radicalize a generation of Rohingyas who were forced to flee to Bangladesh for safety. During operation *Nagamin*, which was a crackdown in several frontier areas including the northern Rakhine State, approximately 220,000 Rohingya left the country (for details see US government 1999; Nemoto 2013). In the early 1990s they were followed by what is often estimated as a further 270,000 Rohingya who sought refuge during operation *Pyithaya*. These campaigns were designed to deny the Rohingya their claims to residence in Myanmar. Large

[6] The links between these Myanmar groups and the broader global Islamist thrust is the subject of on-going speculation. Such links, where they may exist or have existed, have yet to create Rohingya capacity for terrorist attacks like we see elsewhere in Southeast Asia (such as in southern Thailand or Indonesia). Selth (2004) wrote a considered treatment of the relevant issues, dating from the early phase of the 'Global War on Terror'.

numbers of people who fled during these campaigns, perhaps as many as 500,000, are still in Bangladesh. Since then the Myanmar government has maintained its vigil against what is perceived to be a long-term threat of further and repeated incursions from these marginalized communities. There is also unsubstantiated talk that such groups receive support from sympathetic governments and groups in the Middle East. If that is true, the Myanmar government has, through its policies, helped to create the conditions for breeding such resentment. For instance, as Yegar argued '[a]t the end of 1989, the government of Burma/Myanmar began to settle Buddhists in Muslim areas of Arakan/Rakhine by displacing the local population' (2002: 63). The years since then left Myanmar's Muslims, like most others, waiting for better political options. Their conditions remained tenuous throughout the period of military rule when the government continued to marginalize Muslims, especially in the townships of northern Rakhine State.

Electoral Politics

If the goal of government policies over these decades was to evict the Muslim population from northern Rakhine State, they have succeeded only partly. This region remains the cauldron for Muslim political activity in Myanmar, with as many as one million Rohingya, Kaman and others living in areas near the state capital, Sittwe. Because of these circumstances, Matthews has argued that in Myanmar 'the question of the minority religions [is] a political as well as [a] cultural or ethnic one' (1995: 287). Creating tolerance among non-Muslim populations has proved difficult, with the disenfranchisement of Muslims persisting alongside their inconsistent acceptability in the national political conversation (see ICG 2013). With recent changes to the political landscape, most notably through the implementation of an electoral system under the 2008 Constitution, Myanmar's Muslims face new political and social challenges. Their short-lived opportunities for increased representation at the local and national levels have been overshadowed by campaigns of violence and discrimination. With the results of the 7 November 2010 general elections, and the various mechanisms through which Muslim leaders sought to consolidate their status in the country, this discussion stretches standard expectations about the role of minorities in Myanmar society.[7]

It is through the 2010 general elections that Muslims in Myanmar were first forced to interact with the wide-ranging transformation of national politics (see Tables 4.1, 4.2, and 4.3). Under these conditions, great uncertainty pervaded all political discussions. It remains far too early to adjudicate the final trajectory of the changes that are underway, to say nothing of the prospects for success in rehabilitating a political system that suffered through almost five decades of military rule, and where Burman chauvinism became the standard (as explained by Walton, 2013). It is also premature to make strong judgements about how Myanmar's Muslim political experiences compare with those of others, particularly in South Asia. In response to the incremental opening of new spaces for political activity, different Muslim political groups have emerged, while older organizations have been forced to adjust to the demands of unfamiliar political processes. Until the general elections of 2015, advantages of incumbency enjoyed by the USDP, a direct successor to the mass organization convened by the former military government, frustrated many of the alternative political contenders, including the premier opposition party NLD. To explain the Muslim politics that gained some prominence from 2010 to 2015, this chapter introduces what were three distinctive outlets for Muslim political energy: the National Democratic Party for Development (NDPD), USDP, and the Kaman National Progressive Party (KNPP). While these were not the only political parties that include Muslim members, they each highlight different aspects of the evolution of Muslim participation in what is a rapidly changing political order.

National Democratic Party for Development

The NDPD, founded in Yangon on 4 June 2010, and chaired by Maung Maung Ni, presented a slate of 22 Muslim candidates for

---

[7] The data on the 2010 election results presented here is drawn from my 'Myanmar political cultures' dataset that has consolidated information from ALTSEAN-Burma (2010), Irrawaddy (2010), and the Union Election Commission, among other sources.

the 2010 election in Yangon and Rakhine State. Two members were elected to the Rakhine State legislature: Aung Myint (also known as Zarhidulla) to the first Buthidaung constituency, while Borshir Ahmed was elected to the second constituency.[8] Aung Myint received 34,158 votes, defeating the USDP candidate who received a close-run 31,678 votes. In the second constituency, Borshi Ahmed won with 27,942 votes, defeating the next placed candidate who received 23,417 votes. These hard-fought contests have not, however, led to strong representation in the Rakhine State Hluttaw.[9] In 2014, I was informed by senior figures at that Hluttaw that the two Muslim representatives have not sat since the Rakhine State's anti-Muslim violence of 2012. The NDPD also contested seats at both the national and local levels in Yangon, but only in the two townships where the Muslim population is most heavily concentrated, Mingalar Taung Nyunt and Pabedan. In Rakhine State they campaigned for other seats including Maungdaw, Buthidaung, Sittwe, Kyauktaw, and Mrauk-Oo. Among all the Rakhine State seats that they contested, they lost to the Rakhine Nationalities Development Party (RNDP) on seven occasions.[10] The USDP defeated their candidates in thirteen constituencies, including some very close contests like the one between Abdul Tahil who

[8] Many Myanmar Muslims are known by two names: a Burmese name and an Arabic one. In this chapter I have opted to present both names at the first mention and to subsequently refer to them by the name with which they are most commonly known. This is most often the Burmese name, although there are some exceptions.

[9] In Myanmar there are fourteen State and Region Hluttaw, or legislatures, formed by the 2008 Constitution. After the 2010 election they were dominated by the USDP, although in some areas such as the Rakhine State, ethnic interests won sufficient seats to hold senior cabinet positions at the State level.

[10] The RNDP has, more recently, been accused of leading the violent campaigns against Muslims in what they perceive to be Rakhine-only areas. In 2013, at the Australian National University's Myanmar/Burma Update, Oo Hla Saw, the General Secretary of the RNDP, was confronted by a large group of Rohingya activists. While they managed to discuss their disagreements in a cordial fashion, the emotions of the Rohingya were very apparent. Rakhine nationalist politicians are often blamed for inflaming the sentiments of their supporters and working to purge the remaining Muslim households from towns like Sittwe.

received 47,802 votes in the Pyithu Hluttaw seat for Buthidaung, which Shwe Maung (also known as Abdul Razak) won with 51,985.[11] Indeed, all of the Buthidaung contests in 2010 were relatively close, with margins of victory of less than 10 per cent. There were claims that the USDP disrupted party campaigning activities in Maungdaw Township, although the Union Election Commission later rejected an appeal on these grounds.

In 2010 the NDPD ran a significant, multi-sited campaign. Its Chairperson, Maung Maung Ni, contested the Pyitthu Hluttaw seat for Sittwe. He received 14,916 votes but was comprehensively defeated by Maung Nyo from the RNDP who received 40,023 votes. In the lead-up to the election, Maung Maung Ni presented the party's platform on radio and television on 8 October 2010. An account of these statements was published in the next day's *New Light of Myanmar* (Maung Maung Ni 2010), a government-run newspaper which has long been highly censored. In an impressive re-interpretation of a stale genre, Maung Maung Ni's statement mimicked much of the rhetoric of the State Peace and Development Council era, invoking the non-disintegration of the Union and perpetuation of sovereignty, among other standard lines. Yet, in a break from the ordinary rhetoric, he mentioned religion on six occasions and made much of the value of 'mutual help and mutual understanding among the national brethren and religions'. He also suggested that the NDPD was determined to 'constantly oppose any acts of terrorism and leftist or rightist extremism'. In Maung Maung Ni's words, 'with regard to human rights, we will guarantee the people to enjoy social, economic and political freedom, rights to press, mobilisation, religion, profession and living freedom'. This effort to win votes for the party culminated in the enthusiastic motto: 'people born in the Union, regardless of race and religion, may enjoy equal rights!' This aspiration was endorsed in the context that 'all national brethren live together through thick and

[11] The Pyithu Hluttaw (People's Assembly) is the lower house of the Myanmar Pyidaungsu Hluttaw (Union Assembly) in Naypyidaw. From 2011 to 2015, Shwe Mann, formerly a top-ranking general in the military government, chaired the joint house. Khin Aung Myint, a former general and Minister of Culture, chaired the upper house, or Amyotha Hluttaw (National Assembly).

thin in the successive eras and all walks of life regardless of race and religion took part in the independence struggle'.

Even though the NDPD struggled for electoral success in 2010, the party, through the efforts of Maung Maung Ni and his team, continued to maintain a high profile. In July 2012, at a time of significant violence in Rakhine State, the NDPD submitted a paper to the Pyidaungsu Hluttaw as a 'presentation for the native inhabitants (whose faith is Islam) residing in the Rakhine State' (NDPD 2012). This short account of important historical, cultural and political information sets out the details of many 'indigenous Muslims' and their contributions to national life. It included a list of the elected representatives for the Parliament or Hluttaw. This list explained that Muslims were elected to various legislative roles on nineteen occasions from 1936 to 1962, with figures such as Sultan Ahmed (from Maungdaw), Abdul Gaffar (from Buthidaung), Abdul Borshor (from Buthidaung), and Sultan Mahmood (from Buthidaung) achieving regular electoral success. In the BSPP-era, Muslims were elected to the Hluttaw in 1974 and 1978. During the 1990 election held under the auspices of the State Law and Order Restoration Council, five Muslim candidates were elected from township level seats in Maungdaw, Buthidaung and Sittwe. Such calls for more inclusive policies have yet to bear fruit.

In 2014 the NDPD demanded the inclusion of the term 'Rohingya' as a category in the census (Muddit 2014). In association with the Democracy and Human Rights Party (DHRP), a newer party seeking to champion Muslim rights, the NDPD sought to present a persuasive historical and political justification for Rohingya belonging. It is relevant that during its establishment phase in 2012, the DHRP was forced, under pressure from the Union Election Commission, to expel some of its executive committee members who had listed their ethnicity as 'Rohingya'. The party's chairperson, Kyaw Min, was one of the successful candidates of an earlier era: he had been elected in 1990 from Buthidaung but had never been able to take his seat. He was later jailed in 2005 with a 47-year sentence for his labour activism, but was released in the general amnesty of 2012. It is in this context that both the NDPD and the DHRP have sought to present themselves as representatives of the Muslims of Rakhine State. They fielded candidates in the 2015 general elections, none of whom were elected.

Union Solidarity and Development Party

As the party of the national government from 2011 to 2015, and the lineal successor of the former military regime, the USDP chose some candidates that reflected a more diverse ethnic and religious background for the 2010 general election. It presented five Muslim candidates for seats in northern Rakhine State, in the townships of Buthidaung and Maungdaw. Four of them won, with Shwe Maung and Aung Zaw Win (also known as Zaw Ki Ahmed) taking seats in the Pyithu Hluttaw, while Zayad Rahman (also known as Htay Win) won a seat in the Amyotha Hluttaw, and Zar Hein Gir (also known as Aung Myo Min) won a seat in the Rakhine State Hluttaw. In all cases, the candidate with the second-highest vote tally was from the NDPD, and in the seat that the Muslim USDP candidate lost—a Rakhine State legislature seat in Buthidaung township—it was the NDPD that prevailed.

The three Muslim candidates successful in their election to the Pyidaungsu Hluttaw in 2010 are worth discussing in more detail. Before his election to the Pyitthu Hluttaw, Shwe Maung was the Managing Director of Cyber Base Technology. Like the other Muslims elected to represent Rakhine State in Naypyidaw, his nationality and religion is listed, officially, as 'Bama/Muslim'. He holds a Bachelor of Engineering from the Yangon Institute of Technology, and has been an active member of the Buthidaung and Maungdaw local political scene for many years. On joining the Hluttaw he became a member of the Reform and Modernisation Assessment Committee, a powerful oversight body chaired by Aung Thein Linn, who is a senior figure in the USDP and who served as Mayor of Yangon from 2003 to 2011. For his public profile, Shwe Maung maintains a robust social media presence across Facebook, Twitter, and YouTube. He has also proved controversial. In early 2014 he was summoned for questioning over his comments about alleged violent incidents in Rakhine State. In this challenging situation, Shwe Maung appeared to receive high-level backing from USDP allies who determined that he remained a useful, if outspoken, voice, in their efforts to present the transformation of Myanmar politics as legitimate and representative. It is apparent, however, from discussions with other government representatives in Naypyidaw that Shwe Maung is deemed a divisive figure. He has been roundly criticized for what is perceived to be an audacious defence of Rohingya interests. He was not endorsed to contest the 2015 general election.

The other Muslims elected at the national level under the USDP banner are similarly interesting. Aung Zaw Win was elected to the Pyitthu Hluttaw seat for Maungdaw where he won with a huge margin: 137,691 votes to the 68,523 taken by Nurul Hauk of the NDPD. Aung Zaw Win is the Chairperson of Shine Construction, a major Yangon-based building contractor. He holds a Bachelor of Science from Sittwe University. He has been a long-term supporter of government economic and political activities in northern Rakhine State, including road construction. For the Amyotha Hluttaw, Zayad Rahman won Constituency 7 in the Rakhine State, based in Maungdaw. He holds a degree in geology from Yangon Arts and Science University, and was a Director of Liberty Trading Company, Managing Director at Unigrade International Company, while also previously serving as the Deputy Chairperson of the Union Solidarity and Development Association (USDA) for Buthidaung and Maungdaw. His businesses focus on the export of pulses, beans and fisheries products, and on the importation of steel, spices and pharmaceuticals. These businesses are headquartered in Yangon, with a trading presence in Peninsular Plaza, the heart of Myanmar's commercial and cultural activities in Singapore. Neither Aung Zaw Win nor Zayad Rahman contested the 2015 poll.

Kaman National Progressive Party

With the weight put on 'national race' status in Myanmar politics, the KNPP, registered in Yangon and led by Chairman Zaw Win and General Secretary Tin Hlaing Win, has a particular advantage. The Kaman claim indigeneity in Rakhine State, based on their long history of settlement, going back to the seventeenth century. According to one media report, '[t]he Kaman are a Rakhine ethnic subgroup that are believed to be of Indian descent and they primarily practise Islam' (Myo Myo 2010). The party's central executive committee comprises retired government officials and businessmen. In the 1990 election, the Kaman National League for Democracy (KNLD), as it was then known, took one seat in the People's Parliament with the campaign of Shwe Ya who won the Sittwe (1) constituency.

Since then it has sought to rebuild its presence, and draw support from other 'national races' in Rakhine State. In a campaign statement broadcast on radio and television in October 2010, party General

Secretary Tin Hlaing Win announced that as 'a national race party, we will give top priority to having equal rights for all national races without putting narrow-minded concepts in the fore' (Tin Hlaing Win 2010). Though the party failed to win seats in 2010, the party Chairman, Zaw Win, has a strong track record, including in government service. He is a former joint Director of the Yangon Division High Court. Zaw Win told *Mizzima* (2010) in the lead-up to the election that:

> In Arakan State, Muslims are not allowed to travel freely ... So, if we win some seats, we'll address these and other problems. Though we should limit the rights of people who are not Burmese citizens, all Burmese citizens should get their deserved rights.

Such sentiments are politically potent in circumstances where the overall situation of Muslims has continued to deteriorate.

In 2010, there were also some Muslim candidates who stood for election as independents. These included Arman Hinzar (also known as Sein Hla) in Sittwe's contest for the Pyithu Hluttaw seat, although he was ultimately unsuccessful. The challenge for all political parties and candidates will be to adequately reconcile the need to campaign on local issues with the challenges facing the nation more generally, especially in the context of the Buddhist-Muslim fault-line. As the KNPP's statements show, there are major challenges campaigning on behalf of Muslims even when they can claim 'national race' status. In late 2012 a group of prominent Muslims from Mandalay registered another political party. They had originally wanted to call it the Pathi National Congress, in recognition of the generic term '*pathi*' often used for Myanmar Muslims. The fact that this designation is not one of Myanmar's national race categories encouraged the Union Election Commission to disallow the party name. The party planned to present candidates at the 2015 general elections but was disallowed again.

Plurality of Muslim Politics

The threat that future conflict between Muslims and Buddhists poses for the sustainability of Myanmar's transformation is clear. With over 100,000 people displaced from their homes in northern Rakhine

State in 2012 and 2013, and new flare-ups of violence elsewhere in the years since, there are major challenges to the management of religious diversity in Myanmar. Since 2012 much of the political interest has centred on the mobilization of political forces against Muslim minorities. The '969' movement, a nationalist and Theravada Buddhist chauvinist organization, has challenged the foundations of pluralist tolerance in Myanmar (see Ramakrishna 2013). While it remains difficult to estimate the number of supporters of '969', their paraphernalia and distinctive logo are seen all over the country. It is taken as a marker of Buddhist affiliation in a context where some have claimed that the Muslim '786', a symbol for *halal* food, was being used to differentiate Muslim-friendly shops. Nowadays this Muslim designation is less commonly seen on shops around the country. In a quiet way, there has been a deliberate effort to downplay any Islamic aspects of this communal feud. Nonetheless there are efforts underway to further stymie Muslim choice, including in sensitive areas like marriage (see Kyaw Phone Kyaw 2014).

This provides considerable ammunition for those among the Muslim leadership who perceive pervasive discrimination. In the context of the 2010 election there was dissatisfaction with the government's unwillingness to produce election materials in languages other than Burmese. This has implications in many parts of the country although perhaps the most significant challenges emerge in parts of the northern Rakhine State where literacy in the national language is low. One report noted that:

> The UEC [Union Election Commission] only published ballots and voter instructions in the Burmese language, which posed a significant barrier in ethnic areas where some people cannot read Burmese, due to poverty and policies of discrimination, which limit access to educational opportunities in these areas. Illiteracy in the Burmese language was serious problem for many Muslim voters (Burma Fund UN Office 2011: 19).

While illiteracy is a less significant concern in the parts of Yangon where Muslims have congregated—which tend to be in the Burmese-speaking downtown and directly adjacent zones—there are calls for greater representation. In this context language and culture are deeply political, and such cultural claims are founded in the oppression and discrimination that Muslim minorities continue to feel.

In Yangon, the politics of many Muslim groups are shaped by their exposure to a cosmopolitan and pluralist society where different ideas of interaction have emerged. There is now a widespread appreciation that the history of interaction between different ethnic groups in this part of the country has been a positive one, helping to draw different groups in to regular conversation. Unless a new inclusive sentiment emerges in Yangon politics, it will remain difficult, if not impossible, for Muslims to get elected. The major parties running candidates in Yangon will continue to look for more deliberately 'mainstream' options, especially to those candidates who can appeal to a wide range of Buddhist interests. In some parts of the city there may be ethnic candidates, particularly Kayin, who can do well. Yet it is outside Yangon that Muslims have faced the most strident and discriminatory campaigns in the years since the 2010 election. The mobilization of anti-Muslim groups has been particularly apparent in some of Myanmar's 'heartland' areas, and in places where military bases exert a strong influence on local politics and economy. It was in 2013 that violence in Meiktila, a town a few hours from Mandalay, became emblematic of the rush of some Buddhists to target their Muslim neighbours. These efforts undermined confidence in the long-term security of the Muslim population.

To make this story of Muslim politics more complete it is worth seeking to interpret the overall picture of Muslim politics at this point in Myanmar's political history. The 2015 election shows the very limited extent to which new spaces for Muslim political activity have emerged. For now, some lessons can be drawn.

First, there is reluctance to embrace Muslims in Myanmar, although many positive efforts are underway. Many Muslims speak fluent Burmese, even in their interactions with each other, and while there are groups who also speak Urdu, Punjabi, Bengali or Chittagonian, they are much less prominent in the national conversation. The Burmanized Muslims are now the largest cohort, especially since teaching in other languages in schools was banned during the socialist period (see Berlie 2008). Educated Muslims will also often speak English, sometimes the product of time spent elsewhere in Southeast Asia, particularly in Malaysia and Singapore, or of stints in the Middle East. There are those who will have learned Indonesian or Malay as part of this exposure, and there are groups of Myanmar Muslims who comfortably consume news and entertainment from Southeast Asia's Muslim majority countries,

Table 4.1 Pyithu Hluttaw constituencies in Rakhine State with Muslim candidates, 2010 election

Party	Constituency and Candidate	Religion	Votes
	Sittwe		
Rakhine Nationals Progressive Party	Maung Nyo	Non-Muslim	40,023
Union Solidarity and Development Party	Kaung San She	Non-Muslim	20,168
National Democratic Party for Development	Maung Maung Ni	Muslim	14,916
Independent	Arman Hinzar (or Sein Hla)	Muslim	11,839
Kaman National Progressive Party	Zaw Win	Muslim	2,621
National Unity Party	Oo Saw Maung	Non-Muslim	2,483
	Buthidaung		
Union Solidarity and Development Party	Shwe Maung (or Abdul Razak)	Muslim	51,985
National Democratic Party for Development	Abdul Tahil	Muslim	47,802
Rakhine Nationals Development Party	Ba Thein	Non-Muslim	15,564
Independent	Aung Hla	Non-Muslim	14,558
	Kyauktaw		
Rakhine Nationals Progressive Party	Tha Sein	Non-Muslim	44,104
Union Solidarity and Development Party	MaungTharzan	Non-Muslim	22,288
National Democratic Party for Development	Maung Sein	Muslim	14,967
National Unity Party	Hla Tun Oo	Non-Muslim	4,037
	Maungdaw		
Union Solidarity and Development Party	Zaw Ki Ahmed (or Aung Zaw Win)	Muslim	137,691

(Contd.)

Table 4.1   (*Contd.*)

Party	Constituency and Candidate	Religion	Votes
National Democratic Party for Development	Nurul Hauk	Muslim	68,523
National Unity Party	Kyaw Aye	Non-Muslim	5,114
	Thandwe		
Union Solidarity and Development Party	Ye Tun	Non-Muslim	16,233
Rakhine Nationals Progressive Party	Tin Win	Non-Muslim	10,285
National Unity Party	Ba Saw	Non-Muslim	8,095
Rakhine State National Force of Myanmar	Maung Maung Thein	Non-Muslim	6,883
Kaman National Progressive Party	Tin Hlaing Win	Muslim	5,120

Source: Author.

and also from South Asia. Some Muslims will also have learned Arabic and/or Urdu, especially those who have been funnelled through the regional Islamic education system. Nonetheless, their strongest linguistic and cultural aptitude will often be in Burmese, and in interacting with their own country's diverse peoples.

Second, many Muslims are looking to vote for Muslims, even in competition with each other. Across South Asia the style of communal politics that has been most prevalent focuses on religious socio-cultural niches. Such blocks are usually tied to a dominant, national-level political party that can take advantage of the predictable flow of votes. In Myanmar's case, the 2010 election saw Muslim voters opt for Muslim candidates standing for the USDP in large numbers; this is similar to the pattern for other minority groups.[12]

[12] While there is no good evidence of mass ballot irregularities in Muslim-dominated constituencies, there are circumstantial indications that the USDP used its government links to ensure victory in some strategic areas. It seems likely, given the relative isolation and lack of external scrutiny, that such violations were particularly prevalent in places like northern Rakhine State.

Table 4.2   Amyotha Hluttaw constituencies in Rakhine State with Muslim candidates, 2010 election

Party	Constituency and Candidate	Religion	Votes
	Sittwe		
Rakhine Nationalities Progressive Party	Aye Maung	Non-Muslim	40,164
National Democratic Party for Development	Maung Maung Tin	Muslim	24,583
Union Solidarity and Development Party	Chan Tha	Non-Muslim	21,757
Kaman National Progressive Party	Hla Toe	Muslim	3,969
National Unity Party	Tun Oo Kyaw	Non-Muslim	2,896
	Buthidaung		
Union Solidarity and Development Party	Maung Aye Tun	Non-Muslim	48,120
National Democratic Party for Development	Mustapha Kamil	Muslim	44,126
Independent	Tun Min aka Amtiyias	Muslim	25,640
Khami National Development Party	Maung Kyaw Khine	Non-Muslim	10,922
National Development and Peace Party	Ali Hussein	Muslim	2,740
	Kyauktaw		
Rakhine Nationalities Progressive Party	Khin Maung (or Aung Kyaw Oo)	Non-Muslim	41,057
National Democratic Party for Development	Maung Maung Lay	Muslim	14,978
Union Solidarity and Development Party	Kyaw Yin	Non-Muslim	12,757
Mro or Khami National Solidarity Organization	San Thar Aung	Non-Muslim	9,995
National Unity Party	Tun Linn	Non-Muslim	9,718

(*Contd.*)

Table 4.2   (*Contd.*)

Party	Constituency and Candidate	Religion	Votes
Rakhine State National Force of Myanmar	Myint Zaw	Non-Muslim	3,794
	Maungdaw 1		
Union Solidarity and Development Party	Zayad Rahman (or Htay Win)	Muslim	72,177
National Democratic Party For Development	Soe Win	Muslim	38,699
National Unity Party	Ba Thein	Non-Muslim	2,079
	Maungdaw 2		
Union Solidarity and Development Party	Maung Thar Khin	Non-Muslim	64,564
National Democratic Party For Development	Taw Yu Baydein	Muslim	30,887
United Democratic Party	Faral Zulhak	Muslim	1,396
	Rathidaung, Poonagyun		
Rakhine Nationalities Progressive Party	Khin Maung Latt	Non-Muslim	57,405
Union Solidarity and Development Party	Aung Zaw Win	Muslim	26,661
National Unity Party	Talai Shay	Non-Muslim	14,149
Khami National Development Party	Maung Thar Tun	Non-Muslim	3,710

Source: Author.

This was in harmony with the pattern for the country as a whole, in an election that was neither free nor fair. Such patterns led to the election of some Muslim candidates, but also to the defeat of the NDPD, which has pushed a more explicitly religioun-based political agenda. The strong ties that many Muslim voters have to their local mosque also mean that religious teachers and other powerbrokers can offer strong signals about communal needs.

Third, for Muslims who are seeking to be elected, there remain major obstacles especially when it comes to acceptance as political

Table 4.3   State Hluttaw constituencies in Rakhine State with
Muslim candidates, 2010 election

Party	Constituency and Candidate	Religion	Votes
	Sittwe 1		
Rakhine Nationals Progressive Party	Tha Lu Che	Non-Muslim	16,998
National Democratic Party for Development	Khin Maung Myint	Muslim	14,493
Union Solidarity and Development Party	Kyaw Zan Hla	Non-Muslim	12,620
Kaman National Progressive Party	Kyaw Nyein	Muslim	1,976
National Unity Party	Ne Aung Kyaw	Non-Muslim	1,567
	Sittwe 2		
Rakhine Nationals Progressive Party	Aung Mya Kyaw	Non-Muslim	24,211
Union Solidarity and Development Party	San Shwe	Non-Muslim	14,345
Kaman National Progressive Party	Aung Hla Tun	Muslim	3,795
National Unity Party	Maung Kyaw Zan	Non-Muslim	2,030
	Buthidaung 1		
National Democratic Party for Development	Aung Myint (or Zarhidulla)	Muslim	34,158
Union Solidarity and Development Party	Maung San Shwe	Non-Muslim	31,678
Mro or Khami National Solidarity Organization	K Paught	Non-Muslim	4,510
	Buthidaung 2		
National Democratic Party for Development	Borshir Ahmed	Muslim	27,942
Union Solidarity and Development Party	Barshi Armad	Muslim	23,417
Rakhine Nationals Progressive Party	Tun Aung Thein	Non-Muslim	8,936

(Contd.)

Table 4.3   (*Contd.*)

Party	Constituency and Candidate	Religion	Votes
	Maungdaw 1		
Rakhine Nationals Progressive Party	Saw Nyein	Non-Muslim	22,712
Union Solidarity and Development Party	Aung Tun Hlaing	Non-Muslim	7,319
National Democratic Party for Development	Mei Lon	Muslim	5,401
Mro or Khami National Solidarity Organization	Kyaw Tun Naing	Non-Muslim	4,501
National Unity Party	Tun Sein	Non-Muslim	2,065
Rakhine State National Force	Hla Saw	Non-Muslim	1,533
	Kyauktaw 2		
Union Solidarity and Development Party	Zar Hein Gir (or Aung Myo Min)	Muslim	71,508
National Democratic Party for Development	Khin Maung Myint	Muslim	38,867
National Unity Party	Tun Maung	Non-Muslim	2,263
	Maungdaw 2		
Union Solidarity and Development Party	Mra Aung	Non-Muslim	52,923
National Democratic Party for Development	Chay Kauk Ali	Muslim	31,320
National Unity Party	Chit Tun Aung	Non-Muslim	2,205
National Development and Peace Party	Ohman Pip Has	Muslim	690
	Rambree 2		
Union Solidarity and Development Party	Kyaw Khin	Non-Muslim	14,649
Rakhine Nationals Progressive Party	San Khin	Non-Muslim	5,162
Kaman National Progressive Party	Tun Myint	Muslim	1,239

(*Contd.*)

Table 4.3   (*Contd.*)

Party	Constituency and Candidate	Religion	Votes
	Mrauk-U 2		
Rakhine Nationals Progressive Party	Kyaw Thein	Non-Muslim	20,518
National Democratic Party for Development	Nu Arlaung	Muslim	6,935
Union Solidarity and Development Party	Maung Than Sein	Non-Muslim	6,095
Mro or Khami National Solidarity Organization	Ba Bwe	Non-Muslim	2,646
National Unity Party	Tha Zan Hla	Non-Muslim	2,495
Rakhine State National Force	Aye Kyaing	Non-Muslim	1,876

Source: Author.

leaders by Myanmar's non-Muslims. While the NDPD, the DHRP, and the KNPP are gently explaining their Muslim perspectives, it is the USDP that supported all of the Muslims elected to serve in Naypyidaw in 2010. Notwithstanding this modest success, Muslims are challenged by the need to find a formal status that will protect them in Myanmar's new constitutional system. Religious identity in the country has been so thoroughly politicized that it would take significant changes to the national mood for there to be any acceptance of a greater role for Muslims in society more generally. For Muslims to take on such prominence would ultimately require a de-emphasis on their religious identity and the re-imagination of their Myanmar citizenship. It is the issue of citizenship, and contention about the perceived loyalty of Muslims to the country and its system, that counts. In this context Kipgen has argued for reconciliation and a consociational democracy (2013). In the same optimistic vein, Parnini has suggested that:

> The recent democratization in Myanmar will open up new avenues for resolving the Rohingya refugee crisis through viable political means, diplomatic breakthroughs and intensified bilateral negotiations between Myanmar and Bangladesh (2013: 296).

Yet, the barriers that will need to be overcome before such reconcilia-tion and resolution is possible are significant. The level of anti-Muslim sentiment that has emerged means that the plural identities of Myanmar's Muslims are under grave and growing threat.

* * *

Muslim political activity, like most minority politics in Myanmar, will rarely, if ever, prove determinative in an election. The number of Muslim voters is relatively low and it cannot be assumed that there is any overall coherence to their political opinion or voting behaviour. In the future the dynamics of bloc voting, that may have been relevant in 2010, will likely have been overtaken by other approaches to mobiliz-ing such niche cohorts for electoral success. The NLD, to say nothing of some minority, regional and sectoral political parties, will all be looking for Muslim voters at prospective future elections but have not offered Muslim candidates.

Looking closely at the political and electoral dynamics in areas where Muslims are culturally and economically important, helps to introduce a new appreciation of their agency and activism. As a promi-nent minority across many parts of the country, the politics of Muslims will matter in the nascent transition to a more inclusive political and social order. That order will only prove sustainable if new compro-mises with Muslim identity politics emerge. The idea that Muslims could be more effectively brought inside the 'national races' categories is one option, although the prevailing rejection of any inclusion of the Rohingya makes that doubtful. As Zainuddin puts it, 'up to this point it seems the Rohingya need to rely on their own strength, and cannot expect any help from outside, including from Bangladesh who are their neighbours' (2000: 53). Under these conditions, many Muslims are likely to find that religious politics remain highly-charged and that they continue to be excluded from 'national race' consideration (see also the discussion in Willis 2014). This will lead to further grievances among those who perceive that there is no long-term future in a Myanmar dominated by Buddhist interests galvanized in the '969' mould.

There are other electoral implications, including those for Myanmar's major political players. Aung San Suu Kyi has been heavily criticized by the international community for her unwillingness to speak up for Muslim minorities especially when they are facing severe violence (see Lee 2014). In a passionate appraisal of this issue, Green argues that '[i]t is Aung San Suu Kyi's general refusal to speak out against the crimes endured by the Rohingya that has provided cover for David Cameron and the international community's failure to intervene' (2013: 96). In this context Green goes on to suggest that '[r]acism is Burma's political fault-line and while the epicentre might reasonably be understood as the ethnic cleansing of Burma's Rohingya community in Arakan [Rakhine], the central fracture itself must be understood as institutionalized Islamophobia, deeply embedded and historically informed' (2013: 97). Even after her 2015 general election success, the conundrum for Aung San Suu Kyi and other Myanmar politicians is that they risk alienating the Buddhist majority by appearing too cosy with Muslim interests. During a period of great political uncertainty, the risks to individual politicians and to entire political parties are immense. There is a chance that future Myanmar elections will be decided by the electorate's appreciation of anti-Muslim solidarity.

Clearly, the question of better integrating Myanmar's Muslims has long-term political consequences. To the extent that Muslim politics are important to Myanmar's future, they will need to be understood as one part of an historically-defined but ever more complex political terrain. As Myanmar continues to become enmeshed in the global political and economic system it faces the need to draw Muslims into the political mainstream more adequately. This might be predicated on a more sympathetic approach towards resolving their citizenship status and improving their other opportunities. Boosting the ranks of Muslims in the Myanmar bureaucracy could be a first step, and helping improve their prospects for career progression would be helpful. If, in the years to come, Muslim politics prove tolerable to Myanmar's other populations, then Muslim politicians will have found a desirable middle ground.

5 Houses of Islam

Muslims, Property Rights, and the State in Myanmar

JUDITH BEYER[*]

On a street in downtown Yangon stands a four-story house that is like many in the area, but has its very own story to tell. In this house live Auntie Karima[1] and Uncle Said, an elderly Muslim couple, with their adopted children.[2] Under the portico, in front of the house, tea stalls and small makeshift eateries provide temporary

[*] This chapter is based on data collected during six months of ethnographic fieldwork in Yangon (Myanmar), between December 2012 and December 2013. My research was financed by the Max Planck Institute for Social Anthropology, Halle/Saale. I wish to thank Melissa Crouch from the Centre for Asian Law (National University of Singapore); the Indian Ocean Studies Group at the Martin Luther University Halle-Wittenberg (Germany); and Natasha Pairaudeau and Julie Stephens from the Centre for Economics and History, as well as Saumya Saxena in Cambridge (UK), for their comments and suggestions.

[1] All names used in this chapter are pseudonyms. 'Auntie' and 'Uncle' are polite forms of address when a person is younger than the addressee (as was the case here). They are used as alternatives to the Myanmar terms 'Daw' (for a woman) and 'U' (for a man).

[2] Auntie Karima has raised over ten children in her house so far, among them Buddhists, Muslims, Christians, and Hindus; all of them are grown-up already. Although busy with her family and the businesses she runs, she prays

rest and offer mohinga (Burmese fish noodle soup) or *dosa* (Indian pancakes) to passers-by. The ground floor opens towards the street and is divided into one-room shops where various services are available. Beyond the main entrance, an old, stained wooden board on the wall to the left lists the names and owners of the businesses that used to be based here. About twenty people had their private companies in this house as indicated by the abbreviation 'Ltd.' behind their names. Some wooden plates have been removed from the board, rendering the stories of some former inhabitants invisible.

Climbing the stairs to Auntie Karima's flat on the second floor for the first time in February 2013, I duck underneath hanging laundry and pass by storage boxes in the shared hallway. I notice the tiny golden Buddha statues and fresh flowers, placed on altars installed above the doors. Each door leads into a maze of flats and rooms of which only the smallest part is visible from the stairwell. I continue to the second floor and, before entering my hosts' apartment, I pass through another shorter hallway from which a number of tiny rooms branch off to both sides. There is one shared toilet for all the inhabitants of these rooms. Before my hand can reach through the iron gate at the end of the hallway to knock on the door of Auntie Karima's flat, her daughter opens the door: 'Please, come in.'

* * *

In this chapter, I use the example of Auntie Karima (65) and Uncle Said (68) of the Kalai Memon Muslim community, to describe and analyse the transformations of property in Myanmar's former capital, Rangoon/Yangon.[3] This case study illustrates the ongoing struggle between government and community interests; between the

---

every morning at 4 am for one hour, reads the *Qur'an*, and goes for a walk in a nearby park. By the time I left in December 2013, she was contemplating the adoption of three young children from Burmese families in the northern part of the country, whose parents had died. Uncle Said teaches English and is an active member of several Muslim community organizations.

[3] The name of the city was changed in 1988 along with other towns. I use Rangoon when referring to pre-1988 and Yangon when referring to post-1988 events.

application and enforcement of state laws and their disregard; as well as the application and negotiation of non-state norms and principles, such as Muslim understandings of community and solidarity. It also traces the personal struggles of owners, tenants and squatters trying to obtain, renovate and sell property or simply secure a place to live. Through this, my chapter provides an example of Muslims' responses to broader trends and patterns in the country, particularly in Yangon. Among these historical moments are the granting of land to immigrant settlers at the beginning of the nineteenth century, the disposal of land after the Second Anglo-Burmese War, land speculation in the beginning of the twentieth century, the nationalization campaign of the 1960s, and finally the recent introduction of new land laws and foreign investment laws.[4] The contemporary context is marked by an increasing need for real estate. With the end of international sanctions, new foreign investments have poured into the country. Alongside tourism and real estate purchases by 'cronies' (businessmen on good terms with the outgoing military establishment), this has led to skyrocketing land and property prices, rent rates, the launching of modernization projects and the general development of the city. These recent developments make an investigation into property and its historical trajectories important and timely.

In tracing the change of property regimes over time, I rely on different historical sources: colonial-era publications by officers of British India, academic publications on the history of the country, doctoral dissertations, colonial-era legislation and reports, documents on the history of the Muslim Kalai Memon community written by community members, as well as the oral history of Auntie Karima and Uncle Said. I do not treat any of these historical sources as more 'authentic' or important than the other. The focus of this chapter is to show how state policy on property, designed by the colonial, the socialist, the military and the current state, has impacted Muslim people's lives from an anthropological perspective.

There has been much critique within anthropology of the study of property relations through a state-centred lens—the predominant

---

[4] See The Farmland Law No 11/2012; The Vacant, Fallow and Virgin Lands Management Law No 10/2012; The Foreign Investment Law No 21/2012; Foreign Investment Rules Notification, 31 January 2013.

approach from the eighteenth century onwards (see Geisler 2006). Anthropologists have also investigated the working of property in stateless societies, albeit often under different paradigms and assuming that property that is neither 'stately' nor 'private' must be 'communal'. Legal anthropologists have argued that property should be viewed in a much broader context than simply the 'Big Four' categories of open access, common property, state property and private property (see Benda-Beckmann 2001: 296). In more recent legal anthropological debates, the state continues to play a role, but no longer as 'the sole legitimate font' in which property is a mere tool of state regulation (Benda-Beckmann et al., 2006: 5). Rather, the state is seen as one among many potential actors with an interest in holding the 'bundle of rights', a metaphor used to describe property in its characteristic as a *relation* between different actors.[5] In Myanmar, 'the state' has always been and remains a driving force when it comes to property. However, this does not render all non-state actors entirely passive. This chapter shows how people like Auntie Karima accept, adapt and navigate through the different property regimes, finding alternative spaces to carry on with their individual and community lives.

Family Histories on the Second Floor

Auntie Karima's flat is light and spacious. I take off my shoes and sit down on a divan, and while waiting for coffee to be served, my eyes wander along the walls of the living room: a large picture of the *ka'aba*,[6] a copy of the *hadith* (sayings of the Prophet Muhammad) resting on a piece of cloth, various family photographs, a large clock, a cupboard with festive china, a *Qur'an* on the side table, next to it an old brochure about yoga. Auntie Karima waits patiently until I have oriented myself and while her daughter serves coffee and brown sticky rice with coconut ('Burmese chocolate'), she explains what I have seen by telling me 'We are Muslims.'

---

[5] The term 'bundle of rights' dates back to Henry Maine (1986 [1861]) and has been adapted by other legal and social anthropologists to describe phenomena such as marriage (see Leach 1961).

[6] The *ka'aba* is the sacred building in Mecca that all Muslims face when undertaking their daily prayers.

After several visits, I come to appreciate the history of her family's arrival in Myanmar in 1905 and with it the history of part of Yangon's diverse Muslim community. The ancestors of Auntie Karima and her husband came from the port city Thatta, which used to be the capital of the Indian province of southern Sindh.[7] The city is located close to Karachi in contemporary Pakistan. Uncle Said recalls the story of conversion and forced migration of their community, the Kalai Memon[8]:

Kalai Memon came to Burma from India, but actually they are from Sindh, Pakistan. They had a partition ... so, we are from Thatta. Thatta is a town, 70 miles from Karachi. So our ancestors were Hindus. Our ancestors became Muslim under some saint; I don't know the name of that saint.[9] So he made us Muslim. So at that time, since we changed our religion, most of the Hindus became our enemies, because they don't like their religion to be changed by anyone. So maybe there was some massacre ... so some ran away. Some remained there. Those who remained there, they are called Sindhi Memon. Because it is in Sindh province in Pakistan. Those who ran away up to Kutch in Rajastan in India, they were called Kutchi Memon. Most ran away until Gujarat [province], they are called Kalai Memon. In Gujarat, there is a sub-province called Kathiawar.[10] Those people who ran away to Kathiawar are called Kalai Memon. From Kathiawar, the British took over

---

[7] The city is said to be the ancient Patala, conquered by Alexander the Great. See for example Burnes (1835: 27).

[8] All conversations with Auntie Karima and Uncle Said were in English—which they both spoke fluently. Among each other and with most of their community members, they speak Memon. Some in their community, however, have a better command of Urdu. The younger generation of Kalai Memon increasingly uses Burmese language, but there is an expectation that people speak Memon within the community. In this chapter, paragraphs in italics indicate direct speech, which has been transcribed from audio recordings.

[9] Histories of the Memon diaspora communities on the Internet seem to agree that a saint called Pir Yusuffuddin Saheb converted the trading-class Lohanas from Lohanpur in Sindh to Islam in the fifteenth century. Various translations of the word 'Memon' are available, one of them from the Urdu word 'Momin' ('the one who believes in God'). See, for example, the Chicago Memons (2014), the Memon World (2014), or Moomal's (1996) account of the Kuch Memon community in South Africa.

[10] Now a province in western India at the Arabian Sea coast in the state of Gujarat.

India, Burma, everything. And Burma was a very fertile country … so our forefathers, I don't know – my grandfather or her grandfather [nodding towards his wife] *– they came to Myanmar; at that time it was Burma. And they spread throughout Burma. So actually we are from Pakistan, but you can say we are from India. Whatever, so this is the real history. We are Khatiawar, this is why we are called Kalai. Kalai in Sindh language means 'I leave you' - meaning 'gone.' Kalai means 'gone' in Sindh. Our ancestors' houses were burnt, people were killed, everything. Here also you must have heard, Rakhine people* [meaning Rohingya], *they ran away … because when it comes to your life and your property, you throw away your property and you run away. Now these Rakhine people they run … as far as Australia … by boat or anything they can get - they also go away.*

The Memon are often described as a 'merchant class' or 'sailor businessmen' whose extensive networks spread across the Indian Ocean. Despite their conversion to Islam in the fifteenth century, Memon communities living in India were classified as 'Hindu' by the British colonial power, for example, when it came to the application of personal status laws regarding matters of succession and inheritance (Rankin 1939: 101–2).[11] They were to become one part of the 'Indian community' that the British shipped across the Bay of Bengal from

[11] In 1847, the Chief Justice of the Supreme Court in Bombay, Sir Erskine Perry, decided in a case involving Khoja and Kutch Memon, that the Hindu customary law of excluding females from any share in a paternal estate shall be applied to the case, although the parties are both Muslims. The groups had originally been Hindu before their conversion and had retained, so they argued, Hindu customary law in certain aspects of their life (see *Hirabai v Sonabai*, 1847. This is similar to Lord Dunedin who argued that 'the converts had retained their Hindu law relating to the exclusion of females from succession, and that that law had been engrafted as a custom on the Mahomedan law although not in accordance with the rules of the Koran.' The argument in this case was later extended to other cases involving Muslims which 'appear to pre-suppose as the ground of his [Sir Erskine Perry's] decision a view that the Khojas and Memons had adopted not only this custom but the whole of the Hindu law to which it owes its origin' (Beaman 1913). In doing so, the judges rendered Hindu customary law more important than Shari'a, and Hindu identity and religion more important than Muslim identity and religion, at least in areas concerning personal status. This changed only in 1937, with the establishment of the Shariat Act (India), which abolished the application of customary law for all cases of succession and inheritance.

1840 onwards.[12] Together with all other people from India, no matter which class, caste, or religion, they are referred to as *kula lu-myo*.[13] Auntie Karima recalls what her grandfather had told her from the early days of his arrival:

My grandfather was a lord in India and he was brought here by force by the British. My family settled in Aung Lan Myo in Upper Burma where they were given land. My grandfather took cottonseeds from India and was the first to introduce cotton to this country. My family were businessmen and knew how to start a business. They started with a small factory, but were soon prohibited

[12] A general problem in assessing the situation of Indian Muslims is that many publications on the 'British Indians' or 'Burmese Indians' do not differentiate between those who were of Muslim faith and those who were Hindus. The religious orientation of Indians who came to Burma was often not explicitly discussed. Judging from the census in the nineteenth and early twentieth centuries, carried out by the British in Burma, there was a significant number of Muslims who had come from India, which is why I engage with this literature here. Literature on (ethnic) minorities is often only concerned with those groups who resided in the country prior to British occupation, which means that the Muslims from India, who came to the country in the 19th century only, rarely feature in this body of literature. An exception is Yegar (1972), whose publication is a historical account of Muslims in Burma exclusively up until the 1970s.

[13] According to The Anglo-Indian Dictionary (1996 [1886]), the term *kula* is a 'Burmese name of a native of Continental India; and hence misapplied also to the English and other Westerns who have come from India to Burma; in fact used generally for a Western foreigner... But the true history of the word has for the first time been traced by Professor Forchhammer, to *Gola*, the name applied in old Pegu inscriptions to the Indian Buddhist immigrants, a name which he identifies with the Skt. Gauda, the ancient name of Northern Bengal, whence the famous city of Gaur.' Note that *kala* is pejorative, as it translates as 'black'. Burmese give the latter term to people with (South) Indian ancestors who have a darker skin color. Yegar mentions that in the days of the Burmese Kingdom the descendants of Arab, Persian and Indian Muslim traders were referred to as 'Pathee or Kala' (Yegar 1962: 6), but he also notes the earlier translation 'to cross over [the Bay of Bengal]'. In his glossary, Amrith defines the term *kala* as a 'Burmese term used to describe Indians, originally a term denoting 'foreigner', but it assumed pejorative connotations' (2013: 287). 'Foreigner' is also sometimes translated as *kula phyu* (lit. white foreigner) in Myanmar.

to engage in trade. When the Prince of Wales visited Aung Lan Myo in 1906,
my grandfather gave him a rousing welcome as he was from a family of
lords and knew how to welcome royalty. He was then permitted to work as a
businessman with cotton. He traded for and with the Steel Brothers Company
and the Bombay Burma Company, which were the two biggest companies at
that time. He started with cotton but then expanded to other crops.

During British colonial times in Burma (1824–1948), some of the 'Burmese Indians' who arrived were highly educated and served in the colonial administration as soldiers or private merchants. Like Auntie Karima's grandfather, many had private businesses in India and managed to re-establish themselves in Burma. Muslims from India, like the families of Auntie Karima and Uncle Said, were by no means the first Muslims to arrive in the Buddhist country. Chinese travellers found Arab and Persian trade colonies along the coasts of Myanmar as early as 860 CE (Yegar 1962: 2; Leider 1998). In 1795, a British officer who visited Rangoon on his way to the Court of Ava, wrote that he could hear 'the solemn voice of the Muezzin, calling pious Islamites to early prayers'.

Indian Muslims in the nineteenth century came as part of a colonizing mission. Next to educated elites who spoke English and helped to administer the colonial state, British forces were in need of labourers and preferred non-Burmans of Indian origin over the local population. In contrast to the educated elites who settled in Upper Burma, the *chettiar* moneylenders (see Amrith 2013: 119-122; Charney 2009:10) and indentured labourers from India settled in Rangoon, turning it into an Indian city or—put derogatively—'an asylum for fraudulent debtors and violent and unprincipled characters from every part of India' (Pemberton 1835: lii; see also Tinker 1993).[14]

Property in Rangoon during British Colonial Times

Rangoon had been a small town before the arrival of the British. The numbers of its estimated population in 1823 fluctuated between 9,000 and 30,000 people. In 1856, there were 46,000 people living

---

[14] In 1804, the number of Muslims living in Rangoon was recorded as 5,000, compared to around 500 Christians (including non-Europeans). The number of Europeans, in comparison, was just 25 (Pearn 1939: 78).

in the city and by 1921 this had grown to around 98,000 people.[15] The city is located on a peninsula hugged by the riverbed of the Hlaing River (now known as Yangon River) to the south and the west. The river empties into the Gulf of Martaban of the Andaman Sea to the southeast of the Bay of Bengal. The famous Shwedagon Pagoda attracted religious pilgrims from inland. According to legends, it was erected during the lifetime of the Buddha. The pagoda continues to dominate the city until today. In the eighteenth century, the settlement became a trading hub when the monarch established connections with the European trading companies, which began to export teak in large quantities.

Before the annexation of Burma, '[t]he Burmese Government [i.e. the Burmese King] had never given land to foreigners and rarely permitted permanent buildings to be erected; anyone who erected such a building did so at his own risk and by the custom of the country was liable to see it destroyed or appropriated at the discretion of the Burmese authorities.' (Pearn 1939: 180). In 1839, foreigners still needed the express sanction of the King to buy property in Rangoon (Pearn 1939: 147). Relations between the King of Burma and the Governor of India deteriorated over a housing dispute in 1840 when the city governor demanded that an assistant to the British Colonel, who preferred to live in Rangoon rather than in the capital Ava, should vacate the house in which he was living at the time. The assistant left not only the house, but also the country, following his Colonel. Up until 1851, British subjects (including Indians) living in Rangoon had no Indian Government official to respond to their problems in the city.

As Rangoon became a military hub as it prepared for the looming war with the British (Pearn 1939: 151), houses were no longer renovated or new buildings constructed because the inhabitants were under 'the impression that the town might be entirely removed by order from Court [of the King of Burma]' (1939: 152). Instead, in 1841, the King issued an order to fortify Rangoon and he stayed in the city for a year to observe the construction process. As Burmans moved to the new city, the foreign mercantile community was left alone close

[15] See Yin May (1962: 32); Zin New Myint (1998: 69); cited in Kraas, Yin May and Zin Nwe Myint (2010: 27).

to the riverside, isolated from the King's new city (1939: 156ff.). When the British annexed Lower Burma in the Second Anglo-Burmese War in 1852, Rangoon was invaded and destroyed by Indian troops of the East India Company.

Rangoon became the capital of British Burma and was populated first by Indian soldiers. Montgomery, Fraser, and Dalhousie, the three British colonial administrators responsible for the development of Rangoon, designed a town-plan for a city that was to accommodate 36,000 people. It was based on 'a general British philosophy of colonial urbanism' (Hemingway 1992: 34) and did not take any pre-war arrangement into account. It was oriented towards the river and the sea, set up to function as a port city of significant commerce and as an example of successful colonial modernization. Lord Dalhousie, who was Governor General of India from 1848 to 1856, was responsible for the naming of streets, among them the 'Mogul street', named 'after the Muslim merchants who settled in that quarter of the town' (Pearn 1939: 188). When the new rulers of Rangoon planned the city, they declared all land government property, which was later to be distributed to private citizens under the auspices of the government. Land and property became a commodity:

> It is to be distinctly understood that all persons now occupying houses and land in Rangoon only occupy and hold the same on sufferance; present permission gives them no legal right to the property. ... All these matters will be arranged after peace has been restored either by British Commissioners, or the Burmese authorities, as the case may be. (Laurie 1853: 148–9; cited in Pearn 1939: 176)
>
> No buildings now existing or which may hereafter be built without sanction from the authorities will be considered to entitle the occupants to property in the soil they cover. (Phayre in a letter to Dalhousie, dated December 25, 1852; cited in Hall 1932, 11)

Dalhousie and Phayre did away with property rights, assuming that only when a Burmese occupied a plot of land and thereby had physical possession of the property, did he or she intend to keep it.[16]

---

[16] Hemingway reports that at one point, Phayre discussed 'to follow Burmese practices in property law. However, this attempt was certainly not made in Rangoon where all land was assumed to be government property and previous rights of tenure were disallowed' (Hemingway 1992: 94).

Europeans residing in Rangoon demanded the recognition of existing occupancy, and Persians, Armenians and Indians demanded the maintenance of former rights in the land, although the authorities rejected these claims (Pearn 1939: 191). No such requests from the Burmese appear to have been recorded. Captain Phayre, who became Commissioner of the new province Pegu (Bago), within which Rangoon was to be administered, proposed to sell outright the freehold of the land in the town at fixed rates. He preferred this method of disposal, to sale by auction, as being fairer to the poor (Pearn 1939: 191). An annual land-tax would be imposed and there would in addition be a monthly municipal tax varying according to the size of the land. The Governor of India accepted Phayre's views about the propriety of selling the land regardless of former occupancy but the prices, which Phayre wished to fix, were considered to be much too low.

The town magistrate exercised the powers of municipal administration. He was in charge of the allotment of town and suburban building-sites and of the collection of municipal and provincial taxes. Any occupier whose building or land was 'filthy and unwholesome' was liable to be fined by him. The magistrate had wide powers of inspection of buildings (Pearn 1939: 216). The first buyers were Indian traders (Chakravarti 1971: 7). The plot where the house occupied by Auntie Karima and Uncle Said is located was classified as a 'first class lot' within the business district.[17]

From 1854 onwards, Phayre introduced the renting of town lots because, until then, no Burmese had bought even the least expensive lot. By 1855, Burmese and non-Burmese squatters, who had been living on the same land before, had rented 823 lots (Hemingway 1992: 77). In 1855, Dalhousie noted that 'the land [which the squatters had occupied] has been readily disposed of either by sale or lease, and the price or rent has been promptly and easily paid' (Pearn 1939: 197). Hindu, Christian, Jewish, Muslim, and Chinese communities received a number of free land grants to build their places of worship.[18] All

---

[17] All in all, there were five classes of lots. First class lots along the river were the most prestigious and largest in size (up to over 2000 m^2). The other lots differed from the first category in regard to size, decreasing with each class. See Hemingway (1992: 50) for details.

[18] Government [of India] to Phayre, India Political Proceedings (IPP). 200/38, September 16, 1853. No. 124.

were exempt from taxation. In addition, some religious communities, such as Christians and Muslims, bought land for graveyards. While some of them still have the original land grants from those days even today, many only own copies made by the Yangon City Development Council (YCDC) and many others have no documentation at all. This poses a problem whenever community members pursue any sort of alteration to established property, be it restoration, renovation, modernization, extension, renting, or selling.

By 1872, nearly all land of any value in central Rangoon had been allocated, and so the policy of leasing was introduced to avoid the complete alienation of the public land within the town. Leases were granted for fifteen years at most, and generally, for only five years— this short-term lease policy turned out to be a severe handicap to the development of the city (Pearn 1939: 260).

In 1874, a municipal committee was established and led by the Chief Commissioner. The colonial officials appointed its members with two seats out of twenty five reserved for Muslims. The two Muslims ran unopposed, as did most of the other candidates, indicating that the interest among those local residents eligible to become members was not very high. The Committee was authorised to levy taxes on houses and land, amongst others. Its general aim was to govern the city, in an effort to decentralize certain aspects of colonial governance in British India.

By the 1880s, Burma had become the third great destination for Indian labour, and it would attract between 12 million and 15 million labourers from 1840 until 1940 (Amrith 2013: 104).[19] The British India Steam Navigation Company introduced sailings between Rangoon and Madras on a fortnightly basis: 'As the great rivers Kaveri, Krishna, and Godavari spilled into the Bay of Bengal, so the sons of their valleys crossed it, pouring in their thousands into Burma and Malaya' (Amrith 2013: 108–9).[20]

---

[19] Amrith calculates that 'from the beginning of organized Indian emigration in 1834 until 1940, well over 90 per cent of *all* Indian emigrants went to Ceylon, Burma, and Malaya. Put simply, the Bay of Bengal region accounts for nearly the sum total of India's emigration history in the age of empire' (2013: 104; italics in original).

[20] The 'sons' Amrith refers to were able-bodied men who came for several years to Burma to work in the rice mills and on the plantations. They

The Government encouraged immigration as the only means of ensuring the cultivation of the land and in 1881, almost 30,000 immigrants, mostly from Madras and Bengal, entered the country.[21] Already then, only 49 per cent of the city population had been born in Rangoon. Of all inhabitants, 44 per cent were Indian.[22] Employment in the rice-mills and saw-mills of Rangoon and in the port was readily available. A large part of the incoming population stayed in very bad conditions in so-called 'lodging-houses' with low ceilings where there was often no light and circulation of air. The British authorities considered these living conditions responsible for the outbreak of epidemics such as small-pox (see Osada 2011 for details). New laws did not provide for the new conditions developing in Rangoon, and overcrowding became a serious problem.

The city profited from the annexation of Upper Burma in 1885, as the export of rice, timber, petroleum, cotton, spices and textiles increased. Housing conditions, however, deteriorated further with the influx of settlers coming from Upper Burma, who were looking for job opportunities in the south (Charney 2009:6). Officials who wanted to improve the situation were faced with resistance as 'many owners of the most dilapidated dwellings in town collect enormous rents from

---

migrated across the Bay of Bengal from Telugu-speaking areas north of Madras (nowadays Andra Pradesh), from the Tamil region, from Orissa, and from Bengal. They also came overland from Chittagong (Amrith 2013: 119). In general, migration followed seasonal patterns as it was closely related to agricultural labour. These migrants were categorized as 'domestic' migrants since Burma was part of British India since 1886. Many migrants intermarried and have remained in the country ever since. Their offsprings are referred to as 'half-caste' (kabia).

[21] Report on the Administration of British Burma during 1881–2 (Rangoon: Government Press, 1882), India Office Library and Records (IOR) V/10/497, 20; cited in Hemingway 1992: 269.

[22] The census of 1901 shows that 'Indianization' increased in the coming years: of the total population of 293,000 in Rangoon, 165,000 were Indians (56 per cent), compared to 90,000 Burmese (31 per cent). In 1913, there were around 290,000 immigrants arriving from Indian ports, in 1927 around 361,000. Chakravarti notes that '[b]etween 1852 and 1900, Rangoon thus developed from a small town into a city of about a quarter million people—and looked Indian in appearance' (Chakravarti 1971: 8).

these people'.[23] With the failure to enforce laws on registration of lodging-houses, wealthy Burmese and Europeans continued to treat overcrowding as a lucrative source of income.[24]

Many laws and regulations had been adapted from British India. In 1897, a Legislative Council was established for the Province of Burma, and it could exercise legislative power. The same year, a notification under the Land and Revenue Act of 1876 declared that '[f]or two years after arrival to settle, [i]mmigrants of the agricultural and labouring classes from countries outside of Burma' were exempt from capitation tax[25] in order to ease their arrival. One consequence of the rapid population growth was the rise of masonry buildings, with wooden houses giving way. Nevertheless, the short-term leases granted to urban residents prevented any substantial investment in housing (Charney 2009: 19). With land alienation progressing in the countryside, a reclamation scheme regulated that in Rangoon, reclaimed sites of land should be given to the poor. But once the sites had been secured on these favourable terms, they were quickly sold to land speculators, with the result that an area intended for the housing of the poor became 'more and more occupied with buildings utilized for commercial purposes or for letting to tenants'.[26] Some of the reclaimed land was also occupied before it had been equipped with sanitation and other large areas were coming into the hands of builders so that squatters had to move:

> The overcrowding in the town proper was such that by 1911 in one quarter of central Rangoon the density of population amounted to 636 persons per acre (omitting non-residential [sic] buildings and open

[23] Annual Report on the Working of the Rangoon Municipality (1939: 182–3, cited in Pearn 1939: 258).

[24] There are no numbers on how many of the wealthy property owners were Muslim Indian merchants.

[25] See Revenue Department Notification No. 163, in: *The Lower Burma Land Revenue Manual* (1945: 89–90).

[26] See the Annual Report on the Working of the Rangoon Development Trust 1921–2, cited in Pearn (1939: 275). The Rangoon Development Trust (RDT) was formed in 1920 in order to acquire land for development, reclaim water-logged land, build new roads to the suburbs, and provide housing to Rangoon's poorer occupants, but in fact it aided wealthy 'foreigners' (Europeans, Chinese and Indian merchants) (see Pearn 1939: 281; Charney 2009: 21).

spaces) – a density greater than that of the most thickly populated wards of Calcutta and approaching the enormous figures of Bombay. (Pearn 1939: 276)

As time progressed, the migrants, particularly those from India who had been brought to Burma as labour force, refused to subordinate their interests to the colonial measures regulating public health, policing and property. Increasingly fearing violent responses from squatters if evicted from their settlements, the colonial government in Rangoon had to work their rules and regulations around the fact that they simply could not administer the amount of people they had invited to live in the city.

In contrast to this seemingly uncontrolled and uncontrollable population dynamic, the history of the Yangon Memon Jamaat (YMJ), the religious community organization to which Auntie Karima and Uncle Said belong, provides an alternative vision of how Indian Muslims organized themselves and even helped others.[27] The organization was founded in 1909 and took up residence downtown, not far away from the place where Auntie Karima and Uncle Said live today. After its establishment, the first thing the Jamaat did was to provide *kafan* and *dafan* (after-death rituals including washing, wrapping, and burying) for poor Muslims who did not have family in Burma. These services were and still are provided for all Muslims, not only Memons. Another tradition, one that continues until today, is the support of poor children from both 'pure' Memon families and those who have intermarried with non-Memons. The Jamaat opened a *madrasa* (Islamic boarding school) in a neighbouring building and offered Islamic studies and Urdu language lessons to all Muslim children up to the fourth grade. Both buildings were purchased by the organization through donations from its members.

From Inter-religious Riots to Independence

The First World War had a significant impact on sea-borne trade and influenced the reorganization of the Trading Companies. With

[27] The following account is based on a letter written by one of the established community members for a fellow-Memon residing in Karachi (Pakistan) who inquired about the history of the YMJ for a journal article. The document is from 2003 and I received it directly from Uncle Said.

the economic depression setting in, after the war came what Pearn called 'racial antagonism', directed against the Indian labourers who made up almost ninety per cent of the unskilled and semi-skilled labourers of Rangoon. They competed over labour with the Burmese:

> ...on the 26th May [1930] fighting began between Burman and Indian coolies, and grew into a serious communal riot which did not cease until the troops were called out four days later. Many deaths occurred during the rioting; ... Scandalous to relate, although at least 120 deaths occurred, not a man was convicted, not a man was even brought to trial, for his part in this affair: such was the complete breakdown of the system of law and order. (Pearn 1939: 291)

Eight years later, more rioting occurred between Burmese Buddhists and Burmese Muslims who had been living in the country long before the Indian Muslims arrived. In 1929 (or 1931 according to other sources), a Burmese Muslim, Shwe Hpi, had written and published a document that contained highly disparaging references to the Buddha, although it was only noted by the local press in 1938.[28] In a mass meeting at the Shwedagon Pagoda, it was declared that should the government fail to act appropriately, 'steps will be taken to treat the Muslims as Enemy Number 1 who insult the Buddhist community and their religion, and to bring about the extermination of the Muslims and the extinction of their religion and language' (Final Report 1939: x). After having clashed with the police, the Young Monks Association (YMA) attacked Muslims and looted Muslim shops. Over hundred mosques were set on fire (Final Report of the Riot Inquiry Committee 1939: 286). There were also violent attacks against Indian Muslims:

> Soon the whole country was ablaze with encounters between Burmese and Indians augmented by mass attacks on unarmed isolated Indians. Although a few Hindus tried to save their lives on the basis of religion,

---

[28] Maung Shwe Hpi was a teacher in Myedu village in Shwebo district, whose population was mainly Muslim. Their ancestors, in turn, were deported from Thandwe (Rakhine) by the Burmese King in the middle of the 16th century. They were most likely not ethnic Burmans (personal communication with German Myanmar scholar Uta Gaertner, 27 June 2014).

it is doubtful whether any appreciable number of them were spared by the frenzied mob of Burmese. (Mahajani 1960: 79)[29]

Mahajani notes that '[t]he Indian National Congress registered its feeling of grave concern over "the danger to Indian life and property in Burma"' (1960: 80). A member of the Indian Legislative Assembly, to whom the riots had been reported, noted that they needed to be seen as 'a design to turn out all Indians from Burma' (1939: 203–7, cited in Mahajani 1960: 81).

On 23 December 1941, the Japanese launched their first air attack against Rangoon:

> There was a general breakdown of law and order and the Indians, already wary after the riots of the past decade, began to panic. The perception was that the British were about to withdraw from Burma, and that in their absence, Burmese mobs would have free reign to terrorize the Indian population. Suddenly, the Indians began to move northwards. But without the Indians the city simply could not function: they made up almost the entire working class of Rangoon. The dockworkers were the first to abandon their jobs. This meant that essential supplies could not be unloaded from the ships in the Rangoon docks. Many of these vessels became sitting targets for Japanese bombers (Ghosh 2011).

While half of the Indian population began what Tinker has called 'A Forgotten Long March' from Burma to India via the hill tracts, the other half of the Indian population decided to stay in Rangoon (Tinker 1979). Auntie Karima recalls the situation at the beginning of the Second World War:

> *When the Second World War started, the Steel Company and the Bombay Burma Company were closed. There were bombings. My grandfather passed away due to his age around this time, but business continued in the family. My family started a rice mill in Taikkyi—about 40 miles from Rangoon. I was born in Taikkyi in 1948. My father was active in politics during the war and got arrested. When he came free, he decided to move all of us to Rangoon where he had received his school education. The rice mill exists until today, but it is closed now and people are trespassing there although it is still in*

---

[29] Hundreds were wounded and killed. Yegar (1972, 37) speculates that the official numbers as given in the Final Report of the Riot Inquiry Committee (1939) might not contain all the casualties sustained.

> *my family's property. Between 1945 and 1957 my family had businesses in*
> *Rangoon, in different smaller houses.*

Rangoon was severely destroyed during the Second World War: half of the public and commercial buildings and one-third of homes were ruined. About 80 per cent of the city had to be rebuilt (Charney 2009: 58). The Yangon Memon Jamaat continued performing *kafan* and *dafan* to those Muslims who had died during the War. They also continued their charity work with opening a free medical dispensary within their premises, staffed 'with doctors who saw people of every caste or creed'. Medicine was given free of charge.

The country became nominally independent under the Japanese Occupation in 1943. When the British re-occupied the country in 1945, they devalued the newly introduced Japanese currency (the 'Japanese rupee'). As a result, riots broke out and poor rural civilians sought shelter in the city, which had been deserted over the course of the war. Like in former times, 'Rangoon was a veritable metropolis of matting and thatch' (Appleton 1947: 514; cited in Charney 2009: 59).

The country received full independence on 4 January 1948 and Muslims from India, who were living in Burma, could apply for citizenship along with other minorities. The alternative was to receive a foreign registration certificate (FRC), or become stateless. Auntie Karima recalls:

> *Most Indians who had come to Myanmar were low-class workers. What did*
> *they know about citizenship? They did not even register after the government*
> *announced in the newspaper that whoever registered within a certain time,*
> *would receive citizenship. After 1955/1958 [she did not remember exactly],*
> *nobody could become a citizen of Burma and received an FRC instead. My*
> *family and the family of my husband were educated and registered—others*
> *did not even know how to read and did not register.*

Muslim Property under 'Burmese Socialism'

Over a decade after the war, in 1957, Auntie Karima's father, together with two partners, bought a piece of land in downtown Rangoon, close to the river when the city was rebuilt after 1852. The house, which had been erected on this land, had been destroyed in the war and after having torn it down, they built a new house on the same plot:

My father, together with two partners, bought the land. Each had their own businesses, a nylon factory and a weaving factory. After independence, the business went up and it was impressive. In 1959, the new building was finished and we moved in: on the ground floor there were offices for rent to other businesses, on the first floor there were our own offices, on the second floor there were four apartments (two for my father, two for one of the two partners), on the third floor there were also four apartments, all of them taken by the third partner since he had a big family. We owned the house only until 1962. Everyone was very happy.

These years were prosperous ones also for the Yangon Memon Jamaat, who opened a Young Men Memon Association (YMMA), located in the *madrasa*. The club brought old and young men together over sports such as table tennis, billiard and *carrum* [carrom] (a table game common in South Asia). A library was opened with books in Gujarati, English, and Urdu. Debates and religious sermons were held in the building, and the cricket and scout teams of the association competed with other clubs in the city. The *madrasa* relocated to a new and larger building and the curriculum was expanded. In the evenings, book-keeping, typewriting and other vocations were taught to adults who had to work during the daytime. Individual members of the Kalai Memon community, who owned factories, built four mosques in Yangon so that their factory workers had a place to pray.

The overall political situation, however, deteriorated when Buddhism became the state religion in 1961. This led to anti-Muslim riots in Rangoon in late 1961 (Smith 1965: 322). When General Ne Win came to power in 1962, he suspended the Constitution (thereby ending Buddhism's status as the state religion[30]), dismantled Buddhist institutions, and proclaimed that Burma was to be turned into a socialist state. The only party would be the 'Burmese Way to Socialism Party'—all other political parties were declared illegal. Private businesses, regardless of size, including general stores, department stores, brokerages, wholesale shops, and warehouses

---

[30] After the adoption of the 1947 Constitution on independence, which recognized 'the special position of Buddhism as the faith professed by the great majority of the citizens of the Union'. The second paragraph declared '[t]he state also recognizes Islam, Christianity, Hinduism and Animism as some of the religions existing in the Union at the date of the coming into operation of this Constitution.'

were nationalized, beginning with foreign businesses (Chinese, Indian, Eurasian[31]) (Charney 2009: 81–2). This ended the dominance of foreign commercial interests in Burma's economy at the time (Ooi 2004: 58). Thus, while the well-being of Muslims came under threat in 1961 during the riots, their property rights were infringed upon during socialism where they became targets not because they were Muslims, but because they were 'foreigners' owning businesses and property. Ten years after the event, Yegar writes in regard to the Muslim population in Burma that '[v]ery little is known as to how deeply the Muslims in Burma were affected by the military rule of General Ne Win who seized power in a military coup in March, 1962, and to what extent their organisational life and religious and cultural activities were affected' (Yegar 1972: x). This is, to some extent, still valid today as field research, especially conducted by foreigners, has been extremely difficult to pursue over the last decades. Before I was introduced to Auntie Karima by a local friend of mine, I asked whether her family was rich, knowing that they owned a house in downtown Yangon. My friend answered 'not as rich as she is supposed to be'. When I later asked Auntie Karima about the 1960s, I understood his comment. She said:

> Everything was nationalised. The army came at noon and took over the key and closed the offices. We had to leave immediately. We could only keep the apartments to live in.

A similar fate awaited the *madrasa* run by their community organization: the school was nationalized and taken over by the government, like all other schools, in 1965. At least one of the four mosques of the Kalai Memon community was closed, or as Auntie Karima put it, 'martyred' (Ar., *shahid*), in the Ne Win era. Auntie Karima recalls how her father managed to secure an income after he was deprived of his business:

> My father found work as an accountant in a governmental position since he and one more person were the only ones that could properly do the job. The other accountant was Mr Chaudry, a Bengali. From 1964–66, every 15 days a steamer named 'Monguadi' came and took every Indian who had an FRC (Foreign Registration Certificate] and a birth certificate with them— the Hindus were the first to emigrate. The capacity of people per ship was

---

[31] Meaning Anglo-Burman in this context.

2,500. There were two steamers, one going one direction, the other the other direction. These two steamers came for two years on this 15-day schedule: India took back all its citizens [mostly to Orissa and Madras]. Others pretended to be Indian and went also. Most of them were Oriyas. The steamer came until 1972 regularly, but not every 15 days. After that, migration became less.

Uncle Said recalls the impact this change in policy had on his immediate family:

had seven brothers—all of them left. The first two in 1966 to India, the second two left in 1971 to Bangladesh, and the last three went between 1980 and 1983 to Pakistan.[32] My family had a 300-acre rubber plantation which was nationalized in 1966.

The 1980s are remembered as particularly hard times for the Memon community in Yangon. In 1971, the Jamaat provided service to the refugees from the Bangladesh Liberation War, who had fled to Burma via Arakan. These were Pathans, Punjabis, Mahjirs, Sindhis and Memons. Although the funds of the Jamaat were meagre during these years, the organization hosted refugees in four apartments that were allotted for them. In a letter addressed to fellow Memons in Karachi, the writer describes that they were properly clothed and fed until their papers were cleared to proceed to Pakistan:

We are very proud to say that only the Memon community could stand high in doing this Yeoman Service [loyal help] in the name of Islam and humanity.[33]

The Memon's *madrasa* was appropriated by the state and turned into a state school. Moreover, their application to renew the licence of their men's association was denied, and so it was closed in 1974. That same year, the 1974 Constitution was introduced, and Article 161 noted that:

Every citizen's income, savings, property and residential buildings lawfully earned and acquired by his diligence and manual and mental contribution, instruments of production permitted to be owned within the framework of the socialist economic system, and other lawful possessions shall be protected by law.

[32] The family had connections to other South Asian countries through his brothers' wives.

[33] 'Yeoman' is a late medieval English term for landholder.

However, all other articles of the 1947 Constitution that had guaranteed the right to private property (arts. 17(I), 23) had been removed. It was during these years that Auntie Karima and Uncle Said were married in an arranged marriage after which they moved into the house they still occupy today. Uncle Said recalled:

> *Karima and I got married in 1971 and moved into the upper floor [the third floor] of this house. The floor beneath us was occupied by the Andaman islanders.*

Finding a Home in Auntie Karima's House

In 1857, when the British government established a detention colony on the Andaman Islands, located at the juncture of the Bay of Bengal and the Andaman Sea (see Anderson 2010 for details), Burma began sending life-term prisoners there. After independence from Britain in 1947, the Andaman Islands remained under Indian administration. It took almost twenty years until the Burmese government decided to accept the offsprings of those they had sent to the Islands. When in 1966 several hundred native Burmese people, all of them born on the Islands, were repatriated to Burma, many of them were placed in vacant flats or other confiscated property that had been nationalized, but never been put to use. One of those houses was the house of Auntie Karima's father. She explained:

> *When the Andaman people arrived in Burma, they spoke only Urdu, they used to play only Indian songs in the beginning—there are two or three older ladies living in this house who still speak Urdu but the rest of them are all 'Burmanized.' Some went back because they could not stand the city life in Rangoon—although in those times, between 1966 and 1988, you would not see a car within five minutes—there were only buses in downtown Rangoon. Our neighbour [Ma Mala] was a child when she came from the Andaman Islands to Rangoon, still, she is inclined to go back. She says 'my parents made me come here.'*

When I met Ma Mala in the following week in Auntie Karima's house, she told me about her grandfather who had been sent to the Andaman Islands in 1900. She repeatedly mentioned how much she would like to return to her family's spacious house on the island, where curries tasted good and the air was fresh. This is unlike Yangon, where she showed me the tiny, dark flat she calls home. Leaving Auntie Karima's place, we passed through the common hallway where many inhabitants from the second floor had gathered around a TV set, watching the South East Asia Games.

When I returned to Auntie Karima's flat, I shared my thoughts with her about the living conditions I had seen: the narrow, dark ceilings, the lack of light and air, and the obvious poverty. She remarked 'and she is more of a citizen than us'. She then told me how in 2004, she and her husband moved from the flat on the third to the second floor. Auntie Karima was able to do this only by buying her own property back from the people who had been put into her family's house in 1966. With her money, several Burmese families from the Andaman Islands moved out, but many more are still there.

Not only the house itself, but also the pavement out front has been carved into tiny compartments with vendors, some from the Andaman Islanders community, claiming usage rights to a particular space on the pavement. Auntie Karima expressed sympathy towards them as they lack a regular income and cannot afford to rent a place. She buys food from them, allows them to live for free, and invites some of them regularly to her place. This complex arrangement can neither be analysed by drawing recourse to the labels 'legal' and 'illegal', nor would it be sufficiently covered by delineating property into 'private', 'state' or 'communal'. Neither tenants nor squatters, these people share their lives with Auntie Karima door-to-door in a form of neighbourliness that is based on fateful circumstances and Auntie Karima's conviction that the poor deserve to be helped.

Renovation, Rent Control, and Religion

Having relocated from the third to the second floor, Auntie Karima joined forces with a fellow businessperson from the neighbouring Chinese community and turned the now-empty third floor into a guesthouse. As there are only very few people who still possess the original land grants or documents that indicate them as legitimate owners, I asked Auntie Karima how she had proved to the authorities that the third floor was actually her property, a prerequisite when trying to obtain a permit for renovation and opening a business such as a guesthouse. She explained that in cases like hers, people present tax receipts showing that they have been paying fees to the Yangon City Development Council every month. Initially, they thought that only Chinese tourists would take advantage of the central location of the guesthouse, but increasingly, western tourists, mostly backpackers, show up on her doorstep, too. In the last two years since the country has opened up, a massive influx of foreigners—investors, NGOs, and tourists alike—have entered Yangon. The notorious lack of living space in the city, which by now has between four and five million inhabitants, has created a problem for those who need a place to sleep, be it for a night, a week or a year.[34]

Besides her guesthouse, Auntie Karima owns an import-export business, currently exporting broomsticks from the Delta to Saudi Arabia and tea leaves to India. In terms of bureaucracy, in her opinion, it has become easier because the paperwork has been reduced over the last few years:

> In former times it took so long to file the necessary documents that by the time you had obtained everything, the ship had already left. Now it's easier, but it's a lot of work, still. Eventually I will hand over the tea leaves business to another friend.

She also runs a travel agency located in one of the houses of the Jamaat, to which she pays a small monthly rent. At present, the YMJ owns eight buildings in downtown Yangon. Mostly Buddhist Burmese people live in them and they pay no rent to the Jamaat. Uncle Said explained:

> We do not have proper rent control here and most of the tenants are Myanmar Buddhists. We cannot go against them. And we do not have the time. We have to go to the court and go after them ... and as it is, we get enough money from our donations.

The YMJ continues working through charity, which currently includes, for example, stipends to 'old-aged Memons and mixed Memons, even

[34] In 2013, property prices in downtown Yangon exceeded those of New York City. Prior to the lifting of heavy international sanctions, some Burmese military generals invested in property. Many hotels and large businesses are in the hands of (former) military personnel. For example, UNICEF reportedly pays $87,000 per month for a villa owned by a former military general in an exclusive neighbourhood in Yangon. See Kyaw Hsu Mon (2014).

to widows of Memons or mixed Memons, for their upkeep.' The elderly also receive food aid in the form of rice and cooking oil every two months. Stipends are also given to poor children of Memon and 'mixed Memon' background from kindergarten up to postgraduate courses. Medical aid is given for free to the needy and 'houses are purchased or leased for Memons who for unforeseen disaster are immediately in need of it'. Moreover, those who have failed in starting a business may receive start-up grants from the community. Finally, Islamic studies are being taught in one of their *madrasas* for about 250 non-Memon students in both Burmese and Urdu languages. English language lessons and Arabic are also offered. The community life also includes cultural activities such as celebrating *Eid-ul-Fitr* together or holding an 'Urdu symposium' during the winter months where prizes are given to talented poets. They cover these expenses through the philanthropic work of community members. Despite these wide-ranging activities, Uncle Said emphasized that they take care to keep a low profile: *Muslim organizations have to stay low-key. We should not come in the eyes of the government, otherwise they will say 'from today, it is closed until further notice.' And what will we do? What should we do? This is a phase, you know ...*

In 2006, the YMJ premise in downtown Yangon encountered difficulties exercising its property rights, when the community tried to register its building as damaged with the city authorities, in order to be allowed to renovate it. Although they do possess the necessary documents, the authorities did not grant the re-classification of the property. This is a common procedure and does not concern Muslim communities only. The house hosts offices and meeting rooms and the third floor is used as a dormitory for male Muslims (which they refer to in Burmese as *musafir khana*) from all over Myanmar who can stay there for a minimal charge. Sometimes, the floor is rented out to poorer Muslims from their community or other Muslim communities for marriages or other functions, also at a low price. The entire building is in need of renovation.

***

Since British colonial times, property regimes in Yangon have been both complex and fragile, mirroring the country's political processes of transformation that produced them. By exploring the 'work of property' (Verdery and Humphrey 2004) from British colonial times until today, this chapter focused on individual actors like Auntie Karima and Uncle Said, who have to 'make do' with changing property regimes, amidst insecurity and injustice. In their edited volume, anthropologists Verdery and Humphrey link the concept of property to a variety of themes ranging from different forms of economy to gender, work and personhood. The work of property in a particular context, they argue, has been interpreted in the literature in light of getting access to scarce resources, the rise of liberal democracy or as a form of appropriation (2004: 3–4). Since colonial times, Burma/Myanmar has witnessed a continuous transformation of property initiated by 'the state'. While a significant amount of academic writing on property regimes has criticized the focus on the role of the state in guaranteeing or distributing property rights, in the case of Myanmar such a state-centric view is helpful: many changes in government, especially throughout the twentieth century, have always affected or were directly aimed at property regimes. These changes ranged from the initial free land grants to religious communities, to forcing owners to give up their business property, to opportunities to invest in the booming property market after the country 'opened up' in 2011. The possibility of bypassing the state or even openly protesting against its policies or laws has been and continues to be minimal. I therefore suggest understanding the concept of property in the context of Myanmar as a relation between changing forms of state apparatuses and a body politic, consisting of citizens as well as non-citizens.

When my visit to Auntie Karima's house ended one evening, she told me that the YCDC intended to demolish the portico in front of the house to make room for parking lots. As part of recent reforms, the government has embarked on road widening initiatives that displace sidewalks (and the porticos above them). Auntie Karima showed me the letter from the YCDC announcing that the portico would be removed. As we went outside onto the portico where her family cooks in the dry season, dries the laundry and tends the plants, Auntie Karima explains: 'For us, we will manage, but they (pointing towards her neighbours whose part of the portico is separated by a brick wall) will suffer. They live there with fifteen people in one small room. What they will do without the outside space, I do not know.'

I peek across the balcony to the very left and see the four lanes of Strand Road and behind them, the Yangon River where container ships depart for the Andaman Sea, dwarfing the ferries and small wooden boats criss-crossing to Dala, a small town on the other side. We talk about the many new parking spaces that have been built recently to accommodate the influx of imported cars. 'But they want more,' Auntie Karima says. As I utter a quiet curse, she hastens to add:

> Don't feel sorry. We are used to it. The government has taken much much more than this from us. In 1964, they took our factory, our shops, everything. We had nothing to eat. We survived only hardly, but we survived. So this is nothing new ... gradually, it will change. There is pressure now from so many countries, but actually, they do not care about the world. The previous head of government [General Than Shwe] said 'the world can go to hell, we have enough rice, we can survive.'

Her comparison of the military government's behaviour to the new government was illuminating, contextualizing the wide range of new laws regulating land and property, seemingly in line with its policy of 'opening up' the country to foreign investment, tourism and general democratic change. The new state laws, however, only cover a small percentage of *de facto* existing property relations on the ground.[35] Auntie Karima's house is a case in point. From the sidewalk up to the unoccupied fourth floor, several different types of ownership can be diagnosed, all of which have in common that the right of possession cannot simply be proven by a standardized bureaucratic act. The 'bundle of rights' in place instead, ranges from customary regulations such as the distribution of space on the sidewalk for tea stalls or how the common hallway is being used, to state laws regarding socialist-era expropriation and state resettlement policies that led to a loss in both property and ownership rights to control or dispose of her family property. But the 'bundle of rights' is also shaped by the personal decision-making processes of Auntie Karima in the way she tried to 'make do' with fateful circumstances and how she related to the

---

[35] The new Draft Condominium Law, for example, is directed at buildings that are erected on freehold land or land that was granted to the residents. The majority of all buildings in Yangon, however, are built on leased land 'meaning owners of condo apartments do not own the land it sits on' (Consult Myanmar 2014).

'Andaman occupants'. She also reacted quickly when state legislation allowed for the developing of tourist infrastructure in response to the end of international sanctions, and the influx of tourists. If we return to the concept of property as a 'bundle of rights', she has increased the bundle by now, also owning a jointly run guesthouse. Diversification of ownership might be a strategic move, concerning the fact that the contemporary state is often unpredictable as its predecessors have been, when it comes to property. Although the 2008 Constitution now guarantees private property again (art 37(c)) and the right to ownership as well as the use of property (art 372), complaints about land grabs are common, also in neighbouring Dala across the river.[36] In Yangon, around ten per cent of the inhabitants live in slums (Gómez-Ibanez et. al. 2012: 9), and many of them have been evicted in the course of 'modernizing' the city in the last two decades (see Skidmore 2004). The demolishing of the portico will not only violate Auntie Karima's ownership rights, but also the 'Andaman Islanders' usage rights of their part of the portico, as well as the customary regulations of the tea stall owners who will lose both their established locations and their regular customers once the sidewalk is gone.

Uncle Said joined us on the portico to say goodbye to me as the *muezzin*[37] had started calling all Muslim men to evening prayer. He heard what Auntie Karima told me about the city government's plan to demolish the portico and added: *We live here, because most Memons are here, our mosque is here. We cannot move because the government does not allow the building of new mosques. We want to be near our culture.*

To be 'near our culture' has become especially relevant in the last two years in which the country has witnessed an increase in ethno-nationalist rhetoric in which Buddhist supremacy is often coupled with downgrading Muslims as the 'dangerous Other'. The general atmosphere in Yangon during the stay of my fieldwork was tense in the sense that the downtown areas, but also other quarters such as Sanchaung, had become religiously segregated, with

---

[36] Article 37, (a) regulates that 'The Union is the ultimate owner of all lands and all natural resources above and below the ground, above and beneath the water and in the atmosphere in the Union,' indicating that customary land regulations are not taken into account.

[37] The *muezzin* is the person at the mosque who leads the call to prayer.

ethno-nationalist '969' plaques and stickers posted on restaurants, taxis, and above street signs, indicating which places were 'Buddhist' (see Nyi Nyi Kyaw, this volume). Not only Muslims, but also Christians and Buddhists expressed their insecurity and confusion in light of these developments.

From an anthropological perspective, it is not useful to find out how Auntie Karima and Uncle Said or other members of the Yangon Muslim communities 'feel' about the waves of anti-Muslim violence that have hit the country in Rakhine and other places since 2012. When asked directly, my Muslim informants stressed 'Yangon is different' than the other parts of the country. They are, however, very much aware of the situation in Rakhine State, as Uncle Said's historical account of the flight of the Kalai Memon indicated. There, he directly linked the persecution of his own community to the situation in contemporary Rakhine State, arguing that people will leave their property behind, once their life is in danger.

The Kalai Memon Jamaat in Yangon is a tightly knit community, which has set up internal modes of taking care of its members and other Muslims by providing social security, education, and even alternative forms of dispute resolution such as a get-together for all male members of the community where they discuss problems. These measures are efforts to remain independent and to stay out of the state's reach. While Muslims like Auntie Karima and Uncle Said have found ways to continue as a community, the reality that they cannot build new mosques, combined with their desire to stay downtown, will be a source of future tension due to the growing price of land and the increasing regulation of property by the state.

6 Muslim Women's Education in Myanmar

PHYU PHYU OO

In Myanmar today, many Muslim women are uneducated or unable to finish their education due to a variety of challenges. Too often, social, cultural and religious customs and practices limit the paths a Muslim woman may take, as does the lack of economic opportunities. Being an Indian Muslim woman, I have experienced some of the religious and social constraints that prevent Muslim women from making their own decisions and pursuing higher education. I have observed my peers encounter many of the same challenges. The purpose of this chapter is to consider the value and opportunities for women to obtain education—both Islamic and modern— in Myanmar. It also sets out to explore the perceptions of Muslims in Myanmar about the value and role of Islamic education, in comparison with education offered by government schools. I describe the social pressures and religious constraints placed on women (particularly Indian Muslims) in Islamic communities in Myanmar and argue that these combine to hinder education and employment opportunities for Muslim women. Finally, I conclude by identifying areas for future research and policy reform that would help Muslim women to begin to overcome these barriers and exercise their independence in decision-making about their own education and careers.

The research for this chapter is primarily based on empirical data gathered from interviews with 42 Muslim women and three religious leaders within conservative[1] and liberal[2] Muslim communities. These interviews were conducted between October and December 2013, primarily in Yangon, which remains the largest city in Myanmar (although Naypyidaw is now officially the capital city). Interviews were conducted in Burmese language with Muslim women aged between 18 to 60 years old, from a variety of socio-economic backgrounds. The interviews focused on their educational and professional experience, their motivations to pursue education, the level of support from their parents, and their experiences of primary education and secondary education (where relevant). The interviews also explored the attitudes and perceptions of their families and Muslim neighbours about education for women. Interview participants who had children were also asked about their attitudes towards their own children and whether they allow, or will allow, their daughters to make their own choices regarding their education and future. I compliment this empirical research with reflections on my own experience as a Muslim woman growing up in the Indian Muslim community in Yangon.

[1] I use the word 'conservative' in this chapter to refer to people in Muslim communities who adhere to tradition and strict Islamic practices in Myanmar. For example, religious leaders in these communities may teach that Muslims need to study only the *Qur'an* and not attend government schools to receive a broader education. Often their beliefs concern how women should act or dress, such as that women should wear the *burqa* (a cloth tailored to cover the entire body in order not to be seen by men). Religious leaders have a significant influence over their followers to persuade them follow the same set of traditions and religious beliefs.

[2] I use the word 'liberal' to refer to Muslims who are more tolerant, open, and flexible with regard to their religious practices and traditions. Leaders of such communities may teach the members of their community that it is best to receive both Islamic education and government-run education, and most of the time they encourage their followers to study at the graduate level. They also allow their members to live in a way that is consistent with Burmese culture, such as wearing Burmese traditional clothes, which for women usually includes a long, fitted skirt known as a *longyi* and a blouse with short sleeves.

This chapter therefore provides new empirical research on Muslim women, which has been an understudied area in Myanmar.[3] From these interviews, I will demonstrate in this chapter that there are several different reasons why Muslim women are often prevented from seeking higher education, and why Muslim women themselves may not see the value in education. I begin with a brief overview of Islam in Myanmar, noting the differences between the Indian Muslim and Burmese Muslim communities in particular. I then consider two main types of education for women: Islamic education and education in government-run schools. I identify the specific constraints on accessing higher education, and the possible ways these may be overcome. I argue that parents and religious leaders have the potential to play a key role in the process of encouraging and opening up opportunities for Muslim women to obtain education.

Myanmar and Islam in Historical Perspective

Located in Southeast Asia, Myanmar (formerly known as Burma) is one of the least developed countries in the world. Previously ruled by a military regime, in 2011 it came under the control of a quasi-civilian government led by the current President, Thein Sein. The estimated population from the 2014 census is 50 million. According to the 1983 government census (which is not considered to be a reliable source), Muslims were estimated to represent four per cent of the population, although other sources estimate a higher figure. Most of the people practise Buddhism, while small minorities follow the Muslim, Hindu and Christian faiths. The education and health systems are extremely underdeveloped, and the country is now in the process of reforming these major social services required for the country's development. Although the Burman people form the largest ethnic group, there are many ethnic minorities in different parts of the country, the major ones being Karen, Shan, Rakhine, Mon, and Chin. The dominance of Burmans politically over other ethnic groups has been

---

[3] The one exception to this is Lambert (2011), whose masters thesis provides a descriptive overview of the lives of Burmese Muslim women who have settled in the United States.

the cause of considerable tension between the government and ethnic minorities, which still continues. Recently, Muslim communities have faced anti-Muslim riots, which began in 2012 with protests and violence against the Muslim Rohingya people of Rakhine State (see Nyi Nyi Kyaw, this volume).

Yet Muslims have had a long presence in Myanmar. Myanmar has a history of Muslim traders passing through, and some settling in, the area. Muslims started arriving in Myanmar between the seventh and eighth century BCE, as Arabs and Persians came for trade. They settled in Myanmar and continued their work as traders. Others served the Burmese kings as military personnel, often holding positions in royal families as advisors, administrators, port authorities, mayors, and traditional medicine men (Yegar 1972). Muslims settled in certain parts of Myanmar such as the city of Taungoo (Bago Division), the Yamaething Township, and the city of Meiktila (Mandalay Division). They married within their communities, or to people from Burma. Depending on the couple who married and their families, in such a case of a mixed marriage either the bride or the groom would convert to Islam or Buddhism. Burmese Muslims came to be known as 'Zerbadis', a term that describes the children of a marriage between a Muslim man and a Burman woman (Selth 2010).

The Burmese kings gave equal opportunity to followers of Islam by allowing them to build mosques and perform religious duties. One key example is that King Mindon, during his rule (1854 to 1878), built the Peacock rest house in the Holy City of Mecca for the Muslims from Myanmar who went there to perform the *hajj* (pilgrimage to Mecca). He also arranged for the construction of a mosque for the Muslim community in Mandalay (Thant Myint U 2007: 136).

During British colonial rule, the population of Muslims in Burma increased due to the migration of large numbers of Indian Muslims looking for work (see generally Chakravarti 1971; Egreteau 2011). In the documentation and records of British colonial authorities, it was assumed that many Muslims at this time were Indian (see Keck, this volume), although there were also many other Muslim communities present. Further, as Crouch (chapter 1, this volume) has pointed out, the studies that have been conducted on Muslims in Burma often refer to the connection between Islam and South Asia.

Under British rule, economic pressures and nationalism contributed to the rise of anti-India and later, anti-Muslim sentiment. At that time, India was still under British control, and as part of British India, Burma was a key part of the business, trade and labour markets in the region (Turnell 2009). Most of the businesses in Yangon were dominated by Indians, in contrast to many Burman people at the time who struggled to make a living. It was difficult for Burmese people to find employment, since there was competition from Indian labour in every sector and Indians were usually cheaper to hire than Burmans. These pressures precipitated the anti-Indian riots of 1930 and the anti-Muslim riots of 1938 (Charney 2009). In the 1940s and 1950s, and again in the early 1960s, large numbers of Indians left Burma (Egreteau 2011: 40). Today, there are an estimated 2.5 to 3 million people of Indian background in Myanmar, although few still have ties to India itself (Egreteau 2011: 41).

In the lead-up to independence from the British, and for several years after independence, Burmese Muslims made particular efforts to differentiate themselves from foreign (non-Burman) Muslims. This division has been maintained and resulted in the formation of two main Muslim groups, one Burmese Muslim and the other Indian Muslim.[4] After migration to Burma, Indian Muslims maintained their culture including the use of Urdu language, clothing, and attendance at the mosque, and they therefore remained distinctive in society. Today, these two Muslim groups lead their respective communities in their own ways, and different cultures and perceptions characterize these two groups. The Indian community remains convinced that Indian culture is their culture, Indian language is their language, and Indian dress is their dress. Although Burmese Muslims maintain Burmese customs in part, as a way to show their unity with Burman nationals, Burman sentiment turned against those viewed as foreigners, including Muslims of all ethnic groups.

---

4 While I recognize the diversity within the Muslim community, as aptly described by Selth (2010), in this chapter I use the term 'Burmese Muslim' to refer to any Muslim other than Indian Muslim (although in reality those who identify as 'Burmese Muslim' may have ancestors from other ethnic groups of Burma).

Education Opportunities for Muslims

The tension between these two Muslim communities has had an impact on the education of Muslims since the country became a British colony. Under the British regime, the education system was ruled by wealthy Indians, and Burman nationals, including Burmese Muslims, resented the influence of Indians over the education system. At that time, the *madrasas* (Islamic boarding schools) were dominated by Indian Muslims who used the schools to maintain and promote Indian culture. In December 1929, at the Burmese Muslim Educational Conference for all Muslims, Burmese Muslims proposed that Burmese language should be taught as a second major subject after Arabic in all *madrasa* (Pathi U Ko Ko Lay, n.d). This proposal was rejected by the more powerful Indian Muslim representatives at the conference. They insisted that Muslim children must study Urdu as their second major language, because at the time it was the language spoken by the majority of the Indian Muslim population in Burma.

As a result, Burmese Muslims formed the Myanmar Muslim Educational Society (MMES) and one of their objectives was to encourage the teaching of Burmese language in Islamic schools, in addition to Arabic. Their activities were mostly ignored, however, since Indian Muslims were very wealthy and powerful enough to dominate the education system for Muslims (Pathi U Ko Ko Lay, n.d.). Through the leadership of these two Islamic groups in Myanmar, two Islamic societies with very different attitudes about educating the new generation emerged. As a result, depending on which community they belong to, Muslims in Myanmar may choose either to educate their children in an Islamic school or to educate them in both Islamic schools and state schools. The latter is possible because Islamic education classes are usually held early in the morning or late in the afternoon or evening. Many Indian Muslim families choose Islamic education only, while Burmese Muslims often encourage their children to attend both Islamic and government schools.

Islamic Education in Islamic Religious Schools

In Islamic religious schools, known as *madrasa*, students learn to recite the *Qur'an* as well as what is and is not prohibited by the teachings of Islam. Hundreds of *madrasa* operate throughout Myanmar

(Sulaiman 2008). A student, male or female, who completes the 30 chapters of the *Qur'an* is regarded as a *hafiz*. Once he or she can recite the *Qur'an* in Arabic, the student is given the title *mawlawi*. It is very common to find a *hafiz* or *mawlawi* in most Muslim families, and a person who has obtained this status is regarded with great honour and respect. Many Muslim families choose to support their children to become a *hafiz* or *mawlawi* because they believe that a person who has this training can save the family members from their sins and bring them to heaven.[5] Some students may also choose to continue their graduate Islamic study outside the country such as in India or Pakistan after they complete the tenth standard.

The language of instruction in many *madrasa* across Myanmar is Urdu, and students are usually also required to learn to read in Arabic, although there are other *madrasa* that use Burmese language. Burmese Muslims argue that speaking Burmese helps Muslims to explain the Islamic religion to the non-Urdu speaking majority. Indian Muslims, who still financially control many *madrasa*, reject that view. Study at a *madrasa* is usually limited to learning the *Qur'an* and religious practices, and does not include general education such as science or mathematics. In some Islamic schools, the curriculum and teaching methodology is very traditional, although such methodology is also very common across all the education sectors in Myanmar. Teaching is one way: students do not usually ask the teacher questions about the topic for the lesson. Students are required to memorize information and it is not a matter of understanding instructions and processes. In some schools, students are beaten if they do not memorize the teachings. Sometimes this causes stress for children who beg their parents not to send them to school, for example, if they have not finished their homework and fear they may be punished. Most parents, however, do not interfere with the school's teaching methods, which are viewed as necessary to become a good Muslim. In this way, a child who lives with fear will learn the *Qur'an* very quickly before his tenth year and practise Islamic teachings. The students also believe that what they are doing is necessary to becoming a good Muslim. Children taught in this kind of conservative religious schools often develop a

---

[5] This statement is based on interviews with Muslim families and personal experiences among Muslim communities.

conservative view of Islam, and bring their family members to the same faith. The career opportunities for a student who graduates from an Islamic religious school are limited, and the only option is to become a teacher at a *madrasa* or a leader of daily prayers at a mosque.

In recent decades, one reason for the conservative nature of some mosques is the *Tablighi Jemaat* movement, which has had an influence in some Islamic religious schools in Myanmar. The focus of the *Tablighi Jemaat* movement is generally to foster and restore Islamic practices among Muslim communities. It encourages students to travel to different parts of the country in order to teach the main Islamic beliefs and practices to other Muslim communities. Many parents from conservative Muslim communities believe that this practice will help their children become 'good Muslims'. However, *Tablighi Jemaat* activities, rather than restoring Islamic beliefs, have often led to the development of conservative religious practices within the Muslim community in Myanmar, as I discuss in more detail later. The advocacy of certain practices, such as requiring women to cover their head with a headscarf and wear loose clothing that covers their entire body, has had a significant influence on some communities.

In addition, another reason for the conservative nature of Islamic education is that the Myanmar government does not influence or regulate education in *madrasa*. Although Muslims in Myanmar are permitted to attend education at government schools, some courses of study are limited to Buddhist students and this is a significant disincentive for Muslims who hope to pursue higher education. For example, Muslim students face extreme difficulties, and in some cases are not allowed, to train for military careers as doctors, nurses, or engineers, which are considered to be the most respected, secure, and well-paid forms of employment.

The Government Education System

Although the general education system of Myanmar was once highly respected by neighbouring countries, today it is recorded as one of the weakest in the world. Basic education is divided into three stages: primary education is five years; secondary education is four years; and upper secondary education is two years. This means that students usually complete their schooling when they are just 16 or 17 years old.

Primary education is compulsory for all citizens and the enrolment rate for children of primary school age has been estimated at 90.2 per cent (UNICEF 2011: 44). The actual attendance rate may be much lower, however, especially in rural areas.

The main reasons that students do not complete primary education are affordability and access. The rates of enrolment after grade five is significantly lower (UNICEF 2011). It is estimated that only 58.3 per cent of children attend secondary school. The remaining children are either out of school working or attending primary school at an age older than the system intends. Nevertheless, both girls and boys generally have an equal opportunity to enrol in primary education in government schools.

After the completion of upper secondary school, students are allowed to apply to enter university. There are 164 universities and colleges throughout the country as officially documented by the Ministry of Education (Ministry of Education 2014a). Students can choose to study medicine, dentistry, pharmacy, paramedical services, engineering, foreign languages, economics, and other major subjects such as physics and zoology. Apart from tertiary studies, other technical and vocational training are available—in nursing, tourism, arts, music, and tailoring—led by government and private organizations.

Medicine and engineering are the most popular disciplines in Myanmar and require a high score on the university entrance exam. Parents customarily encourage students to try to be admitted to a medical or engineering university because these are viewed as providing the best education in the country and the most secure career opportunities. Unfortunately, women do not have equal opportunity to be admitted to medical universities because the score required for women to gain admission is significantly higher than for men. In December 2013, at the first 'Women's Forum Myanmar' organized by Women's Forum for Economy and Society, opposition leader Daw Aung San Suu Kyi made reference in a speech to this problem:

> She said Burmese women were well qualified, often comprising the majority of top students in schools. 'But there's discrimination against them,' she added. 'In certain faculties, girls are required to get more marks than boys in order to enter.' Women applicants are required to earn significantly higher marks than men if they seek to study six

> subjects at universities, including medicine and law, activists say. The
> policy was put in place because women currently outnumber men in
> these faculties. (Michaels 2013)

This policy was introduced because women usually outnumber men
in gaining admission to medical universities. My own experience
illustrates this. At the time I applied for admission to medical universities, the required score for women was 410 while the required
score for men was set lower at 375. Despite the fact that I scored 385,
which is higher than that required for men, I was rejected because I
did not meet the higher score for women. Hence, I applied instead for
pharmacy, which needs a lower score than medicine, so that I could
still be part of the medical profession. The reason usually given by
the government for the difference in scores for men and women is
that the country needs more male doctors in order to fulfil the gaps
of health professions at rural and hard to reach areas. It is also felt
that it is not suitable for women to travel or work alone in these
remote areas.

Another reason for the difficulties in access to university degrees
is that universities in Myanmar have often been closed for long periods of time. After the 1996 riots between students and the military
government, universities were closed for over two years and moved
to remote areas of the city (Selth 2010; see also Crouch 2014b: 544–7).
The curriculum for disciplines such as law and engineering was also
changed, and the entrance score for many university degrees was
significantly reduced. As a result, more students were admitted and
the prestige of being admitted to engineering and law declined. This
meant that there was a dramatic increase in the number of students
who enrolled and graduated with university degrees, but that these
degrees were increasingly seen as worthless in terms of job prospects.

Various challenges face the higher education system today: a basic
lack of funding, a lack of management capacity and international support, and mediocrity of teaching methods. The examination system is
badly managed: it is very easy to pass the exam because students are
questioned only on selected topics given to them in advance. In some
universities, teachers do not punish students if they open books and
copy the answers during the exam. This has downgraded the value
of a university degree and hence employment opportunities after
school have also suffered. Many male and female graduates end up

in low-paid jobs since university education does not prepare them to apply for employment opportunities that require a high level of skill and training. Such opportunities require a high level of education, such as a medical degree, or these positions are often given to students who have received their education and degree abroad, because it is acknowledged that these degrees provide a more rigorous education. Very few parents can afford to send their children abroad to complete their graduate studies. Some parents, who feel that university education in the country is worthless, do not allow their children to continue to study and encourage their children to start a business or work to contribute to the family income.

In this section I have identified the broader challenges and trends in university education in Myanmar. I now turn to the education of Muslim women in particular.

The Education of Muslim Women in Myanmar

The education opportunities for Muslim women may differ depending on whether they are part of the Burmese Muslim or Indian Muslim community. Some Burmese Muslims encourage their children to study the *Qur'an* at home or in Islamic school, while also allowing their children to obtain education at a government school. They believe that the *Qur'an* encourages all Muslims to be educated, and this includes both Islamic education and modern education such as science and mathematics. They also encourage their young women to attain a modern education and to continue with their education until graduation, rather than drop out early. However, the main purpose of women's education in Burmese culture is limited to developing their ability to read and write. It rarely prepares them to enter the workforce because it does not expect or encourage women to do so. This reality hinders young women, who are not motivated to expand their knowledge and develop a career path. Even if they choose to work, many hold low-level jobs and usually lack motivation to look for better opportunities because their understanding of the role of women in Myanmar, culturally, is centred on becoming married and providing for their husbands.

In contrast to the Burmese Muslim community, parents in Indian Muslim communities often choose a *madrasa* for their children's education, believing it will help their children to maintain their culture as Indians and their faith in Islam. In the past, *madrasa* accepted both male and female students, although girls were not allowed to continue studying past tenth grade. According to the teachings of some religious leaders, once a girl reaches puberty she is not permitted to be seen by men and must cover her whole body. More recently, some *madrasa* have specifically opened for girls, regardless of age, and it is staffed by female teachers so that they can acquire Islamic education and earn the title of *hafiz*.

The reality, however, is that conservative religious leaders and parents are concerned that modern education at a government school will diminish faith in Islam and their traditions. Hence studying at Burmese government schools is prohibited by many Indian Muslim religious leaders and by some conservative Indian Muslim communities in Myanmar. Their attitude towards women is very restrictive and they do not encourage women to study.

In addition, Muslim women themselves may also not see the value in education. One example is a female teacher I interviewed who volunteers at a tailoring school for the poor. She held the view that higher education may not be helpful for women. She said: My parents stopped educating me because the [Muslim] community did not allow it, and I still think they were right as education at university level wouldn't have been useful on the day I got married and became a housewife.[6]

The link she makes between university education and its irrelevance to the role of a married woman is clear. This teacher has two daughters whom she decided to educate up to tenth grade, although she herself only received education up until fifth grade. She went on to express her views that university education would not be useful for their future, but that it would be better for her daughters 'to study a vocation such as tailoring'. Another way to read her comments is as an indictment of the quality of the Myanmar government education system, which is extremely poor by international standards and has become one of the factors contributing to the under-education of Muslims in Myanmar.

---

[6] Interview with Daw Ni La Win, a voluntary teacher at a tailoring school for the poor, 1 December 2013, Yangon.

Still, some Indian Muslims, both men and women, attend government schools to attain modern education in addition to Islamic education. However, very few are admitted to college and generally end their education at the lower secondary level. This is for a range of reasons, including fear of the influence of Burmese culture on their own community, the students' own lack of motivation to continue, lack of parental encouragement, and little prospect for employment opportunities afterwards. Nowadays, larger numbers of Muslim women are participating in the workforce than in the past. However, many remain trapped in a traditional frame of mind, unaccustomed and lacking the confidence to voice their own ideas or to question authority figures.

Barriers to Women's Higher Education

There are particular social and religious constraints that hinder Muslim women's attainment of higher education in Myanmar. As in some other Islamic communities, the lives of Muslim women in Myanmar are often governed by the male head of the family, and their day-to-day life and choices may be strongly influenced by their father or male guardians. There are several factors which influence and hinder the educational opportunities of women in Myanmar in particular. In the following section, I identify and discuss the major barriers to higher education for Muslim women in Myanmar.

Parental Influences and the Culture of Male Dominance in Muslim Communities

Within Muslim communities, parents hold the greatest responsibility for the education or under-education of Muslim women in Myanmar. They may be influenced by several factors when they decide whether their children should attain education in a state school or not. However, their decisions are largely based on perceptions guided by religious leaders, other members of the community and respect for cultural constraints, in addition to concerns about the quality of the government education system of Myanmar and the cost of education.

Islamic religious leaders are often authoritative voices among Muslim communities of Myanmar and their influence also has an impact on the educational status of Muslim people in Myanmar.

There are generally two groups of Islamic leaders who are dominant in Myanmar and two different Islamic societies have formed under their leadership. Liberal religious leaders mostly appear in Burmese Muslim communities and are the ones who encourage education for their communities in both Islamic subjects and modern education such as sciences and mathematics, regardless of gender.

The other kind of religious leaders are more conservative and are generally found in the Indian communities. They teach the members of their communities that children should only study at Islamic schools. The attitude that Muslims should avoid government schooling began to develop along with the spread of *Tablighi Jemaat* practices among Muslims in Myanmar. The practice of *Tablighi Jemaat* movement has been described as 'a quietist, apolitical movement of spiritual guidance and renewal' (Metcalf 1996). Its origins can be traced back to the Indian subcontinent (Metcalf 1982), but it now has branches and influence among Muslim communities across the globe (see Sikand 2002). One of the central tenets that drives the *Tablighi Jemaat* is the idea that Muslims have a responsibility to share with fellow Muslims the main practices and principles of Islam. It is believed that as Muslims teach other Muslims about the Islamic faith and life, they are also refining and perfecting their own faith and the practise of Islam (Metcalf 1996). It has had particular consequences and influence on women in Muslim communities.[7] The influence of the *Tablighi Jemaat* movement has been felt across Southeast Asia (Noor 2012), including in areas such as Southern Thailand (Noor 2009a), Java, and Indonesia (Noor 2009b).

Tablighi Jemaat groups in Myanmar are mainly comprised of conservative Muslim people and religious leaders and they have convinced parents and their communities of many problematic ideas including that they should not send their children to Myanmar state schools to obtain modern education. They reason that the faith of the children will weaken because they will learn about Buddhist practices and other cultures in the government school. These religious leaders are highly influential among the Indian Muslim communities and

---

[7] See for example Ali (2011), who uses the case study of the *Tablighi Jemaat* in Australia to demonstrate that the increasing turn to Islamic piety among Muslim women is part of an effort to respond to the challenge of modernity.

elders of the families. Many parents follow this ideology and believe that their children cannot become good Muslims if they are sent to study at a government school.

Some religious leaders also believe that young Muslim women must be protected from seeing men and they should not be allowed to attend school with young men. Women instead are taught that they must stay at home until they are married. If they want to go out among men, they must protect themselves by dressing in full-body covering, such as those worn by women in Arab countries. The power of this concept has increased and many girls or women nowadays in Indian Muslim communities have started to wear the *burqa*, a cloth tailored to protect the whole body, either as a religious belief or as a fashion statement. The practice of wearing the *burqa* started along with the *Tablighi Jemaat* practice and sales of these garments have become quite high at shops and food stores run by Muslim traders in Yangon.

Being a Muslim woman who grew up in the Indian community in Yangon, I have experienced various types of social pressures that hinder Muslim women from being the decision-makers of their lives. Muslim women tend to believe that they have no influence in the community or in the family, and that those decisions that impact their life will be made by the father or the eldest male of the family. Since the same pressures are found in the families of their peers within the Muslim community, women rarely try to challenge the will of their parents and family. Few exceptions can be found among conservative families. One example of an exception is the case of my cousin who, against the wishes of his elderly parents, decided to educate his daughter and allow her to complete her secondary school education at a government school. Due to the weak education system of Myanmar, however, he let his daughter continue toward graduation at a private school after she finished her government secondary school.

In my own experience, although I was raised within the Indian Muslim community, I had the chance to complete graduate study because I had a supportive father who valued education. I was also motivated to continue my study, like my brothers had been able to do, despite the cultural constraints and the pressure of an arranged marriage. This is because I always wanted to prove to the community that it is possible to be independent as a Muslim woman and to make decisions free from traditional influences. This was not the case for my older sisters, however. They both left schools after reaching upper secondary level and my parents arranged marriages for them.

One of the social and cultural pressures Muslim women face concerns early marriage, and it is common in conservative Indian Muslim communities. Parents or elders in the family usually make the arrangement for their daughter's marriage when she reaches her fifteenth or sixteenth birthday, or before turning twenty. Almost all the girls raised in conservative families have only one clear expectation and that is to be married. Arranged marriages are common among Indian Muslim communities in Myanmar. 'Love marriages', that is, when the boy and girl choose each other free from the influence of their parents or the community, are regarded as disrespectful to the community. Thus, parents want to protect their daughters from falling in love and they prefer that their daughters stay at home as they mature rather than continuing study at schools. It has become a custom to stop educating daughters after the completion of primary or secondary education. On the other hand, girls themselves accept that education is not necessary for their life since they will get married one day and have a family. In some families, young girls themselves ask their parents to stop educating them so that they could learn household work instead. This shows that when women marry young according to custom, their example influences younger members of the community and helps perpetuate the notion that girls were born to be married within that society.

Women who grow up in more liberal Muslim communities have better opportunities to attain education. However, they are still influenced by cultural traditions similar to those that influence Myanmar women. It is important to note certain characteristics and traditions of Burmese women because it reflects the values of Muslim parents and women who tend to follow Myanmar traditions. The traditions of Burmese women are not remarkably different from other Asian countries, and they do not share equal opportunities with men. Since childhood, they are taught that Buddhist males are always superior to Buddhist females. In some specific religious activities and places, only men are allowed to go or to perform such religious duties. Although in recent days more and more women can be seen at work, it was quite different in the past. In almost all households, fathers are usually regarded as the household authority. The mother usually serves as a housewife and takes care of their children. They defer to their husbands and sons on all matters. At mealtime, women serve their husbands first and always eat the leftover food after the men have finished eating. They justify this behaviour with the saying, 'the husband is god, the son is master'. Daughters have to help their mothers with household work and take care of their younger siblings whenever they are free from school. Once they can read and write, they are sometimes not allowed to continue school because mothers think it is unnecessary for a girl to achieve a higher level of education or to work. Daughters expect to be trained as a housewife and to marry a good man who they can depend on for their income.

Burmese parents pay attention to the conversations of neighbours about their daughters since a girl's reputation can have an important impact on whether she marries someone who is perceived as a good man. This is why women cannot enjoy their freedom when they are young and parents may try to protect their daughters when they reach puberty by stopping their education or by having a male family member accompany them whenever they go out, in order to prevent them from dating and having pre-marital sex. Generally, Muslim families who are descendants of minor ethnic groups that existed in Myanmar, before Indians migrated during the British Raj, treat their women according to Burmese customs. Consequently, Muslim women grown up in these families may be allowed education, but higher education opportunities are still limited.

The geographical location of the Myanmar education system contributes to parents' perceptions that it is not an appropriate environment for their daughters. As late as upper secondary education, a girl can study at a girls' school where she is not in contact with the opposite sex. University, however, is co-ed. Until 1995, universities were located in well-developed areas of the city and not far from home for most students. After the 1996 riots, the universities closed for two years and moved to more remote and undeveloped areas of the city. Some Muslim parents feared that they would lose the ability to monitor their daughters' activities, increasing the risk that they might develop illicit relationships with boys. My parents are among those who decided not to continue their daughters' (my two sisters) education because of the location of universities, as well as the perceived weakness of the education system. In some families, girls might be given the option to study through distance learning or at a private school, but the quality of distance education is extremely low.

Poverty and Illiteracy

In poor Muslim families, the literacy rate is very low for both men and women. I conducted interviews among Muslim women (above the age of 18 years old) who are acquiring vocational training such as tailoring and volunteering as teachers. According to the interviews, most were unable to complete their primary education because they were very poor and struggling to help their family earn a daily income. Many children born to fathers and mothers who both work in low-paid jobs also themselves have to struggle to help make ends meet for the family. Their average income per day can be estimated as US$ 2 per day (2000 kyats).[8]

Although primary education is meant to be free, there are associated costs such as books, school activities and extra tuition in government schools. The costs increase with each level of study. In very poor families, parents prefer their children to work as soon as they grow up so that they can help provide living essentials.

The Lack of Role Models

The attitude that women do not need to pursue higher education and that early marriage is preferable has limited the number of educated female role models who are able to challenge cultural norms and provide inspiration to young girls. Generally, the only role model of independent women that young Muslim girls see are others who have married young and serve their husband and family, dependent on others for their security. Mothers are major contributors to this perception and they often share these ideas with their daughters. Since they themselves have the perception that acquiring higher education would not be helpful for a girl, the same understanding is passed on to their daughters and their motivation to obtain education decreases.

---

[8] See more at: http://www.aseanbriefing.com/news/2013/04/16/minimum-wage-levels-across-asean.html

Unfortunately, in most Muslim communities, mothers are not educated and have also adopted the view that educating women is fruitless and potentially harmful to the face of the family. I am one of the very few role models in my community, because I completed a university degree and am now employed in a full-time job with a well-known organization. Many of my female cousins envy me and regret not pursuing higher education. When I asked how they plan to educate their daughters, they said that they want their daughters to achieve a higher level of education. However, they also mention the constraints they face. For example, it may be very difficult to convince the father and some male elders in the family, and without their permission they will not be able to do anything. Even if they try, they do not have resources such as money and information because men are the leaders of the household and they are also the financial supporters of the family. One example of the power of role models can be seen from within my family. A few of my relatives have adjusted their behaviour based on my own example of obtaining higher education and having my own career. A female relative of mine commented that she was determined to educate her daughter because I proved that it could lead to a better life.

However, my own example also shows how going against cultural norms could prove difficult. My parents and I faced significant criticism from my extended family and community. For example, my aunt, the elder sister of my mother, scolded my mother because she permitted me to become educated and failed to arrange my marriage. The pressure led my mother to try to force me to get married and have a family. I had to fight to convince my mother that I would be strong and capable enough to live on my own and to make my own decisions. Without role models, however, it is unlikely that many young women will seek further education when it results in such a negative reaction from family and neighbours.

Fear of the Influence of Burmese Culture

As stated above, government education was designed for all citizens and the schools teach Burmese culture and Buddhism as part of the curriculum. Other religions, such as Islam, are not taught. For this reason, Muslim religious leaders and parents fear that their children will lose their interest in Islam if they attend these schools. This belief became especially strong when the government schools implemented daily Buddhist prayers, recited in the morning before classes begin. Many parents asked their children not to say the Buddhist prayers, not to make friends with Buddhists and not to eat their food.

The fear of Burmese culture influencing Muslim children is so strong that it sometimes affects a child's ability to graduate. The mother of one of my nephews, for example, stopped sending him to the private pre-school because the school rules did not allow food from home to be brought into the school, but required children to eat the (non-*halal*) food that the school provided. This policy alarmed parents who wanted their children to consume only *halal* food, in accordance with the practice of Islam. A similar situation was described by U Aye Lwin, a prominent liberal Muslim religious leader. He said, 'Parents are over anxious about Burmese cultural influences and their children marrying non-Muslims. One parent came to school to submit the resignation for his daughter who was studying at the primary level because he had been informed that a male Buddhist student had proposed to her.'[9]

Parents who do send their children to government schools may try to control their children with very rigid rules. During my student life, I never dared to make friends with boys or to invite them to my family home because I was afraid that my parents and grandparents would take me out of school and arrange for my marriage, as had been done for my peers among my relatives. In seeking to follow family rules, Muslim children tend to isolate themselves from children of other ethnic and religious backgrounds at school. It is common in primary and secondary school that Muslim students make friends only with other Muslim students. Thus, even if there are model students in the school from other cultures, Muslim students are not encouraged to mix with them.

Lack of Employment Opportunities

In Myanmar today, many Muslims, both men and women, struggle to obtain employment either in the government sector or the private

9   Interview with Al-Haj U Aye Lwin, Chairman Executive Committee, Islamic Development Bank (IDB) Scholarship Programme Implementation Committee, Yangon, Myanmar, November 2013, Yangon.

sector. The isolation of Muslim societies from other communities is due in part to their physical appearance and choice of dress, which is often regarded negatively by other non-Muslim communities. For example, I was once interviewed at a famous clinic in Yangon for the position of pharmacist. The first question I was asked was whether I would be flexible enough to deal with other staff in terms of religious practices and eating habits, since I would be the only Muslim employed in the department. Due to such challenges, many Muslims chose to find employment within Muslim communities, working in shops and on construction teams owned by Muslim businessmen.

Government employers may also limit the entrance of Muslims into certain professions and sectors. For example, Muslim people are not allowed to be employed in the military, even if they hold a national identity card. My dream was to be a military doctor, but there was no way to realize this dream because my national identity card shows my religion as Islam. Moreover, there is rarely a chance to be promoted to a higher position in government employment when one is a Muslim. The limitations in employment are a concern among the Muslim communities and many are concerned that they will never be able to be promoted or hold a higher position, even if they are fully qualified for the job.

These concerns lead many students to drop out of university because of the perception that there will be no opportunities for them after graduation. Instead, Muslims may start their own business or contribute to the family business. When it comes to women, parents think that sending their daughters to university is all risk and no reward, and hence may decide not to do so. Although with the expansion of international investment and international non-government organizations in Myanmar, there are more and more opportunities for Muslim women, the attitudes about acquiring education have remained unchanged and young Muslims are not qualified to compete when the opportunities come.

Overcoming the Challenges Faced by Muslim Women

No scholarship currently exists on Muslim women in Myanmar and the scholarship that does exist generally focuses on women in Myanmar who are ethnically Burman and Buddhist (as pointed out by Crouch, this volume). This chapter has aimed to begin to fill this gap, but also to suggest areas for further research and policy reform. I therefore conclude this section by identifying and outlining suggestions that may have implications for public policy, as well as ways in which international donors could support local initiatives to empower women.

Informing Parents about the Benefits of Modern Education

Promoting and increasing the literacy of young women in Muslim communities depends on the education and desire of their parents. In a Muslim family, the father or male elders are often the most powerful and the decision whether a young women should receive an education is determined by them. Through campaigns or workshops, the benefits of education and examples of the negative impact of a lack of education could be shown to them, for example, how uneducated Muslim women are vulnerable to abuse, and how their lack of knowledge affects opportunities for the next generation. Since one of the major concerns of Muslim parents is the influence of Burmese culture and the risk of girls marrying non-Muslims, parents need to be reassured that students will be allowed to maintain their Islamic practices while also studying in a government school.

It is also necessary to educate mothers about the rights of women through women's forums so that they can relay these ideas to their husband, relatives, and daughters about the importance of education and challenge the opinion of conservative religious leaders. There are some educated Islamic leaders who are trying to change the perceptions of conservative families and encourage modern education in this way.

Strengthening the Modern Education System

The modern education system of Myanmar is of poor quality and the new democratic government is seeking to strengthen it. Meanwhile, greater numbers of private local and international schools are being opened, including some international schools led by Muslims for modern education. Muslim parents are more in favour of sending their children to these schools. However, the costs of the schools are not affordable, except for upper class families. It is expected that many schools will expand and improve in quality in the near future, and government education will be strengthened and made more afford- able. Along with the improvement in the education system, the edu- cation of Muslim women should be promoted. Moreover, with more educated Muslim people, the education system in *madrasa* may also be strengthened and the bias against modern education may weaken.

Generating Role Models

Seeing the achievements of educated Muslim women will inspire other women to seek education and change their perceptions of women's place in society. Once parents are informed about the ben- efits of education and the education system is strengthened, it is likely that more role models among Muslim women will appear. This will motivate Muslim women to reassess traditional customs such as early marriage, which may limit their opportunities to pursue education. As they are educated and their concepts change, there is no doubt a new generation of young women will move into higher levels of education and professional standing.

Improving Financial Assistance

The reality is that some families cannot afford to send their children to school because they are poor. When a choice must be made, they will send their sons to school rather than daughters because they believe that their young men will be the leaders and breadwinners of a family. Although support from trust funds and non-governmental organiza- tions exist for the poor to continue their education, it is still limited. For example, the Chulia Muslim Religious Trust Fund[10] (CMRTF) has increased its financial support from less than a hundred students . to more than 200 students of poor Islamic background to continue

[10]   The Chulia Muslim Religious Trust Fund was founded in 1972 by a group of men from the Chulia Muslim community; later on this trust fund was also supported by the other Muslim communities. It provides financial assistance to the poor, regardless of whether they are Muslim or non-Muslim, including assistance to find shelter or housing, obtaining medical treatment, and attaining modern education. The Trust Fund also offers computer train- ing and vocational trainings for the poor.

university education. However, the support provided is a fixed amount and it usually only fulfils 50 per cent of a student's needs. There is also voluntary vocational training available, such as tailoring for women; however, the need is more than what has been provided and many more women are on waiting lists. Fund providers must be encouraged to allocate some of their funds to scholarships and bursaries for poor students to achieve university or vocational training.

Promoting Awareness about Employment Opportunities

Nowadays, employment opportunities for Muslim women have increased since international companies started investing in Myanmar and international non-governmental organizations expanded their activities for the development of the country, where less discrimination will be affected on grounds of religious influences and traditional appearances. However, very few Muslim women are employed and some educated women are not employed because they have received little guidance on possible career opportunities. One Muslim woman who had graduated with a degree in Industrial Chemistry said that she is still unemployed because she does not know how to apply for a job, or which job would suit her.[11] Women who have strong professional experience must therefore lead awareness programmes to promote job-seeking skills among Muslim women and encourage them to find employment. Moreover, they need support and guidance from various people such as their parents and Islamic associations, which could organize women's development programmes in order to help them identify suitable career pathways.

* * *

Muslim women in Myanmar are often in a highly vulnerable position and subject to the strong influence of the male family members and religious leaders. Few Muslim women fight against the traditions and customs of their community in order to acquire higher education

[11] Interview with Ms Aye Thida, a young educated woman from a conservative Muslim community, who was motivated to pursue employment (November 2013, Yangon).

and make their own decisions about their future. Many more Muslim women have grown up in conservative Muslim families and have little hope of receiving education or having the opportunity to seek employment. I have shown that for some Muslim women, their aim in life, which is ingrained in them since childhood, is to become a housewife like their mother and to raise a family. This ideology that guides daily life presents many barriers against education and employment that will be difficult to overcome. The issues identified in this chapter, and the suggestions for reform, need to be acted upon in order to allow a new generation of Muslim women to receive higher education, to reduce their dependency, and increase their independence and ability to choose their own future.

III

Uncertainty, Security, and Violence

III

Uncertainty, Security
and Violence

7 Islamophobia in Buddhist Myanmar

The 969 Movement and Anti-Muslim Violence
Nyi Nyi Kyaw

In June and October 2012, there were two waves of conflicts involving Buddhists, Rohingya and non-Rohingya Muslims in Rakhine State. Since then, Myanmar has faced sectarian riots in other parts of the country, which are unprecedented in its history since it gained independence in 1948. The timing of the riots—from Rakhine State (June and October 2012), to Meiktila (March 2013), Okkan (April 2013), Lashio (May 2013), Kanbalu (August 2013), and Mandalay (July 2014)—has led many sequence theorists to argue that the violence spread across the country due to the situation in Rakhine State.

Against the backdrop of Myanmar's democratization or political liberalization since 2011, some people have proposed structure-focussed theories to explain the situation. Many, if not most, argue that the political liberalization and freeing up of society and the media have played a significant role. Other historical explanations identify that this political opening has reopened old wounds and trace Islamophobia back to colonial times.

Adequately explaining the reason for these riots during this time of transition is a distinct challenge. In general terms, on the one hand, the outside world and international media tend to depict these communal or sectarian conflicts as *anti-Muslim*, reflecting the fact that the brunt of the riots were against Muslims in areas of Myanmar where they constitute a minority group, except in northern Rakhine. Those accounts also highlight the ineffectiveness or alleged involvement of the security forces, most, if not all, of whom are supposedly Buddhists (Human Rights Watch 2012, 2013b; Gittleman et al. 2013). On the other hand, local Myanmar media, reflecting popular opinion, claim that Muslims provoked the riots and highlight intercommunal tensions between Muslims and Buddhists. Local perceptions of the riots, before it spread beyond Rakhine State, suggested that illegal Rohingya Muslims were the main perpetrators. However, this claim was weakened when riots targeting non-Rohingya Muslims broke out in other parts of the country.

This led some people to claim, based on conspiracy theories, that old-school cliques were responsible, that is, those who had been reluctant participants in the new so-called civilian establishment and wanted to revert back to the authoritarian past. This explanation proved very popular among democracy activists and dissidents. A warning also frequently followed: if the Myanmar government does not stop these riots, it may be seen as digressing from its steps towards democracy. This explanation emphasized the role of the government in ensuring that the rule of law and the security of its citizens were maintained and it has been most frequently pronounced by Aung San Suu Kyi on various occasions as the major cause of the violence.

Another theory among these agency-focussed explanations popular in the international media is the role of the Buddhist nationalist 969 movement in stoking Islamophobia and leading to anti-Muslim violence. While the 969 movement played a role in sectarian violence in Myanmar in 2012 and 2013 through its anti-Muslim incitements, it is difficult to prove that its leaders were actively involved in the violence. So far, no hard evidence of their direct involvement has emerged. However, that the moral support given by this movement and its central message, which breeds Islamophobia among Buddhists, leads to anti-Muslim violence is undeniable. Most writings on the numerologically intriguing 969 movement are concerned with only its de facto ideologue and propagandist—the ubiquitous and media-friendly Buddhist nationalist monk U Wirathu[1]—and his call

---

[1] The monk's Dharma name is U Vicittābivamsa although he is mostly known by his pseudonym, Wirathu.

for Buddhists to stop transactions with Muslim businesses in order to protect the Myanmar Buddhist race and religion. That the origin of the 969 movement lies in Mawlamyine in 2012, and was inspired by an obscure book written and published in 1997 by Nha-phat-hla[2] U Kyaw Lwin, a late director-general of the Ministry of Religious Affairs, suggests this is a new or recent phenomenon.

This chapter aims to analyse this movement, to identify how it operates and to consider its influence, particularly the way it has affected Buddhist attitudes towards Muslims in Myanmar. Its central thesis is that the 969 campaign of Islamophobia invigorated a deeply held siege mentality with roots in colonial times. Its Buddhist audience were made to believe that Buddhism and Buddhists in Myanmar are under threat from Islam and Muslims in Myanmar and elsewhere. Contextually, despite repeated promises by President Thein Sein and by the Speaker of the Parliament Thura Shwe Mann, that they would check the spread of hate messages in Myanmar, the 969 campaign has grown across Myanmar due to tacit official approval, if not outright support.

In order to understand the 969 campaign, this chapters draws on original speeches [in Burmese] made by monks associated with the 969 network, which are sold on the streets of Yangon as videos. These tapes are aimed at Buddhists, and may be listened to by people in teashops or at home. Buddhist sermons in Myanmar follow a common format. A Buddhist monk will narrate a story from the Buddha's life and identify lessons for the audience, or recite and expound a particular passage from the scriptures. There are usually intervals or sessions during which the monk stops, asks the audience to repeat what he has just said and then allows the audience to respond. However, 969 propagandist monks sensationalize their sermons by stories of Buddhist women forcibly converted to Islam and often harassed by their Muslim husbands, and by conspiracy theories of the Muslim plot to Islamize Myanmar. Through such methods of sensationalist interaction, these sermons offer a persuasive message to their audience. I also draw on a range of media reports on the 969

---

[2] Nha-phat-hla is an honorific title that literally means 'two-sided'. In Buddhist understanding, it refers to *lokiya* (mundane) and *lokuttara* (supermundane), which means 'good' or 'beneficial for' both worlds.

movement which, although these are usually less inflammatory than the tapes or sermons, also constitute a crucial part of anti-Muslim discourse in Myanmar.

Buddhism in Myanmar and the Role of Buddhist Monks

It has often been said that in Southeast Asia a Buddhist 'thinks of his whole way of life as Buddhist—his individual, family and village' (Lester 1973: 3). The role Buddhism plays in politics in countries with Buddhist majorities has been a particular feature of Buddhism in the region. Keyes has identified the close connection between Buddhism and social life, noting that Buddhism 'has never been separate from the social world in which Buddhists live' (Keyes 2007: 147). One of the most popular Buddhist preacher-cum-writers in Myanmar is the monk known as Mettashin Shwe Pyi Thar Ashin Zawana.[3] In his book 'Lifeblood of Myanmar' (*Myanma-to-e A-thak*) (2003), he argues that Buddhism is an essential part of Myanmar. One of the world's foremost comparative scholars of Southeast Asia, the late colonialist-cum-scholar J.S. Furnivall (1956: 12) also argued that 'it is Buddhism that has moulded social Burman life and thought and, to the present day, the ordinary Burman regards the terms "Burman" and "Buddhist" as practically equivalent and inseparable.'

The 969 movement which is led by Buddhist monks cannot be analysed without a discussion of the paramount role of Buddhist monks in Myanmar's predominantly Buddhist society. More than one hundred years ago Fielding-Hall (1898: 145) described the position of monks in the following way: 'The king is feared, the wise man admired, perhaps envied, the rich man is respected, but the monk is honoured and loved. There is no one beside him in the heart of the people.' Spiro (1982: 396) also concludes that 'there is probably no other clergy in the world which receives as much honour and respect as offered to the Buddhist monks of Burma.'

---

[3] In 2014, Mettashin Shwe Pyi Thar Ashin Zawana, who used to be a prolific writer of best-selling books on Buddhism, left the monkhood.

Indeed, the Buddhist monkhood or Sangha is designated as one of the Three Gems of Buddhism in whom Buddhists go for refuge. This is evident from the following three lines which are chanted as prayers by both Buddhist monks and laypeople in Theravāda countries, including Myanmar:

Buddham Saranam Gacchāmi (I go for refuge in the Buddha!) .
Dhammam Saranam Gacchāmi (I go for refuge in the Dhamma!)
Sangham Saranam Gacchāmi (I go for refuge in the Sangha!)

This concept of the Buddhist trinity has led Shwe Sone Chaung Sayadaw Ashin Vicitta Linkara (2013: 112) to write that '[a] disrespect of the Sangha is tantamount to that of Lord [Buddha]'. Moreover, of the three Gems, in real life Buddhists are only able to encounter the Sangha since the other two elements refer to the no-longer-physically-existent Buddha and the non-human Buddhist Dhamma scriptures. Since both the Sangha and lay Buddhists are human, they understandably form an interdependent relationship.

This suggests that the Buddhist Sangha evokes a similar charisma of the kind first identified by Max Weber (1948), that is, both institutional and personal charisma. Based on this, Hiroko Kawanami (2009) claims that some influential monks may possess both types of charisma: the monastic order's institutional charisma, and their own personal charisma. She also comments on the nature of power in Myanmar: 'Power in traditional societies such as Myanmar is deeply engrained in religious and political culture, and requires a moral and other-worldly dimension in understanding its exertion in society' (Kawanami 2009: 212). In other words, monks as guardians of Buddhism possess tremendous power in Myanmar society which puts them more or less on par with official elites, especially in Buddhist affairs, since they are the very Gem of Buddhism. For these reasons, Smith (1965: 186) concludes that: 'Popular reverence for the monks makes their influence considerable in whatever area they choose to exert it, including politics'.

However, the view that monks must not participate in politics via voting is widely held and accepted in Myanmar. Indeed, since 1936, Myanmar Buddhist monks have not been allowed to vote in elections, let alone contest them, unlike their Sri Lankan counterparts. In 1936, an order of the Burma Legislative Council banned monks from being elected to the house (Larsson 2015; Smith 1965). Again in 1946, another debate about whether to allow monks to vote in Legislative Council elections was resolved in the negative despite two disparate views. In the debates, senior Sangha members argued that 'priests should be aloof and isolated from mundane matters' and 'politics bred anger and ambition and the emotions from which priests should strive to keep free', while their younger counterparts claimed that the Sangha's main duty was 'not escape from the world but service to humanity' (Maung Maung 1989: 122).

On one hand, this non-participation of monks in Myanmar's politics as either voters or professional politicians or parliamentarians has been one of the most significant facets of Myanmar's politics, especially since the twentieth century.[4] Yet monks have also come to take on a political role at certain times in post-colonial Myanmar. The political role of Buddhist monks in post-colonial Myanmar and Sri Lanka was noted by Edmund Leach (1973: 35) who argued that:

> Logically, this would imply that everyone who aspires to be a good Buddhist, but more particularly anyone who becomes a monk, should be totally disinterested in politics. Formal doctrine, as enunciated by present-day Buddhist monks, makes this quite explicit. Yet both the historical and contemporary facts are quite otherwise.

Especially in times of political and social crises, monks in Myanmar have proven to be the forerunners of, or participants in, public agitation for change or improvement. Both positive and negative examples of monks' engagement in politics can be found in Myanmar.

One of the most prominent examples of monks' *positive*[5] participation in politics is the Saffron Revolution of September 2007. According to a collection of articles by monks and people who were

---

[4] It has become a custom to include one or more sentences on the vital role of the Buddhist monastic order and Buddhism in Myanmar's history in almost all writings about the country. The most comprehensive studies of Buddhism, its authority in society and its involvement in various ways in politics in different epochs of Myanmar since pre-colonization are those of Sarkisyanz (1965), Schober (2010), Smith (1965), Spiro (1982), and Turner (2014).

[5] A detailed account of the Saffron Revolution is available in Lintner (2009) and Fink (2009b).

involved in, or bore witness to, the Saffron protests of September 2007, the main reason for the monks' involvement was as a 'service to humanity' (Ashin Pyinnya Nanda 2013). Photos of Buddhist monks chanting the *mettā sutta* (the Buddhist scriptural discourse of loving kindness) in the streets in non-violent protests against the political and social situation in Myanmar were widely featured in the international media. This was sparked by the harsh treatment meted out by the authorities against some monks in Pakokku in early September, and the crushing of these protests by authorities led to an international outcry. A separate example is the work of the famous philanthropist Sitagū Sayadaw Ashin Nyanissara, who was very active in supporting survivors of Cyclone Nargis in May 2008, which led to the deaths of thousands of people and caused major destruction to towns and villages (Jaquet and Walton 2013). Another example is the health and education work of a well-respected monk, Ashin Sandadika.

However, their role in politics has at other times been negative, resulting in violence (Keyes 2007). This was captured by Edmund Leach (1973: 31) in his comments regarding Buddhist nationalist movements: 'I claim that when a whole political movement prides itself in its 'nationalism' it is always seeing itself as being on the defensive or in opposition, and even the most aggressive actions against neighbours are justified by the plea of self-preservation'.

Various comparative examples of the dark side of the Buddhist Sangha in Sri Lanka and Thailand have been noted by Bartholomeusz (2002), Jerryson (2011), and Schober (2006). Apart from the monks' social and moral authority derived from their religious legitimacy, Buddhist monasteries' physical and organizational structures are significant factors in their influence on any social and political movements. Although Smith (1965) was writing about monks' involvement in politics in colonial times, his argument regarding their mobilizational advantage and the strong organizational structure of Buddhist monasteries (in which hundreds of monks resided) is still relevant. Indeed, monasteries in present Myanmar have become more numerous and larger over the years to accommodate the Sangha which is estimated to be 500,000-strong.

The Buddhist Sangha therefore possess the ultimate moral authority and orginazational efficiency as well in Myanmar society.

I now turn to consider in more detail the roots of anti-Muslim attitudes among Buddhists in Myanmar.

Historical Fault Lines between Buddhist Monks and Muslims

In Burma, it has been said that the most tragic and abrupt event in
its history was the overthrow of the Burmese Konbaung kingdom and
the Buddhist ecclesiastic authority that was a crucial part of it (Gravers
1999; Taylor 2009). Therefore, the subsequent history of Burma in
the colonial period has been labelled a 'tragic narrative' that 'was a
deeply traumatic and emasculating experience' (Ikeya 2011: 4).

Out of this history has arisen the tendency to blame everything
that goes wrong in present day Myanmar on the period of British
colonization. This attitude and strategy has been notably adopted
by the Myanmar armed forces for decades. The interpretation
of Myanmar's history by successive commanders-in-chief has
emphasized the perception that Burma has had to shoulder chronic
problems of civil war, ethnic issues and the like brought about by
colonizers. By adopting this rhetoric, the Myanmar armed forces
avoid responsibility for not being able to solve the problems left by
the British, and denying their complicity in exacerbating old problems or creating new ones. A speech of the present Commander-in-
Chief, Senior General Min Aung Hlaing,[6] which was delivered on
Armed Forces Day, 27 March 2014, is one recent example in which
he blamed the British for the problems facing Myanmar today. Many
annual speeches given by his predecessors on Armed Forces Day
had adopted a similar rhetoric.

The British colonized the whole territory of Burma, the geo-
political body presently known as Myanmar, after waging three
Anglo-Burmese wars and completed its imperialist project in late
1885. With the opening of the Suez Canal in 1869 and growing
international demand, the British tried to commercialize and

---

[6] Senior General Min Aung Hlaing's speech is reproduced, though not
verbatim, on page 8 of the state-owned newspaper *Myanma Alin* (the New
Light of Myanmar) issued on 28 March 2014.

develop the Burmese agricultural sector. They brought in cheap labour from India, which was already under their rule, and colonial Rangoon became more like an Indian city than a Burmese one as the largest proportion of its population was Indian. Moreover, Burma was ruled as a province of India under the British Raj which made Indian immigration easy and unhindered because the two formerly different territories were now the same colony. The growing nationalist sentiment agitating for Burma's separation from India, and increased competition between blue and white-collar Indian labour and their Burmese counterparts, resulted in Indophobia, which did not discriminate between Indian Hindus and Indian Muslims. The myth of the deracination of the Burmese/Bamar Buddhist race due to ceaseless Indian immigration and increasing Indo-Bamar inter-religious and inter-communal marriages rose to prominence in the 1920s and 1930s. This was used in agitations for separating Burma from India and limiting Indian immigration. Eventually, Burma was freed from India in 1937, when it was made into a separate colony. This growing Indophobia and increased economic competition for scarcer jobs in the aftermath of the Depression resulted in two bouts of anti-Indian disturbances in 1930 and 1938, the first being anti-Indian and the second anti-Indian Muslim (Chakravarti 1971; Mahajani 1960).

Egreteau traces this phenomenon of Indophobia to colonial times and concludes that it has gradually transformed into the Islamophobia seen in Myanmar nowadays. He argues that 'after years of 'Burmanisation' processes, Burmese old-age 'Indophobic' sentiments have turned towards more 'Islamophobic' tendencies, now explicitly targeting the Muslim communities of Indian origin' (Egreteau 2011: 33). However, a qualification is needed regarding the term 'Muslim communities of Indian origin' as Egreteau's argument seems to miss an important fact that the distinction between Indian and non-Indian Muslims is blurred in present-day Myanmar. In the eyes of the 969 preachers, all Muslims in Myanmar, regardless of their racial origins and ethnic backgrounds, follow the same religion and pose a threat to Buddhism and Buddhists. Therefore, it might be truer to argue that Islamophobia in present-day Myanmar does not target only Indian Muslims but all Muslim groups.

Similarly, monks' anti-Muslim attitudes and activities also originated in colonial times. Amidst apocalyptic fears of the extinction of
Buddhism and its majority adherents in Myanmar, monks in colonial
Burma did the same as the 969 preachers and Ashin Wirathu are now
doing, that is, issuing calls for the boycotting of Muslim businesses,
which occurred in Mandalay during and after anti-Muslim riots of
1938 (Maung Maung 1989). Indeed, the first manifesto of *Dobama
Asiayone* (Our Burman Association) issued on 30 May 1930, which
is regarded as the forerunner of the Burmese nationalist movement
agitating for independence from Britain, called for the boycotting of
Indian (both Hindu and Muslim) shops (*Dobama Asiayone Thamaing
Pyusuye Apwè* 1976). It can even be argued that the Burmese nationalist movement, which later fought for and gained independence from
the British, originated in Indophobia. Another influential monks'
organization, officially called the All Burma Young Monks Association
(ABYMA) but better known by its Burmese name *Yahanphyu Aphwe*,
which was influential in post-independence Burma until the early
1960s, was also founded in Mandalay amidst anti-Muslim riots in
1938. Regarding the *Yahanphyu Aphwe* in Mandalay, Smith (1965:
189) writes: 'The basic aim of the founder, U Zawtika, was to unify
the monkhood in the fact of the threat which the Indian Muslims
were thought to pose to Buddhist religion and Burmese culture.
The growth of the organization was disrupted by World War II,
but has grown substantially since independence'. Another monks'
organization in Yangon called the *Thathana Mamaka* (Young Monks
Association, YMA) was also involved in the 1938 riots according to
the Final Report of the Riot Inquiry Committee (1939), formed in the
aftermath of the riots.

These Islamophobic sentiments, which were rooted in colonial
times and continued until the first years after independence, seemed
to have faded into the background on the coming to power in 1962 of
the military coup regime. The Ne Win regime (1962 to 1988) emphasized unity rather than diversity, which might have been a reason
why communal divisions were not exploited for political purposes.
Nevertheless it was highly xenophobic and/or Islamophobic, but
more economic nationalist than religious nationalist. Although Ne
Win hated Chinese and Indian communities for their economic
wealth and used them as scapegoats whenever he faced economic

problems, even then, he did not explicitly highlight religious differences. In general, the whole country suffered political repression under one-party rule and social and economic hardships due to the government's mismanagement.

One area in which Ne Win was blatantly xenophobic was the creation of barriers to stop Muslims from entering the public sector. This is in contrast to the pre- and post-independence period when Burma had several prominent politicians and cabinet ministers who were Muslim. Gradually, under Ne Win, Muslims became a sociopolitically marginalized group and it became increasingly difficult, if not impossible, for them to be promoted to senior government positions. Of all the organs of public service then in Burma, the armed forces, which had had a number of Muslim officers until the 1960s, became increasingly anti-Muslim, especially in its admission system. Since most, if not all, senior government positions were then filled by active or retired armed forces officers, the fact that Muslims were not able to join the armed forces meant that it was impossible for them to attain a high office in the government. However, anti-Muslim disturbances were less common under the socialist government.

The situation drastically changed with the coming to power of another military regime which increasingly misused religion in its propaganda. Indeed, the previous regime led by Ne Win had used religion in its fights against communism. The Burmese armed forces published a pamphlet called *Dhammantaraya* (Danger to Dhamma) in 1959, when Burma was being ruled by the caretaker government headed by Ne Win. It portrayed communism as an imminent threat to the majority faith, based on notes written by a participant of a series of classes on ideology given by Thakin Soe, the ideologue of the Communist Party of Burma (Bo Bo 2010; Mehden 1960). A Director of the Department of Psychological Warfare and Policy in the armed forces, who was also an adjutant to Ne Win, Colonel Dhammika U Ba Than, wrote in a self-satisfied way of the *Dhammantaraya* campaign: 'This served as a punch at their [communists'] ideological solar-plexus, and they are yet to recover from that terrible blow. The Defence Services just stimulated the "religious nerves" and all it cost them was a few thousand kyats' (1962: 71).

Indeed, it was Dhammika U Ba Than's admission that the armed forces were directly involved in the psychological warfare against communists by abusing religion for political purposes—a practice which is banned by all three constitutions of Myanmar. This ploy came to be used in the following decades by successive psychological warfare officer corps. The armed forces, especially their intelligence and psychological warfare corps, also came to hijack the colonial-era myth of the fear of extinction of the Burmese Buddhist race due to demographic pressures posed by Indian migrants, especially in the 1990s when Myanmar conducted a propaganda war in the state newspapers on almost a daily basis. A series of fourteen articles titled *Amyo-pyauk-hma So-kyauk Hla-pa-thi* (We Fear Deracination!) were published in February and June 1989[7] in the state newspaper *Lôk-tha Pyi-thu Ne-sin* (Working People's Daily). These articles traced colonization and xenophobia and finally discussed various pieces of Myanmar citizenship legislation before and after independence. By invigorating the colonial-era myth of deracination and arguing that Buddhism is still under threat from Islam and Muslims (especially Rohingya), the articles defended the discriminatory 1982 Citizenship Act as a Buddhist bulwark against illegal migrants.[8] This was clear evidence of the sustainability of the colonial-era myth of deracination, at least at the official level, which created a Burman Buddhist siege mentality that saw itself on the verge of extinction from the world, first by the Indian race and then the Muslim world. The old Buddhist word *Dhammantaraya*, which was used in 1959 by the armed forces, was again used in an article in the May 1992 issue of the monthly magazine *Myet-kin-thit* (Greener Pasture), which was known to have close ties to military intelligence. The article that appeared in it, entitled *Dhammantaraya Rohingya*, argued that the Rohingya were

---

7 The first seven articles (Nos 1–7) were published from 20–26 February 1989, and the last seven on 3, 5, 8, 9, 13, 20, and 28 June 1989, all in the *Lokt-ha Pyi-thu Ne-sin*, the Working People's Daily.

8 We can see the same line of argument being used in defense by the present Myanmar government and people in response to the calls by the international community to amend or repeal the 1982 citizenship law, which is beyond the scope of this chapter.

a danger to the Dhamma (Po Kan Kaung 1992). In short, the *Lôk-tha Pyi-thu Ne-sin* and the *Myet-kin-thit* articles effectively portray Muslims (including Rohingya) as a demographic threat to Myanmar and Buddhism.

The abuse of the history of colonialism for the political advantage of the armed forces and officials of successive Myanmar governments are the two major structural or contextual factors which have played roles in the emergence of the 969 propaganda and its acceptance by certain sections of Myanmar society, despite the country's recent steps to democratization.

The 969 Movement: The Numerological Bases of 786 and 969

Although 969 propagandist monks and their lay Buddhist support-ers, including Myanmar authorities, deny its anti-Muslim raison d'être, reality demonstrates otherwise. While most journalistic writings emphasize the call for the shunning of transactions with Muslim businesses as the main strategy of the movement, many of them fail to point out the most important factor behind the emer-gence of the movement. Indeed, according to 969 preachers, the emergence of the mythical symbol 969 was inspired by the Islamic symbol 786 used by Muslim shops in Myanmar. An explanation of the 786 symbol is necessary because, according to the founders of the 969 movement, the 786 symbol is one of the reasons for the 969 movement.

Many shops owned by Muslims across Myanmar display the numerical sign 786 (in English) or ၇၈၆ (in Burmese) or ٧٨٦/<٨٦ (in Arabic). It is used in some parts of the world, mainly by South Asian Muslims, as a numerical representation of the first verse of the *Qur'an* which reads *Bismillah hi rahmani rahim* meaning 'In the Name of God, the Most Gracious, the Most Compassionate'. This verse is also usually quoted by Muslims when they begin reciting the *Qur'an*, at the start of each chapter, or when they do good deeds.

Before taking a look at how the number 786 is derived from a verse of the *Qur'an*, we need to know the Arabic Abjad numeric system which gives values of 1, 10, 100, or 1000 to each of the twenty-eight letters of the Arabic alphabet, as shown in Table 7.1.

Table 7.1   Arabic Abjad Numerals

	1	2	3	4	5	6	7	8	9
1s	ا	ب	ج	د	ه	و	ز	ح	ط
10s	ي	ك	ل	م	ن	س	ع	ف	ص
100s	ق	ر	ش	ت	ث	خ	ذ	ض	ظ
1000	غ								

Source: Chrisomalis (2010: 163).

According to Abjad, the numerical value 786 is obtained by adding up the respective values of the letters which spell the Qur'anic verse *Bismillah hi rahmani rahim*, as shown in Table 7.2.

Prior to the 1990s, it was the norm for Muslim-owned food shops to display easily identifiable signs of 786 or ٧٨٦/<٨٦ in order to inform Muslim customers that they prepared and sold *halal* food. The granting of *halal* certification to food shops and industries, regardless of whether they are Muslim-owned or non-Muslim-owned, by Muslim religious bodies is a recent phenomenon which only appeared in the 1990s. Non-Muslim shops which sell *halal* food but do not have *halal* certification normally write on their signboards and/or menus that customers of any religious faith may consume their products, which means the meat they use is *halal*. Signs usually used in other countries—'Halal' in English and 'حلال' in Arabic, which mean it is permissible or lawful according to Islam—are not common in Myanmar.

Indeed, the display of 786 signs by Muslim shops and businesses is common in South Asia. For example, these signs are widely used in shops and homes in Pakistan and some people even start their personal letters with 786, in honour of God, although the sign is not

Table 7.2   How 786 is Calculated

ب	س	م	ا	ل	ل	ه	ا	ل	ر
2	60	40	1	30	30	5	1	30	200
ح	م	ن	ا	ل	ر	ح	ي	م	
8	40	50	1	30	200	8	10	40	T=786

Source: Author.

officially endorsed. The custom is not usually found in Southeast Asia, such as in Indonesia. One exception, however, is that some Indian Muslim shops in Singapore and Malaysia do use this sign. It is likely that Muslims in Myanmar inherited the practice of using 786 due to their strong education links with South Asia, where most of the *ulama* (Islamic religious leader) in Myanmar who study abroad are trained.

Despite the common practice of writing 786 on Muslim properties, shops, wedding invitations, documents and notices, there is a lack of knowledge among most Myanmar Muslims about the numerical theory behind the symbol. According to the *Mufti* of the Islamic Religious Affairs Council[9] (IRAC) of Myanmar, Omar Myint Naing (2013), Myanmar Muslims customarily use this sign because they may consider it to be in honour of the first verse of the *Qur'an*, they may not be able to write in Arabic, or they may be afraid that writing the verse in Arabic in public places and documents may be sacrilegious.

Leaving aside the 786 sign, I now turn to the popular emblem of the 969 movement, which is featured below in Figure 7.1. Although the 969 leaders have never claimed that this emblem is based on the Buddhist flag, in fact, its background is the same as the Buddhist flag except that it uses the colour pink instead of orange. The official colours of the Buddhist flag in Myanmar, which uses pink instead of the orange found in Buddhist flags elsewhere, are contained in detailed instructions on the use of the Buddhist flag issued by the *Naing-ngan-to Sangha Mahanayaka Apwè* or State Sangha Mahanayaka Committee (abbreviated *Ma-Ha-Na*) (State Sangha Mahanayaka Committee 2008: 96).

Although writing the numerical symbol 786 has a long history in Myanmar, 969 in its present form has a relatively short life. It is not written in Arabic numerals but in its Burmese counterpart (၉၆၉), as seen in the emblem below. Although the 969 emblem was officially launched on the Thadingyut Full Moon Day in 2012, which fell on

---

9 The IRAC is one of the five active Islamic organizations recognized by Myanmar authorities as representative of Myanmar Muslims. The other four are the *Jamiat Ulama-El-Islam*, All-Myanmar Maulvi League, All-Myanmar Muslim Youth (Religious) Organisation and the Myanmar Muslim National Affairs Organisation.

Figure 7.1   969 Emblem

Source: Author.

30 October, what it refers to—the Buddha, Dhamma, and Sangha—is the same age as Buddhism. 969 is a composite of 9, 6, and 9 which refer to the numbers of qualities of Buddha, Dhamma, and Sangha respectively.[10] The movement uses this symbol because its leaders want to convey the message that it represents the Three Gems of Buddhism and, symbolically drawing on the qualities of the Holy Trinity, indicates to Buddhists that it is a noble endeavour.

According to the Secretary of the 969 movement, Ashin Thaddhamma, the lion, elephant, horse and ox in the emblem, which are again based on the Pillar of Ashoka, are symbols of bravery, strength, speed and forbearance respectively (Galache 2013).

[10]   A detailed discussion of the qualities of Buddha, Dhamma, and Sangha is available in the Department for the Promotion and Propagation of the Sāsanā (2002: 117–24).

Moreover, certain instructions that came with the launch of the emblem ask that persons who hang it on the walls of their shops and homes pray and that it be used to show Buddhist unity across Myanmar. Finally, they warn against non-Buddhist use of the emblem for any reason and request that legal action be taken against non-Buddhists who misuse it.

In these ways, 969 leaders adopt symbols and rituals for their movement that are familiar to Buddhism. Although the 969 emblem has never been officially endorsed, a Muslim man who allegedly removed one from a betel shop in Kyaukyi, Bago Division, on 20 April 2013, was sued by the local police chief on 22 April. He was found guilty and given a prison sentence of two years with labour on 23 April, under article 295 (A) of the Penal Code, which criminalizes deliberate and malicious acts intended to outrage the religious feelings of any class by insulting its religion or religious beliefs. This demonstrates the willingness of certain local authorities to support the 969 movement by characterizing such behaviour as a criminal offence (*The Voice Daily* 2013).[11]

The Spread of Islamophobia by the 969 Movement

Despite the claim that the 969 movement only aims to protect Buddhism in Myanmar, the purpose and goals of the campaign are not entirely clear. When it claims that Buddhism must be defended, the faith itself becomes a designated referent object under genuine or imagined threats from someone, some group, some event or some process. Both implicitly and explicitly, for the 969 movement's leaders and supporters, the threat is Islam and Muslims both within and without Myanmar.

The 969 leader, Ashin Thaddhamma, argued that the defence of Buddhism was the ultimate aim of their self-proclaimed Buddhicization project (Kyaw Phyo Tha 2013). Here the 'defence of

---

[11] Indeed, the same article (295 (A)) was used to jail a Muslim woman riding a bicycle in Okkan. She was said to have bumped into an 11-year-old novice monk and her sister allegedly verbally abused the novice, and after this incident occurred, anti-Muslim disturbances broke out in Okkan.

Buddhism' means specifically Myanmar Buddhism, not Buddhism throughout the world. According to him:

> Burma is the only country in the world where Theravada Buddhism flourishes very well.[12]
>
> When our Buddhists are less interested in the faith, our religion will be under threat. Apart from Buddhists, who else will take care of Buddhism? That's why we are working hard to make people more interested in the religion. (Kyaw Phyo Tha 2013)

This paranoid or apocalyptic view is also espoused by another 969 leader, Ashin Wimala Biwuntha, who told an audience at a Buddhist temple in Mawlamyine in June 2013: 'We Buddhists are like people in a boat that is sinking. If this does not change, our race and religion will soon vanish' (Kyaw Zwa Moe 2013). Elsewhere, Ashin Thaddhamma denied the inherent Islamophobic agenda of the 969 campaign:

> It's just speculation. We have nothing to do with saying 'no' to other religions. We are just working for Buddhism. People may have different views on what we are doing. We are not trying to defeat other faiths, just strengthen our own. (Kyaw Zwa Moe 2013)

Despite this denial, in one of his media interviews, Ashin Thaddhamma openly claimed that Muslims conspire to shop only at Muslim-owned shops, and said (in Burmese): 'In order that they know each other, they are intentionally using this 786 number' (Htet Naing Zaw 2013).

The vice-presiding monk of Mya Sadi Nan Oo Monastery in Mawlamyine, Ashin Yaywata, also questioned the use of the 786 sign by Muslims in Myanmar:

> I want to ask, who started this practice? For years, Muslims have refused to buy anything from Buddhist shops, even from betel nut sellers. They use 786 to support each other, so we have to do the same thing. (Kyaw Zwa Moe 2013)

---

[12] This claim shows obvious neglect of the fact that Sri Lanka and Thailand still exist as places where Theravada Buddhism is the religion of the majority of the population. Indeed, it is similar to that made by certain fundamentalist Buddhist monks in Sri Lanka who imagine that their country is the only place where pristine Theravada Buddhism still exists. See Schonthal (this volume).

Indeed, the argument that 969 was created to counter 786 is not plausible, because Buddhist shops commonly displayed other Buddhist symbols before the emergence of 969. Generally, Buddhist shops in Myanmar display အရဟံ (the first quality of Buddha meaning the Worthy One) or ဗုဒ္ဓံ ဓမ္မံ သံဃံ (Buddha, Dhamma, Sangha). This practice has never aimed or claimed to compete with or counter the use of 786 by Muslims. Like their Muslim counterparts, Buddhist shops use either of the two Buddhist symbols to pay homage to the religion of their affiliation and practice.

In video files of the sermons of the 969 leaders from Mawlamyine and other Buddhist monks who have participated in the 969 preachings, the messages are openly and inflammatorily anti-Muslim. In media interviews, Ashin Wirathu is more anti-Muslim than other 969 preachers, partly due to his celebrity status among journalists, both local and international. Although he does not hold any official position in the 969 movement, he is widely regarded as the movement's de facto leader or most important propagandist. Examples of his inflammatory anti-Muslim speeches widely available in English-language media are:

> Over the past 50 years, we have shopped at Muslim shops and then they became richer and wealthier than us and can buy and marry our girls. In this way, they have destroyed and penetrated not only our nation but also our religion. (Fisher 2013)
>
> Muslims are fundamentally bad. Mohammed allows them to kill any creature. (*The Diplomat* 2013)
>
> [The Halal way of killing] allows familiarity with blood and could escalate to the level where it threatens world peace. (Hodal 2013)
>
> With money, they become rich and marry Buddhist Burmese women who convert to Islam, spreading their religion. Their businesses become bigger and they buy more land and houses, and that means fewer Buddhist shrines. (Szep 2013)[13]
>
> They're [mosques] like enemy base stations for us. (Szep 2013)
>
> If we are weak, our land will become Muslim. (Fuller 2013)
>
> Muslims are like the African carp. They breed quickly and they are very violent and they eat their own kind. (Tin Aung Kyaw 2013)

---

[13] Although this claim by Ashin Wirathu of Muslims buying land so that fewer Buddhist shrines could be built is, indeed, unfounded even for a casual onlooker in Myanmar which has innumerable Buddhist shrines, it could have worked to increase Islamophobia for his enthusiastic followers.

The most anti-Muslim rhetoric of the 969 movement is the accusation made by its leaders that 786 stands for a total of 21 (that is, 7+8+6 = 21). The widespread conspiracy theory behind this is that the number 21 refers to the Muslim plot to Islamize Myanmar by the end of the 21st century and so Muslims are characterized as a threat to Myanmar which is predominantly Buddhist. This accusation is supported by two claims made by the 969 leaders: Muslims within Myanmar implement this Islamization project, and they are financially supported by other rich Muslim countries. It is expected that extremist movements like 969 would use such rhetorical tactics to magnify an issue or problem. However, if we look at this particular rhetoric about a Muslim plot to Islamize Buddhist Myanmar from the spectrum of power relations in Myanmar, in which Muslims constitute a politically and socially marginalized minority, we can see how this claim can potentially enrage many from the majority Buddhist population.

According to the 969 movement, Myanmar Muslim men contribute to the mass Islamization of Myanmar because they marry both Muslim and non-Muslim women, convert non-Muslim women to Islam and have many children with them. In fact, in Myanmar, it is widely believed that Muslim men are more fertile than Buddhist men. Some also believe that Muslim men usually practise polygamy although there are no reliable marriage statistics that either prove or disprove this suspicion. According to the 969 rhetoric, these two social concerns are perceived as a real threat to the security and future of Buddhists in Myanmar because Muslim men are allegedly waging a *Love Jihad* or *Romeo Jihad* against Buddhists, a conspiracy theory popular among certain Hindu nationalist groups in India (Gupta 2009; Rao 2011). This has often been exaggerated to generate fear and concern. For example, Ashin Wimalar Biwuntha, a 969 leader said, 'Muslim men try to win the love of poor Buddhist women for their reproductive tactics. They produce a lot of children, they are snowballing. We have a duty to defend ourselves if we don't want to be overwhelmed'. (*The Diplomat* 2013)

Established on 27 June 2013,[14] a popular campaign by *Amyo Ba-tha Tha-tha-na Ka-kwaè-saung-shauk-ye Apwè* (abbreviated *Ma-Ba-Tha*,

---

[14] *Ma-Ba-Tha*'s Upper Myanmar branch, of which Ashin Wirathu has been an active executive member, was also formed in Mandalay on 15 January 2014.

or known in English as the Patriotic Association of Myanmar, PAM)[15] has called for the banning of intermarriage between non-Buddhist men and Buddhist women, but not vice versa, in an offshoot of the popular myth discussed above. *Ma-Ba-Tha* claims that Buddhist women find themselves at a great disadvantage when they inter-marry with non-Buddhist men whose religious laws do not approve of interfaith marriage. Although the campaigners do not openly say that it targets intermarriage between Muslim men and Buddhist women, it is common knowledge in Myanmar that this is the case. Campaigners affiliated with *Ma-Ba-Tha*, who are mainly monks, have claimed that they have already collected millions of signa-tures in support of the draft law which was prepared by *Ma-Ba-Tha* and sent to the Myanmar parliament but is yet to be debated and approved.

Although the interfaith marriage bill alone was most commonly known, there were three other bills called for by *Ma-Ba-Tha*: the reli-gious conversion bill; the monogamy bill; and the population control bill. Responding to the Buddhist nationalist organization's petition backed by 1.3 million signatures of Myanmar people, in March 2014 President Thein Sein appointed a special commission to draft the bills on religious conversion and population growth. The Supreme Court of the Union was concurrently given the responsibility of draft-ing the two bills on interfaith marriage and monogamy (Weng 2014). The four bills were drafted and printed for public consultation in the government newspapers in early December 2014. These bills have since been approved by the Myanmar parliament in 2015.

Although the other three bills are new, it must be noted that this campaign by *Ma-Ba-Tha* to ban or make illegal interfaith marriages between non-Buddhist men and Buddhist women is not new. It is just a repetition of that which emerged in the colonial era when Buddhist nationalists made interfaith marriage a very thorny issue and used it to call for separation from India. At that time, after its colonization,

---

[15] This is the English translation of the organization's name given on its official website at www.pam.org.mm. However, the literal translation of its Burmese name, *Amyo Ba-tha Tha-tha-na Ka-kwaè-saung-shauk-ye Apwè* is the 'Organization for the Protection of Race, Religion, and Sāsanā', which clearly shows it is imbued with a defence and security mentality.

Burma was ruled as a province of British India until 1937. Buddhist nationalist elites and politicians popularized the myth of deracination by arguing that, unless Burma was separated from India, the Burmese Buddhist race would be swamped by Indians and disappear from the earth (Chakravarti 1971; Ikeya 2011). A counter-argument could clearly be made that the myth is no longer relevant because Myanmar has been an independent nation since 1948. A colonial-era myth expressed in the metaphor *Mye-myo-ywe Lu-myo-ma-pyôk Lu-myo-hma Lu-myo-pyôk-m*—The Earth Will Not Swallow a Race to Extinction but Another Will!—has been adopted as the official motto by the Ministry of Immigration and Population in Myanmar which was established in 1995 by the State Law and Order Restoration Council. This motto by implication refers to the threat of a takeover by Indians and Muslims and demonstrates how deeply this agenda has penetrated the mainstream as the motto of an official government ministry.

The Organization of the 969 Movement

The 969 movement was only officially launched in October 2012 by a hitherto unknown young monks' association based in Mawlamyine called *Tha-tha-na Pālaka Gaṇavācaka Sangha Apwè* (Defenders of Sāsana and Religious Teachers Network). Its leadership is composed of five monks—Myanan Sayadaw Ashin Thaddhamma, Hitadaya Sayadaw Ashin Wimalar Biwuntha, Ashin Wizza Nanda, Ashin Ganda Thara, and Ashin Pandita. It does not have a chairperson but Ashin Thaddhamma, who designed the 969 emblem, is said to be its secretary (Galache 2013). Apart from those five monks, the movement does not have a clearly visible organizational structure.

Aside from Ashin Wirathu, who still receives both international and local media coverage, the 969 leaders and their activities and sermons have featured little in the media. Further, because of international attention to the notorious 969 tapes and videos, since mid-2013 such materials have become harder to find. For example, 969 video tapes were very visible in the streets of Yangon, Mandalay and other cities and towns across the country between 2012 and mid-2013. But since late 2013 they have become relatively harder to find. This has led some to conclude that the 969 movement is declining or is not as active as before. However, this is not the reality. The 969 movement's head organization, *Tha-tha-na Palaka Gana-wasaka Sangha Apwè*, maintains its own Facebook page, which is updated on an almost daily basis with photographs of 969 leaders' travels to many places as far away as Shan State, Rakhine State, Kachin State, and Yangon, Mandalay and Sagaing Regions. Notably, 969 leaders travel in motorcades guarded from the front and rear by their lay supporters on motorcycles waving Buddhist flags and 969 emblems who are greeted by Buddhists on both sides of the streets. Moreover, the photographs also show that 969 sermons are usually attended by hundreds of lay Buddhists, if not thousands. This is one indication that this movement is not declining at all but growing.

Another noteworthy fact about the 969 organization is that most of its leaders are part of *Ma-Ba-Tha* which has various chapters in cities and towns across the country. It has relied on the extensive *Ma-Ba-Tha* networks afforded by the overlapping executive membership of 969 and *Ma-Ba-Tha*. Amidst heightened questions from the international community and certain sections of Myanmar society who dislike the hate messages being spread by the movement, the supreme *Ma-Ha-Na*, which is authorized to oversee all Sangha bodies in Myanmar, issued an order dated 2 September 2013 and signed by all 47 members of the Committee which banned new monks' associations, including 969. However, the vice-chairperson of the State Sangha Mahanayaka Committee (Yangon Division), Ashin Baddanda Guna Linkara, has admitted that the Committee ideologically agrees with 969's defensive strategy from the Muslim threat and was only unable to provide official approval to the monks' drafting of an anti-interreligious marriage bill (Ferrie and Oo 2013). Therefore, the 969 movement has gained the implicit approval of the State Committee, if not its outright endorsement. It was the second time the State Committee issued an order banning 969, although it was slightly unclear whether the ban was made on 14 or 24 August 2013 (*Associated Press* 2013; May Sitt Paing 2013).

Apart from the supreme *Naing-ngan-to Sangha Maha-nayaka Apwè*, President Thein Sein has repeatedly promised in his monthly speeches that he will not tolerate any form of inflammatory hate speech. However, no concrete action has been taken by him or the cabinet. Although the Speaker of the Pyithu Hluttaw (Lower House), Thura U Shwe Mann, confirmed this view during his trip to the US in June 2013, no action has resulted. Moreover, the Myanmar Ministry of Religious Affairs has only said it would not provide any official recognition to the 969 movement (May Sitt Paing 2013). The only organization that has taken action is *Ma-Ha-Na* which issued the above-mentioned order in an attempt to ban the 969 movement. But the order was only concerned with the official formation of monks-only associations, and so because 969 and *Ma-Ba-Tha* have lay members and are not registered as official organizations, they have evaded the ban. Moreover, at the first anniversary of *Ma-Ba-Tha* held in Yangon on 21 June 2014, Bamaw Sayadaw Ashin Kumara Bhivamsa, the chair of *Ma-Ha-Na*, stated that *Ma-Ha-Na* and *Ma-Ba-Tha* would have to cooperate for Buddhist affairs (Sanay Lin 2014). In other words, *Ma-Ha-Na* recognizes *Ma-Ba-Tha* as a comrade in promotion of Buddhism. Since 969 leaders sit on the executive committee of *Ma-Ba-Tha*, it means they are indirectly recognized and protected by *Naing-ngan-to Sangha Maha-nayaka Apwè*.

Moreover, the 969 leaders have been able to travel freely and widely in Myanmar and give their sermons since March 2014, even in a place like the northern Rakhine State where inter-communal tensions run high. Therefore, even if it cannot be stated without concrete evidence that the 969 movement has enjoyed official patronage from the Union government, it can at least be said that it has been given free rein.

The Popularity of the 969 Stickers

One of the key aspects of the 969 movement has been the distribution of 969 stickers. This raises the question: why have the 969 stickers been so popular in Myanmar? Most media reportage on the 969 movement has portrayed it as an extremist or fundamentalist anti-Muslim movement. Yet the media has also pointed out that this message of hatred has been spread simply by the use of 969 stickers of various sizes and shapes, which can be seen widely across Myanmar. Some news stories on the Meiktila riots also stated that the 969 symbol was sprayed on Muslim properties during the riots. These claims have contributed to the notoriety of the movement in the international community and have effectively led to a singular, limited understanding of the symbol as an anti-Muslim sign. However, portraying it in this way, while partly reasonable and true, has failed to point out some other factors which might have played roles in the popularity of the 969 stickers.

From my own observations growing up in Yangon and visiting other cities, Buddhist homes and shops have always displayed various Buddhist religious photos, artefacts and objects, especially on Buddhist altars, well before the emergence of 969 stickers. For example, in Buddhist homes there are usually photos of famous Buddhist monks and Burmese occult masters or *weikzas*, such as Bo Bo Aung and Bo Min Khaung. Other items that are often found in Buddhist homes include banyan leaves from Bodh Gaya on which Buddha images are usually printed; and bank notes touched by famous monks, such as the late Tharmanya Sayadaw U Vinaya, which are believed to carry virtue or magical powers. A series of paintings which have the slogan: 'May Whoever Happens to Be at This Home/Shop/Car Be Full of Peace and Serenity Since This Home/Shop/Car is under Lord Buddha's Loving Kindness!': appeared in the 2000s, and are very popular. They can be seen hung on the walls of homes and shops and in cars. Displaying such Buddhist photos, objects and artefacts has constituted a core part of Myanmar Buddhist culture, as can be observed by anyone living in or visiting the country. In other words, these objects denote the banality of Myanmar Buddhist culture (Billig 1995). The emblem of the 969 movement, which refers to the Three Gems with the Buddhist flag in the background, has therefore appropriated a wholesome Buddhist symbol that is familiar to Buddhists in Myanmar. Some Buddhists have stated that they keep 969 labels because they believe they bring virtue (*Mizzima News* 2013). The 969 movement identifies with everyday Buddhist symbols and is therefore numerologically and mythically attractive. The 969 sign is therefore an ironic mix of both ordinary Buddhist practise and highly controversial attitudes towards Muslims.

Likewise, even when a Buddhist home or shop displays a 969 sticker, this does not mean that that particular home or shop is an active campaigner or supporter of the movement because, as previously argued, this is part of Myanmar Buddhist culture. Furthermore, even when someone ardently campaigns for or supports the movement, this does not mean that either he or she is violently anti-Muslim. It appears that there are many levels of campaigning, supporting, and implementing the 969 agenda among Myanmar Buddhists; for example, a Buddhist shop with a 969 sticker might have displayed it just to show that it is Buddhist-owned or to compete with nearby Muslims shops in a religious way by encouraging Buddhist buyers who form the majority of Myanmar's population.

Other possible contributing factors in the popularity of 969 stickers in Myanmar include the novelty and colourfulness of the stickers, the aggressive campaigning of the movement's leaders and Ashin Wirathu, and the Myanmar Buddhist backlash against the international community's portrayal of 969 as a violent anti-Muslim movement. The last factor can be clearly supported by the almost country-wide condemnation of the *Time* magazine cover story[16] which portrayed Ashin Wirathu as the face of Buddhist terror. In terms of local reactions, many Buddhists felt insulted by the cover story because it was perceived to denigrate their peaceful Buddhist faith. Accordingly, this story attracted a series of criticisms from a large number of columnists in the Myanmar local media, as well as from the President.

Moreover, not all Buddhists in Myanmar agree with the 969's agenda and campaign, and not all Buddhist homes and shops display its stickers. While local and international journalists must have noticed the highly obvious 969 stickers throughout Myanmar, they might have failed to notice the shops and homes which do not have them. There still exists a majority of Myanmar Buddhists who do not follow the 969 campaign, but it is unclear whether they *silently* approve the message of the 969 campaigners. There is of course a difference between indifference, remaining passive, and actively supporting the movement.

Moreover, the 969 propaganda is conveyed mainly through public Buddhist sermons given in the streets which have been fashionable for almost a decade. This means that even an ordinary Buddhist listener, who has made no judgements about, and has no prejudice against, Muslims is highly likely to be swayed by the sensationalist,

---

[16] The cover story titled 'The Face of Buddhist Terror' by Hanna Beech was featured with a cover photo of Ashin Wirathu in the Europe, Middle East and Africa, Asia, and South Pacific editions of Time (Vol. 182, No. 1) issued on 1 July 2013.

extremist rhetoric of 969 preachers after listening to their sermons. To obtain official permission to hold such sermons in the streets by Buddhist monks is not difficult nowadays, especially for 969 monks. To date, no monks affiliated with the 969 movement have been reportedly denied permission to deliver their sermons. This has added strength to the argument that Myanmar officials have played at least an implicit role in having allowed hate speech to spread across the country, although other factors have played their own roles. The fact that leading 969 preachers were *officially* allowed to give their anti-Muslim sermons at various towns in Rakhine in 2012 and 2013, where Muslim-Buddhist relations were at a record low, shows the partiality of Myanmar authorities who are understandably biased towards the Buddhist majority (Weng 2013).

Asked about the role of 969 in sectarian violence, Myanan Sayadaw Ashin Thaddhamma, a major 969 preacher well-aware of the symbolic way the emblem has been used in sectarian violence, categorically rejected the allegations (Kyaw Phyo Tha 2013). Ashin Thaddhamma was seen to be only self-defensive and evasive, not taking responsibility for the role that the 969 campaign might have played in breeding Islamophobia among Buddhists. While I have demonstrated that the 969 sign is complex and has multiple and at times ambiguous meanings, it is clear that it has played some role in stoking anti-Muslim sentiment and exacerbating the violence that has taken place against Muslims.

* * *

This chapter has argued that the 969 movement and its Islamophobic agenda have fuelled sectarian conflict in Myanmar by reviving, though in a novel way, a siege mentality among Myanmar Buddhists which had its roots in colonial times. By considering the spread of anti-Muslim discourses by 969 monks, this chapter has identified the social and political factors in Myanmar that have allowed the movement to grow.

This chapter has demonstrated that there are a range of explanations for the emergence of the 969 movement, including the recent shift to democratization and the greater political and social freedoms now evident in Myanmar. It has also identified that the message of the 969 movement has created Islamophobia among Myanmar's Buddhists, who have called for immediate action to defend Buddhism and Buddhists in Myanmar. Mythical and numerological bases, coupled with daily Buddhist symbolic practices, have played a role in popularizing the movement. Although the government, and President U Thein Sein in particular, has criticized the actions of the hate-mongers in the aftermath of sectarian conflicts across the country, there has been little or no control or monitoring of the spread of Islamophobic securitization within the country. This failure to act is one of the reasons for its continued growth.

The increasing importance of figures such as Ashin Wirathu in local media and at various Buddhist sermons across the country is another pressing issue and, backed by President Thein Sein's office as a Son of Lord Buddha, his role in Myanmar Buddhist politics is unlikely to decline in the near future. Indeed, we could even argue that this monk's and other 969 propagandists' ubiquity throughout the country is more evidence of the growing influence of the movement. At the same time, the Buddhist majority, which has been largely silent about the 969 campaign, is expected to remain silent partly due to other pressing issues, such as land confiscation, poverty, and the war in Kachin State. This suggests that despite the prohibition on monks being involved in politics officially, their unofficial role in politics in Myanmar is much more concerning. In the absence of a strong response from the government, this has only exacerbated the precarious position of Muslims in Myanmar.

8 New Technologies, Established Practices

Developing Narratives of Muslim Threat in Myanmar

MATT SCHISSLER

During the first week of July 2014, violence between Buddhist and Muslim communities wracked Mandalay, Myanmar's second largest city, leaving two persons—one Buddhist, one Muslim—dead and property belonging to both sides destroyed. '[S]cores of Buddhist men on motorcycles converged on a Muslim neighbourhood in Mandalay brandishing swords, yelling anti-Muslim slogans and ransacking Muslim shops... set off by reports that a Muslim man had raped a Buddhist woman,' opened the coverage by the *New York Times* (Fuller and Moe 2014). 'Facebook Post Stokes Anti-Muslim Violence in Mandalay,' ran the headline for another news story, as it adduced the violence as deriving from the Facebook posts of a leading nationalist monk famous for his virulent anti-Muslim sermons (Mezzofiore 2014). Though not the first such violence in Myanmar, the incident marks the first time violence was explicitly connected to uses of social media. While coverage from other news outlets was slightly more cautious in drawing such causal connections,[1] civil

---

[1] The *New York Times*, for example, noted that Facebook posts about the incident shared by a prominent Buddhist leader, 'appeared to have partly spurred the violence.' See Fuller and Moe 2014.

society, religious leaders, and even Myanmar's central government
seemed to take a similar position, with the latter going so far as to
shut down access to Facebook for two nights because it 'could lead to
a bigger conflict'.[2]

Locating the cause of riotous violence in a social media post can
seem misplaced in a country where only a fraction of the population is
estimated to have access to the Internet.[3] Mobile phones and Internet
access are widespread in Mandalay, but other recent instances of violence have been experienced at times in places in Myanmar where
Internet access has not yet expanded. Since June 2012, large scale
violence has occurred in Rakhine State and central Myanmar, where
140,000 and 3,000 people remain displaced, respectively (UNOCHA
2014; Si Thu Lwin 2014). Smaller scale incidents involving the destruction of mosques, homes, and shops belonging to Muslims have also
occurred in areas as diverse as Shan and Kachin states in northern
Myanmar, the former capital of Yangon, and Bago Region and Kayin
State to the east.

New telecommunications infrastructure is under development,
however, and will soon make mobile phone and Internet access available for the majority of Myanmar's population, along with concomi-
tant media and communication platforms. The pace of this growth
is expected to be rapid, and while it is important to adopt a critical
eye when appraising pronouncements of a future for Myanmar that
is technologically determined,[4] it is also important to consider the

---

[2] Disruptions were quickly noted after the second night of violence (*Eleven
Myanmar* 2014b). Government authorities later confirmed that they were responsible for this disruption (*The Irrawaddy Blog* 2014).

[3] Estimates on the exact percentage of the population that has access to the
Internet vary. In a forum involving government, civil society and technology
companies during July 2014, for example, government attendees estimated
connectivity at less than 5 per cent. Market research companies, meanwhile,
have estimated the number as just 1 per cent, while the Myanmar Computer
Federation estimates 25 per cent of the country is already online. Whatever
the actual percentage is, it is quite low, but changing rapidly. See for example,
We Are Social 2014; *The Star* 2014.

[4] Eric Schmidt, chairperson of Google, for example told a group assembled at the Yangon ICT Park in March 2013 that the country is set to 'leapfrog
20 years of difficult-to-maintain infrastructure and go straight to the most

material effects of these technologies. Scholarship in the field of the history of technology is a persuasive reminder that it *matters* how technologies are able to accomplish particular purposes, both those they are designed for and those unforeseen, processes which interact with and help to constitute politics (Hecht 2001: 267). Thus the adage: '[t]echnology is neither good nor bad; nor is it neutral', and technology may reflect, strengthen, perform, and change existing power relationships (Allen and Hecht 2001: 1, 10).

Significant changes to Myanmar's technological and media environment are underway but still nascent; understanding their emergent interrelationship with Buddhist-Muslim violence is as much an anticipatory concern as it is yet an empirical one. Therefore, in an effort to open the way to further inquiry, this chapter will consider the potential alignments between newly-arriving technologies and those everyday communication practices developed as a part of surviving under, and sometimes contesting, decades of authoritarian rule in Myanmar. This approach is loosely based upon a similar project undertaken by the anthropologists Robin Jeffrey and Assa Doron, who explored the transformations wrought by rapid increase in mobile phone access in India by first asking how ideas and information had been communicated in the past. In doing so, Jeffrey and Doron were able to identify ways in which cheap mobile phones materially disrupted established practices; they then discussed the implications of these disruptions for gender and social relations as well as overtly political undertakings such as election campaigning (Jeffrey and Doron 2012; 2013).

What, then, are established communication practices in Myanmar that might be disrupted—or align particularly powerfully—with the growing use of new technologies and media that will arrive along with telecommunications infrastructure? In order to illustrate potential interactions between these established practices and new technologies, and consider their potential relationships to anti-Muslim antagonism and violence like that experienced in

---

modern... We have a chance to see how a new nation can shape itself, not just its own destiny, but also its relationships with neighbours, its economic growth and what I believe will be its extremely rapid social development.' See Schmidt 2013.

Mandalay, this chapter will make use of existing anthropological literature as well as my own experiences living in a working class neighbourhood along the Yangon River. Although this was not a pre-meditated ethnographic undertaking, while actively participating in a variety of civil society initiatives that seek to, *inter alia*, promote peace and prevent Buddhist-Muslim conflicts, I began employing a methodological approach of 'observant participation' (Vargas 2008: 165) in line with what some have described as an 'activist' or 'engaged' scholarship (Hale and Calhoun 2008). Wherever possible, observations discussed below are selected from those already published in occasional posts to a popular blog.[5] While other reflections will also be included, those experiences already subjected to online discussion, debate, and re-interpretation are particularly well suited for a chapter concerned with the circulation of discourses on social media.

New Technologies

During the year 2012, when I first moved into western Yangon, only one friend in my ward had a mobile phone; within less than two years, nearly all of them did. This is an experience in the country's urban centre, but it is being replicated nationwide. Myanmar's erstwhile state monopoly over telecommunications is breaking up and mobile phones, once available to only the handful that could afford expensive SIM cards, are becoming more common. In 2013, an estimated less than four per cent of the population had mobile phones, though government statistics claimed 10 per cent—still the lowest penetration rate of any country in Asia save for North Korea (Ferrie 2013). In early 2014, two international telecoms companies, Ooredoo and Telenor, received operating licenses to establish new infrastructure across Myanmar; Ooredoo's publicly stated target is to extend coverage to 97 per cent of the population within five years (*Reuters* 2014). Telenor's goal is 90 per cent (Srisamorn 2014). The target set by U Thein Sein,

---

[5] The posts were first shared on Facebook, and then kindly published by *New Mandala*, a Southeast Asia focused blog affiliated with the Australian National University. See http://asiapacific.anu.edu.au/newmandala/author/matt/.

Myanmar's President, is slightly more modest: 80 per cent of the population by 2016 (*Eleven Myanmar* 2014a).

In 2014, meanwhile, the costs of mobile phones and tablets that can handle basic Internet functions are dropping precipitously. Myanmar's regional neighbours are useful indicators in this respect and, where they have seen increased mobile access, that now also entails access to the Internet (We Are Social 2014). Elsewhere in the region, too, Internet access has meant large percentages of the population using social media such as Facebook and Twitter. A journalist commenting on recent data about the use of social media in Asia perhaps put it best: Facebook is not a website visited by Internet users, 'Facebook *is* the Internet' (Russell 2014, emphasis added). This is likely to hold true in Myanmar, with social media not as one website among many but as the dominant platform by which people make their way online.

In Myanmar, social media is already extremely popular. One regional marketing company, for example, identifies 1,240,000 Facebook users in the country (We Are Social 2014: 132). If the current estimate that approximately one per cent of the population has access to the Internet is accurate, this would represent more than two Facebook accounts for every Internet user in Myanmar. The messaging application known as Viber, meanwhile, boasts an even wider user base in Myanmar at five million users (Millward 2014). Underscoring the popularity of social media, Facebook is already used as a communication platform for government leaders and politicians, civil society, the private sector, and journalists. Government departments including the office of Myanmar's President regularly issue information and statements via Facebook. The President's spokesperson is known as the 'Facebook Minister,' for example, and winners of bids for offshore oil and gas concessions were recently announced by a ministerial Facebook status update. It is no wonder then that Myanmar journalists often scoop stories by trawling their newsfeeds.

Even Myanmar's monastic community, which lives an otherwise ascetic life, uses social media to access and disseminate information. At an event I attended to discuss harmony between religious communities, for example, a Buddhist leader criticized American diplomats in attendance for bias in their criticisms regarding religious violence. 'I also follow the US Embassy Facebook page,' the monk said to those assembled. 'One month ago, the US embassy issued the statement regarding the attack on a mosque, without confirming the information. But I was very sorry not to see a statement issued regarding the attack on a very dutiful soldier in Rakhine State' (Schissler 2014a). A few chairs to his left sat U Wirathu, the religious leader whose Facebook posts have been credited with sparking the riots in Mandalay during July. In March 2014, U Wirathu had 29,958 followers on Facebook and was leading 'media trainings' to instruct attendees in how to use social media (Long 2014).

There are perhaps deceptively simple technological reasons for why Facebook may become particularly popular in Myanmar, unlike in China with its diversity of social media platforms (Fong 2012). Facebook can be installed on phones and tablets by users and phone shops, to be easily mastered by people not otherwise familiar with using the Internet to search for news and information. In a country where the speed of Internet connectivity can be infuriatingly slow, the standalone Facebook apps on mobile devices will often load when other sites will not. Perhaps most important for Burmese language users, it is relatively easy to use and read Burmese script on Facebook, an issue that has long plagued users of SMS messaging, email, and even word processing software. Twitter, conversely, does not lend itself as well to use in Myanmar language, at least at the present moment. Those who have experienced the frustration of waiting for an Internet page to load in Myanmar, or the bewildering helplessness of trying to read a Burmese language page or document without Unicode or the correct fonts installed,[6] will know these are sufficiently compelling technological factors to determine choice of platform. These issues are being rapidly addressed, but it may not matter; if Facebook is already the platform where all your friends are, it is reasonable to assume that you, too, will join them there. Even more so if the company pursues special arrangements with mobile network providers to enable users to access Facebook without incurring any extra charges or requiring a data plan, as it has in other emerging markets (Deibert 2013).

---

[6] The process of making the Myanmar alphabet legible electronically has been an inconsistent one, and as of 2014 the majority of users continued to use font-based approaches rather than Unicode, creating a mishmash of legibility that technology companies have yet to resolve.

At the same time, care should be taken not to over-centralize analysis on any one platform. Facebook may decline in popularity, as some have recently predicted (Cannarella and Spechler 2014), and other applications will grow in popularity. Facebook and Viber are two units of analysis salient in the present moment, but the concerns of this chapter will be relevant for other platforms were they popular instead, or when they become so. It is, ultimately, important to approach the concept of 'technology' without prefiguring those considered to be most important (for example, 'social media'). The reality invariably will be one in which multiple technologies are interacting with one another and with the existing social and power relations that they are simultaneously helping to re-shape (Sterne 2003). Myanmar's telecommunications infrastructure is growing and this will introduce mobile phones, Internet access, and a host of applications and media sources not previously encountered by most people in the country, along with other important changes such as expansion of roads and electrification that are necessary to power and maintain a new grid. This will be happening at the same moment that Myanmar's economy is opening up to globalization and people will be making use of a host of other material objects and technologies not previously encountered widely.

Established Practices

This section will explore two long-established communication practices in Myanmar—rumours and the maintenance of plausible deniability—and their potential to align or be disrupted by new technologies and media. These are two strategies that contribute to managing risks, constructing communities, and accessing and disseminating information. This is not to drape over these strategies an ascribed functionality or, on the other hand, assume wholly autonomous agency for those employing them. But these strategies cannot be reduced to mechanical reactions, thoughtless reflexes, or the product of ignorance and low levels of formal education, though Myanmar's national education system is in disarray. Instead, this section will examine them as *habitus*, Bourdieu's formulation for history turned into nature, those practices that are both spontaneous, in that they are the immediate product of individual choices, and non-spontaneous, in that they are always rooted in those past conditions and structures that guide social action (Bourdieu 1995). *Habitus* is a useful heuristic for considering communication practices in Myanmar because it emphasizes that they are techniques of the body that both dictate, and may be altered by, uses of new technologies (Sterne 2003: 380). 'The "book" from which children learn their vision of the world is read with the body,' Bourdieu notes (Bourdieu 1995: 90), just as, in updated form, there is always a person whose fingers are tapping on a tablet or a keyboard (Sterne 2003: 381).

The first potential alignment between existing practices and new communications technologies was reaffirmed for me in discussions following a presentation of some of the early thoughts that motivated this chapter, at a January 2014 conference hosted by the National University of Singapore (NUS). 'Don't you think you may be overplaying this whole Facebook thing? I would not expect it to become a form of vernacular media,' a participant with a research focus on South Asia asked following my presentation. 'In Pakistan, social media is the least popular method. It is mass SMS messaging that is used to share information'. As we continued this discussion over the lunch break, the Myanmar heads around the table shook vigorously. 'Nobody will use mass SMS messaging in Myanmar,' another participant, a Muslim woman who lives in Yangon, told our colleague. 'People are afraid to receive such messages, because they could be punished. But it is no crime to log into Facebook. You are simply scrolling down the page, and you see what other people share'.

To note that logging into Facebook is no crime is an example of new technology aligning with older practices that are deeply embedded within Myanmar. Information on social media platforms can be consumed by individuals who, though they have held the information in their hand, never have to lay claim to it as such. My Myanmar colleague at NUS was thus indirectly invoking Goffman's framework for ratified and unratified participants in an exchange—those who are addressed and drawn in to communicating and those who remain outside yet listen in (Goffman 1981: 131–2). Applied to social media in Myanmar, this would mean that one may access information while maintaining the plausible deniability of a bystander, one who overhears communication but is not involved and thus not at risk. On social media this distance may be maintained while the message is nonetheless held close and engaged, with an intimacy and freedom to extend the encounter that is unavailable to a bystander who must position their body close enough to hear and, eventually, decide if they will risk entering into the exchange. It is understandable that SMS messages might be seen as the opposite given that the recipient is addressed directly, their participation ratified—an intimate encounter with information that risks culpability should the exchange face sanction later.

One may strengthen plausible deniability further by using fake identities online. Where companies such as Facebook officially seek to require the use of real names, this is only of limited distinguishing value, given that people in Myanmar rarely use surnames. Even for those whose social media identities correspond to real identities, one need only scroll down a page where others are sharing potentially illicit information. Others who are willing to share such information and take the risks, do so, or do so with an account that is unattached to any traceable identity. If sharing objectionable material is a crime, it is the crime of the original poster, not the user who scrolls by. This is a new version of the aphorism related by Christina Fink in *Living Silence*, her 2001 book about everyday life during military rule: 'We have no mouths, only ears' (Fink 2001: 128).[7]

Maintaining plausible deniability was then a mechanism for containing and controlling risk; with this maintained, one could push the boundaries of safety and acceptability. Fink describes, for example, a strategy used during the 1980s in which student activists used seemingly innocuous book sharing networks to establish precarious, but no less important, feelings of collective solidarity. After finishing a given text, the reader would add a short comment and the name of their hometown, and then pass on the book. 'For those who had developed political ideas,' noted Fink, 'knowing they had similarly-minded peers in other parts of the country was very important. They often felt isolated among their own schoolmates'. One could glance over the geography of previous readers to feel the presence of a community; but one needed not take risks to do so, beyond possessing a piece of nondescript literature (Fink 2001: 184). In another more overtly

---

7 For an updated look at the uses of plausible deniability by social activists, see Prasse-Freeman 2012: 388.

political strategy, students distributed pamphlets by placing them in stacks on the top of buses, to be scattered as the vehicles pulled away (Fink 2001: 188). Sharing pamphlets is the crime of the distributor, not the bystander who stoops to pick up an unknown piece of paper. Bystanders may briefly read the message and maintain positioning as unratified and inculpable, unless and until they decide to pocket the message and declare their involvement in the exchange. The same pamphlet may be encountered on Facebook and consumed at leisure, the phone or tablet pocketed without any analogous declaration.

The second established practice that is likely to align with newly-arriving communication technology is the long-standing salience of rumour in Myanmar, as a way to convey information word-of-mouth, outside of formal media or any organized authority.[8] Anointing this the 'dominant form of discourse' during life under authoritarian rule, Monique Skidmore described rumour as a way to build community and a sense of intimacy, and a way to provide clarity and make sense of a world that could otherwise seem unintelligible and opaque (Skidmore 2003: 13; 2004: 45). Rumour could also enable decision-making under difficult circumstances. 'Rumours are extremely important,' Skidmore noted, 'because they are one of the few forms of mundane information that allow individuals and families to speculate on outcomes, to gamble on courses of action, to assess options, and to weigh probabilities' (Skidmore 2003: 13).[9] It is no wonder, given long-standing media censorship and state propaganda, that people in Myanmar developed such alternative approaches for transmitting and sharing information.[10]

This latter use of rumour has been particularly evident to me at tense and bewildering moments. On 20 March 2013, for example, a mob of an estimated 1,000 people rampaged through the Muslim areas of Meiktila, a town in central Myanmar. Later, we would learn

[8] This draws upon a definition of rumour offered by Pamela Donovan, which she contrasts against legends, myths, gossip, hoaxes and conspiracy theories: see Donovan 2007.

[9] See also Leehey 2010: 27.

[10] This is consistent with one of the most common explanations for why rumours spread and are relied upon, though this is not the only reason: see Donovan 2007.

that at least 44 people had been killed, including some 20 children massacred in a school (Physicians for Human Rights 2013a), more than 10,000 people displaced,[11] and 800 buildings razed (Human Rights Watch 2013a). In the days after, smaller instances of violence occurred in other areas of Myanmar (Phelan 2013). As violence seemed to be spreading to other areas beyond Meiktila, the feeling of tension in my neighbourhood was palpable. That night, questions about violence had a visceral urgency: Were there really riots in other parts of Yangon, as we had heard? Were homes being looted in the southern end of our township, at that very moment? As my neighbours and I stood on the street and discussed these things that night, we had agreed to watch and listen and warn each other if needed. I had shared information from a news story just published that evening, saying that rumours of riots in the other townships were spreading, but untrue. How, though, could one really know, and plan appropriately? The news media was unreliable, referencing a government source would prompt derisive laughter; accessing dependable information was difficult. What sources could be trusted? We had all felt more secure when an auntie on our block announced that she had spoken with people in the area in question. 'I called my friend who works in the market there,' the auntie told us. 'She closed her shop but she said there is no fighting' (Schissler 2013a).

The above analysis highlights the everyday practices of collecting information and of piecing together those available sources and things said or unsaid to construct an intelligible whole. Most illustrative of this are the regular interactions at the steps of my building, with neighbours and friends selling fruit and other wares from street stands there. These conversations about quotidian topics are also exercises in sharing information and talking over the news, international and local, from sources accessed online, on the radio and in print journals, and shared, re-shared, and discussed throughout the day (Schissler 2013c). All people do this of course, but there is an important corollary to rumour as the dominant form of discourse: people with decades of experience using rumour to manage life and maintain community in an environment of restricted information are perhaps *more* adept at gathering such collections

---

[11] A year later, more than 3,300 remained displaced. See Si Thu Lwin 2014.

and producing narratives than people accustomed to living with free media and without censorship. In the context of literature produced within this milieu, Jennifer Leehey has amply illustrated the skill required to both produce and interpret texts created in light of these constrictions (Leehey 2010). Broadly applied, James Scott's concept of *metis* provides the vocabulary for identifying the practical skills and acquired intelligence inherent in such communication strategies (Scott 1998: 313).

This last recognition is important, finally, because *metis* complicates the assumption underlying explanations like those given for the July riots in Mandalay, where it was said that an untrue rumour spread on Facebook and so incensed the city that a riot spontaneously burst forth. This is an assumption about society in Myanmar as credulous to the point of gullibility and thus ripe to be misled by rumours, spread with new technologies. There are certainly people in Myanmar who fit this description, as there are in any place, but identifying existing communication practices highlights that a more careful consideration of the uses of new technologies will be necessary. On the night of violence in Meiktila, for example, my friends and I stood on our corner discussing rumours of riots in other parts of Yangon. 'Did you check on the Internet? I heard they are fighting in Mingalataungnyunt [eastern Yangon]. Is it true?' a friend had asked me. As we discussed this rumour we considered what might be happening, sifting through the information we had available; hearsay, a media report, Facebook, and then, finally, a mobile phone call to the ostensibly afflicted location (Schissler 2013a). For me, the experience drove home what it is to function in an environment of limited and unreliable information. My friends handled it with the implicit skill, *metis*, that comes from regular practice.

Developing Narratives of Muslim Threat

To say that telecommunications infrastructure will bring new forms of media and they will become widely used in Myanmar is not controversial; it is already happening, as the high profile examples of government agencies, politicians, and religious leaders using Facebook demonstrate. But these illustrate social media as an alternative publishing platform for those in positions of authority, both within the state and without. The above discussion of established communication practices is important because it highlights how these new technologies are likely to be used by millions of ordinary people in Myanmar, as they engage the everyday processes of exchanging pieces of information and assembling and reassembling these into intelligible pictures of the world. If people incorporate new technologies into their everyday processes of communication and information gathering, what, if anything, will change? Jeffrey and Doron emphasize this as a matter of new possibilities: 'The new tool accords the possibility of... sav[ing] money independently of a spendthrift husband, infect[ing] others with commitment to a cause, or communicat[ing] with a sweetheart without approval of the family.' It was the cumulative effect of these changed dynamics that they found to have had deep reverberations across Indian society (Jeffrey and Doron 2013: 11, 14).

When the goal is to understand the development of violence and Buddhist-Muslim antagonism, however, it will not be sufficient to search for the *effects* of new technologies, for this would presume their centrality. In his exploration of the relationship between growths in televised media and Hindu nationalism in India, Arvind Rajagopal highlights the importance of instead considering the interrelationship between possibilities attendant to new media technology and the particularities of a given historical moment. In India, new possibilities created by growth in print media and audio-visual broadcasting did not *cause* Hindu nationalism, but neither could nationalism be understood without considering the new technology (Rajagopal 2001). In Myanmar, it can be similarly said that political contests and conflicts will unfold in light of what newly arriving technologies make possible. This could be said of most new communication technologies in most places most of the time, but exploring existing communication practices helps to highlight why it may be significant in Myanmar: new technologies likely to reshape the everyday production of narratives are arriving at precisely a moment when narratives about the country, its past, and its future are being wrenched open and contested with new force and possibility.

After more than sixty years of military rule, Myanmar is at the final stage of a seven-step 'roadmap to Discipline Flourishing Democracy,' which has featured a shift to law-making in parliament and the release of political prisoners, ceasefire negotiations with ethnic armed groups, reduction of pre-publication censorship, and the lifting of bans on public assembly, unions and political organizing. These changes have been hailed as the country's 'perestroika' and a 'Burma spring' (Selth 2011; Della-Giacoma 2011), and bring with them fraught contests for power between a military that is ostensibly retreating to its barracks yet backing a ruling party, and an opposition that is both fractured and led by a national icon and Nobel prize-winner Daw Aung San Suu Kyi. In an email missive circulating among political activists in early 2014, a friend characterized this as two bulls racing towards each other on a field; I share this vision, playing out on a field being experienced in daily life as a dissolution in the markers of certainty (Lefort 1988: 19). These changes have also enabled western countries to remove or weaken economic sanctions, a process that, along with domestic economic reforms, has touched off an intensified re-engagement with global flows of capital and culture. Telecommunications infrastructure is thus both a metaphor for the country's re-encounter with globalization and part of the material process by which it is becoming possible.

The state and society in Myanmar will be experiencing a media and technology upheaval at the same time they are, with an unusual lateness, encountering the fullness of contemporary globalization with which societies throughout the rest of the world have been contending for decades. Coca-Cola for example, an oft used marker for the spread of global capital and culture (Foster 2008; Lowe 2012), ended its 60-year absence from Myanmar in 2012, leaving North Korea and Cuba as the only remaining markets in which Coke is not officially sold (Jordan 2012). This encounter is bringing long-absent investment capital and development activity. But, in a place with an established cadre of crony capitalists and a state that rationalizes use of force more than it regulates, it is also opening the way for extraction of natural resources and expropriation of land that is leaving most of the country far behind.

Consideration of the developing conflicts between Buddhist and Muslim communities in Myanmar must take these broader issues into account. It is not sufficient to locate inquiry exclusively in the history of relations between communities or the individual antagonisms within the hearts of people in Myanmar, just as it is not sufficient to seek out effects caused by new technologies and media. Arjun

Appadurai, for example, has argued that the encounter with globalization generates a sense of social uncertainty that undergirds collectivized violence. Appadurai sought to understand the regularity of mass violence against civilians during the 1990s, identifying it as produced by the loss of national economic sovereignty inherent in the logic of globalization, a loss that is simultaneously a challenge to the conviction that national identity will remain fixed and permanent so long as its geographic boundaries are defended. In such contexts, exclusion and violence against minorities are not spontaneous outbursts but projects that create the 'macabre form of certainty' needed to restore majority identities that have been made newly vulnerable (Appadurai 2006: 5–7).

The point is not to argue that Myanmar's re-encounters with democracy or globalization make violence inevitable. Indeed this would be too similar to those problematic interpretations of Buddhist-Muslim violence as tragic growing pain and the inevitable dark side of new freedoms, political conflict, or a weak state. Quite the opposite: 'These account only for the characters,' Appadurai notes. 'We need to look elsewhere for the plot. And the plot—worldwide in its force—is a product of the justified fear that the real world game has escaped the net of state sovereignty and interstate diplomacy' (Appadurai 2006, 43). Appadurai's theatre metaphor is similar to one employed by Paul Brass, whose study of Hindu-Muslim violence in north India is also instructive (Brass 1997; 2003). For both Brass and Appadurai, violence is a production that must be mobilized, contingent on the construction of ideological scripts of fear and antagonism. These are not 'age old hatreds,' though they are historically situated, but narratives that are promoted by organized political forces.

This script for fear and antagonism is evident in Myanmar. 'Fear is not just on the side of the Muslims, but on the side of the Buddhists as well,' Daw Aung San Suu Kyi told the BBC during an October 2013 interview. 'There's a perception that Muslim power, global Muslim power, is very great' (*BBC News* 2013). She was pilloried for this interview,[12] but her description was important for

---

[12] David Blair of the Telegraph (UK), for example, called her remarks 'deeply disturbing' and went on to mock the idea that a Buddhist majority could fear a Muslim minority. See Blair 2013.

it summarized a fear that is being mobilized, and located it as both surrounding Myanmar's borders and embodied in a domestic minority. Organized political forces calling for the protection of 'race and religion'[13] have gained increasing prominence as they have identified Islam as an existential threat to Buddhist nationhood, and Muslims within Myanmar as the vanguard. These groupings have undertaken popular national campaigns calling for the boycott of Muslim-owned businesses, passage of national laws restricting inter-faith marriage, and the restriction of citizenship for Muslims (see Nyi Nyi Kyaw, this volume). Though at times seeking to position themselves as officially non-partisan, they have nonetheless received public support from a wide array of public and political figures, government officials, the state body that oversees Myanmar's monastic order, and some members of ethnic armed groups.

The most virulent examples of this discourse have attracted international attention, such as the rhetoric of U Wirathu, the Buddhist leader whose posts were credited with sparking the July riots in Mandalay and whom a Time Magazine cover story had earlier branded the 'Face of Buddhist Terror' (Beech 2013). But a narrative of global threat must be given certitude through circulation and interaction in everyday life. Propaganda and organized campaigning are necessary but not sufficient; they also rely on what Appadurai calls 'little stories,' those individual pieces of information and quotidian conflicts that are both interpreted in light of the larger script and fixed within it as the illustrations that imbue it with personalized meaning (Appadurai 2006, 91).

The relationship between narratives deployed by organized political forces and circulation in everyday life has become particularly apparent to me over the last two years, as I have spent evenings sitting on the street corners in my ward, eating, drinking rough tea or beer, and discussing a variety of issues. I have similar discussions in the neighbourhood teashops, where I sit nearly every morning, and in other regular interactions with friends and neighbours. My friends in

---

[13] These include the '969' movement, named for Buddhist numerology; the 'Organisation for the Protection of Race and Religion', often referenced by its Myanmar language abbreviation 'Ma Ba Tha;' and a handful of nationalist youth organizations.

the neighbourhood are electricians, carpenters, trishaw or van-for-hire drivers (not owners), wage labourers, and seamen on container ships. Religion, politics, and history are not uncommon topics, though as the tension in the overall milieu has increased I have become more cautious about the friendly debates over Buddhist-Muslim relations in which I once participated.

In these conversations, I have noted a variety of discourses that repeat and illustrate misperceptions about Islam and fear of—and antagonism towards—Muslim communities. The first time Islam arose as a topic, a friend told me that the symbol '786', which is often displayed at Muslim-owned businesses, meant that Islam would take over the world in the twenty-first century, 'because seven plus eight plus six equals twenty-one'. Such claims are repetitions of those made by nationalist leaders, which combine to envision Myanmar as the final missing link in a contiguous chain of Muslim countries that have been steadily expanding from northern Africa to Mindanao. 'Look at Indonesia,' I am implored to remember. 'It used to be a Buddhist country, now it isn't' (Schissler 2013b). The invasion described is one of population growth, creeping in from Malaysia and Bangladesh and with Muslim men given rewards for marrying and converting Buddhist women and incentives for having large families.

'My father is Buddhist but my mother is Christian. If my father was Muslim, this could not be,' another friend explained as we debated the credibility of these threats. But there is a slippage between the abstract and historical and those 'little stories' that are personalized and local. Forced conversions are a tragedy that is described as happening to specific Buddhist women in specific places, nearby; actual Muslim families with multiple children are pointed out as proof of looming population growth. Anecdotes of revulsion at butchering during Eid al-Adha are used to demonstrate a tendency towards violence inherent in Islam, while Muslim prosperity is highlighted to illustrate ascendant Muslim dominance within Myanmar. Many Muslim families are poor, but many others are involved in aspects of the economy that are highly visible; construction companies, import-export businesses, sites of wealth which one may encounter on an everyday basis. Personal experiences of disrespect in a place of work similarly confirm individual qua collective victimization. 'On my ship, the Muslim seaman rudely threw away my pork curry before I had finished it,' another friend recounted to me, an experience that would have represented an additionally powerful attack had the tanker been Muslim-owned (Schissler 2013a).

Disruptions and Possibilities

Understanding the production of Buddhist-Muslim antagonism in Myanmar will thus require seeking to discover if and how new technologies are re-shaping both the efforts of organized political forces to produce narratives of fear and antagonism, and the circulation of those 'small stories' that repeat and illustrate them. In Myanmar, new technologies and media are only just arriving and, as such, disruptions and possibilities are only just emerging. This chapter has argued that new technologies will be actively used as a part of narrative production, as people collect and share the news and information that is used to make sense of an uncertain world. Before closing, this chapter will consider some of the ways that new technologies have already begun to be involved in narrative production in Yangon.

These closing observations are not meant to be a comprehensive explication of the ways that new technologies are or may become significant, just as the point of the preceding section was not to extrapolate conclusions regarding currents in national opinion. This chapter is, after all, drawing primarily from experiences in just one neighbourhood in one city in Myanmar. Instead, this chapter will close with examples that are sufficient to illustrate connections between those organized efforts to call forth scripts of anti-Muslim fear and antagonism, their reinforcement through repetition and illustration in everyday discourse, and potential disruptions and possibilities attendant to new technologies and media.

Telecommunications infrastructure will offer materially effective tools for gathering the constituent pieces that combine into narratives about the world. These networks will bring James Scott's distance-demolishing technologies (Scott 2009), with the potential to stretch communication across geographic space, as with the auntie who called another part of the city to confirm news about rumoured riots; she had only purchased her mobile phone a few months earlier. SMS messaging and Viber will assist with this. Social media can demolish distance as well. Some would expect communication with new technologies such as social media to be primarily phatic (Miller 2008; Leibold 2011). But much of everyday conversation is phatic, and yet important feelings and information are conveyed; the same can be said of communication with new technologies. Rumour and information gathering as *habitus* also explains why it is reasonable to anticipate that new technologies will be incorporated into these existing practices: as the residuals of those sedimented histories that combine to produce a practice persist, so should the practice.

Simultaneously, uses of new technologies will assist with the restructuring of *habitus* (Bourdieu 1995: 78). The regularity of communication on Viber and with Facebook may, for example, enable individuals to push boundaries and establish that previously verboten activities are possible without fear of sanction. My Myanmar interlocutors at the NUS cafeteria table may, then, come to be incorrect; as the necessity of plausible deniability for surviving under a capricious regime is experienced as less necessary, use of direct messaging via SMS or platforms like Viber may increase. Conversely, as these platforms are used they may assist with reducing the felt need for plausible deniability. There is a kind of exhilaration that accompanies the act of sharing when such acts were previously proscribed. This feeling can become a sense of obligation or responsibility when the information shared is a warning, such as a call for defending nation and religion against an existential threat.

To the extent that people employ new technologies for the everyday act of sharing information, these technologies may strengthen the persuasive power of the individual pieces of information that are exchanged. Information sourced from friends and family is often stamped with an implicit imprimatur of truth, whether it is rumour or whether it is news. News stories and state propaganda may still be beyond credulity, but they gain credibility when re-transmitted by friends and family. Social media can both supplement and simulate the inter-personal practice of collecting information, an online mechanism for sharing and accessing information word-of-mouth, tap-by-tap. On Facebook, one interacts with 'friends,' after all, who make comments and post links. The latest incarnation of Facebook adds to this still, by aggregating posts by 'friends' discussing the same topic. Information gains credibility through repetition (Begg et al. 1992). In real life this can take time, and time can serve as a diluent. With new technologies, repetition can happen with new reach, pace, and regularity (Osborn 2008).

New technologies also reinforce the in-built credibility of word-of-mouth information with videos, photographs, and links to other information sources. Earlier in the day after the violence in Meiktila, for example, a friend had emailed me a Facebook link to a grainy video of men with automatic weapons and faces masked by scarves, accompanied by a Burmese-language audio track threatening revenge for violence against Muslims. 'The Muslims are going to be really angry now,' he had said as he called to make sure I had seen the video. 'I just want to let you know to please be careful'. The video was clearly a fake, and in a Facebook post a few days later I wondered why it had been taken seriously in spite of its conspicuous dubbing and low quality (Schissler 2013a).

At other times, I have had real-life debates about the likely veracity of such videos, often with neighbourhood friends that share my scepticism but nonetheless feel compelled by the emotional pull of the footage. In May 2013 a video was making the rounds, purporting to be of a Buddhist beheaded by Muslim extremists in southern Thailand. 'I don't know if the person in the video is really Buddhist or not. But I saw it and when I see things like that, I feel it,' a neighbourhood friend told me as we had discussed the video on the corner one afternoon, motioning a punch as he spoke. Later, after anti-Muslim riots in Lashio were said to have resulted from rumours of violence against a Buddhist woman by a Muslim man, we had agreed to be cautious about what to believe and not to spread misinformation. 'If I don't see it with my own eyes,' he had said, 'I won't do anything'. A few minutes earlier, another of the friends sitting with us had been earnestly attesting to the reliability of a video showing a monk killed in Meiktila. 'Do you want to watch it? I have it on my phone,' he told me. 'Everyone does' (Schissler 2013b).

It would be easy to explain the pull my friends identified in these videos as the product of low education levels or the nascent familiarity audiences in Myanmar have with parsing multi-media content. Surely, a population that has not had ready access to such media will find it particularly compelling. There *is* something additionally persuasive about information conveyed via multimedia—but this is true for all audiences, not just those in Myanmar. In my own political context in the US, for example, the moving pictures and inflammatory language of televised political attack ads help decide elections. Perhaps that is the point: Myanmar audiences will now be encountering those visual presentations of information and ideas that are powerful for audiences the world over.

The above analysis indicates that new technologies will enable information and ideas to be shared and narratives developed across distances, at greater speeds, and with new credibility and persuasive power. These possibilities are inherent in new technologies, but to focus on them exclusively is to assume a kind of false consciousness for people in Myanmar in which Buddhist-Muslim conflicts are primarily a function of 'untrue' information made newly available and accepted. This is, after all, the premise underlying the government's decision to temporarily restrict access to Facebook after the Mandalay riots. But considering new technologies in light of the production of broad scripts of Muslim threat makes clear the radical insufficiency of focusing on individual little stories, because it is not their discrete presence or absence that completes or alters the script. On reflection, it is not likely that my friend felt compelled to email me and then follow up with a phone call because the grainy video he had shared was dispositive evidence of an imminent threat. It need not be; the virtual terrorist figures it presented were a synecdoche for a threat already established and located in Muslim bodies throughout Myanmar. That the faces of the figures were masked and bereft of any visual connection to the disembodied Burmese language dialogue dubbed over the video is a kind of confirmation that the particular fact of their bodies did not matter, only the threat that they signified.

I have certainly learned this during neighbourhood conversations, where early on I had to take care in contesting the veracity of individual stories. At first, this decision was a practical one: my language skills could only reach so far into a nuanced discussion of information sources. Such discussions also always risked dead-ending with reference to another source who was an eye-witness, at which point I would need to accept the story or find myself in the uncomfortable position of impugning the word of a friend or family member of a friend. Over time, however, it became clear that the individual stories were not the crux of the matter; it was their aggregate power that proved larger points about Islam and Buddhist-Muslim relations. Indeed some of the information was true, discussed on our corners and referenced on Facebook. By all accounts, a monk *was* killed in Meiktila. The video shared phone-to-phone by my friends was compelling, but it was no more untrue rumour than the news from Muslim countries that I see regularly discussed in Burmese on Facebook. Atrocities by ISIS in Syria and Iraq; abductions and murders committed by Boko Haram; violence in the Central African Republic; these are just news stories, neither falsity nor the virulent hate speech that attracts international media attention—but they nonetheless support a presentation of Islam as violent and threatening (Schissler 2014b).

Like the video of anonymous masked men, news stories about violence and Islam reinforce the larger script of Buddhism under threat. These connections are made by organized political forces and in everyday conversations but, once established, the connection no longer need be explicitly invoked. Such stories, on my Facebook news-feed and in my ward, are merged into a sonic background in which their recurrence is significant not for their detail but for their tonal consistency. As a daily occurrence, such stories become a mnemonic recitation that confirms both the existence of the threat as perceived and, also, of the community of perceivers. Just as the terrorist figure in the video is synecdoche for threatening Muslim bodies in Myanmar, the individual who repeats the story is synecdoche for a nationalist movement qua nation that shares the same concern. Posts on social media are mnemonic insofar as, encountered in their frequency, they are a persistent reminder of the membership and vigilance of a community that shares this perception of threat, just as this is confirmed in the regular encounter with iconography of nationalist organizations or in the nodding of heads at sermons, public talks, or around the teashop table. Bystanders that encounter these mnemonics are thusly reminded not just of the plot, but of their simultaneous smallness and role within something larger.

As telecommunications infrastructure arrives, people in Myanmar will be encountering ideas and information in new ways and more often. They will be able to participate in these encounters, shaping, sharing and repeating them, and it will all be faster and reach further than ever before. *Habitus* formed out of decades of life under authoritarian rule will change. This chapter, however, helps clarify future research necessary for understanding inter-relationships between new technologies and production of Buddhist-Muslim violence and antagonisms throughout Myanmar. That is, future inquiry will need to consider not just the effects of technology and media on the ways people encounter news and information, but whether and how new subjectivities—individual and collective—are emerging that would not or could not have emerged in their absence; are new media technologies significant as a matter of convenience, as James Holston has put it, or something else (Holston 2014: 899)? Even without new technologies, for example, it is possible for people in Myanmar to encounter news and information about the apocryphal threats Buddhism faces from Islam, as is made clear by the occurrence of violence in places and at times that predate the expansion of telecommunications infrastructure. But as the above discussion begins to indicate, the introduction of new technologies is entailing profound changes that matter not just for their functional effects but also affect, imbricated in the everyday ways people in Myanmar are seeking to navigate an uncertain re-encounter with globalization and democratic politics. Consideration of new possibilities attendant to telecommunications infrastructure, then, will need to look beyond simply those acts that become possible, and ask what, if anything, is changing in both the ways that people develop the narratives that organize their worlds, and in the content of the narratives themselves. Technologies matter, as Hecht says; will the production of Buddhist-Muslim violence be any different?

9 Making the Muslim Other in Myanmar and Sri Lanka

Benjamin Schonthal

In June 2014, an idyllic and normally peaceful resort district on the southwest coast of Sri Lanka became the site of violence between local Muslim communities and mobs claiming to act in defence of Buddhism. Observers disagreed about the proximate cause of the violence. Some Buddhists pointed to popular anger over an alleged assault by three Muslim men on a Buddhist monk and his driver. Others saw the violence as catalyzed by incendiary anti-Muslim speeches given at a large rally protesting the alleged assault. In one particularly fiery speech, the secretary general of Sri Lanka's most active Buddhist nationalist group, the *Bodu Bala Sena* (BBS, Army of Buddhist Power), warned Muslims and 'any other outsiders' that any future assaults on Sinhalese would be dealt with directly by Buddhists themselves.[1] Within hours of the speech, groups of thugs attacked Muslim-owned shops and homes in Dharga Town, a suburb of the municipality of Aluthgama. Three days of riots followed. Four people died and over 100 people were injured. Many more thousands, mostly Muslims, were forced to abandon their homes to escape rampaging crowds.

---

[1] The terms used for Muslims and outsiders were *marakkala* and *paraiya* respectively, both derogatory terms. Full videos of the speech are available online at YouTube: http://www.youtube.com/watch?v=YFeaR9acsvM.

Among the many disturbing images that came out of the June 2014 riots in Aluthgama, Dharga, Welipenna, and Beruwala, was a photo circulated on Twitter which depicted a pamphlet that had been posted on Aluthgama's walls and lamp posts in days following the violence. The pamphlet advertised another Buddhist rally in the town of Mawanella, some 200 kilometres inland from the riots. Titled 'We condemn the killing of Sinhalese Buddhists in Aluthgama,[2] the poster read:

> A group of Buddhists including Buddhist monks have been taken to the hospital and are still receiving treatment after being targeted in a Muslim terrorist attack in the Aluthgama area on June 15, 2014. Moreover, there was also significant loss and damage to some Buddhist temples.
>
> To all those devoted to their country (S: *jātimāmaka hitavatuni*), today the followers of Mohammed have placed their hands on the robe of the Buddha. O' honorable people, fear and shame have flowed from this. This is not a minor act, but an egregious crime that will affect every single one of us tomorrow.
>
> *This is the country of we the Sinhalese....*
> *This is the country of our birth and death....*
>
> Against this foolish attack we will hold a special Satyagraha at Mawanella on June 17, 2014 at 3:30 in front of the clock tower. We invite all of you to [attend] this supremely patriotic event out of love for the *Sāsana*.

The poster was signed by a group previously unknown to journalists and scholars, calling itself the 'Mahasen 969.' Depending on how one chooses to translate it, the name either means 'the 969 Great Force' or '[King] Mahasena's 969'—Mahasena being an ancient Sinhalese king described in Sri Lanka's famous fifth-century Buddhist chronicle, the *Mahavamsa* (Mahanama 1912: 267–71). In either translation, it is an ominous moniker, one that suggests that at least some Sri Lankan Buddhist activists have begun to shape themselves in the image of the 969 (see Nyi Nyi Kyaw, this volume).

This pamphlet, along with other stories of contact between the 969 and BBS—including a visit by the BBS to Myanmar in March

---

[2] Call for protest in Manhalla on Twitter, '*Alutgama sinhala bauddha ghātanaya helā dakimu...*' posted 17 June 2014, https://twitter.com/aufidius/status/478836465858670592.

2014 and a visit by U Wirathu to Colombo in September 2014 which culminated in a written memorandum of understanding between the BBS and 969 (Scobey-Thal 2014; Perera 2014)—suggest that it is no longer adequate to look at anti-Muslim violence in Sri Lanka and Myanmar in isolation. Even if Buddhist nationalists in the two countries have thus far collaborated only in words, one can nonetheless see the beginnings of a more popular cross fertilization occurring. People in both countries, Muslims and Buddhists, are beginning to see their own actions in a broader regional framework.

This observation places new burdens on scholars to look more closely and critically at the similarities between violence in Sri Lanka and Myanmar. What are the similarities and links between Buddhist nationalist groups and anti-Muslim propaganda and violence in both locations? Are there parallel or interlinked causes that might be giving rise to these types of nationalist groups and these types of conflicts? How is it that, at this point in time, Muslims in Myanmar and in Sri Lanka have come to be cast as opponents or threats to Buddhism? Why is it that this particular image of a monolithic Muslim 'other' has gained such broad acceptance among certain sections of Myanmar and Sri Lankan society?

This chapter takes some initial steps towards answering these questions by exploring how it is that, at this moment in time, 'Muslims', contrived as a singular communal bloc, have come to be identified by Buddhist nationalist groups in both countries as a problem for the post-war nation (in the case of Sri Lanka) or a gradually democratizing nation (in the case of Myanmar).[3] Although this chapter begins with the familiar characterization of violence in Myanmar and Sri Lanka as religiously inflected, that is, 'Muslim-Buddhist' in nature (to use the hyphenated adjective employed by many media reports), this chapter takes a slightly more circumspect approach to the role of religion in these events. Not only does this chapter think comparatively about Myanmar and Sri Lanka, it also reflects on how, in both cases, a particular 'Muslim-Buddhist' framing of tensions and violence has come

---

[3] For the sake of consistency, I use the term 'Sri Lanka' to refer to the island country at all phases in its history. Prior to 1972 the island was referred to officially as 'Ceylon'. Similarly, I use 'Myanmar' anachronistically when referring to the country before 1989, when it was known as 'Burma'.

to be seen by many as persuasive. To do this, it explores certain political, historical, legal, and discursive processes through which Muslims and Islam have been portrayed as 'threats' to Buddhism, monolithic groups who must be challenged and defended against, on both sides of the Bay of Bengal.

In recent years, this 'othering' has occurred with unprecedented intensity and vitriol. While tensions between those who self-identify as Buddhist and as Muslim have a longer history in both places, extending back to British colonial era, recent conflicts have taken particularly ominous forms, both in terms of the intensity, spread, and persistence of the violence associated with them, and in terms of the stark framing of that violence in religious terms: in the discourse of nationalist propaganda, popular media and (increasingly) outside observers, recent violence is interpreted not as a conflict between certain communities of Buddhists and Muslims, but between Buddhists and Muslims *writ large*, or between Buddhism and Islam. The starkness of this new framing is especially obvious in the case of Sri Lanka where, as many have observed, the end of the island's bloody civil war in 2009 has not led to the end of social violence and perceived enemies, but to the rapid and crude identification of 'Islam' or 'Muslims' as a new, urgent post-Liberation Tigers of Tamil Eelam (LTTE), threat.

In what follows, I concentrate on three distinct historical and contemporary stimuli that have contributed, in similar ways, to the portrayal of Muslims as a monolithic 'other' in both Myanmar and Sri Lanka. These stimuli include violent separatist struggles, multi-faceted legal infrastructures for governing religion, and new forms of Buddhist nationalism. To be sure, these are not the only stimuli. Nor are they the only compelling similarities between the two countries: Myanmar and Sri Lanka have a long history of Theravada Buddhist monastic interchange; they both have a deep legacy of British colonialism (although Ceylon's history of colonial rule remains longer than that of Myanmar); they even manifest similar Buddhist-Muslim demographics.[4] However, more than these other points of comparison, the

---

[4] In the absence of reliable census data, scholars estimate Myanmar's Buddhist population at between 65 and 75 per cent and its Muslim minority at between 4 and 10 per cent; Sri Lanka's most recent census places its Buddhist population at 70 per cent and its Muslim population at 10 percent.

three stimuli mentioned above appear to have contributed directly, in parallel ways, to the construction of Muslims as 'other': the context of separatist struggles contributed to the imagining of Muslim social identity as separate and monolithic; the treatment of religion in constitutional law and personal law systems has contributed to the imagining of Islam as excessively rigid and even threatening to other religious identities; and the context of recent Buddhist nationalism has contributed to the perception of Muslims as part of a global Islamic threat. Through examining these three stimuli, this chapter illustrates the ways in which violence in Myanmar and Sri Lanka—and its stark religious framing— is not simply comparable but (increasingly) co-referential. This violence also draws upon and emerges from analogous political, historical, legal and discursive causes.

Separating and Singularizing Muslims

If one follows reports of violence in Myanmar and Sri Lanka, one sees a general tendency on the part of Buddhist nationalist groups (as well as many media outlets) to talk about Muslims as though they are a singular, monolithic religio-ethnic community. In Myanmar, 'Muslim' is collapsed with 'Rohingya'; in Sri Lanka notions of Muslim religious identity are collapsed into notions of Muslim-ness as an ethnic identity (Egreteau 2011: 46–8; Haniffa 2007). Although not altogether unsurprising—nationalist discourse and media reports always caricature social realities—the presentation of Muslims as a singular homogenous group has deeper roots in the history of separatism in both countries than in an analysis of on-the-ground facts. Although Rohingya Muslims living in Arakan constitute the most populous and (in recent international media coverage) most visible community of Muslims in Myanmar, Muslim communities in Myanmar are not limited to the Rohingya alone. There are significant populations of Shan, Chinese, Kaman Muslims, and Burman Muslims who live in other parts of the country as well (Crouch, chapter 1, this volume). Even within Arakan, Rohingya are not the only ethnic group who practise Islam. Similarly in Sri Lanka (as I discuss below), there are a variety of Muslim communities and a variety of types of Islam practised. In both Sri Lanka and Myanmar, a history of minority nationalist movements and separatist struggles have contributed significantly to the deliberate ignoring and over-writing in popular political discourse of this complexity. In Myanmar, some of the most important struggles have centred on the independence of Arakan, now Rakhine State.[5] In Sri Lanka, the key struggle has been the push for the independence of the northern and eastern regions of the island by the LTTE.

It is important to remember that the modern history of Myanmar's Muslims is not co-extensive with the history of Rohingya Muslims, nor can it be narrated exclusively from the perspective of events in modern-day Rakhine State. However, by the same token, the history of Muslim 'othering' in Myanmar has evolved especially in reference to separatism in that region. In what remains the only definitive study of Muslims in Myanmar to date, Moshe Yegar observed that Myanmar's Burman Buddhist majority have tended to imagine Muslims as 'a minority that prefers separatism' (Yegar 1972: 112). This association of Islam with separatism emerged primarily in the context of territorial competition in Arakan. Up until the late-eighteenth century, the Arakan region had been politically independent from Rangoon and Mandalay, a region controlled by Buddhist kings and influenced heavily by Muslim sultans. The fact of this pre-colonial independence of Arakan served as a common conceit of propaganda for two types of independence movements that took shape in late-colonial and independent Burma: a local Buddhist-led struggle for regional autonomy for Arakan, conceived initially as a separate polity but later as a state within the Union of Burma; and a local Muslim-led struggle for an autonomous polity which would specially protect and secure the religious and cultural rights of local Muslim communities, who had, over time, formed a majority there.

These competing separatist struggles date back at least to the 1940s, when inhabitants of Arakan were recruited into the war efforts of Japan and the British. During the Japanese occupation, local Buddhists, including prominent Buddhist monks, fought as Japanese proxies. Local Muslim communities in contrast, were armed and mobilized by the British as Force V fighters, independent militias tasked with undertaking guerrilla-style attacks on Japanese forces (Selth 1986). Armed and mobilized against each other, Arakan's

---

[5] In this chapter, I use the term 'Arakan' to refer to the region prior to 1988.

Muslims and Buddhists became deeply polarized. Not only were antipathies deepened, but Muslim and Buddhist communities were geographically separated, ghettoised: Muslims fled northward to avoid the anti-Muslim violence associated with the Japanese offensives and Buddhists fled southward to flee the anti-Buddhist violence associated with guerrilla counter-offensives (Yegar 2002).

In the years following the end of World War II, a variety of small but vocal separatist movements grew on both Muslim and Buddhist sides. These groups added to the dozens of ethnic militias that sprung up in Myanmar in the second part of the twentieth century. Muslims in Arakan began to form a diverse array of political and cultural organizations such as the North Arakan Muslim League (NAML) and military organizations such as the Mujahid, with the goal of creating an autonomous polity.[6] At the same time, local Buddhists also began demanding limited political self-rule for Arakan as a federal state. If groups such as the NAML viewed the sovereignty of Arakan in religious terms, local Buddhist separatists tended to view territorial independence in terms of history and class struggle, as a struggle against to reclaim a kingdom that had been overrun by Burman usurpers (Yegar 2002: 67, fn 1). Aside from a few brief moments when the two groups flirted with collaboration, Muslim-led and Buddhist-led movements treated the other as competitors and potential usurpers. Moreover, there was also considerable disagreement and in-fighting among self-declared Muslim and Buddhist movements and actors (Yegar 1972: 97).

Even if different communities of Muslims in Arakan were divided over how and/or whether to separate from Rangoon, from the 1950s onwards, the association of Islam and separatism seemed to grow in the popular imagination. Competition between Rohingya and Rakhine separatists certainly contributed to this perception. However, the association seems to have been further solidified through the increasing centralization and 'unification' efforts mounted by the Burmese state, efforts that tended to portray Rohingya as Muslim interlopers from Bengal rather than *bona fide* citizens of Burma. In one particularly notorious episode from the 1970s, the *Naga Min* (or Dragon King)

---

[6] For a semi-comprehensive list of Muslim separatist groups in Arakan since independence see Berlie 2008: 57–9.

campaign, the Burmese government declared hundreds of thousands of Rohingya Muslims to be illegal residents, refusing them citizenship and creating the beginnings of what would be decades of statelessness (that continues today). In writing the Rohingya out of Burmese history—a process that included omitting them from the official list of national ethnic groups in the 1974 Constitution and 1982 Citizenship Law—the governments in Rangoon and later Naypyidaw have composed a self-fulfilling story about Rohingya separatism. By denying the Rohingya a home in Myanmar/Burma, they have all but guaranteed the persistence of separatism among the Rohingya—a separatism that is often portrayed, both deliberately and inadvertently, as a religious (Muslim) movement. By analogizing Rohingya separatism to regional and international Muslim terrorist groups, the ruling regime has further solidified a popular association between Rohingya separatists and Muslims in general (Selth 2004; Yegar 1972: 110–12). In this way, the alienation of Rohingya in the Burmese nationalist project has ensured the persistence of self-declared Muslim political and military groups in Rakhine State and, by extension, the endurance of a distorted (and false) imagination regarding the homogeneity, 'foreignness' and separatist inclinations of all Muslims in Myanmar.

As in Myanmar, the Sri Lankan Muslim community is diverse in terms of language, geography, ethnic background and theological commitments. Although Tamil is the first language for most Muslims in Sri Lanka, there are some who feel more comfortable in Sinhala or English—and many Muslims speak multiple languages fluently. While it is beyond the scope of this chapter to elaborate at length, it is important to note that significant differences exist in the professional, economic and cultural situations of Muslims in the island's Northern Province, the Eastern Province and in the urban areas of the Central and Southwestern Provinces (particularly around Colombo and Kandy) (Ismail 1995; McGilvray 1998; 2008; 2011). This difference extends to notions of ethnicity as well. Most Muslims in Sri Lanka, if pressed for deep genealogical histories, would likely identify as descendants of Arab traders to Ceylon, a socio-cultural history designated by the term 'Moor'. Others, a smaller number, identify as Malays (descendants of Javanese Muslims who came during the Dutch colonial period). In addition to these larger groups, there are also smaller numbers of Bohras, Khojas, and Memons, who originate from Bombay and Gujarat. To these differences, one should also add substantial differences in interpretations and varieties of Islam on the island, from followers of local Sufi Sheiks, to self-declared traditionalists or 'ordinary' Muslims (Tamil: *cunnattu*), to members of the several different reformist or piety movements that have taken shape on the island since the nineteenth century, some of which are similar to those seen in other parts of Southeast Asia (McGilvray 2011).

In Sri Lanka, as in Myanmar, the diversity of Muslim life has, in many cases, been overlooked in favor of a more monolithic view of Muslim-ness, shaped and sharpened by struggles for political autonomy and the creation of a separate state. Here the most important struggles were not those waged by Muslims themselves but those waged by members of the island's larger Tamil ethno-linguistic population (18 per cent of the population[7]), which, since the colonial unification of the island in the nineteenth century, had been concerned with securing greater degrees of self-determination through legal, political and eventually military action. Tamil nationalism in Sri Lanka has a long and complex history. Yet its defining feature has been the more than 30-year long war (ending in 2009) fought by the LTTE, for a Tamil homeland in the northern and eastern parts of the island. Although not often recognized, the Tamil nationalist struggle had a major influence on consolidating ideas about what it meant to be Muslim in Sri Lanka.

The links between Sri Lankan Muslim identity and Tamil nationalism date back to the late-nineteenth century, when British colonial administrators began gradually and cautiously expanding the number of Sri Lankan members in the island's Legislative Council. The Legislative Council was a small and relatively weak body, but British governors sought to give it an air of legitimacy and a degree of local buy-in by appointing Sri Lankans as local members who could represent a particular 'race' (DeSilva 1973). Initially, the body included one member of the Sinhalese, Tamil, and Burgher communities. As the century progressed, however, debates began to take place on the question of whether Sri Lanka's Tamil-speaking Muslims ought to

---

[7] The term 'Tamil' is itself a complex term of identity as well. Many in Sri Lanka divide the category into two: Sri Lankan Tamils who trace their ancestry back many centuries and Indian Tamils who are descendants of nineteenth and twentieth century migrant labourers from Tamil Nadu.

have separate representatives in the slowly expanding Council. In the 1880s, observing that most Muslims spoke Tamil as their first language, important Tamil political leaders, such as Ponnambalam Ramanathan, claimed that the island's Muslims were a natural part of the Tamil race; therefore, they rationalized, it was perfectly adequate to have a Tamil-speaking Christian to represent Tamil-speaking Muslims in the Legislative Council (Ismail 1995). For many Tamil political elites, Muslims were, in essence, Tamils of another faith. This assertion—of the Tamil-ness of Sri Lanka's Muslims—continued to influence certain strands of Tamil nationalist politics in the mid-twentieth century. Periodically from the 1950s to the 1970s, Tamil nationalist leaders used claims of Muslims' Tamil-ness to support the idea that federalism in Sri Lanka should include regional autonomy for the northern and eastern regions because both regions had Tamil-speaking majorities (Wilson 2000: 82–110). (Less emphasis in their rhetoric was placed on the fact that Tamil-speakers in the Northern Province were mainly Hindu and Christian, while Tamil-speakers in the Eastern Province were mainly Muslim). Similarly, from the 1980s onwards, the LTTE drew upon this argument frequently in order to justify their vision of a single state of Tamil Eelam, which encompassed both the Northern and Eastern Provinces. Muslims who did not agree were branded as traitors, leading, among other things, to a mass expulsion of Tamils from Jaffna in 1990 (Wilson 2000; Kodikara 1989).

Sri Lankan Muslims responded to these attempts to co-opt Muslim-ness into Tamil racial (and later, national) identity by explicitly defining Muslim identity as based not just on a shared religion, but on a shared ethnicity. This project of what one might call encouraged conflation has been so effective that in Sri Lanka today most people understand the designation 'Muslim' as referring to one's ethnic composition as much as his/her religious affiliations. If Rohingya Muslims are considered ethnically Rohingya[8] and religiously

---

[8] This is a matter of some contention. There are many in Myanmar who insist that Rohingya is a made-up ethnic category, generated by the group in order to disguise what is in essence a (foreign) Bengali ethnic identity. For this chapter, the point is irrelevant. The more important issue is that all observers posit an essential link between ethnicity and religion.

Muslim, Sri Lanka's Muslim community tends to be considered both ethnically and religiously Muslim. While large numbers of Muslims in Sri Lanka are clearly connected by history, genealogy, and other factors that might be taken as proxies for something like ethnicity, the unproblematic and unreflective conflation (and consolidation) of religion with ethnicity under the sign of Muslim-ness has arisen as a result of a particular history. A religio-ethnic identity was forged in opposition to Tamil separatist nationalism as a way to challenge Muslims' co-optation into it. In the early twentieth century, in opposition to the claims of Ramanathan (which I described above), the president and co-founder of the Ceylon Moor's Union (CMU), I.L.M. Abdul Azeez wrote a refutation of the argument that Muslims were part of the Tamil race. In it he explained that Muslims, although they spoke Tamil, derived from a different genealogy than Tamils: they were the progeny of Arab traders who had first arrived on the island centuries ago; they had separate customs, physical features and shared a common 'Arab blood' (Ismail 1995: 68). As such they constituted not simply a distinct religious group, but an entirely separate racial community—race being the operative category through which the British understood and recognized Sri Lankan social identity (Rogers 2004).[9] By the mid and late twentieth centuries these same arguments about the distinctiveness of Muslims as a religio-ethnic group blended with distinct political projects. They helped to challenge the attempts of Tamil nationalists and the LTTE to claim Muslims as part of the Tamil nation. These arguments also served the purposes of the new Muslim political parties that would take shape in the 1980s and 1990s, particularly the Sri Lanka Muslim Congress (SLMC), the largest political party in Sri Lanka that claims to represent Muslim interests: by claiming shared religion *and* ethnicity, these parties were able to assert a double-claim to group representation (O'Sullivan 1999; Knoerzer 1998).

In Myanmar and Sri Lanka, the imagined and asserted singularity and homogeneity of Muslim communities, to which journalists and

[9] At various points in Sri Lankan history this argument about the racial distinctiveness of Muslims who descended from Arab merchants has been encapsulated in the word 'Moor', the preferred term of self-designation for those Muslims who identify with this genealogy.

Buddhist nationalists frequently appeal, did not emerge inevitably and naturally from observations about the ways in which Myanmar and Sri Lankan people live. These assertions have their own history, one that is linked to particular struggles for political autonomy and territorial separatism. In the case of Myanmar, popular impressions about the singularity of Muslim religious communities were in large part distilled with reference to Rohingya Muslim separatism in Arakan.[10] In Sri Lanka, by contrast, Muslim leaders actively shaped the terms of their own corporate identity in ethnic terms to fend off attempts at cooptation by Tamil nationalists, including the LTTE. While not being the only determinant of Muslim 'othering' in the Bay of Bengal, these separatist struggles and nationalist movements clearly gave added impetus to the discursive and political construction of Muslim communities as distinct, even monolithic. These assertions of Muslim corporate unity, which in certain contexts served to empower disempowered and numerically small groups, have fed back into exclusivist nationalist discourses in troubling ways.

Law and the Fragmenting of Muslim Identity

If separatist struggles in Myanmar and Sri Lanka worked to solidify notions of Muslim communal identity as singular and coherent, the legal structures of Myanmar and Sri Lanka have also worked to encourage the ideas about the necessary singularity of the beliefs, rituals, institutions, practices, and customs that this presumably singular social group observes. In these cases the effects of law have had less to do with the impacts of litigation and legal action—particularly in Myanmar, where people tend to avoid relying on civil courts—than with law's discursive functions, its tendency to serve as an authorized language that calls into being and renders legitimate certain 'truths' about the social universe it purports to govern. Legal discourse in Myanmar and Sri Lanka tends

---

[10] Other attempts at asserting Muslim political agency were made just following independence in the somewhat short-lived activities of Rangoon-based Burmese Muslim groups such as the Burmese Muslim Association (BMA). However, it appears that the effects of Arakan separatism on the public perception of Muslim identity were larger and more lasting than these groups.

to call into being three separate 'truths' about Islam: (1) the idea that Islam is an individual religion, freely chosen, voluntary and analogous to other types of religious traditions, (2) the idea that Islam is a minority faith and therefore ought not challenge the primacy of Buddhism, and (3) the idea that Islam is also a communal religion, which imposes on its members a distinct (and presumably single) system of norms. Moreover, in both Sri Lanka and Myanmar, these legal 'truths' have been used to confirm the (falsely assumed) monolithic nature of Islam as well as to confirm their own perceptions about the problematic place of Islam and Muslims within the political-legal frameworks of Myanmar and Sri Lanka, insofar as, in the rhetoric of some, Islam(1) and Islam(2) remain in tension with and compromised by Islam(3).

These first two discursive renderings of Islam are visible in the supreme laws that are currently operating in Myanmar and Sri Lanka: the 2008 Constitution of Myanmar and the 1978 Constitution of Sri Lanka. Both constitutions constitute the legal status of Muslims in two ways. On the one hand, the religious rights of Muslims are grouped together with the religious rights of all citizens and are rendered as generic guarantees for all individuals to freedom to believe, manifest, change and teach one's religion.[11] On the other hand, these generic guarantees exist alongside special constitutional provisions that specify the privileged status of Buddhism. Myanmar's Constitution recognizes 'the special position of Buddhism as the faith professed by the great majority of the citizens of the Union' (art 361). Sri Lanka's Constitution recognizes 'the foremost place' of Buddhism and obligates the state to 'protect and foster' it (art 9). These constitutions were drafted at different points in time and were not designed with reference to each other; nevertheless, as with other constitutions in the Buddhist-majority countries of Southern Asia, they both combine general religious rights provisions with special Buddhist prerogatives.[12]

The third discursive rendering of Islam, as an autonomous community governed by a singular set of norms, is visible in the separate statutory systems of Muslim Personal Law, first introduced by the

[11] Myanmar Constitution, art. 34, 348; Sri Lankan Constitution, art. 10, 12, and 14(1)(e).

[12] For more on these constitutional comparisons in Buddhist Southern Asia, see Schonthal 2014.

British, that continue to govern marriage, inheritance, divorce, and religious trusts in Myanmar and Sri Lanka. As in other British colonies, these structures of 'Anglo-Mohammedan Law' did not conform intimately to the full range of practices and customs of Muslim communities, but were confected by British legal draftspersons in consultation with particular clerical elites as a hybrid legal instrument that combined elements of English Common Law with elements of Muslim traditions.[13] The resulting product was half good-faith attempt at legal accommodation and half contrivance, an instrumental codifying of an otherwise broad theological principles and contextual jurisprudence into a 'reified and static entity' referred to as 'the' Muslim Law (Kugle 2001: 258). The creation of this written Muslim law discursively stabilized notions of Islam in a similar manner to the way that separatist politics stabilized notions of Muslim communal identity. In Myanmar this system of Muslim personal law has its roots in Section 13[c] of the Burma Laws Act of 1898 which specifies that 'Mohammedan Law' should be used to resolve disputes between two Muslim parties in all matters of 'succession, inheritance, marriage or caste, or any religious usage or institution.' Three further acts spell out the details of that law[14]:

The Kazis Act (No. 12 of 1880)
The Mussalman Wakf Validating Act (No. 6 of 1913)
The Mussalman Wakf Act (No. 42 of 1923)[15]

The Kazis Act, although largely unimplemented, permits the head of state to appoint and remove Muslim judges, or Quazis, anywhere in the country if such a person is needed to perform marriages or 'certain other rites and ceremonies'.[16] The Mussalman Wakf and Wakf Validating Acts provide for the creation by Muslims of special religious charitable trusts, or Wakfs, and set out the terms for maintaining, auditing, and overseeing those trusts. These principles

---

[13] One important distinction between Myanmar and Sri Lanka is that while Hanfi is the main school of jurisprudence (*maddhab*) in Myanmar, in Sri Lanka it is Shafi'i.

[14] See Crouch, chapter 3, in this volume. Crouch demonstrates that contrary to the claims of Hooker (and, although not mentioned, Yegar 2002), Muslim Personal Law did not stop functioning in 1962.

[15] The complete texts of all acts are available in the appendix to Yegar 1972.

[16] Preamble of Kazis Act.

of Muslim marriage and divorce have not been codified in a statute, but elaborated through a mixture of case law and colonial-era legal textbooks (Crouch, chapter 3, this volume).

Similarly, in the case of Sri Lanka, the parameters of Muslim personal law are spelled out in three statutes:

Muslim Intestate Succession Ordinance (No. 10 of 1931)

The Muslim Marriage and Divorce Act (No. 22 of 1955)

The Muslim Mosques and Charitable Trusts or Wakfs Act (No. 51 of 1956)

The first statute, a short one, specifies that Muslim inheritance and property law will apply to all cases in which a Muslim person dies without having written a will. The second outlines the specific rules for contracting and registering marriages, initiating and arbitrating divorces, dealing with maintenance payments and *kaikuli* ('hand gifts' given by the parents of the bride to the couple as a dowry), and appealing and challenging decisions. The third statute lays out rules relating to the maintenance, administration, and management of donations to mosques and Muslim religious charities (*wakfs*) and the resolution of disputes related to those issues. In contrast to the legal status of Muslims in Myanmar and Sri Lanka's constitutions, when it comes to matters of marriage, divorce, inheritance, and *wakfs*, Muslims assert legal claims as members of a presumably singular and self-evident faith community governed by a presumably singular system of religious law, embodied in case law and/or encoded in textbooks and statutes.[17]

Legal discourse in Myanmar and Sri Lanka, and the 'truths' it appears to support, renders Muslims in three ways: as generically 'religious' citizens (vis-à-vis constitutional fundamental rights), tolerated minorities (vis-à-vis constitutional prerogatives for Buddhism) and autonomous communities (vis-à-vis Muslim Personal Law). However, at the same time, in both places, Buddhists frequently claim that the autonomy of Muslims (as validated in Muslim Personal Law) is incompatible with or threatening towards Islam's other legal statuses, as an individually chosen belief and as a minority faith. One

---

[17] It should be noted here that a key difference between the personal law regimes in Myanmar and Sri Lanka is the recognition of Buddhist personal law in Myanmar (Kyaw 1994; Ikeya 2013; Huxley 1988).

place where these claims are particularly visible is in the on-going campaigns in both countries to pass laws that would place new limits on when and how a person may legally convert from one religion to another.[18] While the draft bills are written in formally neutral language, campaigners clearly see the bills as actively preserving Buddhism's status as the 'majority' or 'foremost' religion by preventing conversions from Buddhism to Islam or Christianity. The campaign in Myanmar, which is gaining momentum as this chapter goes to press, has been organized by the Organization for the Protection of Nation, Race and Religion—or in the Burmese acronym, *Ma Ba Tha*—a Buddhist-led Burmese nationalist group with links to the 969 movement (see below). The ongoing campaign in Sri Lanka, which reached its highpoint in 2004 but which continues in more muted form today, was spear-headed by the *Jathika Hela Urumaya* (JHU, National [Sinhala] Heritage Party), a Buddhist nationalist party consisting of mainly Buddhist monks. Although Islam remains a primary concern in the development of the Myanmar conversion bill, concerns about the proselyting activities associated with Christianity were the initial motivator for designers of the Sri Lankan bill; since 2009, however, proponents of a Sri Lankan conversion bill have increasingly conceived it as a protection against conversions to Islam as well (Berkwitz 2008; Deegalle 2004; DeVotta and Stone, 2008).

Although the two conversion bills were drafted separately and without reference to the other, campaigners in both countries identify and seek to criminalize a similar offense: 'forcible' or coerced conversions, which do not conform with an understanding of religion—or Islam (1)—as individual, chosen, and voluntary. The Myanmar bill establishes Registration Boards at the township level that are tasked with determining 'whether the [person requesting conversion] truly believes in the said religion' (art 5(d)) and/or

---

[18] This section draws upon the unofficial translation of the Myanmar draft conversion law translated by the Chin Human Rights Organization (www. burmalibrary.org/docs18/2014-Draft_Religious_Conversion_Law-en.pdf [accessed 19 June 2014]) and the official Sinhalese and English drafts of the Sri Lankan conversion bill ('Prohibition of Forcible Conversion of Religion Bill, presented by Ven. Dr. Omalpe Sobhitha Thero.' *Gazette of the Democratic Socialist Republic of Sri Lanka* 28 May 2004, Pt. II).

whether the person has converted 'under inducement, intimidation, undue pressure or duress' (art 10(b)). The Sri Lankan bill created a similar duty of oversight for the local Divisional Secretary in order to prevent the use of physical 'force', monetary 'allurement' or miscellaneous 'fraudulent means' in the conversion process (art 2, read alongside art 8). In both cases, prison sentences and large fines apply to violators.

Myanmar and Sri Lankan supporters of conversion legislation insist the dangers posed by coerced conversions are not only a violation of one's (individual) religious rights or a threat to the pre-eminence of Buddhism, but even more significantly a danger that one might become 'captive' within a bounded and singular system of Muslim norms, which the government is legally obliged to enforce through the regimes of Muslim personal law. More specifically, in both contexts, a frequently occurring trope is the image of the Buddhist women who marries into a Muslim household and, once converted to Islam, becomes locked into a system of community and state-imposed norms and laws. Take, for example this exchange I had with a senior member of the BBS:

> A: [If] a Sinhalese woman marries a Muslim man, her right is not protected because she has to marry under the Muslim law. So she comes under the Quazi courts. And then she cannot get back to the normal legal system because she is... under the Muslim law.
>
> Q: But she has certain rights. I mean, she would have consented to that?
>
> A: The problem is if she decided to change, if she [wanted to get] divorced. But still that divorce is not decided by the normal system.[19]

Similarly, in the Myanmar case, the proposed bill on conversion obligates the Registration Boards to consider explicitly the implications of conversion on matters of property, divorce and inheritance. Supporters of the Myanmar conversion bill have pushed the legislation as a broader package of four proposed laws, which includes laws prohibiting polygamy (a limit widely seen as an attempt to limit Muslim polygamous marriages), limiting the size of families and banning interfaith marriages entirely (Weng 2014). Underlying all of

---

[19] Interview with Dilanthe Withanage, Colombo, 9 January 2014.

this are fears that the legal status given to Islam—Islam discursively constructed as a community religion that prescribes a single set of normative obligations and boundaries—has the capacity to undermine the voluntary choices of Muslim individuals (or converts) and therefore to drive Muslim populations forward with a 'ratcheting effect': having converted to Islam, they cannot exit. In the minds of Buddhist critics, this ratcheting dynamic leads to a steady and irreversible shift in religious demographics, which threatens to transform Islam from a 'tolerated' minority religion to one that competes with Buddhism for patronage and power.

Formations of Buddhist Nationalism

The case of the conversion bills discussed in the previous section point towards a third crucial factor in the 'othering' of Muslims in Sri Lanka and in Myanmar: in both cases Muslims are increasingly vilified in the speeches, electronic media, and written propaganda associated with aggressive forms of Buddhist nationalism that have arisen over the last few years. In both places, this recent upsurge in nationalism has been led by Buddhist monks. In Myanmar there are two key actors. One is the *Ma Ba Tha*—a national mobilization group led by well-known Buddhist monks and oriented around pro-Buddhist, pro-Burman activism. The other is the 969 movement, a much looser network of Buddhist monks and laity who have been linked to anti-Muslim violence in Rakhine state and other parts of the country. The most visible exponent and spokesperson of the movement is the Mandalay-based monk U Wirathu, who appears regularly in the media. In Sri Lanka the key players are monk-led nationalist organizations that have gained prominence in the country since 2012. These organizations include the *Sinhala Ravaya* (the Roar of the Sinhala Nation), and the *Ravana Balaya* (Ravana's Force). However, the most significant and active is the BBS. The BBS has its headquarters in Colombo and it maintains strong links with Buddhist monastic centres around Sri Lanka. Its spokesperson and general secretary is Galagoda Aththe Gnanasara Thero, a firebrand whose oratory has been associated with riots and anti-Muslim violence in Colombo, Maharagama and (as seen above) Aluthgama.

The agendas of these organizations are similar. On both sides of the Bay of Bengal, Buddhist nationalist groups describe their purpose as the protection and promotion of Buddhism through preaching about the importance of Buddhist values, history, education, sacred sites, and ceremonies. At the same time, these groups regularly insist upon the need to neutralize threats to Buddhism. They routinely single out Myanmar's and Sri Lanka's Muslims as chief among these threats. For Ma Ba Tha, 969, Sinhala Ravaya and the BBS, Muslims threaten Buddhists in multiple ways: demographically (through higher birth rates and greater rates of in-conversion), financially (through controlling industry) and geographically (through engaging in residential and religious building projects near Buddhist sacred sites). However, a key point of similarity among these groups is the manner in which they construct the Muslims not only as a domestic threat, but as a part of a broader regional or transnational conspiracy to Islamicize the Buddhist world.

A number of media and scholarly analyses of Buddhist nationalist movements in Myanmar have highlighted the ways in which local Buddhism-Muslim violence has been interpreted as part of a broader conflict between Buddhism and Islam. By some accounts, even the name of the '969' movement—which refers to the nine qualities of the Buddha, the six qualities of his teachings and the nine qualities of the Buddhist monkhood, respectively—was conceived in opposition to another three-number code that holds salience for Muslims throughout South Asia, the 'Muslim' number 786. It is common for Muslim businesspersons to display the number 786 at the front of their shops or on shop windows to indicate that the business is *halal* and Muslim-owned.[20] In an analysis of popular discourse about Buddhist-Muslim violence in Lashio in June 2013, Matt Schissler recounted the ways in which certain residents of Yangon framed the conflicts in a global light. Schissler narrates how one Buddhist acquaintance interpreted the number 786—and its three-number sum of 21—as a secret code revealing Muslim ambitions to take over the world within 21 centuries following the death of the prophet. Schissler reports that the same person went on to voice alarm that the Islamic takeover

[20]   On the significance of 786 vis-à-vis 969 see Nyi Nyi Kyaw, this volume.

was already underway, insisting that Indonesia had once been a 'Buddhist country' and was now dominated by Muslims and lamenting that Myanmar's relative lack of military power (compared with that of the U.S., for example) left it vulnerable to Muslim aggressors such as Osama Bin Laden (Schissler 2013b). This perspective has been popularized and disseminated through monks like U. Wirathu, who refer to a 'master plan' designed and financed by Muslims worldwide to transform Myanmar into an Islamic state. In his logic, the protection of Buddhism is intimately linked with the reduction of Muslim demographic, financial and religious influence in Myanmar. If Muslim influence continues to grow, they will eventually become more powerful than Buddhists. In an ominous quote recorded by one BBC reporter, Wirathu warned: 'Muslims are only well behaved when they are weak...When they become strong, they are like a wolf or a jackal; in large packs they hunt down other animals' (Fisher 2013).

Similar tropes of a global Muslim conspiracy appear in the discourse of the Buddhist nationalist groups in Sri Lanka. In an interview in January 2014, the chief executive officer of the BBS, Dilanthe Withanage explained to me that what linked together the 969 movement and BBS was the fact that they both responded to 'global level Islamicization' and that both Myanmar and Sri Lanka were undergoing a similar type of Islamicization process. In a quote that corresponded amazingly closely with the quote by Wirathu mentioned above, he said:

> When [Muslims] are two per cent or three per cent [of a country], they are very silent. When they reach ten per cent, they try to use different forces like [promoting] halal [certification, a phenomenon challenged by the BBS]... to penetrate into the society. When that comes, problems happen. [The] problems in Burma and here are almost the same.

Withanage and others insist that there is a gradual spread of Muslim influence in Sri Lanka, one that, if unchecked, will lead to the ultimate transformation of the island—or at least, Muslim-majority parts of the island—from a *dhammadīpa* or 'island of [Buddhist] dhamma' into an 'Arabian kingdom' (*Mahalaya* 2013).

Concerns with this potential Islamicization can be seen clearly in a cartoon contained in the eponymous newspaper published by the nationalist group, the *Siṅhala Rāvaya*. The cartoonist depicts the teardrop-shaped island of Sri Lanka held in the tentacles of large octopus wearing the distinctive skull-cap (*taqiyah*) of a Muslim man. The cartoonist labels each of the octopus' tentacles with a different feature of Muslim 'control' over Sri Lanka: sharia law, monopolized [financial] markets, economic power, population, control of land, conversion to Islam, 'cunning cooperation' with Sinhalese political

Figure 9.1   Octopus's Tentacles read (counter clockwise)
  shari'a law
  monopolizing markets
  economy
  population
  land
  Islamic conversions
  cunning cooperation
  competition for schools
Source: Cartoon in newspaper, *Siṅhala Rāvaya* Sep 2013, p. 5.

leaders and competition for schools. These topics include the major themes of discontent and objects of opposition for Sri Lanka's Buddhist nationalist groups. These groups worry that Sri Lanka's Muslims will try to slowly introduce more and more features of *shari'a* law in the country, either through expanding the ambit of Muslim Personal Law or through government funding or endorsement of halal certification processes for consumer goods and restaurants. They vex over Muslim influence in certain economic markets, such as export trade, and link Muslim success to hazy global networks of cooperation. They express concern with the growth and spread of Muslim populations, particularly on the East Coast—a concern that was inflamed by recent census statistics (the first complete national census since 1981), which estimated the island's Muslim population at nearly 10 per cent, approximately 2.5 per cent up from the previous data. They also imagine Sri Lankan Muslims making use of vast sums of petrodollars from the Middle East to improve the standards of their own community, and further influence the highest rungs of educational and political power.[21]

The rendering of Muslims as part of a global Islamic threat is not simply a convenient narrative conceit for Buddhist nationalists in Myanmar and Sri Lanka. By portraying Muslims as a 'threat from without' rather than a 'threat from within', these groups tap into deeper cultures of Sinhalese nationalism that draw a rigid distinction between autochthony and foreign-ness, *bhumiputra* (a Sanskrit compound, vernacularized into Sinhala, meaning 'sons of the soil') and *mleccha* (a similar vernacularized Sanskrit term, meaning foreigners and/or barbarians). In both cases, the implied argument is that full political rights belong only to those who are properly 'of the soil'; and that it is the duty of the *bhumiputra* to struggle against all would-be 'invaders', a list that includes (in Myanmar) British, Chinese, Thai and Indians and (in Sri Lanka) British, Portuguese, Dutch and Tamils. By rendering Muslims as *mleccha*, Buddhist nationalists in Sri Lanka have analogized Muslims to colonists, ancient aggressors, and

---

[21] There have been instances of Muslim-majority states giving direct aid to Muslim-majority communities, particularly in the aftermath of the Boxing Day Tsunami of 2005. However, the imagination of these dynamics in the Buddhist nationalist imaginary far exceeds the reality.

purportedly rival 'races'. They have also implied that resolution lays only in two options: vanquishing or domination.

* * *

As this chapter goes to press, the Mahasen 969 remains a mystery. In the end, there was no rally in Mawanella. Seeing the pamphlets described above, a Senior Superintendent of Police successfully petitioned for a court order preventing any rallies in Mawanella town. He met with Muslim and Buddhist groups at the police station in Mawanella and ordered local officers to forcibly stop any would-be protesters (DailyFT 2014). While the prevention of the Mahasen 969's rally might be considered a victory, it is a small victory. Reports of vandalism, violence and tensions continue to flow out of Sri Lanka. Similar reports are arising daily in Myanmar's English news media. Violence shows little sign of burning out in either place. On the contrary, violence against the Muslim 'other' in one country seems to be taking inspiration from the other.

In this chapter, I have tried to think comparatively and regionally, while reconsidering the 'religious' nature of violence between Buddhists and Muslims. This has led me to consider certain similarities in historical, political, discursive, and legal stimuli that fed into the construction of Muslims as a unified 'other' that could pose a threat to Buddhists. In doing this, I hope to contribute to a certain comparative awareness between scholars and observers of Sri Lanka and Myanmar; I also hope to pique a historical awareness among those who might too readily and easily code what's happening in the Bay of Bengal as a conflict between *the* Buddhists and *the* Muslims or between Buddh*ism* and Islam. This is not to say that pointing to religion is entirely unwarranted. Indeed, there are good reasons to take seriously the religious aspects of the conflicts: these reasons could include the self-designations of the actors, the imagery and symbolism associated with them, the visible presence of orange-robes and *taqiyah* at rallies and riots, and so forth. Nevertheless, we ought to make these attributions carefully and deliberately, while being mindful of the politics and histories of using these categories.

I began this analysis with the observation that violence in Myanmar and Sri Lanka have taken similar forms and might be becoming more co-referential. I examined this question with a purposeful eye towards comparison, which led me to identify three distinct stimuli that appear to have contributed to the process of 'othering' Muslims in both places: the influence of separatism on the imagined singularity of Muslim communities, the influence of law on the perceived threat posed by Islam, and the influence of Buddhist nationalists on the impression that local Muslims are part of a global Islamic conspiracy. In identifying and exploring these common stimuli, I hope to lay some initial, tentative groundwork for broader critical comparisons between Sri Lanka and Myanmar. I do not mean to exaggerate the limits of comparative inquiry: compared to Sri Lanka's Muslim communities, the struggles of the Rohingya in Myanmar appear much more dire; similarly the climate of illiberal democracy in Sri Lanka cannot compare to the militarized autocracies of General Ne Win (1962–88) or General Than Shwe (1992–2011), or the quasi-civilian rule of President Thein Sein (2011–present). Nevertheless, increasingly, scholars need to be thinking beyond these differences—profound though they may be—in order to take seriously the real and consequential similarities which are working in parallel and intersecting ways to make violence a disturbingly regular occurrence.

10 The Global and Regional Dynamics of Humanitarian Aid in Rakhine State

ALISTAIR D.B. COOK

In June 2012, riots broke out in Rakhine State in response to the gang rape and murder of a Buddhist woman and the subsequent killing of ten Muslims, who were not Rohingya, following a public call for retribution. Violence escalated and relations between Buddhists and Muslims hit a new low. In October 2012, riots and organized violence broke out again, displacing more people. These two periods of violence disproportionately affected Muslims, with more than 140,000 people estimated to be displaced. These riots caught international attention and prompted diplomatic activity in response to the plight of the Muslim community across the Muslim world. In August 2012, the first high-profile visit to Rakhine State by the international community was a delegation including Turkish Foreign Minister Ahmet Davutoglu together with Mr Ekmeleddin İhsanoğlu, Secretary General of the Organization of Islamic Conference (OIC), and the representatives of the Member States of the OIC Contact Group on Rohingya Muslims.

International responses from the Muslim world to the 2012 violence can be classified into three main categories. First, aid originating from Muslim-majority countries may follow the traditional sovereignty norm of non-interference in the domestic affairs of another state, similar to other developing states. With this approach, aid funds are channelled through international organizations like United Nations (UN) agencies or state-based organizations such as the Myanmar Red Cross. Second, international aid and assistance has been generated by Western-based Muslim Faith-Based Organizations (FBOs)[1] to run field programmes in Rakhine State. These organizations generally follow international humanitarian principles of humanity, independence, neutrality and impartiality, although such programs demonstrate greater sensitivity to Islam, such as the provision of food packages during Ramadan. To date, non-Western Muslim FBOs have not had established field programmes in Rakhine State. Third, some aid organizations have responded with a combination of these two approaches, where funds from Muslim-majority countries are used to support the individual aid programs of Muslim FBOs in Rakhine State. In Myanmar, all FBOs face the same challenges as other humanitarian organizations as a result of the general suspicion surrounding the activities of 'foreign' organizations, such as the need to constantly renegotiate access and operate with restricted access to a population of concern.

Public opposition to international humanitarian aid in general has affected the work of both religious and secular International Non-Government Organizations (INGO), with the most high profile case affecting the work of Médecins Sans Frontières (MSF, also known as Doctors Without Borders). In November 2013, there was public disagreement in local media reports and online social media reports that the secular Medecins Sans Frontiers was 'biased' in the delivery of humanitarian assistance in favour of Muslims affected by the violence. In turn, Peter-Paul de Groote, the head of mission for MSF in Myanmar, wrote an opinion piece in the *Myanmar Times* (MT) to

---

[1] Faith-based organizations are best understood along a spectrum of religious expression from the religious orientation of an organization to those explicitly faith-based. They can be evaluated on three main categories: organizational control, expression of religion and programme implementation (Bielefeld and Cleveland 2013: 446–7). These categories can help identify whether a particular group is targeted explicitly or implicitly; for example, whether an FBO provides meals based on a faith-based diet only to those of that faith or provides aid to anyone regardless of faith.

articulate the independence of the organization. The disagreement concerned the outbreak of violence on 2 November between Muslims and Buddhists in Rakhine State in which two people died and five others were in need of hospital treatment. This raised local suspicioun that all foreign aid agencies, not just assistance from the wider Muslim community, were pro-Rohingya, to the detriment of local Rakhine Buddhists. Camp authorities telephoned MSF and, with permission from Rakhine State health authorities, MSF transported three injured Muslims to hospital. After the Muslims arrived at the hospital, there were reports that this illustrated MSF 'bias'. However, MSF publicly refuted this allegation and noted that it works with the state health authorities particularly in remote areas. These areas are where the Muslim minority are located, and state health officials were also targeted by groups preventing them from delivering humanitarian assistance to Muslims (De Groote 2013). The loudest voices came from the Rakhine majority who called for humanitarian assistance to be distributed equally between the two communities. In response, MSF publicly affirmed that they 'see patients not politics' (de Groote 2013). It is within this context that Western-based Muslim FBOs are building a field presence in Rakhine State. As there is a low-level of trust between the Myanmar government and 'foreign' organizations, many INGOs including Muslim FBOs have invested in developing personal relations with government officials and decision-makers in an effort to sustain and possibly expand access. As this chapter will demonstrate, Western-based Muslim FBOs are no different in wanting to gain and improve access through demonstrating their credentials and trustworthiness as well as developing partnerships with other INGOs to provide assistance in Rakhine State. This chapter will also illustrate the challenges for the diverse network of INGO activity.

Alongside the different aid responses from across the Muslim world to the 2012 Rakhine State violence is the long-standing disenfranchisement of the Rohingya Muslim community. On the side of Rakhine Buddhists, a sense of victimhood has heightened the sense of grievance because Rakhine State is the second least developed state in Myanmar and poverty levels are high. As a result of the extreme levels of poverty experienced in Rakhine State, many in the majority Rakhine Buddhist population feel equally needy to other communities. This feeling is compounded by the perception that many

Rohingya are illegal migrants receiving humanitarian assistance to the detriment of what they perceive as the 'local' population. There is an estimated 200,000 displaced in Rakhine State and Bangladesh along its border with Myanmar in the Chittagong Hills Tract. In all these areas, INGOs face challenges to accessing the population of concern. The restrictions on access for aid organizations by the Myanmar, and local Rakhine, government is motivated by a traditional security framing of the Rohingya population. Rather than viewing Rohingya from a position of humanity, they are framed as a threat to the integrity of Myanmar as a Buddhist-majority state, as recipients of special privileges from the international community, and as a destabilizing force to Bangladesh because of the supposed drain on its limited resources.

While the political changes in Myanmar began in 2010, this traditional security perspective has remained unchanged. Public opinion across Myanmar, particularly of the Rakhine people, is not supportive of efforts to improve the conditions of those in need of humanitarian assistance in Rakhine State, and rejects the need to address the issue of statelessness and recognize the Rohingya as a people of Myanmar (Callahan 2007: 32–3). This chapter will demonstrate that technical aid programmes will face a continued need to re-negotiate access to the Rohingya community, and unless the conceptual and political questions are addressed, this situation is unlikely to improve. After a brief history of Rakhine State, I explore the dominant mindset of the Union government and state government, and how it has affected the perception of humanitarian aid. I then consider the gap between the perceptions of humanitarian aid on the ground and the emergent functional relationships within the global humanitarian community to address this challenge. I conclude by arguing that without a substantive shift in government mind-set, new humanitarian actors entering the system will face the same challenges other humanitarian actors have faced in the past. Access to the Rohingya will be contingent upon personal relationships with government officials by humanitarian aid agencies as well as continued donor assistance.

A Brief History of Rakhine State and the Rohingya

Rakhine State lies in the west of Myanmar along the border with Bangladesh, where the local population consists of a Buddhist majority with a significant Muslim minority. The history of the Rohingya, who are officially referred to in Myanmar as 'Bengalis', is closely related to Bengalis but also draws historical links from the Middle Eastern traders who came to Rakhine State. The state has been a part of many disputes between kings and leaders of Bengal and Tripura. Alongside the various conflicts came a variety of influences, most notably, Buddhism and Islam. Islam entered Myanmar exclusively through immigration and exogamy because of the country's forbidding territory, relatively less external commercial interest and because Buddhism remained a popular religion with the masses and not just of the royal court (Yegar 2002: 20–1).

Under colonial rule, Burma was initially governed as a province of British India and there was significant migration from India and modern-day Bangladesh. With the onset of the Second World War and the Japanese invasion, Myanmar remained under Japanese control from 1942 until 1945, when the Japanese were driven out by the British. The British had made a promise to the Rohingya that they would establish a Muslim national area in northern Rakhine State (Yegar 1972: 96). Based on this promise, some Rohingya mobilized themselves politically and approached President Jinnah of the newly-created Pakistan to propose the integration of northern Rakhine State into Bangladesh (then East Pakistan). This attempt to break off the Muslim area of northern Rakhine State to integrate into Bangladesh contributed to the animosity between the Rohingya and the rest of Myanmar, particularly the Rakhine Buddhists (Coursen-Neff 2000).

In the initial post-independence era, the Burmese Prime Minister U Nu and President Sao Shwe Thaike were said to have acknowledged the Rohingya claim to be a separate ethnic group within Myanmar (Lwin 2012). However, this recognition was denied by the military government when it took power in 1962 and this denial continues. When President Ne Win conducted the widely discredited 1964 census, it revealed widespread emigration from Rakhine State to other parts of Myanmar. In response, government officials prohibited any travel by Muslims east of Akyab District near the Bangladesh border and between villages. The Myanmar government mandated the Rakhine Buddhists with enforcement of the new rules creating greater division between Muslims and Buddhists in Rakhine State (Ragland 1994: 306). Indeed, after the 1962 military coup the police force was initially majority Burman and developed a sense of exclusiveness as police were encouraged to see themselves as part of the new military regime. The opportunity for promotions and jobs in the civil service reduced, leaving more police officers to work in their own communities across Myanmar (Selth 2012: 66).

Since the 1962 military coup, the military governments have been proactive in initiating various policies that discriminate against the Rohingya. These policies range from omitting them from the census to verifying citizenship identification and forced labour. In 1977, Operation Naga Min (Dragon King) was launched with the aim of checking all identity cards. These cards are all colour-coded, pink for those who are full citizens; blue, for those who are associated citizens; green, for those who are naturalized citizens; and white for foreigners (Ahmed 2001: 2). In Operation Naga Min, Muslims in Rakhine State who had legitimate identification cards had them taken away on the pretext of being updated, only to never get them back or altered from citizens to foreigners. Furthermore many were forcibly displaced, villages burned and many fled across the border into Bangladesh. These refugees were later repatriated to Myanmar as part of a bilateral agreement between both governments. Successive governments have contested that the Rohingya are not an ethnic group but are Bengali Muslims who first entered Myanmar during British colonial rule and have been a threat to Myanmar since its independence. The government also argues that the vast majority claiming Rohingya identity is part of an ongoing influx of Bengali Muslims entering Myanmar illegally. This is contested by the Rohingya themselves, foreign governments and international organizations.

However, the Burma Citizenship Law No 4/1982 created obstacles for a 'foreigner' to be granted Burman nationality, with the Muslim Rohingya community as the main target, to delegitimize the Rohingya claims to citizenship. The discredited 1983 census showed the official figures of 567,985 Bangladeshis, 428,428 Indians, 42,140 Pakistanis, and 28,506 Nepalis. An estimated 1 million Burmese of Indian origin remained in Burma in the early 1980s (Taylor 2006; Thet 2008, Egreteau 2011).

By the 1990s, the military junta stepped up their campaign of targeting the Rohingya and systematically denied them human rights, including the removal of citizenship rights, forced labour, and forced relocation. In 1992 the military junta established the NaSaKa, a border security force combining the police, army, customs, and immigration offices, mandated to police the Bangladeshi border and control the movements and population growth of the Rohingya in northern Rakhine State (Cheung 2011: 52). The NaSaKa was largely controlled by Burmans, and was known for its human rights abuses such as taxing marriage registration multiple times, detention and rape of women on the pretext of checking family lists at NaSaKa camps, and implementing the model village program to encourage Buddhist migration to land confiscated from the Rohingya (Islam 2007). The NaSaKa were also widely known for corruption and the taking of bribes to expedite the official documentation process.

By the 2000s, the NaSaKa began to more strictly enforce land use policies, which led to a number of Rohingya evictions, including the demolition of houses built on land registered as paddy fields or shrimp farms (Islam 2007). In early 2007, the military government designated an area along the Bangladesh-Myanmar border, called Taungbro sub-district, to promote cross-border trade with Bangladesh. This area saw many Buddhist families brought in from other states in Myanmar to settle in this new model village (Bosson 2007), as part of the government's policy of promoting Buddhist migration into northern Rakhine State.

The policy of encouraging Buddhist migration from other parts of Myanmar coupled with the fear of mass Muslim migration into Rakhine State led to the local Rakhine Buddhist population's development of a sense of victimhood. This is rooted in the Burman's domination of Rakhine State since independence, along with the encouraged Buddhist migration from elsewhere in Myanmar (largely Burman, as the largest ethnic group) entwined with fears of increasing Rohingya domination (Bachtold et al. 2014: 47). Low level economic and social development has made Rakhine State home to the country's second highest rate of poverty (UN 2012: 3), which further exacerbates tension. Following the 2012 riots and subsequent violence, the Myanmar government decided that the Buddhist and Muslim communities were to be separated 'for their own safety' (UN 2012: 8), which can also make aid appear biased towards a particular community. The Rakhine Buddhists have access to state apparatus, albeit of poor quality, whereas the Rohingya face severe restrictions over access to healthcare, food, and water to name a few provisions delivered by the state. INGOs therefore fill the gap in these services by distributing aid to the Rohingya. However, the local Rakhine Buddhist community sees this as ignoring the extreme poverty faced by many people in Rakhine State, and not just the Rohingya. One of the subsequent central government responses was to disband the NaSaKa border security force in mid-2013 and replace it with the Hlun Thein (Security Force).

Prior to the disbanding of the NaSaKa, in 2012, a 25-member Commission of Inquiry (CoI), which included three Muslim (non-Rohingya) members, was established by President Thein Sein to investigate the root causes of the violence, verify loss of life and property, examine efforts to restore peace and promote law and order, find means to provide relief and resettlement, develop short and long-term strategies to reconcile differences, establish mutual understanding, and advise on promotion of social and economic development (COI 2013: i). After several delays, the Commission published its findings in 2013. The report documented Rakhine fears and perceptions of the violence that occurred, but recognized the need for non-discriminatory policies particularly over births and marriages, and the need to adequately provide for the, disproportionately Rohingya, Internally Displaced Person (IDP) communities, both of which have been identified as report strengths. However, the omission of the history of discrimination, unsubstantiated allegations that Islamic leaders and their Islamic *madrasa* (boarding schools) bred intolerance and radical ideas, the need for justice and accountability measures for human rights abuses by state actors, and the revision of the 1982 Citizenship Law have been identified as key weaknesses in the report (Stein 2013). However, presently, tension and large numbers of displaced persons remain and a concerted effort to address these root causes remains wanting. There is little evidence the recommendations of the report have been implemented to date or that the commission addressed many of the fundamental issues it should have set out to accomplish.

Facts, Perception, and Aid

While objective facts are oftentimes trumped by perception in international relations (Selth 2008: 380), the strategic mindset of the ruling elites at both state and national levels in Myanmar view external actors with suspicion and are no different when considering international aid. Prior to the 1988 pro-democracy protests in Myanmar, the general strategic assumption was that the greatest threat to the state was found within and along Myanmar's borders with the various non-state armed groups. With this mindset, the involvement of other states was viewed through their perceived support for proxy wars with various armed groups, such as the Chinese funding the Burmese Communist Party, Western governments funding humanitarian activities along the Thai-Myanmar border or Muslim-majority countries like Saudi Arabia funding the purchase of weapons by Rohingya insurgents (Selth 2008: 381–4). The latter has facilitated the idea that Myanmar Muslims are an enemy within (Selth 2004: 111–3).

However, since the 1988 pro-democracy protests, the perception has been that other states have sought to influence the internal affairs of Myanmar. This was a result of increasingly powerful rhetoric used by United States politicians in the aftermath of the pro-democracy protests and the placement of five US naval vessels off the coast of Myanmar in September 1988 (Selth 2008: 381–2). Throughout the 1990s, the ruling military in Myanmar saw its national security through these lenses of fearing an enemy within and external aggression from a major power. While the fear of US invasion and the potential for reciprocal action by the Chinese remained a high strategic concern, the Rohingya along its Western border remained a people-centred strategic concern where the threat came from mass Muslim migration into Myanmar to dominate its Buddhist population.

In the aftermath of the 2008 Cyclone Nargis, the Myanmar military was slow to respond to the humanitarian disaster in the coastal Irrawaddy Division, south of Yangon. The international community sought to assist with relief supplies and aid workers, but it was initially rejected by the Myanmar military. The rejection of international assistance was greeted with disbelief by the international community. This frustration over the poor response led to some countries contemplating unilateral aid drops and the invocation of the Responsibility to Protect (R2P) (Selth 2008: 389–91). While the R2P principles focus on crimes of mass atrocity, the French Foreign Minister Bernard Kouchner has argued that the R2P principle should apply in times of natural disaster when the host government is unresponsive to the needs of its people—an argument now known as R2P-Plus

(Caballero-Anthony and Chng 2009). In 2008, the Myanmar military saw the possibility of intervention from Western states under humanitarian auspices to protect a particular community as a direct security threat to the state so there remains suspicion of humanitarian organizations in Myanmar.

While many INGOs have entered Myanmar since 2011 there remains a suspicion of 'foreign organizations'. Humanitarian aid organizations have had to agree to a more limited range of activities in order to gain some access and build trust with officials for the long-term. The development of relationships with government officials can help improve government policy, build local capacity, and improve the long-term viability of aid programmes and constrain abusive behaviour of local officials who fear exposure over their corrupt practices (Pedersen 2012: 275). In the 2012 riots and subsequent violence, these twin threats of external intervention and internal conflict dovetailed. The deep-seated ignorance and fear of Muslim domination was demonstrated through the mass protests that took place ahead of the Organization of Islamic Conference visit to Rakhine State amid the suggestion of the establishment of an OIC representative office in November 2013. While there is a clear role for the international community, its influence remains limited, and any significant political change is still seen as most likely coming from within the country itself (Selth 2008a: 295). Indeed, this extends firmly into the humanitarian aid field. As a result, all NGOs will likely continue to face similar accusations of bias and periodically need to renegotiate access until the deeper issues of anti-Rohingya and anti-Muslim sentiment are tackled.

Humanitarian Aid from the Muslim World

The breadth and depth of support for humanitarian assistance after the 2012 riots has expanded from the usual donor countries to countries such as Indonesia, Turkey, Saudi Arabia, and organizations such as the Organization of Islamic Conference (OIC) and ASEAN (Lacey-Hall 2012). During the 67th UN General Assembly session in 2012, Muslim leaders from OIC countries called for more action to end the violence in Rakhine State, which the UN Secretary General then discussed with Myanmar President Thein Sein and Ekmeleddin

Ihsanoglu, Secretary General of the OIC. By the end of 2012, partly in response to the Al Jazeera documentary 'The Hidden Genocide', the Myanmar Ministry of Foreign Affairs gave permission to UN agencies, INGOs, diplomatic corps, and Muslim Aid to visit affected areas to observe the situation themselves. Moreover, foreign ministers and high-level delegations from Muslim nations, including Turkey, Indonesia, Malaysia, as well as the OIC were allowed to visit Rakhine State (Kipgen 2013: 305).

One organization that has historically shown support for the Rohingya is the OIC. On 16 May 1978, the OIC issued an official statement to the international community that 'the Muslim Rohingya in Myanmar are currently suffering from huge atrocities, which have been confirmed by various reliable sources' (Parnini 2013: 291). At that time, it did not yet have a humanitarian affairs department; this was only established in 2008. Since 2012, the OIC delegation was granted access to deliver assistance in Rakhine State and members have continued to contribute to humanitarian efforts there largely through contributions to United Nations agencies' programs. In 2013, the OIC made plans to establish a liaison office in Myanmar. However, on 15 October 2013, thousands of Buddhist monks in Yangon and Mandalay marched in protest (Kipgen 2013: 306), and President Thein Sein failed to grant permission for the OIC to open a representative office.

Aside from the OIC, Muslim-majority countries have announced their own aid packages for the Rohingya. Saudi Arabia urged the international community to protect the 'Muslims in Myanmar', as the Saudi King pledged US$50 million in aid for the Rohingyas (Abrar 2013: 5). In September 2012 Saudi Arabia's Ambassador to Myanmar gave a US$1 million cheque to the UNHCR to fund the agency's education and health work in Rakhine State and noted that as both Muslim and non-Muslim communities were affected in the rioting, they would 'receive equal amounts of support' (*Myanmar Times* 2012). This was a clear demonstration that Saudi Arabia was towing the Myanmar government's line in this regard. In 2013 Saudi Arabia granted residence permits to some Rohingya refugees in Saudi Arabia and also established the Global Rohingya Centre, two costly initiatives. It was not only Middle Eastern states that signalled their concern, legislators from the Southeast Asian region through the ASEAN Inter-Parliamentary Myanmar Caucus (AIPMC) who have been the recipient countries for an estimated 87,000 people noted that 'the Myanmar government's policy of segregating Muslim and Buddhist communities in Rakhine State is compounding a humanitarian crisis there, while ASEAN's failure to positively influence the situation points to continued institutional failures in the regional grouping' (Abrar 2013: 5). Western-based Muslim FBOs like Muslim Aid (MA) have launched emergency appeals to provide help and support for the Rohingya people through their own field programmes (MA 2014a). Finally, Myanmar Muslim FBOs have donated and distributed aid to those displaced by the violence in Rakhine State.

With the emergence of responses from across the Muslim world, there are three trends evident in these responses. The structure of aid distribution in Muslim-majority countries like the Gulf States mirror many similar competing mandates found elsewhere between different government agencies. However, what is distinctive is the difficulty in distinguishing between the public and private roles of individual members of the royal families, who are key interlocutors in both government and charitable organizations (Cotterrell and Harmer 2005: 18). Gulf States have primarily been engaged in aid assistance at the regional level rather than the international level. However, there has been a noticeable shift towards greater regional cooperation in aid policy through sub-regional organizations like the Gulf Cooperation Council (GCC), regional organizations like the Arab League (Cotterrell and Harmer 2005: 23) and international organizations like the Organization of Islamic Conference.

Indeed, the aid packages of Muslim-majority countries and Muslim international organizations often exhibit a pro-state bias. This is dominant in South-South relations overall, where developing countries donate to other developing countries and demonstrate adherence to the traditional sovereignty norm of non-interference in another state's domestic affairs. As a result, development aid is often funnelled through recipient government agencies or at least requires approval of UN agencies. This more often than not translates into tacit support for bureaucratic and centralized interests (Burke 2012: 193–4).

In the region, Indonesia spearheaded coordination for a number of OIC member countries that pledged assistance for the Rohingyas. Indonesian Red Cross (PMI) signed a Memorandum of

Understanding with his counterpart in the Myanmar Red Cross chair-person Hla Shwe. Jusuf Kalla said that the mission to assist Myanmar was a first for Indonesia in a neighbouring country, and was the result of cooperation between the Red Cross and the Myanmar government (Taufiqurrahman 2012). This cooperation needs to be seen within the Myanmar government's 'total people's defence' strategy, which envisages drawing on all sectors of Myanmar society, particularly the Myanmar Police Force and other bodies such as the Auxiliary Fire Brigade, but also extending to the Myanmar Red Cross (Selth 2012: 68). It therefore appears that there is a tension for the national Red Cross society between its role as an extended arm of the government and upholding humanitarian principles of neutrality, impartiality, independence, and humanity.

This contrasts to the evolution of western-based Muslim FBOs, which have become increasingly significant within the global humanitarian movement. While there are questionable examples of Muslim FBO involvement with non-state armed groups such as the *mujahedeen* in Bosnia during the 1990s, for the majority of trans-national Muslim FBOs this crisis was a turning point in how they operated in the field (Petersen 2012). In the aftermath of 11 September 2001 terrorist attacks on the United States, heightened suspicion emerged over the activities of transnational Muslim FBOs, and led to the banning of 31 Muslim FBOs by the US State Department for their relations with Al-Qaeda or other purported radical Islamic groups. Alongside the banning of Muslim FBOs, western governments were also increasingly interested in partnerships with 'moderate' Muslim FBOs, as a response to the growing divide between Islam and the West (Petersen 2012: 773). Now, Western-based Muslim FBOs are developing partnerships with secular NGOs or Christian FBOs as a way to distance themselves from the more militant kinds of Muslim FBOs. However, some retain a focus on Muslim recipients rather than a universalist approach, which sets them apart from many other transnational NGOs (Petersen 2012: 771).

In November 2012, Muslim Aid visited Myanmar and met with government ministers to convince them of the organization's need to access Rakhine State and that Muslim Aid is an international humanitarian organization that distributes assistance 'no matter what race, religion or colour the people are' (Azad 2013). In 2013,

Muslim Aid began building a hospital to serve 14,000 displaced persons as well as 6 mobile hospitals to help 12,000 people. Muslim Aid has gained similar recognition to other international humanitarian organizations and it opened up field offices in Sittwe and Yangon to deliver aid, including healthcare, education, and livelihood activities, to internally displaced Rohingya. In 2014 Muslim Aid also signed a Memorandum of Understanding and Cooperation with Al Asmakh Charity Foundation, a Qatar-based charity to 'combine their resources for emergency response and poverty alleviation in Myanmar' (MA 2014a). The MOU is implemented through Muslim Aid delivering an Al Asmakh emergency relief project in Myanmar with the permission of both the national and Rakhine State governments in Myanmar (MA 2013).

However, the pool of funders is broader than the Muslim community, thus having strong implications for the humanitarian work these Muslim FBOs undertake. For example, Islamic Relief Worldwide (IRW) took over from MSF the running of the Leda camp in Bangladesh, which is home to undocumented Rohingya refugees, and ran it along with Handicap International and MA. However, as the IRW project was funded by the European Commission's Humanitarian aid and Civil Protection department (ECHO), the funds could not be used to build mosques or other religious buildings. A compromise was reached whereby local community centres were used for religious activities (Palmer 2011: 103).

Western-based Muslim FBOs may be more trusted by Muslims compared to non-religious western-based aid organizations. They are also able to tap into the community network of mosques and community associations in the same way western-based church groups leverage local Christian communities to facilitate aid delivery (De Cordier 2009: 622; Palmer 2011: 98). However, this association can work both ways particularly when an ethnic and religious group is in the minority with historical tension with the majority population within a state combined with the wider level of tolerance towards that group as part of Myanmar society. In this case, rather than Muslim Aid's credentials as a Muslim charity being the leverage, it is its commitment to the international norms of humanitarianism that led to its successful negotiation of access to the population of concern. Overall, what we have seen with the emergence of Muslim world humanitarianism in response to the 2012 riots and its aftermath is its growing importance in the network of global INGOs with a particular focus on the needs of Muslims, but ready and willing to distribute these supplies to all.

Muslim Aid distributed aid to Rohingyas in two different contexts—Buddhist-majority Myanmar and Muslim-majority Bangladesh. The Rohingya have been a source of tension since the independence of both countries and these relations continue to affect and shape the lives of the Rohingya and others displaced along the Bangladesh-Myanmar border. Finally, the domestic Myanmar Muslim community including both Rohingya living in Yangon and Muslims across Myanmar, through FBOs and the business community, provided much needed support to the Rohingya displaced in Sittwe after the violence. This initial support funded several shipments of rice, which was allowed by the government, but were distributed by local Rakhine State authorities, which meant the supplies may have been the object of corruption. However, subsequent shipments like the three in June-July 2012 were distributed by Rohingya camp leaders. In Sittwe, there is a low-profile presence of Myanmar organizations like Myanmar Resources Foundation run by Myanmar Muslims, which distributes food to those IDPs who do not qualify for UN assistance.[2] Five Myanmar Muslim organizations pooled their efforts together to provide food for the Rohingya during the month of Ramadan in 2012 and formed the All Myanmar Islamic Relief Organization (AMIRO), which includes Jamiyyatul Ulama of Myanmar, Islamic Religious Affair Council of Myanmar, All Myanmar Maulvi Organization, All Myanmar Youth Religious Organization and Myanmar Muslim National Affairs Organization. All these organizations have consultative status with the religious authorities of Myanmar and are authorized to deliver humanitarian assistance (Rahman 2012). However, the AMIRO has also built partnerships with other Muslim FBOs based overseas. During August 2012, the Global Peace Mission (GPM) Malaysia sent a delegation to Myanmar to meet with their counterparts and present US$83,000 to AMIRO's Islamic Relief Committee (Rahman 2012a).

---

[2] Correspondence with an independent NGO focused on northern Rakhine State, 27 August 2014.

While there are multiple avenues through which the Muslim community have mobilized to provide relief for the displaced Rohingyas, the conversation has been directed at the activities of those outside northern Rakhine State. Within northern Rakhine State, no evidence has been uncovered to identify the presence of any Rohingya FBOs or community-based organizations providing relief. It is unlikely that if they did, these organizations would be granted permits to operate under the current conditions. Many Rohingya rely on remittances from extended family members working mainly in Malaysia and Saudi Arabia. The Rohingya community have also raised funds and sent them to Rakhine State through the Hawala system of money brokers. However, this money most likely remains within an extended family or particular village and does not necessarily go to the most vulnerable. According to those familiar with the situation, one community-based organized activity for the most vulnerable occurs during *Eid-ul-Fitr* with the distribution of meat. Before the 2012 riots, religious leaders provided religious education which was the most prominent form of community-based activity present in the Rohingya community in northern Rakhine State.[3]

This investigation into the Muslim humanitarian response to the 2012 riots and subsequent violence demonstrates several emergent trends. Muslim-majority countries which offered to provide aid tended to do so through formal channels, in contrast to Muslim FBOs. Muslim FBOs fell into two broad categories, western-based and those based in Muslim-majority countries. The western-based Muslim FBOs like Muslim Aid are more often found running their own field programmes, and work with other humanitarian organizations to provide the needed relief. There is also a trend for Muslim FBOs to support other Muslim FBOs when they have access to a population of concern. Finally, within the Rohingya community, some families rely on extended families to provide them with overseas remittances. However, community-organizing by Rohingya in Yangon or the Myanmar Muslim community more generally were better positioned and accepted by government authorities to provide relief.

[3] Correspondence with an independent NGO focused on northern Rakhine State, 27 August 2014.

Regional Humanitarian Aid and
Myanmar–Bangladesh Relations

Since 2009, there has been a revival of bilateral negotiations between Bangladesh and Myanmar, beginning with the bilateral visits of their foreign ministers. The repatriation of the remaining Rohingya refugees from Bangladesh to Myanmar was a priority item in the agenda (Parnini et al. 2013: 138). Bangladesh sought to resolve the issue quickly, while Myanmar sought documentation so it could determine who its citizens were. Although Bangladesh often complains about sharing responsibility for the Rohingyas, the responsibility has actually been borne by other stakeholders in Bangladesh. The US Committee for Refugees reported that while Dhaka claims it is an economic burden caring for the Rohingyas, Bangladesh has borne little of the cost, with the exception of US$2.5 million that Bangladesh spent prior to UNHCR involvement on the provision of aid to the Rohingya (Parnini et al. 2013: 138).

By the end of 2014, an agreement by President Thein Sein to cooperate with Bangladesh in resolving the Rohingya issue only saw the agreed return of 2,415 documented Rohingya after verification. However, a similar agreement was made in 2005 and only 90 Rohingya returned to Myanmar (Parnini et al. 2013: 295) out of an estimated 200,000 displaced in Bangladesh. As a result, the prospects remain dim for the Rohingya with a restrictive aid environment and continued statelessness. In 2010, only some 28,000 remained in two camps, Nayapura and Kutupalong, in Southeastern Cox's Bazaar, but there are an estimated 200,000 Rohingya residing in the surrounding areas in villages and towns, who were repatriated to Myanmar but have since returned to Bangladesh (Cheung 2011: 52). In the aftermath of the 2012 riots, Bangladesh shut its border to prevent the passage of Rohingya to seek humanitarian aid and protection (IRIN 2012). In February 2014, in an effort to further dissuade Rohingya refugees from fleeing to Bangladesh, the Bangladesh government issued an order for Muslim Aid Bangladesh and other charities to stop their Rohingya humanitarian projects in Teknaf Uppazilla of Cox's Bazaar District with immediate effect, illustrating the highly insecure aid environment in Bangladesh for displaced Rohingya (MA 2014).

For Bangladesh, the displaced Rohingya are no longer a simple humanitarian tragedy; rather they are a potential threat to Bangladesh's internal stability and a source of interstate tension between Myanmar and Bangladesh (Rahman 2010: 234). This mirrors the traditional security mindset dominant in Myanmar on the displaced Rohingya. There is no institutional mechanism for Refugee Status Determination (RSD) in Bangladesh, and it is not party to the UN Refugee Convention or Protocol. It is a member of the executive committee of UNHCR since 1995, so there is potential persuasive power of the UNHCR to use its good offices to ensure that the basic principles of the refugee system are upheld, primarily the right of non-refoulement (Rahman 2010: 238). However, as *ad hoc* institutional practices rather than formal state policy responses dominate the Rohingya response, Bangladesh's policies towards the Rohingya fluctuate in line with domestic public opinion and are characterized by generally applicable punitive immigration measures, and reluctance to negotiate a long-term, sustainable solution, relying instead on short-term solutions such as humanitarian aid (Cheung 2011: 51). As a result, the Rohingya continue to live as a stateless population in Bangladesh describing themselves as 'caught between a crocodile and a snake' (MSF in Cheung 2011: 53). While the vast majority of asylum seekers fled to neighbouring Bangladesh, some fled further away to Malaysia. In Thailand, Chris Lewa, coordinator of the Arakan Project, reports that the conditions for the 1,700 or so Rohingya men who reach Thai shores and find themselves in immigration detention centres are appalling (Green 2013: 95). In the two years since the outbreak of violence in 2012, over 87,000 people—mostly Rohingya but also Bangladeshis—have fled to Thailand, Malaysia, Indonesia, and further afield (UNHCR 2014). This illustrates the ramifications and regional impact of the displaced Rohingya.

Until policies address the statelessness of the Rohingya and respect their fundamental human rights, many Rohingya will continue to seek protection abroad. Assistance and protection is both a moral and legal obligation of the international community and neighbouring states in particular (Lewa 2001: 11). Since 1992, Malaysian government ministers have understood the Rohingya issue as one that no longer qualifies as solely a domestic political affair. The then foreign minister, Abdullah Badawi, in 1992, referred to the Rohingya crisis as one that 'could no longer be regarded as Myanmar's domestic problem because the action by the Myanmar troops has burdened neighbouring countries and may disrupt regional stability' (Parnini et al. 2013: 289). It is clear that while the ultimate political solution needs to involve many stakeholders, there is wide concern with Myanmar's neighbours, and the international community more broadly, about the humanitarian situation in Rakhine State, particularly regarding the Rohingya, the prospects for a long term sustainable solution, and the implications for the region.

There has been a decline in assistance and interest from the international community for long-term refugees overall and particularly with regard to humanitarian aid to Rohingya refugees spread far and wide. Even for those organizations providing for the Rohingya in Bangladesh, government policy has stymied this assistance. Bangladeshi policy focuses on the security of the host state with the perception that the forced migrants are an existential threat. This framing translates into hostility towards the forced migrants and in turn threatens them with the risk of forced repatriation, closed camps, or non-recognition of their status. Thus, the human security dilemma of the Rohingya affects the bilateral relations between Myanmar and recipient states (Parnini et al. 2013: 287). Similar concerns over refugees are reflected throughout the region like in Malaysia, Thailand and Indonesia, with the overwhelming majority of states being non-signatory to the UN Refugee Convention. These concerns are replicated across South Asia as well where waves of Rohingya fled, beginning in the 1960s (Anwar 2013). Ultimately, as the majority of recipients are developing states, traditional sovereignty norms of non-interference dominate state thinking and unless the numbers of Rohingya arriving on the shores of neighbouring states reach crisis point from their perspective, technical assistance and informal diplomacy will remain the main modus operandi of regional state relations regarding the Rohingya.

* * *

I conclude by identifying three barriers which illustrate the challenges to responding to the displaced Rohingya in Rakhine State. These barriers are conceptual, political, and technical. The 2012 riots and subsequent violence that erupted have illustrated a broader nationalistic trend in Myanmar. At the international level, Bangladesh has adopted a containment strategy to stop the delivery of aid and has seen the periodic closure of its borders with Myanmar. Further afield, Rohingya have arrived in Indonesia, Malaysia and Thailand but while concern is heightened, the traditional sovereignty norm of non-interference remains dominant. All neighbouring countries have a poor record of upholding international humanitarian law when we consider the plight of the Rohingya and the reception given to them after fleeing violence in Rakhine State. There remains a need to mobilize moderate civil society leaders and groups in Myanmar to push for social change from within. Finally, the third barrier is technical, that is, assistance programmes and capacity building workshops. While this is notionally a 'low-hanging fruit', it has seen INGOs face the necessity of renegotiating Memoranda of Understanding and new restrictions put in place to control their access to the Rohingya and the aid they receive.

In 2012, the United Nations Resident and Humanitarian Coordinator in Myanmar, Ashok Nigam concluded his remarks at a meeting about the humanitarian situation in Rakhine State by quoting Saya Tun Aung Chain, a retired Yangon University history professor who said, 'I would have us think of our being in a continuous process and the solution which we work out not as final but as an interim and on-going solution. An interim solution is easier to work out if there is an understanding that it is part of an on-going process and that it is going to be incremental. Also since we and the world about us are in continual change, no solution can ever be final' (Nigam 2012). The Rohingya situation has deteriorated since the 1962 military coup, with the widespread violence in 2012 demonstrating a new low and the dominance of an anti-Rohingya and anti-Muslim mindset. However, when considering a way forward, some argue that the central government has failed to connect with key local leaders to anchor change in Rakhine State. In general, local Rakhine politicians were also unwilling to take the lead in implementing changes ahead of the 2015 elections and the risks of being perceived as pro-Rohingya (Bachtold et al. 2014: 46). As a result there is no significant political constituency for change in Myanmar.

As a result of the dominant discourse framing the debate on humanitarian aid in Rakhine State as pro-Rohingya, there is a continued need for humanitarian aid actors to develop relationships within the larger humanitarian community, to find new pathways forward to renegotiate field programmes for populations of concern. The emergence of humanitarian actors from the Muslim world taking a more active role in responding to humanitarian crises illustrated one such new way forward as an aid provider and donor source. Muslim FBOs have an important role to play in identifying the shifting needs of the Rohingya, challenging dominant stereotypes in Myanmar and facilitating community organization within the global Rohingya community. However, the impact of Muslim FBOs will depend upon continued access being provided by Myanmar and donor support for the field programmes, a concern for the global humanitarian community. Ultimately it seems Myanmar is clearly dependent on its Muslim regional neighbours—Bangladesh, Malaysia, and Indonesia—as well as its Buddhist neighbour—Thailand—to find a solution, and so the treatment of the Rohingya is likely to continue to test Muslim-Buddhist relations in the region.

11 Myanmar's Muslims, What Do We Now Know?

Clark B. Lombardi

To say that Myanmar's Muslim community has been woefully understudied is an understatement. Fortunately, new scholarship, including the scholarship collected in this volume, has begun to fill in some of the lacunae in our knowledge of this fascinating and diverse community. Already it is providing insight into the community, helping highlight its extraordinary vulnerability and providing policy-makers with some important information as they try to help Myanmar develop institutions and policies that will protect the community. Even as this new research has filled in gaps, however, it has highlighted a number of areas in which broader understanding of the Muslim community is still thin or non-existent. This volume simultaneously expands our knowledge and points out areas where more research is necessary.

Prior to this volume, one could find remarkably little research published on the Muslims of Myanmar since 1972. In 1960, an Israeli diplomat who had not yet completed his master's thesis in history was posted to what was then Burma. He proposed to write a thesis on the Muslim communities of the country. This proposal accepted, Yegar struggled to find published scholarship or raw data that would help him understand these communities. He ultimately produced not only his master's thesis, but a very useful, though necessarily short, book that catalogued the current state of knowledge about the history of Burmese Muslims up to the coup of 1962 (Yegar 1972). Yegar's book, finally published in 1972, made clear that the Muslim community in Burma had always been remarkably diverse and divided. This was a result of both geography and politics. Myanmar is wedged between three parts of the world with large and diverse Muslim populations: Central, South, and Southeast Asia. It is also on sea routes that were plied by Muslim merchants not only from these regions, but also from the Middle East and Muslim East Africa. In the nineteenth century, Burma was integrated into the British Empire, which exercised dominion over most of the world's Muslims, and facilitated the movement of Muslims across the many regions of the Empire. Over the course of history, groups of Muslims had moved into what is today Myanmar. They had come at different times and in different ways, and at the time Yegar wrote, they were distributed geographically in different parts of the country. Given the lack of accurate census data, it is not clear exactly how large the Muslim community was. Nevertheless, it appeared that taken together, Burma's diverse Muslim communities represented a sizeable minority. It was a community that clearly began to change in 1962 when a deeply authoritarian regime appeared, changing cultural policies and driving many Burmese Muslims of Indian descent into diaspora. A new study, he suggested, would be necessary to explore those changes.

In 1972, Moshe Yegar had pointed out to the world that there was a Muslim population (or arguably a family of Muslim populations) that was hiding in plain sight, was undergoing dramatic change, and deserved to be studied. The world's response was to yawn. In the years following the publication of Yegar's book, there was substantial interest in the study of minority Muslim communities around the world (Haddad 2002; Nielsen 2008). A new peer-reviewed international journal, *The Journal of the Institute of Muslim Minority Affairs* (JIMMA), even appeared in 1989 with a mandate to publish the growing amount of scholarship on such communities (Forbes 1986).[1] Nonetheless,

---

[1] Exemplifying the link between study of Asian Muslim minority communities and a concern about the rise of terrorism in the region, see for example Chalk 2001.

studies about Myanmar's Muslims continued to be noticeably absent from the growing scholarly literature on Muslim minority communities. The JIMMA in its first 25 years of publication produced only one article focusing specifically on a Muslim community living in Burma, which in 1989 was renamed by its government as 'Myanmar' (Forbes 1986).

For the saddest of reasons, people recently have begun to notice and lament the lack of new scholarship into Myanmar's Muslim communities. The country has begun to open up politically and economically. Whatever the benefits of this development, and there are many, it has also unleashed a wave of anxiety and created more space for divisive populist politics than there had been for many years. Muslim Rohingya people who live in Rakhine State have become the victims of violence, some of it organized by shadowy Buddhist organizations that are explicitly hostile to Islam and Muslims. The plight of the Rohingya reminded the world that there were, in fact, Muslims living in Myanmar. As violence has spread and began to touch other Muslims across the country, people have begun to ask questions about the relationship between the Rohingya and other Muslim communities in Myanmar and broader questions about the relationship of Muslim and non-Muslim communities in Myanmar—questions which the existing scholarship is inadequate to answer.

Against this backdrop, in January 2014, the Centre for Asian Legal Studies at the National University of Singapore convened a fascinating and important conference on Islam in Myanmar. The conference was organized by a pair of distinguished scholars of religion and politics in Southeast Asia, including one with deep connections among Muslims within Myanmar and among Burmese diaspora communities. The organizer, Melissa Crouch, provided participants with a bibliography of English language works on Islam and Muslims in Myanmar. She then asked each participant to contribute to our knowledge about Islam and Muslims in Myanmar by updating or supplementing the existing literature. Finally published in this volume, those essays add significantly to our understanding of the history of the Muslim community in Myanmar and of its current predicament.

The essays in this volume help us begin to address some of the important open questions. Why has the academy neglected to study

Burmese Islam or the Muslim communities in Myanmar? What sorts of resource are available for people who wish to focus on these subjects today? Triangulating from journalism and the scholarship that has started to be done in recent years, what do we know about Burmese Muslims that we did not know in 1972? Where might further study best help policy-makers focusing on promoting human rights and democracy in Myanmar? What types of research might most impact scholarship in area studies, Islamic studies, or comparative religion?

Why the Lack of Scholarship?

There are many reasons why Myanmar's Muslim communities failed to attract the type of academic attention that one might expect. Building on some of his own earlier scholarship, Stephen Keck argues provocatively in this book that some policies of British colonial masters were perpetuated by Myanmar's post-colonial rulers and that these policies helped to distract attention from the fact both that there are a lot of Muslims living in Myanmar and that they have played an important part in its history. British colonial modes of conceptualizing their subjects and colonial patterns of governing these subjects strongly influenced attitudes and practices in modern Myanmar. They have also come to influence the way that outside academics think about Burma (Keck, this volume). When the British took over the territory that they knew as Burma, they were confronted with an enormously diverse population. Keck does not make clear whether the solution that the British came up with was rooted in pre-colonial mentalities and practices or, instead, represented something fundamentally new. Irrespective of this, he makes a strong case that, as the British tried to understand, organize, and govern their subjects in British Burma, they conceptualized them as members of linguistic groups who tended to live in particular regions. At least from the colonial period onwards, the Burmese too began to identify and organize themselves politically in similar terms. Subjects who wished to engage with the state, either through cooperation or resistance, tended to accept the primacy of regional and linguistic identity. The embrace of territorial federalism after independence reflects this mentality. So did the rise of regional separatist movements. And it subtly discouraged Muslims living in the country from adopting a transregional Muslim political identity.

In this environment, it was perhaps natural that the academy did not prioritize study of Myanmar's Muslims *qua* Muslims. Indeed, the one monograph that tried to tell the story of Islam and Muslims in Burma was not written by a professional academic, but rather by an Israeli diplomat who happened to have significant talents as a historian. That the academy failed to produce subsequent volumes that built upon Yegar's work, however, cannot be blamed entirely on a blinkered mentality or to scholarly inertia. Even if someone had been interested in studying Myanmar's Muslims, such a person would have found it difficult to carry out such studies effectively. Post-colonial Myanmar was governed by a series of nationalist military regimes that did not encourage any domestic scholarship likely to encourage divisive identity politics. Furthermore, as they grew increasingly xenophobic, these regimes made it difficult for foreign academics to enter the country. The Burmese diaspora appears not to have encouraged or facilitated studies of Islam in Myanmar.

Recently, two things have changed. First, political events have inspired people within and outside Myanmar to return their attention to Myanmar's Muslim minority. Since 2011, Myanmar's authoritarian military rulers have taken steps to loosen their control over Burmese politics and society. While the process of democratization is far from complete, it has led to a significant opening of the political process and an explosion of popular self-expression. This opening has not been entirely benign. Among the troubling voices heard in the new Myanmar are some violent and divisive ones calling for the state to reconstitute itself in a mode that privileges the Buddhist community and its values. In some parts of the country, therefore, Muslim communities have been threatened or attacked. Sometimes the attackers criticize them as 'foreign', and sometimes specifically as 'Muslim'. In such an environment, Burmese Muslims and foreign scholars of Myanmar have been forced to revisit the assumption that Myanmar's Muslims see (or should see) their Muslim-ness as a secondary characteristic—one that has little practical impact on their lives and certainly has less impact than their regional or linguistic identity. Contemporary Burmese Muslims have suffered (or imminently will suffer) because they are Muslim. Do they wish to continue identifying themselves as people to whom their Muslim identity is secondary—people who see themselves primarily as Karen, Bamar, or Shan who just happen to be Muslim?

Second, as political events have highlighted the need for further study of contemporary Myanmar's Muslim communities, it has also created conditions that make at least tentative new studies possible. The political opening has allowed academics to enter the country and has permitted journalists and aid workers to uncover facts that tell us something about the way that Myanmar's Muslims have fared. Crucially too, it has empowered Burmese Muslims to reflect upon their experiences and to speak about them. Taking advantage of these new circumstances, the contributors to this volume, some Burmese and some outsiders, have provided us with important insights about Myamar's Muslim communities and the conditions they live in today.

What New Insights have been Uncovered Recently About the History of Islam in Myanmar and the Current Predicament of Myanmar's Muslims?

The contributions in this volume supplement in important ways the historical information presented in Yegar's history of Muslims in Myanmar and provide some important history for the period after the one that he covers.

Melissa Crouch's chapter on the administration of Islamic law in Myanmar helps us to appreciate that in one respect Myanmar's Muslims were recognized as a community sharing a particular identity and set of needs. The legal system recognized Muslims as a community that shared a right to structure its family relationships according to Islamic law. Her work makes clear that the British authorities had a shallow understanding of 'Islamic law'. Furthermore, there is no significant ethnography and thus we do not know how Burmese Muslim's perceive the courts. Nevertheless, she has done a tremendous service in highlighting the existence of court records that can help us understand, at the very least, the social facts of life in Muslim communities and the attitudes of both Muslims and non-Muslims towards Muslims. Other contributions update the history of Myanmar's Muslim communities to cover events that took place from the 1970s to the present day. Many of these describe powerfully the processes by which Islamophopic and anti-Muslim discourse has spread in Myanmar, particularly in the context of the anti-Rohingya agitation. A number of works situate the experience of Myanmar's Muslims, and particularly the Rohingya's recent experience of persecution, in an important theoretical or comparative context, highlighting how it is facilitated by both a regional environment in which militant Sri Lankan Muslim organizations have sought to export their ideology (Schonthal, this volume) and a technological environment in which intra- and international communication has changed (Schissler, this volume).

Importantly, a number of contributions draw upon a source of information that Yegar left almost entirely unexplored—the testimony of Myanmar's Muslims, both within the country and in the diaspora. In the 1970s and 1980s, the academy embraced new approaches to the study of history. It focused on subjects best accessed through techniques that had previously been underutilized, including oral history. Informed by this development, a number of contributions powerfully describe the experience of being a member of a Burmese Muslim community or as a member of the Burmese Muslim diaspora.

Two major themes emerge in the contributions published in this volume, and particularly in the personal first person accounts of Muslim's daily life in Myanmar. The first key theme is identity. Different chapters focus on 'identity' in different ways. Some focus on the anxieties Burmese Muslims feel as they try to locate Myanmar and its Muslim population within the broader global community of Muslims. Other contributions focus on the challenges faced by the different Muslim communities located within Myanmar as they try to understand their relationship with each other. The Muslim populace in Myanmar is clearly very diverse and it appears also to be internally divided. One thing Muslims apparently share is a sense of disempowerment. Not surprisingly, then, one sees a second central theme, that of growing anxiety. In nearly all the papers, there is a distinct sense of the nervousness, fragility, and vulnerability that Muslim communities in Myanmar are facing and experiencing. It is unclear whether Muslims always felt this way and academics have only recently begun to appreciate it, or whether, instead, Muslims' expressions of anxiety reflect a change in the experience (or mentality) of Muslims living in this fraught period.

Where Should the Study of Myanmar's Muslims Go in the Future?

While the chapters collected here tell us much that we did not previously know, they do not tell us all that we might want to know about Myanmar's Muslim communities. Indeed, even as this volume fills out important details about the history and particularly about the recent experience of Muslims in Myanmar, it also helps us better understand where further study would be productive. It seems clear that studies of Myanmar's Muslim communities could fruitfully be tied into broader academic discussions including comparative colonial history, Islamic studies, comparative religion, politics, and human security studies. It might be useful to structure future research on Burmese Muslims specifically with an eye to answering questions of interest to scholars in those particular fields. In so doing, one would hopefully add nuance to our understanding of the Burmese experience and, at the same time, would enrich the world's understanding of those broader trends.

How has Myanmar's Muslim History been Shaped by Broader Regional and International Trends Over the Course of History and How are Current Trends Shaping Their Experiences Today?

Stephen Keck's chapter situates the experience of Myanmar's Muslims in the context of British colonial history. Melissa Crouch's chapter reminds us that in at least some ways, the community is affected deeply by institutions set up during the Raj to manage Muslim affairs and reflect a uniquely British colonial approach to administering Islamic law. Contributions to this volume that focus on contemporary events highlight the way in which contemporary Myanmar's Muslims are being affected by militant Buddhism and the rise of the internet. All of these remind us that as distinctive as they are, Myanmar's Muslims have always been embedded into transnational networks whose impact on their lives is not fully understood.

It seems crucial to explore still more deeply the ways in which the experiences of Burmese communities have been shaped by broader regional trends during the pre-colonial, colonial and post-colonial period. The makeup of the Burmese Muslim community was shaped by regional trends that promoted the migration of Muslims into and outside of the territory that became part of British Burma and post-colonial Burma. Furthermore, patterns of transnational communication seem to have powerfully affected the way in which this community came to understand itself and came to be understood by their neighbours. Not only did transnational networks help to inform the beliefs and practices of the Muslim community, but, as several contributions to this volume make clear, they appear to have influenced the beliefs and practices of Myanmar's Buddhist community and nurtured and shaped a militant Buddhist ideology that is deeply threatening to Myanmar's Muslim community. Hovering in the background is the threat that Islam's own ever-growing transnational networks, including its militant networks, will become embroiled in the violence that is simmering in the country. More research is needed for us to fully understand the history and impact of regional and transnational religious networks in Myanmar, to predict the trajectory of inter-religious relationships in the country and, if necessary, to respond to further crises.

How do Burmese Muslims Understand and Practise Their Religion and How is Islam in Myanmar Evolving in the Contemporary Period?

The title of this book is *Islam and the State in Myanmar*. Most of our papers have addressed only indirectly the question of what 'Islam' means to these Muslims in Myanmar and whether Muslims' understanding of 'Islam' is changing. Melissa Crouch's essay in this volume talks about what Islam means to the state—at least when the state has promised to resolve an issue according to 'Islamic law'. But we have little understanding of how Muslims feel about the state's interpretation.

There are some indications in this volume that the meaning of Islamic ideas and the nature of Islamic education are contested within the community and indeed, may have divided the community in ways that are dangerous, given the growing strength of Buddhist supremacism. Nevertheless, the chapters here leave us with only a hazy understanding of the contest, and how they might mirror the types of contest that one sees in other countries in South and Southeast Asia.

The contributions also address only indirectly questions of how state regulation or self-censorship impacts Muslims' abilities to perform what they perceive to be their ritual obligations—and thus how it affects the practise of Islam.

Ultimately, the contributions remind us how little is known about religious thought and practice among Myanmar's diverse Muslim communities. We are gaining a better understanding of *Muslims* in Myanmar but not about *Islam* in Myanmar. Indeed, no chapter focuses in detail on describing the religious practices or customs of the Muslim community or of any of its sub-communities. Based on his research some ten years earlier, Yegar in 1972 produced only thin information on the history of Islamic thought and practice in Burma. Not only would we benefit from a richer study of this history up to 1960, but we need to understand whether any changes have occurred since then. Given the remarkable developments in Islam around the world over the past fifty years, it certainly seems likely. So we need more research into both history and contemporary thought and practice: How have religious ideas been transmitted within the Muslim community? How have the teachings of Islam been communicated and interpreted? Are they changing? In which ritual practices are different Muslim groups involved? What are the dynamics of religious transmission? What happened to the Sufi orders, as discussed by Moshe Yegar in his early research?

Obtaining this information will enrich our understanding of the tapestry of Myanmar's population. It will help us understand better what Muslims share with their non-Muslim neighbours and what they do not. It will also help us grasp in a more nuanced way which ideas and practices are shared among Myanmar's different Muslim communities and which are not. At the same time, it will contribute to the broader field of religious and particularly Islamic studies.

Finally, such studies may have significant practical impact insofar as they help clarify what is at stake in the apparently growing tensions between Buddhists and Muslims in Myanmar, and illuminate as well some of the resources available as people try to negotiate a solution to these tensions. Without a more granular appreciation of what Muslims believe and find religiously meaningful, it is hard to understand what beliefs and practices need to be preserved if the community is to thrive. With the completion of this volume, it has become clear that contemporary Burmese Muslims require some form of legal socio-political organization that would help them realize what is important about Islam for them, without threatening what is crucial to other citizens of the state. But without a thick ethnography, it is hard to understand what kinds of compromises could be drawn, as we do not know what the essential things are, what types of values must be respected, nor what types of authority structures must be respected.

What Could Contemporary Muslim Communities, the Government, or the International Community Realistically do to Improve Human Security for Myanmar's Muslims?

Building on the points made in the preceding paragraph, there is another area of research that could fruitfully be carried out among Myanmar's Muslim communities—one that would both help us understand those communities and their predicaments better, and might, at the same time, contribute to a broader area of scholarly enquiry. There is a need for someone to build upon our understanding of Muslim communities. Once one has identified their most significant vulnerabilities, fears and their desires, it will be important to explore what sorts of responses will be most effective. How can one offer this community greater human security in its broadest sense— including both physical and emotional security?

As Myanmar goes through a period of political reorganization, many Muslims have pushed not only for democratization, but for devolution of power to the regions. Such developments may improve the lives of many Burmese. But neither electoral democracy of the sort currently being contemplated, nor territorial federalism, seems likely to solve the problems that Muslims face. Muslims are diverse and do not share all the same desires and aspirations. More important, they are dispersed in such a way that they are a minority in nearly every region of the country.

It would be useful to study the political attitudes and behaviours of Myanmar's Muslim communities and to explore literature in constitutional design and human security studies, to see what sorts of governmental structuring, what sorts of voting system, and what types of rights regime are most likely to provide security for Myanmar's

Muslims while not alienating its non-Muslims. And once structures are in place, it will be crucial to see whether they have fulfilled their promise.

As with the other suggestions for future research listed above, studies of this sort will force people to ask questions that will help everyone better understand Myanmar's Muslim community and its sub-communities. At the same time, it will provide a case study that will help contribute to the greater field of comparative constitutional law and human security studies.

* * *

Over the past seventy years, the academy has neglected to focus much attention on the Muslims of Myanmar. With the exception of a short history of Burma's Muslims published by an amateur historian in 1972, there are almost no studies of this large, diverse and sadly vulnerable community. The contributions in this volume begin to rectify this situation. Hopefully, this new research will inspire further investigations into this community. Such scholarship has the potential to help us understand Myanmar better and should add significantly to broader areas of study in both the humanities and social sciences. Most important, perhaps, is the fact that it has the potential to help Myanmar's Muslims, the Myanmar government, and the international community all to understand better the complexities of Myanmar's Muslim communities and to develop tools to ensure that they are able to flourish in Myanmar as it continues to evolve.

Glossary

Note on the glossary: Most Islamic terms and phrases in Myanmar are borrowed either from Arabic or Urdu. Given the emphasis in this book on the practice of Islam in Myanmar, this glossary includes the terms in Burmese script, with the Romanization in the left column (and therefore may differ slightly from the Arabic or Urdu spelling of terms). Similarly, the explanations for terms in the right hand column relate to Islamic practice in Myanmar. Aside from Burmese terms, words listed in the glossary are marked as follows: Sinhala (SI), Sanskrit (SA) and Tamil (T).

Term in text	Burmese script	Meaning
Amoytha Hluttaw	အမျိုးသားလွှတ်တော်	Upper House, or Nationalities Assembly.
Bismillah hi rahmanirahim	ဗစ္စမစ်လာ ဟိရ် ရဟ်မားန် နိရ် ရဟီးမ်	In the Name of God, the Most Merciful, the Most Compassionate.
Bodu Bala Sena	–	Army of Buddhist Power, a radical Buddhist group in Sri Lanka (SI).
bhumiputra	–	A Sanskrit compound, vernacularised into Sinhala, meaning 'sons of the soil' (SA/SI).
dhammathats	ဓမ္မသတ်	Written law texts (Buddhist), particularly legal rules and reports.

Term in text	Burmese script	Meaning
Dhammantaraya	ဓမ္မန္တရာယ်	Danger to Dhamma (pamphlet title).
Dobama Asiayone	တို့ဗမာအစည်းအရုံး	Our Burman Association
dosa	ဒိုဆာ/ တိုရှည်	Indian traditional snack.
fatwa	ဖသ်ဝါဟ်/ ဖတ်သဝါ	A non-binding Islamic legal opinion, not recognized as law in Myanmar.
fikh	ဖိကဟ်/ ဖေကာ	Islamic jurisprudence.
Eid-ul-Fitr	အီးဒွလ်ဖိသိရ်	The celebration to commemorate the breaking of fast after the end of the month of Ramadan.
Eid-ul-Adha	အီးဒွလ် အသွှာ	The celebration that commemorates Abraham's willingness to sacrifice his son and marks the end of the annual Hajj rites.
hadith	ဟဒီးဆ်	Traditional reports of the words and deeds of the Prophet Muhammad.
hafiz	ဟာဖိဇ်	A title given to a person who has memorised the entire *Qur'an*.
hajj	ဟာဂျ်	Annual pilgrimage to Mecca.
halal	ဟလာလ်	Religiously permissible, often used in relation to *halal* food.
Itsalan Ubade	အစ္စလာမ့် ဥပဒေ	Islamic Law.
Itsalan Thathanayeya Kaungsi Htana Chôk	အစ္စလာမ် သာသနာ့ ရေးရာ ကောင်စီဌာနချုပ်	Islamic Religious Affairs Council.
jameah	ဂျာမေအာ	College or university, also known in Myanmar as *maulvi* schools or *hafiz* schools.

Term in text	Burmese script	Meaning
ka'aba	ကအဗဟ်	A cube-shaped building in the centre of the Great Mosque at Mecca. Muslims face this direction for daily prayers.
kabya	ကပြား	People of mixed blood.
kaikuli	–	'Hand gifts' given by the parents of the bride to the couple as a dowry, a term used by Muslims in Sri Lanka (T).
kafan/dafan	ကဖန်/ဒဖန်	After-death rituals for Muslims, including washing, wrapping and burying.
kula/kala	ကုလား	A term used to refer to Muslims in Myanmar, but many Muslims see this as a derogatory term.
Lôktha-Pyithu-Nesin	လုပ်သားပြည် သူ့နေ့စဉ်	Working People's Daily (newspaper; since 1989 it has been known as The New Light of Myanmar).
Ma-Ba-Tha	မဘသ	Acronym for the organization—*Amyo Ba-thaTha-tha na Ka-kwaè-saung-shauk-ye Apwè*or known in English as the Patriotic Association of Myanmar.
maddhab	မဇဟဗ်	School of law in Islam.
madrasa	မဒရ်ဆာဟ်/ မဒရ်ဆာ	Islamic educational institute, often a boarding school.
mahr	–	Dower, that is, money or other property that a Muslim wife is entitled to from the husband in consideration for the marriage.

Term in text	Burmese script	Meaning
metthab	မက်သဗ်	Place of writing or learning. Refers to an Islamic school for young children.
mawlana	မောင်လာနာ	Term used interchangeably with *maulawi* in Myanmar, but may also refer to a more senior Muslim leader.
Maulawi/maulavi	မော်လဝီ	Muslim scholar who has undertaken about 10 years of Islamic training. The term is also associated with the All-Myanmar Maulvi League.
mettāsutta	မေတ္တာသုတ္တ	Loving kindness (Buddhism).
mleccha	–	Foreigners or barbarians, term used in Sri Lanka (SA).
mufti	မုဖ်သီ	Muslim who has continued further study after completing *maulvi* training (often in South Asia), and has the authority to issue *fatwa*.
muezzin	မုအဇ္ဇင်န်/ မော်ဇင်	The person at the mosque who leads the call to prayer.
musafirkhana	မုစ်ဆဖိရ် ခါနာ	Male dormitory for Muslims, term used in Myanmar.
Myet-kin-thit	မြက်ခင်းသစ်	Greener Pasture (magazine).
Panthay/Panthe	ပန်းသေး	Term used to refer to Muslims of Chinese descent in Myanmar.
pathi	ပသီ	Term used to refer to Burmese Muslims, particularly during the time of the kings; some Muslims identify themselves in this way today.

Term in text	Burmese script	Meaning
pyattôn	ဖြတ်ထုံး	Law reports (during the period of Burmese kings); texts with detailed account of one case or summaries of several cases.
Pyidaungsu Hluttaw	ပြည်ထောင်စု လွှတ်တော	Union Level Assembly, or Union Parliament (2011–present).
Pyithu Hluttaw	ပြည်သူ့လွှတ်တော်	Lower House, or People's Assembly (2011–present).
pongyi	ဘုန်းကြီး	Monk.
Sangha	သံဃာ	Buddhist council of monks.
shahid	ရှဟီးဒ်	Lit. 'to witness', used to refer to a martyr in Islam.
shari'a	ရှရီအဟ်/ ရှရီအတ်	Islamic law.
Tatmadaw	တပ်မတော်	Army, Defence Services.
Taya Yôn Chôk	တရားရုံးချုပ်	Chief Court (1962–72).
Tablighi Jemaat	သဗ် (ပ)လီးဂ်	Islamic religious renewal movement that originated in India in the 1920s.
taqiyah	တက်ကီရာ	Skull cap worn by Muslim men.
Thathana Mamaka	သာသနာ့မာမက	Young Monks Association.
Tha-tha-naPālaka Gaṇavācaka Sangha Apwè	သာသနာ့ပါလက ဂဏဝါစကသံဃာအဖွဲ့	Defenders of Sāsana and Religious Teachers Network.
ulama	အိုလမာ	Islamic religious scholar; in Myanmar, the term may refer to *mawlana/maulvi*, and is also associated with the organization known as *Jamiat Ulama-El-Islam*.

Term in text	Burmese script	Meaning
wakf	၀ါကပ်ဖ	Islamic charitable trust.
weikzas	ဝိဇ္ဇာ	Occult masters.
Yahan phyu Aphwe	ရဟန်းပျိုအဖွဲ့	All Burma Young Monks Association.
Zerbadee/ Zerbadi	ဇိရ်ဘာဒီ	Term used to refer to Burmese Muslims, but considered by many Burmese Muslims to be derogatory.

Bibliography

Abrar, C.R. 2013. 'Multilevel Approaches to Human Security and Conflict Management: The Rohingya Case'. *NTS Policy Brief* (PO13-03). Singapore: RSIS Centre for Non-Traditional Security (NTS) Studies.

————. 1995. *Repatriation of Rohingya Refugees: Regional Consultation on Refugee and Migratory Movements.* Colombo, Sri Lanka: Eminent Persons.org.

Adas, Michael. 1974. 'Immigrant Asians and the Economic Impact of European Imperialism: The Role of South Indian Chettiars in British Burma'. *The Journal of Asian Studies*, 33: 385–401.

Agence France-Presse (AFP). 2012. *Myanmar leader says open to aid for Muslims.* October 21. Available at sg.news.yahoo.com/myanmar-leader-says-open-aid-muslims-152958222.html.

Ahmed, Imtiaz. 2001. *Bangladesh-Myanmar Relations and the Stateless Rohingyas.* http://burmalibrary.org/

Ali, Jan A. 2011. 'Piety Among *Tablīgh* Women'. *Contemporary Islam*, 5: 225–47.

Allen, Michael Thad., and Gabrielle Hecht. 2001. 'Introduction: Authority, Political Machines, and Technology's History'. In Michael Thad Allen and Gabrielle Hecht (eds), *Technologies of Power: Essays in Honor of Thomas Parke Hughes and Agatha Chipley Hughes.* 1st Edition, pp. 1–24. Cambridge, Mass: The MIT Press.

ALTSEAN-Burma. 2010. '2010 Election Watch'. *ALTSEAN-Burma.* November. Available at www.altsean.org/Research/2010/Home.php.

Amrith, Sunil S. 2013. *Crossing the Bay of Bengal: The Furies of Nature and the Fortunes of Migrants.* Cambridge, Mass.; London: Harvard University Press.

Anderson, Clare. 2010. 'Colonization, Kidnap and Confinement in the Andamans Penal Colony, 1771–864'. *Journal of Historical Geography*, 37(1): 68–81.

Anderson, John. 1871. *A Report on the Expedition to Western Yunan via Bhamo*. Calcutta: Office of the Superintendent of Government Printing.

Anderson, Michael R. 1996. *Islamic Law and the Colonial Encounter in British India*. WLUML Occasional Paper No. 7. Women Living under Muslim Law.

————. 1990. 'Islamic Law and the Colonial Encounter in British India'. In C. Mallat and J. Connors (eds), *Islamic Family Law*, pp. 205–23. London: Graham & Trotman.

Anwar, Nausheen H. 2014. 'The Bengali can Return to his Desh but the Burmi can't because He has no Desh'. In Michiel Bass (ed.), *Transnational Migration and Asia: The Question of Return*. Amsterdam: Amsterdam University Press.

————. 2013. 'Negotiating New Conjunctures of Citizenship: Experiences of "Illegality" in Burmese-Rohingya and Bangladeshi Migrant Enclaves in Karachi'. *Citizenship Studies*, 17(3–4): 414–28.

Appadurai, Arjun. 2006. *Fear of Small Numbers: An Essay on the Geography of Anger*. Durham: Duke University Press Books.

Appleton, G. 1947. 'Burma Two Years after Liberation'. *International Affairs* 23(4): 510–21.

Ashin, Pyinnya Nanda. 2013. *Yahanto-mya Hnin Naing-ngan-ye* (Monks and Politics). Yangon: Anagat Kala Sape Saksanye.

Ashin, Vicitta Linkara. 2013. *Sangha Saw-ka Nga-yè-thwa* [If the Sangha is Disrespected, go to Hell!]. Yangon: Zin Yatana Saw Sape.

Associated Press. 2013. 'Senior Myanmar Buddhist Clergy Ban Activist Monks from Forming Own Groups'. 11 September. Available at http://www.foxnews.com/world/2013/09/11/senior-myanmar-buddhist-clergy-ban-activist-monks-from-forming-own-groups/.

Atwill, David G. 2005. *The Chinese Sultanate: Islam, Ethnicity, and the Panthay Rebellion in Southwest China, 1856–1873*. Stanford: Stanford University Press.

Aung-Thwin, Michael and Matrii Aung-Thwin. 2012. *A History of Myanmar Since Ancient Times: Traditions and Transformations*. London: Reaktion Books.

Aye, Nai. 2013. 'Burma expels Rohingya members from political party'. *Democratic Voice of Burma*. 17 May. Available at www.dvb.no/news/burma-expels-rohingya-members-from-political-party/28296.

Azad, Hamid. 2013. Muslim Aid—Myanmar (Interview). Available at www.muslimaid.org/campaigns/current-emergencies/myanmar-burma-appeal/Stefan.

Bachtold, Stefan, Rachel Gasser, Julia Palmiano, Rina M Alluri and Sabina Stein. 2014. 'Working in and on Myanmar: Reflections on a "light footprint" approach'. *Swiss Peace Working Paper* 5/2014. Bern: Switzerland.

Banki, Susan. 2009. Contested Regimes, Aid Flows, and Refugee Flows: The Case of Burma. *Journal of Current Southeast Asia Affairs*, 28(2) 47–73.

Bartholomeusz, Tessa J. 2002. *In Defense of Dharma: Just-war Ideology in Buddhist Sri Lanka*. London: RoutledgeCurzon.

Bayly, Christopher and Tim Harper. 2005. *Forgotten Armies: The Fall of British Asia, 1941–1945*. Cambridge, Mass.: Harvard University Press.

BBC News. 2013. 'Suu Kyi Blames Burma Violence on "Climate of Fear"', October 24. Available at http://www.bbc.co.uk/news/world-asia-24651359.

Beaman, Justice Frank. 1913. Bombay High Court. Jan Mahomed Abdulla Datu vs Datu Jaffar, on 6 August 1913. Available at http://indiankanoon. org/doc/984436/ (accessed 22 August 2015).

Beech, Hannah. 2013. 'The Face of Buddhist Terror.' *Time Magazine* (Vol. 182, No. 1) July 1. Available at http://content.time.com/time/magazine/article/0,9171,2146000,00.html.

Begg, Ian Maynard, Ann Anas, and Suzanne Farinacci. 1992. 'Dissociation of Processes in Belief: Source Recollection, Statement Familiarity, and the Illusion of Truth.' *Journal of Experimental Psychology*, 11: 424–8.

Benda-Beckmann, Franz von. 2001. 'Between Free Riders and Free Raiders: Property Rights and Soil Degradation in Context'. In Heerink, N.H. van Keulen and M. Kuiper (eds), *Economic Policy and Sustainable Land Use: Recent Advances in Quantitative Analysis for Developing Countries*, pp. 293–316. Heidelberg: Physica-Verlag.

Benda-Beckmann, Franz., Keebet von, and Melanie C Wiber (eds). 2006. *Changing Properties of Property*. New York and Oxford: Berghahn.

Berlie, Jean A. 2008. *The Burmanization of Myanmar's Muslims*. Bangkok: White Lotus Press.

Berkwitz, S. C. 2008. 'Religious Conflict and the Politics of Conversion in Sri Lanka'. In Rosalind I.J. Hackett (ed.), *Proselytization Revisited: Rights Talk, Free Markets and Culture Wars*, pp. 199–229. London: Equinox.

Bielefeld, Wolfgang and William Suhs Cleveland. 2013. 'Defining Faith-Based Organizations and Understanding Them Through Research,' *Nonprofit and Voluntary Sector Quarterly* [June], 42(3), 442–67.

Binder, Andrea. 2014. 'The Shape and Sustainability of Turkey's Booming Humanitarian Assistance'. *International Development Policy*, 6(1). Available at http://poldev.revues.org/1741#toctom1.

Billig, Michael. 1995. *Banal Nationalism*. London: Sage.

Blair, David. 2013. 'How Can Aung San Suu Kyi – A Nobel Peace Prize Winner – Fail to Condemn anti-Muslim Violence?' *The Telegraph* (UK). 24 October. Available at http://blogs.telegraph.co.uk/news/davidblair/100242929/how-can-aung-san-suu-kyi-a-nobel-peace-prize-winner-fail-to-condemn-anti-muslim-violence/.

Bo Bo. 2010. 'Raising Xenophobic Socialism against a Communist Threat: Re-reading the Lines of an Army Propaganda Magazine in 1950s Burma Cultures.' In Tony Day and Maya H.T. Liem (eds), *Cultures at War: The Cold War and Cultural Expression in Southeast Asia*, pp. 171–94. Ithaca: Southeast Asia Program Publications.

Bosson, A. 2007. *Forced Migration/ Internal Displacement in Burma with an Emphasis on Government-Controlled Areas*. Geneva: Internal Displacement Monitoring Centre. Available at http://www.ibiblio.org/obl/docs4/IDMC-Burma_report_mai07.pdf.

Bowers, Captain Alexander. 1869. *Report on the Practicability of Re-Opening the Trade Route, Between Burma and Western China*. Rangoon: American Mission Press.

Brass, Paul R. 1997. *Theft of an Idol: Text and Context in the Representation of Collective Violence*. Princeton: Princeton University Press.

———. 2003. *The Production of Hindu-Muslim Violence in Contemporary India*. Washington: University of Washington Press.

Brohm, John. 1957. *Burmese Religion and the Burmese Buddhist Revival*. PhD dissertation, Cornell University.

Brown, Rajeswary Ampalavanar. 2013. *Islam in Modern Thailand: Faith, Philanthropy and Politics*. New York: Routledge.

Bourdieu, Pierre. 1995. *Outline of a Theory of Practice*. Translated by Richard 10th. Nice Edition. Cambridge, UK: Cambridge University Press.

Burke, Adam. 2012. 'Hollow Words: Foreign Aid and Peacebuilding in Peripheral Conflicts'. *Asian Affairs: An American Review* 39(4): 181.

Burma Fund UN Office. 2011. *Burma's 2010 Elections: A Comprehensive Report*. New York: Burma Fund UN Office.

Burnes, Alexander. 1835. *Travels into Bokhara: Containing the Narrative of a Voyage on the Indus from the Sea to Lahore with Presents from the King of Great Britain and an Account of a Journey from India to Cabool, Tartary, and Persia*. London: Murray. Available at https://archive.org/details/travelsintobokho2burngoog.

Butler, Sir Harcourt (Patron). 1927. *Who's Who in Burma*. Calcutta; Rangoon: The Indo-Burma Publishing Agency.

Butwell, Richard. 1963. *U Nu of Burma*. Stanford: Stanford University Press.

Caballero-Anthony, Mely and Belinda Chng. 2009. 'Cyclones and Humanitarian Crises: Pushing the Limits of R2P in Southeast Asia'. *Global Responsibility to Protect*, 1(2): 135.

Callahan, Mary P. 2004. *Making Enemies: War and State Building in Burma*. Singapore: National University of Singapore Press.

———. 2007. *Political Authority in Burma's Ethnic Minority States: Devolution, Occupation, and Coexistence*. Washington, D.C.: East-West Center; Singapore: ISEAS Publishing.

Cannarella, John and Joshua A. Spechler. 2014. 'Epidemiological Modeling of Online Social Network Dynamics'. Department of Mechanical and Aerospace Engineering, Princeton University. Available at http://arxiv.org/abs/1401.4208.

Carroll, Joshua. 2014. 'Myanmar Ploughs Ahead with Census Despite Growing Ethnic Tensions'. *Andalou Agency*. 19 March. Available at www.aa.com.tr/en/news/303054-myanmar-ploughs-ahead-with-census-despite-growing-ethnic-tensions.

Chakravarti, Nalini Ranjan. 1971. *The Indian Minority in Burma: The Rise and Decline of an Immigrant Community*. New York: Oxford University Press.

Chalk, P. 2001. 'Separatism and Southeast Asia: The Islamic Factor in Southern Thailand, Mindanao, and Aceh', *Studies in Conflict and Terrorism*, 24: 241–69.

Charney, Michael. 2009. *A History of Modern Burma*. Cambridge: Cambridge University Press.

Cheesman, Nick. 2014. 'Bodies on the Line in Burma's Law Reports 1892–1922'. In Melissa Crouch and Tim Lindsey (eds.), *Law, Society and Transition in Myanmar*, 77–94. Oxford: Hart Publishing.

———. 2012. *The Politics of Law and Order in Myanmar*. PhD. Department of Political and Social Change, Australian National University.

———. 2010. 'Thin Rule of Law or Un-Rule of Law in Myanmar'. *Pacific Affairs*, 82(4): 597.

Cheung, Samuel. 2011. 'Migration Control and the Solutions Impasse in South and Southeast Asia: Implications from the Rohingya Experience'. *Journal of Refugee Studies*, 25(1): 50.

Chiarella, Gregory M. 2012. 'Sources of Law, Sources of Authority: The Failure of the Philippines' Code of Muslim Personal Law'. *Pacific Rim Law and Policy Journal*, 21(1): 223.

Chicago Memons. 2014. United States. Available at http://www.chicagomemons.com/history.htm (accessed 16 June 2014)

Chrisomalis, Stephen. 2010. *Numerical Notation: A Comparative History*. Cambridge: Cambridge University Press.

CIA. 2014. *Central Intelligence Agency World Factbook: Burma*. Available at https://www.cia.gov/library/publications/the-world-factbook/geos/bm.html.

Coates, Eliane. 2014. 'Sectarian Violence Involving Rohingya in Myanmar: Historical Roots and Modern Triggers.' *Middle East Institute*. 4 August. Available at www.mei.edu/content/map/sectarian-violence-involving-rohingya-myanmar-historical-roots-and-modern-triggers.

———. 2013. 'Inter-religious Violence in Myanmar: A Security Threat to Southeast Asia.' *RSIS Commentaries*. Singapore: Nanyang Technological University. Available at www.rsis.edu.sg/wp-content/uploads/2014/07/RSIS11720132.pdf.

Commission of Inquiry (CoI). 2013. *Final Report of Inquiry Commission on Sectarian Violence in Rakhine State*. Yangon: Republic of the Union of Myanmar.

Consult Myanmar. 2014. 'Condo Draft Law Ready for Parliament This Session: Official'. 2 June. Available at http://consult-myanmar.com/2014/06/02/condo-draft-law-ready-for-parliament-this-session-official/.

Cotterrell, Lin and Adele Harmer. 2005. 'Diversity in Donorship: The Changing Landscape of Official Humanitarian Aid – Aid Donorship in the Gulf States'. *HPG Background Paper*, pp. 1–40. London: Overseas Development Institute:

Coursen-Neff, Z. 2000. *Malaysia/Burma Living in Limbo: Burmese Rohingyas in Malaysia*. New York: Human Rights Watch. Crosthwaite, Sir Charles. 1912. *The Pacification of Burma*. London: Edward Arnold.

Crouch, Melissa. Forthcoming. 'Emergency Powers in Times of Political Transition: Between the Constitution and the Criminal Code in Myanmar'. In Andrew Harding (ed.), *Constitutional Change and Law Reform in Myanmar*. Hart Publishing.

———. forthcoming 2016. 'Islamic Legal Studies on Southeast Asia: A Review'. In Anver Emon, Kristen Stilt and Rumee Ahmed (eds), *Oxford Handbook on Islamic Law*. Oxford: Oxford University Press.

———. 2014a. 'The Common Law and the Constitutional Writs: Prospects for Accountability in Myanmar'. In Melissa Crouch and Tim Lindsey (eds), *Law, Society and Transition in Myanmar*, pp. 141–58. Oxford: Hart Publishing.

———. 2014b. 'Rediscovering "Law" in Myanmar: A Review of Scholarship on Myanmar Law'. *Pacific Rim Law and Policy Review*, 23(3): 543–75.

———. 2014c. 'The Layers of Legal Development in Myanmar' In Melissa Crouch and Tim Lindsey (eds), *Law, Society and Transition in Myanmar*, pp. 33–58. Oxford: Hart Publishing.

———. 2013a. 'Asian Legal Transplants and Lessons on the Rule of Law: National Human Rights Commissions in Indonesia and Myanmar'. *Hague Journal of the Rule of Law*, 5(2): 146–77.

———. 2013b. 'The Constitution, Emergency Powers and the Rule of Law in Myanmar', pp. 46–53. *Panorama: Myanmar in Transition*.

Crouch, Melissa and Nick Cheesman. 2014. 'A Short Research Guide on Myanmar's Legal System'. In Melissa Crouch and Tim Lindsey (eds), *Law, Society and Transition in Myanmar*, pp. 21–32. Oxford: Hart Publishing.

DailyFT News. 2014. 'Danger Averted in Mawanella'. 18 June. Available at http://www.ft.lk/2014/06/18/danger-averted-in-mawanella/.

De Cordier, Bruno. 2009. 'Faith-based Aid, Globalization and the Humanitarian Frontline: An Analysis of Western-based Muslim Aid Organisations'. *Disasters*, 33(4): 608.

Deegalle, M. 2004. 'Politics of the *jathika hela urumaya* Monks: Buddhism and Ethnicity in Contemporary Sri Lanka'. *Contemporary Buddhism* 5(2): 83–103.

Deibert, April. 2013. 'Google "Free Zone" and Facebook "Zero": Products Targeting Developing Populations.' *Innovation Series*. 19 February. Available at http://www.innovation-series.com/2013/02/19/google-free-zone-and-facebook-zero-products-targeting-developing-populations/.

Della-Giacoma, Jim. 2011. 'The Burma Spring.' *Foreign Policy*. 13 October. Available at http://www.foreignpolicy.com/articles/2011/10/13/burma_prisoner_release_spring?page=0,0&wp_login_redirect=0.

Department of Immigration and Citizenship (DIAC). 2013. *Australia's Humanitarian Program: 2013–14 and Beyond, December 2012*. Available at http://www.immi.gov.au/media/publications/pdf/humanitarian-program-information-paper-2013-14.pdf.

Department for the Promotion and Propagation of the Sāsanā. 2002. *How to Live as A Good Buddhist*. Vol. 1. Translated by U Han Htay and U Chit Tin. Yangon: Department for the Promotion and Propagation of the Sāsanā.

Deppermann, Lee J.F. 2013. 'Increasing the ICJ's Influence as a Court of Human Rights: The Muslim Rohingya as a Case Study'. *Chicago Journal of International Law*, 14(1): 291.

Desai, Walter. 1954. *India and Burma: A Study*. Calcutta: Orient Longmans.

De Groote, Peter-Paul. 2013. 'Patients not Politics in Rakhine State'. *Myanmar Times*. 7 November. Available at www.mmtimes.com.

De Silva, K.M. 1973. 'The Legislative Council in the Nineteenth Century'. In K.M. De Silva Kandy (ed.), *University of Ceylon History of Ceylon Vol. 3*, pp. 226–48. Sri Lanka: University of Ceylon.

DeVotta, N and J. Stone. 2008. '*Jathika hela urumaya* and Ethno-Religious Politics in Sri Lanka'. *Pacific Affairs*, 81(1): 31–51.

Dhammika U Ba Than. 1962. *The Roots of the Revolution*. Rangoon: Director of Information.

Dobama Asiayone Thamaing Pyusuye Apwè. 1976. *Dobama Asiayone Thamaing (akyinkyôk)* [Abridged History of Dobama Asiayone]. Vol. 1. Yangon: Sarpay Beikman.

Donovan, Pamela. 2007. 'How Idle Is Idle Talk? One Hundred Years of Rumor Research.' *Diogenes*, 54(1): 59–82.

Egreteau, Renaud. 2012. '"China is Paradise": Migration and Diasporic Solidarities among Burmese Muslim Communities in the Yunnan-Burma/Myanmar Borderlands'. Paper presented at *The Art of Neighbouring: Old Crossroads and New Connections Along the PRC's Borders*, Asia Research Institute, National University of Singapore.

————2011. 'Burmese Indians in Contemporary Burma: Heritage, Influence and Perceptions since 1988'. *Asian Ethnicity*, 12(1): 33–54.

Eleven Myanmar. 2014a. *Myanmar's Mobile Penetration Rate Expected to Reach 80 Percent by 2015–16*. 10 February. Available at http://www.elevenmyanmar.com/index.php?option=com_content&view=article&id=50 17:myanmar-s-mobile-penetration-rate-expected-to-reach-80-percent-by-2015-16&catid=44&Itemid=384.

————. 2014b. *Facebook down in Myanmar after Riots in Mandalay*. 4 July. Available at http://www.elevenmyanmar.com/index.php?option=com_content&view=article&id=6654:facebook-is-down-in-myanmar-after-riots-in-mandalay&catid=44:national&Itemid=384.

Elverskog, Johan. 2013. *Buddhism and Islam on the Silk Road*. Singapore: ISEAS.

Farrelly, Nicholas. 2009. '"Ak47/M16 Rifle—Rs. 15,000 each": What Price Peace on the Indo-Burmese Frontier?'. *Contemporary South Asia*, 18(3): 283.

————. 2008. 'Tai Community and Thai Border Subversions'. In Andrew Walker (ed.), *Tai Lands and Thailand: Community and State in Southeast Asia*. Singapore: National University of Singapore Press.

————. 2014. 'War, Law, Politics: Reflections on Violence and Conflict in Kachin State'. In Melissa Crouch and Tim Lindsey (eds), *Law, Society and Transition in Myanmar*, 305–22. Oxford: Hart Publishing.

Farrelly, Nicholas and Ishrat Hossain. 2014. 'From Bangladesh: Considering Another Side of the Rakhine Conflict'. In Nick Cheesman and Htoo Kyaw Win (eds), *Communal Conflict in Myanmar*. Yangon: Myanmar Knowledge Society.

Fealy, Greg and Virginia Hooker (eds). 2006. *Voices of Islam in Southeast Asia: A Contemporary Sourcebook*. Singapore: Institute of Southeast Asian Studies.

Ferrie, Ared and Min Zayar Oo. 2013. 'Burma Buddhist Committee Bans Anti-Muslim Organizations'. *The Irrawaddy*. 11 September. Available at http://www.irrawaddy.org/archives/43796.

Ferrie, Jared. 2013. 'In Myanmar, Cheap SIM Card Draw May Herald Telecoms Revolution.' *Reuters*. April 24. Available at http://www.reuters.com/article/2013/04/24/us-myanmar-telecoms-draw-idUSBRE93N1AX20130424.

Fielding-Hall, Harold. 1898. *The Soul of a People*, 2nd edition. London: Macmillan & Co Ltd.

Final Report of the Riot Inquiry Committee. 1939. Rangoon: Government Printing and Stationary.

Fink, Christina. 2001. *Living Silence: Burma Under the Military Rule*. Bangkok: White Lotus Press.

————. 2009a. *Living in Silence in Burma: Surviving Under Military Rule.* Second edition. Thailand: Silkworm.

————. 2009b. 'The Moment of the Monks: Burma, 2007.' In Adam Roberts and Timothy Garton Ash (eds), *Civil Resistance and Power Politics: The Experience of Non-Violent Action from Gandhi to the Present*, pp. 354–70. New York: Oxford University Press.

Fisher, Jonah. 2013. 'Anti-Muslim Monk Stokes Burmese Religious Tensions'. *BBC*. 29 August. Available at www.bbc.co.uk/news/world-asia-23846632.

Fong, Henry. 2012. '5 Things You Need To Know About Chinese Social Media.' *Forbes*, 25 October. Available at http://www.forbes.com/sites/ciocentral/2012/10/25/5-things-you-need-to-know-about-chinese-social-media/.

Forbes, Andrew D.W. 1986. 'The Panthay (Yunnanese Chinese) Muslims of Burma'. *Journal of Muslim Minority Affairs*, 7(2): 384–94.

Foster, Robert J. 2008. *Coca-Globalization: Following Soft Drinks from New York to New Guinea.* Palgrave Macmillan.

Fuller, Thomas 2013. 'Extremism Rises Among Myanmar's Buddhists'. *New York Times.* 20 June. Available at www.nytimes.com/2013/06/21/world/asia/extremism-rises-among-myanmar-buddhists-wary-of-muslim-minority.html.

Fuller, Thomas and Wai Moe. 2014. 'Buddhist-Muslim Mayhem Hits Myanmar's No. 2 City.' *The New York Times.* 3 July. Available at http://www.nytimes.com/2014/07/04/world/asia/buddhist-muslim-mayhem-hits-myanmars-no-2-city.html.

Funston, John. 2010. 'Malaysia and Thailand's Southern Conflict: Reconciling Security and Ethnicity.' *Contemporary Southeast Asia*, 32(2): 234.

Furnivall, John S. 1956. *Colonial Policy and Practice: A Comparative Study of Burma and Netherlands India.* New York: New York University Press.

Fytche, Lieutenant-General Albert. 1878. *Burma Past and Present With Personal Reminiscences of the Country.* 2 vols. London: C Kegan Paul & Co.

Galache, Carlos Sardina. 2013. 'Who are the monks behind Burma's "969" Campaign?' *Democratic Voice of Burma.* 10 May. Available at http://www.dvb.no/news/features-news/the-monks-behind-burma's-"969"movement-2/28079.

Garth, Bryant G and Austin Sarat (eds). 1998. *How does Law Matter?* Chicago: Northwestern University Press, American Bar Foundation.

Geisler, Charles. 2006. 'Ownership in Stateless Places'. In Franz Benda-Beckmann, Keebet von, Melanie G. Wiber (eds), *Changing Properties of Property*, pp. 40–57. New York: Berghahn.

Ghafur, Abdul [U Khin Maung Sein]. 2014. *Isalam Ubade [Islamic Law]*. 1st ed. 1984; 3rd ed. 2014. Yangon: Theiddi Myaing Press.

Ghosh, Amitav. 2011. *Exodus from Burma 1941: A Personal Account, Parts 1, 2 & 3*. 21 June. Available at http://amitavghosh.com/blog/?p=432.

Gittleman, Andrea, Holly G. Atkinson, and Marissa Brodney. 2013. *Patterns of Anti-Muslim Violence in Burma: A Call for Accountability and Prevention*. New York: Physicians for Human Rights.

Goffman, Erving. 1981. *Forms of Talk*. Philadelphia: University of Pennsylvania Press.

Gómez-Ibanez, José A, Derek Bok, and Nguyen Xuan Thành. 2012. *Yangon's Development Challenges*. Report prepared for Proximity Designs. March 2012. Available at http://www.ash.harvard.edu/extension/ash/docs/yangon.pdf.

Gouger, Henry. 1860. *A Personal Narrative of Two Years' Imprisonment in Burmah 1824–1826*. London: John Murray.

Government of Myanmar. 2012. *Press Release Regarding the Recent Incidents in Rakhine State of Myanmar*. 21 August. Government of the Republic of the Union of Myanmar.

Gravers, Mikael. 1999. *Nationalism as Political Paranoia in Burma: An Essay on the Historical Practice of Power*, 2nd edition. Richmond: Curzon Press.

Green, Penny. 2013. 'Islamophobia: Burma's Racist Fault-line'. *Race and Class*, 55(2): 93.

Gupta, Charu. 2009. 'Hindu Women, Muslim Men: Love Jihad and Conversions'. *Economic and Political Weekly*, 44(51): 13–15.

Haddad, Yvonne. (ed.). 2002. *Muslims in the West from Sojourners to Citizens*. New York: Oxford University Press.

Hall, D.G.E. 1932. *The Dalhousie-Phayre Correspondence 1852–1856*. London: Humphrey Milford.

Hamilton, Charles. 1979. *The Hedaya, or the Guide*. New Delhi: Kitab Bhavan. First published 1791, republished 1979.

Haniffa, Farzana. 2007. *In Search of an Ethical Self in a Beleaguered Context*. Ph.D. Dissertation Submitted to Columbia University.

Hardy, Peter. 1973. *The Muslims of British India*. Cambridge: Cambridge University Press.

Hale, Charles R. and Craig Calhoun. 2008. *Engaging Contradictions: Theory, Politics, and Methods of Activist Scholarship*. 1st edition. Berkeley: University of California Press.

Harvey, G.E. 1925. *History of Burma (From the Earliest Times to the 10th March 1824)*. London: Longmans.

Hayden, Martin and Richard Martin. 2013. 'Recovery of the Education System in Myanmar'. *Journal of International and Comparative Education* 2(2): 47–57.

Hefner, Robert W. and Muhammad Qasim Zaman. 2007. *Schooling Islam: The Culture and Politics of Modern Muslim Education*. Princeton: Princeton University Press.

Hemingway Maxim, Sarah. 1992. *The Resemblance in External Appearance: The Colonial Project in Kuala Lumpur and Rangoon*. Ann Arbor: UMI Dissertation.

Hecht, Gabrielle. 2001. 'Technology, Politics, and National Identity in France'. In Gabrielle Hecht and Michael Thad Allen (eds), *Technologies of Power: Essays in Honor of Thomas Parke Hughes and Agatha Chipley Hughes*. 1st Edition, 253–95. Cambridge, Mass.: The MIT Press.

Hla Aung. 1958. 'A Brief Note on Legal Education'. *The Burma Law Institute Journal*, 1(1): 89.

Hodal, Kate. 2013. 'Buddhist Monk Uses Racism and Rumours to Spread Hatred in Burma'. *The Guardian*, 18 April. Available at http://www.the-guardian.com/world/2013/apr/18/buddhist-monk-spreads-hatred-burma.

Holston, James. 2014. '"Come to the Street!": Urban Protest, Brazil 2013'. *Anthropological Quarterly*, 87(3): 887–900.

Hooker, M.B. 2003. *Indonesian Islam: Social Change through Contemporary Fatwa*. Honolulu: University of Hawaii Press.

———. 1984. *Islamic Law in Southeast Asia*. Oxford: Claredon Press.

———. 1978. *A Concise Legal History of Southeast Asia*. Oxford: Claredon Press.

———. 1975. *Legal Pluralism: An Introduction to Colonial and Neo-colonial Laws*. Oxford: Clarendon Press.

Htet Naing Zaw. 2013. 'Rakhine pyi-nay atwin 969 tayarpwe myar kyin pa [969 Sermons Held in Rakhine State]'. *The Irrawaddy* (in Burmese), 27 December. Available at http://burma.irrawaddy.org/news/2013/12/27/52748.html.

Human Rights Watch. 2013a. *Burma: Satellite Images Detail Destruction in Meiktila*. Human Rights Watch. Available at http://www.hrw.org/news/2013/04/01/burma-satellite-images-detail-destruction-meiktila.

———. 2013b. *'All You Can Do Is Pray': Crimes Against Humanity and Ethnic Cleansing of Rohingya Muslims in Burma's Arakan State*. New York: Human Rights Watch. Available at www.hrw.org.

———2012. *'The Government Could Have Stopped This': Sectarian Violence and Ensuing Abuses in Burma's Arakan State*. New York: Human Rights Watch. Available at www.hrw.org.

———2002. *Crackdown on Burmese Muslims*. Briefing Paper. July.

Huxley, Andrew. 2014. 'Is Burmese Law Buddhist? Tradition and Transition'. In Melissa Crouch and Tim Lindsey (eds), *Law, Society and Transition in Myanmar*, pp. 59–76. Oxford: Hart Publishing.

————. 1990. 'Khaek, Moro, Rohingya: The Family Law of Three Southeast Asian Muslim Minorities'. In Chibli Mallat and Jane Connors (eds), *Islamic Family Law*. London: Graham & Trotman Limited.

————. 1988. 'Burma: It Works, but is it Law?' *Journal of Family Law* 27: 23.

Ikeya, Chie. 2013. 'Colonial Intimacies in Comparative Perspective: Intermarriage, Law, and Cultural Difference in British Burma'. *Journal of Colonialism and Colonial History*, (Spring) 14(1).

————. 2011. *Refiguring Women, Colonialism and Modernity in Burma*. Hawaii: University of Hawaii Press.

Images Asia and Burma Network. 1997. *Nowhere to Go: A Report on the 1997 SLORC Offensive Against Dupbaya District (Karen National Union 6th Brigade) Karen State, Burma*. April 1997. Thailand.

International Commission of Jurists. 2013. *Right to Counsel: The Independence of Lawyers in Myanmar*. Available at http://icj.wpengine.netdna-cdn.com/wp-content/uploads/2013/12/MYANMAR-Right-to-Counsel-electronic.pdf.

International Crisis Group. 2013. *The Dark Side of Transition: Violence Against Muslims in Myanmar*. Asia Report No 251. 1 October. Brussels, Belgium.

Integrated Regional Interaction Networks (IRIN). 2012. *Bangladesh: Closing the door on Rohingya*. 13 June. Available at www.irinnews.org

Irrawaddy. 2010. 'Burma Election 2010'. *The Irrawaddy*. November. Available at election.irrawaddy.org

Islam, Syed Serajul 2007. 'State Terrorism in Arakan'. In Andrew T.H. Tan (ed.), *A Handbook of Terrorism and Insurgency in Southeast Asia*. Massachusetts: Edward Elgar Publishing.

Islamic Human Rights Commission. 2005. *Myanmar Muslims: Oppressed of the Oppressed*. United Kingdom.

Ismail, Qadri. 1995. 'Unmooring Identity: The Antimonies of Muslim Elite Self-Formation in Sri Lanka. In Pradeep Jeganathan and Qadri Ismail (eds), *Unmaking the Nation*, pp. 55–105. Colombo: Social Scientists' Association.

Jaquet, Carine and Matthew Walton. 2013. 'Buddhism and Relief in Myanmar: Reflections on Relief as a Practice of Dāna'. In Hiroko Kawanami and Geoffrey Samuel (eds), *Buddhism, International Relief Work, and Civil Society*, pp. 51–73. New York: PalgraveMacmillan.

Jeffrey, Robin and Assa Doron. 2012. 'Mobile-izing: Democracy, Organization and India's First 'Mass Mobile Phone' Elections.' *The Journal of Asian Studies*, 71(1): 63–80.

————. 2013. *The Great Indian Phone Book: How Cheap Mobile Phones Change Business, Politics and Daily Life*. London: Hurst & Company.

Jerryson, Michael K. 2011. *Buddhist Fury: Religion and Violence in Southern Thailand*. Oxford: Oxford University Press.

Jerryson, Michael and Mark Juergensmeyer (eds). 2010 *Buddhist Warfare*. Oxford: Oxford University Press.

Jordan, Tony. 2012. 'Coca-Cola Announces Will Return to Myanmar After 60 Years'. *Bloomberg*. 15 June. Available at http://www.bloomberg.com/news/2012-06-15/coca-cola-announces-will-return-to-myanmar-after-60-years.html.

Kabir, Mohammad Humayun. 2003. 'Rohingya Refugees in Bangladesh: Some Issues and Security Implications'. In Omprakash Mishra and Anindyo J. Majumdar (eds), *The Elsewhere People: Cross-border Migration, Refugee Protection and State Response*. New Delhi: Lancer Books.

Kamali, Mohammad Hasim. 2008. *Shar'iah Law: An Introduction*. Oxford: Oneworld.

Kawanami, Hiroko. 2009. 'Charisma, Power(s), and the Arahant Ideal in Burmese-Myanmar Buddhism'. *Asian Ethnology* 68(2): 211–37.

Keck, Stephen L. 2009. 'The Making of an Invisible Minority: Muslims in Colonial Burma'. In *Living on the Margins: Minorities and Borderlines in Cambodia and Southeast Asia*, pp. 221–34. Siem Riep, Cambodia: Center for Khmer Studies.

Keyes, Charles. 2007. 'Monks, Guns and Peace: Theravada Buddhism and Political Violence.' In James K. Wellman (ed.) *Belief and Bloodshed: Religion and Violence across Time and Tradition*, pp. 145–63. Lanham, Maryland: Rowman & Littlefield.

Khan, M. Siddiq. 1936. 'Muslim Intercourse with Burma'. *Islamic Culture*, 10: 409–27.

Khin Maung Kyi. 2006. 'Indians in Burma: Problems of an Alien Subculture in a Highly Integrated Society'. In K.S. Sandhu and A. Mani (eds), *Indian Communities in Southeast Asia*, pp. 625–67. Singapore: ISEAS Publications.

———. 1993. 'Indians in Burma: Problems of an Alien Subculture in a Highly Integrated Society'. In K.S. Sandhu and A. Mani (eds), *Indian Communities in Southeast Asia*, pp. 624–65. Singapore: Institute of Southeast Asian Studies.

Khin Maung Win. 1999. 'Religious Freedom in Burma: A Divisive and Suppressive Practice of the Military Regime'. *Legal Issues on Burma Journal* No. 4 (October), 17–27.

Kiefer, Thomas M. 1972. *The Tausug: Violence and Law in a Philippine Moslem Society*. New York: Holt Rinehart and Winston.

Kim, Hodong. 2004. *Holy War in China: The Muslim Rebellion and State in Chinese Central Asia 1864–1877*. Stanford: Stanford University Press.

Khin Maung Yin. 2005. 'Salience of Ethnicity among Burman Muslims: A Study in Identity Formation'. *Intellectual Discourse*, 13(2): 161–79.

Kipgen, Nehginpao. 2013. 'Conflict in Rakhine State in Myanmar: Rohingya Muslims' Conundrum'. *Journal of Muslim Minority Affairs*, 33(2): 298.

Knoerzer, Shari. 1998. 'Transformation of Muslim Political Identity'. In M. Tiruchelvam and C.S. Dattathreya (eds), *Culture and Politics of Identity in Sri Lanka*, pp. 137–67. Colombo: International Centre for Ethnic Studies.

Kodikara, Shelton. 1989. *Indo-Sri Lanka Accord of July 1987*. Colombo: University of Colombo.

Kozlowski, Gregory. 1985. *Muslim Endowments in British India*. Cambridge: Cambridge University Press.

Kraas, Frauke, Yin May, and Zin Nwe Myint. 2010. 'Yangon/Myanmar: Transformation Processes and Mega-urban Developments'. *Geographische Rundschau* 6(2): 26–37.

Kugle, S.A. 2001. 'Framed, Blamed and Renamed: the Recasting of Islamic Jurisprudence in Colonial South Asia.' *Modern Asian Studies* 35(2): 257–313.

Kyaw, U Aye. 1994. 'Religion and Family Law in Burma'. In Uta Gaertner and Jens Lorenz (eds), *Tradition and Modernity in Myanmar: Culture, Social Life and Languages*, pp. 237–50. Hamburg: Lit Verlag.

Kyaw Hsu Mon. 2014. 'Unicef Rents Rangoon Office from Former General'. *The Irrawadday*. 20 May. Available at http://www.irrawaddy.org/burma/ unicef-rents-rangoon-office-former-general.html?PageSpeed=noscript.

Kyaw Phone Kyaw. 2014. 'Civil society slams "disgraceful" interfaith marriage law plan'. *The Myanmar Times*. 12 May. Available at www.mmtimes. com/index.php/national-news/10312-civil-society-slams-disgraceful-interfaith-marriage-law-plan.html.

Kyaw Phyo Tha. 2013. 'Two Sides of the Sangha'. *The Irrawaddy*. 19 June. Available at http://www.irrawaddy.org/interview/magazine-interview/ two-sides-of-the-sangha.html.

Kyaw Zwa Moe. 2013. 'A Radically Different Dhamma'. *The Irrawaddy*. 22 June. Available at http://www.irrawaddy.org/burma/magazine-cover-story-burma/a-radically-different-dhamma.html.

Lacey-Hall, Oliver. 2012. 'Remarks on a Panel Discussion on "Relief and Humanitarian Assistance"'. *Workshop on Relief, Rehabilitation, Rule of Law, and Sustainable Development in Rakhine State*. Nay Pyi Taw, Myanmar. 22–23 September.

Lambert, Karen Hunt. 2011. *Burmese Muslim Refugee Women: Stories of Civil War, Refugee Camps and New Americans*. Master's thesis, Utah State University.

Lambrecht, Curtis. 2006. 'Burma (Myanmar)'. In Greg Fealy and Virginia Hooker (eds), *Voices of Islam in Southeast Asia: A Contemporary Sourcebook*, pp. 23–9. Singapore: Institute of Southeast Asian Studies.

Larson, G.J. 2001. *Religion and Personal Law in Secular India: A Call to Judgment*. Bloomington: Indiana University Press.

Larsson, Tomas. 2015. 'Monkish Politics in Southeast Asia: Religious Disenfranchisement in Comparative and Theoretical Perspective'. *Modern Asian Studies*, 49(1): 40–82.

Lau, Martin. 2010. 'Sharia and National Law in Pakistan'. In Jan Michiel Otto (ed.), *Sharia Incorporated: A Comparative Overview of the Legal Systems of Twelve Muslim Countries in Past and Present*. Leiden: Leiden University Press.

Laurie, William F. 1853. *The Second Burmese War: A Narrative of the Operations at Rangoon in 1852*. London; Bombay: Smith, Elder & Co. Available at https://archive.org/details/secondburmesewaroolaur.

Leach, Edmund. 1973. 'Buddhism in the Post-Colonial Political Order in Burma and Ceylon'. *Daedalus*, 102(1): 29–54.

———. 1961. 'Polyandry, Inheritance and the Definition of Marriage'. In Edmund Leach (ed.), *Rethinking Anthropology*, pp. 105–13. London: The Athlone Press.

Lee, Ronan. 2014. 'A Politician, Not an Icon: Aung San Suu Kyi's Silence on Myanmar's Muslim Rohingya'. *Islam and Christian-Muslim Relations*, 25(3): 321.

Leehey, Jennifer. 2010. *Open Secrets, Hidden Meanings: Censorship, Esoteric Power, and Contested Authority in Urban Burma in the 1990s*. Doctoral dissertation in Anthropology. Seattle, WA: University of Washington.

———. 2012. 'Reading "Saturn": Interpretive Practice Under Censorship in Burma.' *Journal of Burma Studies*, 16(1): 1–25.

Lefort, Claude. 1988. *Democracy and Political Theory*. University of Minnesota Press.

Leider, Jacques. 1998. 'These Buddhist Kings with Muslim Names. A Discussion of Muslim influence in the Mrauk-U period'. In Richard, Pierre and Francois Robinne (eds), *Études Birmanes. Melanges en Homage à Denise Bernot*, pp. 189–215. Paris: EFEO.

Lester, Robert C. 1973. *Theravada Buddhism in Southeast Asia*. Ann Arbor: University of Michigan Press.

Lewa, Chris. 2001. 'The Rohingya: Forced Migration and Statelessness'. In Omprakash Mishra (ed.), *Forced Migration in South Asian Region*. New Delhi: Lancer Books.

Leyland, Peter. 2009. 'Thailand's Troubled South: Examining the Case for Devolution from a Comparative Perspective'. *Australian Journal of Asian Law*, 11(1): 1–28.

Leibold, James. 2011. 'Blogging Alone: China, the Internet, and the Democratic Illusion?' *The Journal of Asian Studies*, 70(4): 1023–41.

Liebermann, Victor B. 1984. *Burmese Administrative Cycles: Anarchy and Conquest c 1580 – 1760*. Princeton: Princeton University Press.

Lidauer, Michael and Gilles Saphy. 2014. 'Elections and the Reform Agenda'. In Melissa Crouch and Tim Lindsey (eds), *Law, Society and Transition in Myanmar*, pp. 201–24. Oxford: Hart Publishing.

Lintner, Bertil. 2009. *The Resistance of the Monks: Buddhism and Activism in Burma*. New York: Human Rights Watch.

————. 1990. *The Rise and Fall of the Communist Party of Burma*. Cornell: SEAP Publications.

Liow, Joseph Chinyong. 2009. *Islam, Education and Reform in Southern Thailand*. Singapore: ISEAS.

Long, Kayleigh. 2014. 'Monk Expands Teachings.' *The Myanmar Times*. 24 March, 1.

Lowe, Lisa. 2012. 'Metaphors of Globalization'. In Joe Parker, Mary Romero, and Ranu Samantrai (eds), *Interdisciplinarity and Social Justice: Revisioning Academic Accountability*, 37–62. SUNY Press.

Lwin, Nay San. 2012. 'Making Rohingya Stateless'. *New Mandala*. Available at http://asiapacific.anu.edu.au/newmandala/2012/10/29/making-rohingya-statelessness/.

Mahajani, Usha. 1960. *The Role of Indian Minorities in Burma and Malaya*. Bombay: Vora.

Mahaḷayā. 2013. 'kāttaṇkuḍiya arābi rājadhāniyakda?' *Siṃhala Rāvaya* (Newspaper) [undated].

Mahanama. 1912. *Mahavamsa: the Great Chronicle of Ceylon* (W. Geiger. trans.). Delhi: Asian Educational Services.

Maine, Henry Sumner. 1986. *Ancient Law: Its Connection with the Early History of Society, and its Relation to Modern Ideas*. Tucson: University of Arizona Press.

Mathieson, D. S. 2009. 'Plight of the Damned: Burma's Rohingya'. *Global Asia* 4(1): 86–91.

Matthews, Bruce. 1995. 'Religious Minorities in Myanmar: Hints of the Shadow'. *Contemporary South Asia*, 4(3): 287.

Maung Maung. 2008. 'M.A. Raschid'. In Robert Taylor (ed.), *Dr Maung Maung: Gentleman, Scholar, Patriot*. Singapore: ISEAS.

————. 1963. *Law and Custom in Burma and the Burmese Family*. The Hague: Martinus Nijhoff.

————. 1962. *A Trial in Burma: The Assassination of Aung Sang*. The Hague: Martinus Nijhoff.

————. 1959. *Burma's Constitution*. The Hague: Martinus Nijhoff.

Maung Maung, U. 1989. *Burmese Nationalist Movements, 1940–1948*. Edinburgh: Kiscadale Publications.

Maung Maung Ni. 2010. 'National Democratic Party for Development Presents its Policy, Stance and Work Programmes'. *The New Light of Myanmar.* 9 October.

May Sitt Paing. 2013. 'Buddhist Committee's 969 Prohibitions Prompts Meeting of Movement Backers'. *The Irrawaddy.* 10 September. Available at http://www.irrawaddy.org/security/buddhist-committees-969-prohibitions-prompts-meeting-of-movement-backers.html.

McCargo, Duncan. 2012. *Mapping National Anxieties: Thailand's Southern Conflict.* NIAS Press.

McGilvray, D.B. 1998. 'Arabs, Moors and Muslims: Sri Lankan Muslim Ethnicity in Regional Perspective'. *Contributions to Indian Sociology,* 32(2): 433–83.

———. 2008. *Crucible of Conflict: Tamil and Muslim Society on the East Coast of Sri Lanka.* Durham: Duke University Press.

———. 2011. 'Sri Lankan Muslims: between Ethno-Nationalism and the Global Ummah'. *Nations and Nationalism,* 17(1): 45–64.

McKenna, Thomas M. 1978. *Muslim Rulers and Rebels: Everyday Politics and Armed Separatism in the Southern Philippines.* Berkeley: University of California Press.

McLaughlin, Tim. 2014. 'Enumeration of Rohingya a "complete failure", Census Observers Say'. *The Myanmar Times.* 19 August. Available at www.mmtimes.com/index.php/national-news/11424-enumeration-of-rohingya-a-complete-failure-census-observers-say.html.

Mehden, Fred von der. 1960. 'Burma's Religious Campaign against Communism'. *Pacific Affairs,* 33(3): 290–99.

Memon World. 2014. Pakistan. Available at www.memon-world.net/bhistory1.htm.

Mendelson, E Michael. 1975. *Sangha and State: A Study of Monastic Sectarianism and Leadership.* Ithaca: Cornell University Press.

Metcalf, Barbara. 1996. 'Islam and Women: The Case of the *Tablīghi Jama`at,*' *SEHR,* 5(1) *Contested Polities.* Available at http://www.stanford.edu/group/SHR/5-1/text/metcalf.html.

———. 1982. *Islamic Revival in British India: Deoband 1860–1900.* Princeton: Princeton University Press.

Mettashin Shwe Pyi Thar. 2003. *Myanma-to-e A-thak.* Yangon: Chotaythan Sape.

Mezzofiore, Gianluca. 2014. 'Wirathu's 'Buddhist Woman Raped' Facebook Post Stokes Anti-Muslim Violence in Mandalay.' *International Business Times UK.* 2 July. http://www.ibtimes.co.uk/wirathus-buddhist-woman-raped-facebook-post-stokes-anti-muslim-violence-mandalay-1455069.

Michaels, Samantha. 2013. 'Suu Kyi criticizes gender bias in Burma universities.' *The Irrawaddy.* 6 December. Available at http://www.irrawaddy.org/burma/suu-kyi-criticizes-gender-bias-burma-universities.html.

Miller, Vincent. 2008. 'New Media, Networking and Phatic Culture.' *Convergence: The International Journal of Research into New Media Technologies*, 14(4): 387–400.

Millward, Steven. 2014. 'Viber Claims Early Lead in Myanmar with 5M Registered Users.' *Tech in Asia*. 1 August, Available at http://www.techinasia.com/viber-5-million-users-in-myanmar/.

Ministry of Education. 2014a. 'List of Universities, Degree Colleges and Colleges under Respective Ministries.' Department of Higher Education. Available at http://www.myanmar-education.edu.mm/dhel/999-2/ (accessed 2 May 2014).

————. 2014b. Department of Higher Education. Available at http://www.myanmar-education.edu.mm/universities-list-2/.

Mizzima News. 2013. *Yone-kyi-myat-noe 969 nhnit la-gaung ei ga-yat-myar (Believed and Admired 969 and its Controversies).* 5 April. Available at http://mizzimaburmese.com/2013-10-20-17-18-22/2013-10-20-16-34-57/item/11293-2013-10-15-03-02-10.

Mizzima News. 2010. *Kaman National Progressive Party – KNPP.* 12 July. Available at www.bnionline.net/index.php/news/mizzima/8920-kaman-national-progressive-party--knpp.html.

Moomal, Ebrahim C. 1996. *The End of the World. Random, Ramant and Runaway thoughts on the Ultimate Journey.* Pretoria: Laudium.

Morse, Jedidiah and Richard C. Morse. 1823. 'Rangoon'. In *A New Universal Gazetteer.* New Haven: Converse.

Muddit, Jessica. 2014. 'Rohingya call on govt for inclusion in 2014 census'. *Democratic Voice of Burma.* 13 January. Available at www.dvb.no/news/rohingya-parties-call-on-govt-for-inclusio-in-census-burma-myanmar/36023.

Mulla, Sir Dinshaw Fardunji. 2013. *Mulla's Principles of Mahomedan Law,* revised by Iqbal Ali Khan. 20th ed. India: LexisNexis.

Muslim Aid (MA). 2014. *Statement on Closure of Rohingya Projects in Bangladesh.* February. Available at www.muslimaid.org/media-centre/news/muslim-aids-statement-on-closure-of-rohingya-projects-in-bangladesh/.

————. 2014a. *Myanmar Update, June 2014.* www.muslimaid.org/campaigns/current-emergencies/myanmar-burma-appeal/.

————. 2013. *Muslim Aid and Al Asmakh Charity, Qatar sign MOU for humanitarian activities,* 12 February. Available at www.muslimaid.org/media-centre/press-release/muslim-aid-and-al-asmakh-charity-qatar-sign-mou-for-humanitarian-activities/.

Mya Than. 1993. 'Jairampur: A Profile of an Indian Community in Rural Burma'. In K.S. Sandhu and A. Mani (eds), *Indian Communities in Southeast Asia,* pp. 683–706. Singapore: Institute of Southeast Asian Studies.

Myo Myo. 2010. 'Party Works to Enlist Members'. *The Myanmar Times*. 19 July. Available at www.mmtimes.com/index.php/national-news/5088-party-works-to-enlist-members.html.

Myo Win. 2011. *Muslims in Myanmar: An Introduction*. Prepared for Hillary Clinton (unpublished). Yangon: December.

Nardi, Dominic and Kyaw Lwin. 2014. 'Understanding the Myanmar Supreme Court's Docket: An Analysis of Case Topics from 2007 to 2011'. In Melissa Crouch and Tim Lindsey (eds), *Law, Society and Transition in Myanmar*. pp. 95–116. Oxford: Hart Publishing.

Narinjara. 2013. *Ethnic party to scrutinize Kaman population in Burma*. 29 November. Available at http://www.narinjara.com/main/index.php/ethnic-party-to-scrutinize-kaman-population-in-burma/.

NDPD. 2012. 'National Democratic Party for Development'. 4 July. Paper submitted to the *Pyidaungsu Hluttaw*, Yangon.

Nemoto, Kei. 2013. 'The Rohingya Issue: A Thorny Obstacle between Burma (Myanmar) and Bangladesh'. *Burma Library*. Available at www.burmalibrary.org/docs14/Kei_Nemoto-Rohingya.pdf

Nielsen, Jørgen. 2008. 'Review: Islam in Europe.' 62 *Middle East Journal*. 144–8.

Nigam, Ashok. 2012. Remarks at the *Workshop on Relief, Rehabilitation, Rule of Law, and Sustainable Development in Rakhine State*, pp. 22–23 September. Naypyidaw, Myanmar.

Noor, Farish A, Martin van Bruinessen and Yoginder Sikand (eds). 2008. *The Madrasah in Asia: Political Activism and Transnational Linkages*. Amsterdam: University of Amsterdam Press.

Noor, Farish A. 2012. *Islam on the Move: The Tablighi Jama'at in Southeast Asia*. Amsterdam: Amsterdam University Press.

———. 2009a. *The Tablighi Jama'at Movement in the Provinces of Southern Thailand Today: Networks and Modalities*. RSIS Working Paper 174. Available at http://www.rsis.edu.sg/wp-content/uploads/rsis-pubs/WP174.pdf.

———. 2009b. *The Spread of the Tablighi Jama'at Across Western, Central and Eastern Java and the Role of the Indian Muslim Diaspora*. RSIS Working Paper 175. Available at http://www.rsis.edu.sg/wp-content/uploads/rsis-pubs/WP175.pdf.

Nu, U. 1951. *From Peace to Stability*. Ministry of Information: Government of the Union of Burma.

Nyi Nyi Kyaw. 2008. *Rohingya Muslims: Myanmar's Forgotten People*. RSIS Commentaries No 12/2008. Singapore.

———. n.d. *Islamic Education in Myanmar* (unpublished paper).

O'Connor, V.C. Scott. 1904. *The Silken East*. London: Hutchinson & Co.

———. 1907. *Mandalay and Other Cities of the Past in Burma*. London: Hutchinson & Co.

O'Sullivan, Meghan. 1999. 'Conflict As Catalyst: Changing Politics of the Sri Lankan Muslims.' In Siri Gamage and I.B. Watson (eds) *Conflict and Community in Contemporary Sri Lanka*, pp. 53–78. London: Sage Publications.

Office of the UN Special Advisor on the Prevention of Genocide. 2010. *Analysis Framework*. Available at http://www.un.org/en/preventgenocide/adviser/pdf/osapg_analysis_framework.pdf.

Omar Myint Naing. 2013. *786 Khu-hnit-ya-shit-sè-chauk Hu-thi* (What is 786?). Yangon: Kan Sape.

Ooi, Gin Keat. 2004. *Southeast Asia: A Historical Encyclopaedia from Angkor Wat to East Timor*. Santa Barbara: ABC-Clio.

Osada, Noriyuki. 2011. *An Embryonic Border: Racial Discourses and Compulsory Vaccination for Indian Immigrants at Ports in Colonial Burma, 1870–1937*. Moussons: Recherche en sciences humaines sur l'Asie due Sud-Est 17: 145–64.

Osborn, Michelle. 2008. 'Fuelling the Flames: Rumour and Politics in Kibera.' *Journal of Eastern African Studies*, 2(2): 315–27.

Pacitto, Julia. 2013. 'Writing the "Other" into Humanitarian Discourse'. *Refugee Studies Centre Working Paper Series* 93 (August): 1–37.

Palmer, Victoria. 2011. 'Analysing Cultural Proximity: Islamic Relief Worldwide and Rohingya refugees in Bangladesh'. *Development in Practice*. 21(1): 96.

Pan Eiswe Star. 2008. 'Tourism industry not new to the Golden Land'. *The Myanmar Times*. 6–12 October, Vol 22.

Parnini, Syeda Naushin. 2013. 'The Crisis of the Rohingya as a Muslim Minority in Myanmar and Bilateral Relations with Bangladesh'. *Journal of Muslim Minority Affairs*, 33(2): 281.

Parnini, Syeda Naushin, Mohammad Redzuan Othman and Amer Saifude Ghazali. 2013. 'The Rohingya Refugee Crisis and Bangladesh-Myanmar Relations,' *Asian and Pacific Migration Journal*, 22(1): 133.

Pathi U Ko Ko Lay. n.d. *Myanma Naingngan Hnint Islam Thathena* (The Union of Myanmar and the Religion of Islam). unedited version, n. p.

Pearn, Bertie R. 1939. *A History of Rangoon*. Rangoon: American Baptist Mission Press.

Pedersen, Morten B. 2012. 'Rethinking International Assistance to Myanmar in a Time of Transition'. In Nick Cheesman, Monique Skidmore and Trevor Wilson (eds), *Myanmar's Transition: Openings, Obstacles and Opportunities*. Singapore: ISEAS.

Pemberton, Robert Boileau. 1835. *Report on the Eastern Frontier of British India*. Calcutta: Baptist Mission Press.

People's Literature Committee. 1961. *Who's Who in Burma*. People's Literature Committee and House, 54 Merchant Street, Rangoon.

Perera, Yoshitha. 2014. 'BBS – 969 sign pact on anti extremism' *Daily Mirror.* 30 September. Available at http://www.dailymirror.lk/news/53156-bbs-969-sign-pact-on-anti-extremism-.html (accessed 18 February 2015).

Petersen, Marie Juul. 2012. 'Trajectories of Transnational Muslim NGOs'. *Development in Practice*, 22(5–6): 763.

Phelan, Jessica. 2013. "Myanmar: Anti-Muslim Violence Spreads Beyond Meikhtila." *Global Post*, March 25. Available at http://www.globalpost.com/dispatch/news/regions/asia-pacific/myanmar/130325/myanmar-sectarian-violence-meikhtila.

Physicians for Human Rights. 2013a. *Massacre in Central Burma: Muslim Students Terrorized and Killed in Meiktila*. Available at http://physiciansforhumanrights.org/library/reports/meiktila-report-may-2013.html.

———. 2013b. *Patterns of Anti-Muslim Violence in Burma: A Call for Accountability and Prevention*. Available at physiciansforhumanrights.org.

Po Kan Kaung. 1992. 'Dhammantaraya Rohingya (Rohingya as Danger to Dhamma)'. *Myetkinthit*, 25 (May): 87–104.

Prasse-Freeman, Elliott. 2012. 'Power, Civil Society, and an Inchoate Politics of the Daily in Burma/Myanmar.' *The Journal of Asian Studies*, 71(2): 371–97.

Proceedings of the Indian Legislative Assembly. 1939. New Delhi.

Pudjiastuti, Tri Nuke. 2000. 'Problematika Minoritas Muslim di Filipina, Thailand, dan Myanmar: Catatan Pendahuluan' [Problems of Muslim Minorities in the Philippines, Thailand and Myanmar: Preliminary notes). In M. Riza Sihbudi (ed.), *Problematika Minoritas Muslim di Asia Tenggara: Kasus Moro, Pattani, dan Rohingya* [Problems of Muslim Minorities in Southeast Asia: The Cases of Moro, Pattani and the Rohingya]. Jakarta: Puslitbang Politik dan Kewilayahan, Lembaga Ilmu Pengetahuan Indonesia.

Rahman, Ahmad Azam Abdul. 2012. *Rohingya: The Most Persecuted and Forgotten Muslim Minority*. Istanbul: UNIW theunity.org.

———. 2012a. *GPM 2nd Humanitarian Mission to Myanmar: A Preliminary Report*. 29 August. Available at Gpm.com.my

Rahman, Utpala. 2010. 'The Rohingya Refugee: A Security Dilemma for Bangladesh'. *Journal of Immigrant and Refugee Studies*, 8: 233.

Ragland, Thomas. 1994. 'Burma's Rohingyas in Crisis: Protection of "Humanitarian" Refugees under international law'. *Boston College Third World Law Journal*, 14(2): 301.

Rajagopal, Arvind. 2001. *Politics After Television: Religious Nationalism and the Reshaping of the Indian Public*. Cambridge, UK: Cambridge University Press.

Ramakrishna, Kumar. 2013. 'Non-violent Extremism: The Case of Wirathu in Myanmar'. *RSIS Commentaries*. Singapore: Nanyang Technological University. Available at dr.ntu.edu.sg/bitstream/handle/10220/20108/RSIS1452013.pdf?sequence=1.

Rao, Mohan. 2011. 'Love Jihad and Demographic Fears'. *Indian Journal of Gender Studies*, 18(3): 425–30.

Razak, Myat Htoo. 2007. *U-Razak of Burma: A Teacher, A Leader, A Martyr.* Bangkok: OS Printing House.

Report on the Administration of British Burma during 1881–82. Rangoon: Government Press.

Republic of the Union of Myanmar. 2014. *The Population and Housing Census of Myanmar 2014. Summary of Provisional Results.* August. Department of Population, Ministry of Immigration and Population, Myanmar.

Reuters. 2014. 'Ooredoo, Telenor Finally Set to Get Myanmar Telecoms Licences', 29 January 2014. Available at http://www.reuters.com/article/2014/01/29/myanmar-telecoms-idUSL3N0L32U120140129.

Rogers, John D. 2004. 'Early British Rule and Social Classification in Sri Lanka.' *Modern Asian Studies*, 38(3): 625–47.

Rosen, Laurence. 2000. *The Justice of Islam: Comparative Perspectives on Islamic Law and Society.* Oxford: Oxford University Press.

Russell, Jon. 2014. 'Despite Claims of a Decline in the West, Facebook Is Stronger Than Ever in the Rest of the World.' *The Next Web.* 27 January. Available at http://thenextweb.com/facebook/2014/01/27/despite-claims-of-a-decline-in-the-west-facebook-is-stronger-than-ever-in-the-rest-of-the-world/.

Sajāwandī, Sirāj al-Dīn Muḥammad ibn Muḥammad. 1959. *al Sirājiyyah, or the Mahommedan law of inheritance.* With notes and appendix, by Almaric Rumsey. Reprinted from the translation of Sir William Jones, published at Calcutta, in 1792. Lahore: Premier Book House.

Sanay Lin. 2014. 'Ma-Ha-Na ko Ma-Ba-Tha we pan mi ma hôk' [*Ma-Ba-Tha* Will Not Criticize *Ma-Ha-Na*]. *The Irrawaddy.* 21 June. Available at http://burma.irrawaddy.org/news/2014/06/21/60779.html.

Sandy, May. 2012. 'Saudi Arabia donates $1m to UNHCR for health, education'. *Myanmar Times*, 10–16 September.

Sarkisyanz, Emanuel. 1965. *Buddhist Backgrounds of the Burmese Revolution.* The Hague: Martinus Nijhoff.

Schissler, Matt. 2013a. 'Everyday Ethnic Tensions in Myanmar'. *New Mandala.* 27 March. Available at http://asiapacific.anu.edu.au/newmandala/2013/03/27/everyday-ethnic-tensions-in-myanmar/.

———. 2013b. 'Conversations after Lashio'. *New Mandala.* 3 June. Available at asiapacific.anu.edu.au/newmandala/2013/06/03/conversations-after-lashio/.

———. 2013c. 'After the Bombings: 15 October in Yangon'. *New Mandala.* 16 October. Available at http://asiapacific.anu.edu.au/newmandala/2013/10/16/15-october-in-yangon-after-the-bombings/.

————. 2014a. 'Sleeping Dogs'. *New Mandala*. 20 January. Available at asiapa-cific.anu.edu.au/newmandala/2014/01/20/sleeping-dogs/.

————. 2014b. 'May Flowers', *New Mandala*. 17 May. Available at http://asia-pacific.anu.edu.au/newmandala/2014/05/17/may-flowers/.

Schmidt, Eric. 2013. 'Unique Opportunity: Eric Schmidt, CEO, Google, on Unleashing the Power of Information'. Myanmar Information and Communication Technology Park, Yangon, March 22. Available at http://www.oxfordbusinessgroup.com/news/unique-opportunity-eric-schmidt-ceo-google-unleashing-power-information.

Schober, Juliane. 2010. *Modern Buddhist Conjunctures in Myanmar: Cultural Narratives, Colonial Legacies, and Civil Society*. Honolulu: University of Hawaii Press.

————. 2006. 'Buddhism, Violence and the State in Burma (Myanmar) and Sri Lanka.' In L.E. Cady and S.W. Simon (eds), *Religion and Conflict in South and Southeast Asia: Disrupting Violence*, pp. 51–69. Oxon: Routledge.

Schonthal, Benjamin. 2014. 'The Legal Regulation of Buddhism in Contemporary Sri Lanka.' In R. French and M. Nathan (eds), *Buddhism and Law: An Introduction*. Cambridge: Cambridge University Press.

Scobey-Thal, Jake. 2014. 'This Is the Modern Axis of Buddhist Hate'. *Foreign Policy (blog)*. March 7, 2014. Available at http://blog.foreignpolicy.com/posts/2014/03/07/this_is_the_modern_axis_of_buddhist_hate.

Scott, James C. 1998. *Seeing Like a State: How Certain Schemes to Improve the Human Condition Have Failed*. New Haven, Conn: Yale University Press.

————. 2009. *The Art of Not Being Governed: An Anarchist History of Upland Southeast Asia*. New Haven, Conn: Yale University Press.

Seekins, Donald M. 2011. *State and Society in Modern Rangoon*. London: Routledge.

Selth, Andrew. 2012. 'Myanmar's Police Forces: Coercion, Continuity and Change'. *Contemporary Southeast Asia*, 34(1): 53.

————. 2011. 'Thein Sein as Myanmar's Gorbachev.' *Asia Times*. 19 October. http://www.atimes.com/atimes/Southeast_Asia/MJ19Ae01.html.

————. 2010. 'Modern Burma Studies: A Survey of the Field'. *Modern Asian Studies*, 44(2): 401.

————. 2008. 'Even Paranoids Have Enemies: Cyclone Nargis and Myanmar's Fears of Invasion'. *Contemporary Southeast Asia*, 30(3): 379.

————. 2008a. 'Burma's 'Saffron Revolution' and the Limits of International Influence'. *Australian Journal of International Affairs*, 62(3): 281.

————. 2004. 'Burma's Muslims and the War on Terror'. *Studies in Conflict & Terrorism*, 27(2): 107–26.

———. 2003. *Burma's Muslims: Terrorists or Terrorised?* Canberra Papers on Strategy and Defence Number 150. Canberra: Strategic and Defence Studies Centre, Australian National University.

———. 1986. 'Race and Resistance in Burma, 1942–1945'. *Modern Asian Studies*, 20(3): 483–507.

Sen, Ronojoy. 2010. *Faith, Religious Secularism and the Indian Supreme Court*. Oxford: Oxford University Press.

Sen, B.K. 2001. 'Women and Law in Burma'. *Legal Issues on Burma Journal* No.9, August.

Shaw Zan, U and Aye Chan. 2005. *Influx-Viruses The Illegal Muslims of Arakan*. New York: Arakanese in United States.

Shwe Sone Chaung Sayadaw Ashin Vicitta Linkara. 2013. *Sangha saw ka nga-yè thwa* [If you disrespect the Sangha, you shall go to Hell!]. Yangon: Alin Ein.

Si Thu Lwin. 2014. 'A Town Stained in Blood Takes Tentative Steps Toward Peace.' *The Myanmar Times*. 21 March. Available at http://www.mmtimes.com/index.php/national-news/9924-a-town-stained-in-blood-takes-tentative-steps-toward-peace.html.

Sikand, Yoginder. 2002. *The Origins and Development of the Tablighi Jama'at (1920–2000): A Cross-country Comparative Study*. Hyderabad, India: Orient Longman.

Skidmore, Monique. 2006. 'Scholarship, Advocacy and the Politics of Engagement in Burma (Myanmar)'. In Victoria Sanford and Asale Angel-Ajani (eds), *Engaged Observer: Anthropology, Advocacy and Activism*. London: Rutgers University Press.

———. 2004. *Karaoke Fascism: Burma and the Politics of Fear*. Philadelphia: University of Pennsylvania Press.

———. 2003. 'Darker Than Midnight: Fear, Vulnerability, and Terror Making in Urban Burma (Myanmar)'. *American Ethnologist*, 30(1): 5–21.

Sladen, Edward B. 1870. *Trade Through to China: An Address to the Glasgow Chamber of Commerce*. Glasgow.

Smith, Donald Eugene. 1965. *Religion and Politics in Burma*. Princeton: Princeton University Press.

Smith, Martin. 1999. *Burma: Insurgency and the Politics of Ethnicity*. Revised edition. Bangkok: White Lotus.

Spiro, Melford E. 1982. *Buddhism and Society: A Great Tradition and its Burmese Vicissitudes*. 2nd ed. Berkeley: University of California Press.

———. 1974. 'Book Review, The Muslims of Burma: A Study of a Minority Group by Moshe Yegar'. *Journal of Asian Studies*, 33(2).

———. 1977. *Kinship and Marriage in Burma: A Cultural and Psychodynamic Analysis*. Berkeley: University of California Press.

———. 1967. *Burmese Supernaturalism*. Englewood Cliffs: Prentice-Hall.

Srisamorn, Phoosuphanusorn. 2014. 'Telenor on $1bn Roll in Myanmar.' *Bangkok Post*. 8 March.   Available   at http://www.bangkokpost.com/ business/news/398743/.

State Department. 2006. *Burma: International Religious Freedom Report 2005*. United States Department of State. Available at www.state.gov/j/drl/rls/ irf/2005/51506.htm.

State Sangha Mahanayaka Committee. 2008. *Sangha nayaka let swè* [Handbook of Sangha Nayaka]. Yangon: State Sangha Mahanayaka Committee.

Stein, Sabina A. 2013. *Critical Reflection: Presentation of the Report of the Inquiry Commission on the Sectarian Violence in Rakhine State*. Zurich: Swiss Peace and ETH Zurich. Available at www.swisspeace.ch.

Steinberg, David. 2001. *Burma: The State of Myanmar*. Washington: Georgetown University Press.

Stephens, Matthew. 2011. *Islamic Law in the Philippines: Between Appeasement and Neglect*. ARC Federation Fellowship Policy Paper, Melbourne University. Available at http://www.law.unimelb.edu.au/files/dmfile/ Stephens_web2.pdf.

Sterne, Jonathan. 2003. "Bourdieu, Technique And Technology." *Cultural Studies*, 17(3-4): 367–89.

Stockwell, Foster. 2003. *Westerners in China*. London: MacFarland & Company, Inc., Publishers.

Strawson, John. 1999. 'Islamic Law and English Texts'. In Eve Darian-Smith and Peter Fitzpatrick (eds), *Laws of the Postcolonial*, pp. 109–26. Ann Arbor: The University of Michigan Press.

Subramanian, Narendra. 2014. *Nation and Family: Personal Law, Cultural Pluralism, and Gendered Citizenship in India*. Stanford: Stanford University Press.

Sulaiman, Mohammed Mohiyuddin Mohammed. 2011. 'Keeping Islamic Faith and Serving Buddhist State: Muffasir of al-Qur'an in Burmese, (Thiri Pyan Chi) Ghazi Mohd Hashim (1917–1993)'. Working Paper, Universiti Kebangsaan Malaysia (National University of Malaysia).

———. 2008. 'Islamic Education in Myanmar: A Case Study'. In Monique Skidmore and Trevor Wilson (eds), *Dictatorship, Disorder and Decline in Myanmar*, pp. 177–91. Canberra: ANU E-Press.

Szep, Jason. 2013. 'Special Report: Buddhist Monks Incite Muslim Killings in Myanmar'. *Reuters*. 8 April. Available at http://www.reuters. com/article/2013/04/08/us-myanmar-violence-specialreport-idUS-BRE9370AP20130408.

Tagliacozzo, Eric. 2004. 'Ambiguous Commodities, Unstable Frontiers: The Case of Burma, Siam, and Imperial Britain, 1800–1900'. *Comparative Studies in History and Society*, 46(2): 354–77.

Taufiqurrahman, M. 2012. 'Kalla pledges aid to Myanmar Rohingya'. *The Jakarta Post*. 10 September.

Taw Sein Ko. 1913. *Burmese Sketches*, vol. 1. Rangoon: n.p.

Taylor, Robert. 2006. 'The Legal Status of Indians in Contemporary Burma'. In K.S. Sandhu and A. Mani (eds), *Indian Communities in Southeast Asia*. Singapore: ISEAS.

———. 2009. *The State in Myanmar*. 2nd ed. London: C. Hurst; Honolulu: University of Hawaii Press.

———. 2005. 'Do States Make Nations? The Politics of Identity in Myanmar Revisited'. *South East Asia Research*, 13(3): 261.

———. 1993. 'The Legal Status of Indians in Contemporary Burma'. In K.S. Sandhu and A. Mani (eds), *Indian Communities in Southeast Asia*, pp. 667–83. Singapore: Institute of Southeast Asian Studies.

Thailand Burma Border Consortium (TBBC). 2010. *Three Sides to Every Story: A Profile of Muslim Communities in the Refugee Camps of the Thailand Burma Border*. July. http://www.tbbc.org.

Thant Myint U. 2007. *The River of Lost Footsteps: A Personal History of Burma*. London: Faber & Faber.

———. 2001. *The Making of Modern Burma*. Cambridge: Cambridge University Press.

The Diplomat. 2013. 'The Mad Monks of Myanmar'. 9 July. Available at http://thediplomat.com/2013/07/the-mad-monks-of-myanmar.

The Irrawaddy Blog. 2014. 'Lo at Lo Pe Bôk Ko Peik Ta so Tè Yè Hmu Chat Win Kaung.' 2014. *The Irrawaddy Blog (Burmese)*. Available at http://burma.irrawaddy.org/interview/2014/07/04/61420.html.

The Riot Enquiry Committee. 1939. *Final Report of the Riot Enquiry Committee*. Rangoon: Government Printing Press.

The Star. 2014. 'Tech Sector Sizzles as Myanmar Embraces Internet for the Masses. 3 October. Available at http://www.thestar.com.my/Tech/Tech-News/2014/10/03/Tech-sector-sizzles-as-Myanmar-embraces-Internet-for-the-masses/.

The Voice Daily. 2013. '969 *tan-seik pyet-si-thu-ko taung-dan 2-hnit cha*' [Who Destroyed 969 Sticker Given 2-Year Prison Sentence]. 25 April: p 6.

Thet, Lwin. 2008. 'Indians in Myanmar'. In Kesavapany, K., Mani, A. and Ramasamy (eds), *Rising India and Indian Communities in East Asia*. Singapore: ISEAS Publications.

Tin Aung Kyaw. 2013. 'Buddhist Monk Wirathu Leads Violent National Campaign against Myanmar's Muslims'. *Global Post*. 21 June. Available at http://www.globalpost.com/dispatches/globalpost-blogs/groundtruth-burma/buddhist-monk-wirathu-969-muslims-myanmar.

Tin Hlaing Win. 2010. 'Kaman National Progressive Party presents its policy, stance and work programmes'. *The New Light of Myanmar*. 10 October.

Tin Win, U. 1986. *Chaye Kyunnot Akyaung Mathi Kaung Saya Mya* (Good Things to Learn From My Life). 1st edition. Yangon: Paung Laung.

Tinker, Hugh. 1993 [1974]. *A New System of Slavery: The Export of Indian Labour Overseas 1830–1920*. London: Hansib.

———. 1986. 'Indians in Southeast Asia: Imperial Auxiliaries.' In Colin Clarke, Ceri Peach and Steven Vertovec (eds), *South Asians Overseas: Migration and Ethnicity*, pp. 39–56. Cambridge: Cambridge University Press.

———. 1979. 'A Forgotten Long March: The Indian Exodus from Burma, 1942'. *Journal of Southeast Asian Studies*, 6(1): 1–15.

Tin Maung Maung Than. 1993. 'Some Aspects of Indians in Rangoon'. In K.S. Sandhu and A. Mani (eds), *Indian Communities in Southeast Asia*, pp. 585–623. Singapore: Institute of Southeast Asian Studies.

Tin Maung Maung Than and Moe Thuzar. 2012. 'Myanmar's Rohingya Dilemma'. *ISEAS Perspectives*. 9 July. Singapore.

Trager, Frank N. 1966. *Burma: From Kingdom to Republic, A Historical and Political Analysis*. London: Pall Mall Press.

Turner, Alicia. 2014. *Saving Buddhism: The Impermanence of Religion in Colonial Burma*. Honolulu: University of Hawaii Press.

Turnell, Sean. 2009. *Fiery Dragons: Banks, Moneylenders and Microfinance in Burma*. Copenhagen: NIAS Press.

UN Office for the Coordination of Humanitarian Affairs (UNOCHA). 2014. 'Myanmar: Internal Displacement in Rakhine State (1 May 2014)'. Available at http://www.refworld.org/docid/53bbbc6f4.html.

United Nations. 2012. *Rakhine Response Plan (Myanmar): 2012–June 2013 (Revision 16 November 2012)*. Yangon: United Nations.

UNHCR. 2014. 'More than 20,000 people risk all on Indian Ocean to reach safety: UNHCR report.' 22 August. Available at http://www.unhcr.org/53f741fc9.html

UNICEF. 2011. *Myanmar Multiple Indicator Cluster Survey 2009–2010: Monitoring the Situation of Children and Women*. October. The United Nations Children's Fund. Available at http://www.unicef.org/myanmar/MICS_Myanmar_Report_2009-10.pdf.

US Government. 1999. *Burma [Myanmar]: Information on Rohingya Refugees*. United States Bureau of Citizenship and Immigration Services. Available at www.refworld.org/docid/3ae6a6a41c.html.

Vargas, João H. Costa. 2008. 'Activist Scholarship: Limits and Possibilities in Times of Black Genocide'. In Charles R. Hale and Craig Calhoun (eds), *Engaging Contradictions: Theory, Politics, and Methods of Activist Scholarship*, 1st edition, 164–82. Berkeley: University of California Press.

Verdery, Katherine and Caroline Humphrey (eds). 2004. *Property in Question. Value Transformation in the Global Economy*. Oxford, New York: Berg.

Walton, Matthew J. 2013. 'The "Wages of Burman-ness:" Ethnicity and Burman Privilege in Contemporary Myanmar'. *Journal of Contemporary Asia*, 43(1): 1.

We Are Social. 2014. *2014 Asia-Pacific Digital Overview: We Are Social's Snapshot of Key Digital Data & Statistics*. Singapore. Available at http://www.slideshare.net/wearesocialsg/social-digital-mobile-in-apac.

Weber, Max. 1948. *From Max Weber: Essays in Sociology*. Translated, edited, and with an introduction, by H.H. Gerth and C. Wright Mills. London: Routledge, Taylor & Francis.

Weng, L. 2013. 'Extremist Monks Hold Talks Throughout Strife-Torn Arakan'. *The Irrawaddy*. 26 December. Available at http://www.irrawaddy.org/burma/extremist-monks-hold-talks-throughout-strife-torn-arakan-state.html.

———. 2014. 'Monks' Convention in Burma Calls for Restricting Buddhist-Muslim Marriage'. 13 June. *The Irrawaddy*. Available at http://www.irrawaddy.org/conflict/monks-convention-in-burma-calls-for-restricting-buddhist-muslim-marriage.html.

Williams, R.V. 2006. *Postcolonial Politics and Personal Laws: Colonial Legacies and the Indian State*. Oxford: Oxford University Press.

Willis, Nathan. 2014. 'The Potential Role of a Racial Discrimination Law in Myanmar'. *Forced Migration Review*, 45: 82.

Wilson, A. Jeyaratnam. 2000. *Sri Lankan Tamil Nationalism: Its Origins and Development in the Nineteenth and Twentieth Centuries*. London: Hurst & Co.

Win Kyi, U. 1984. *Mahamedin Upaday Aphwint Kyan*. Yangon: Mar Mar Publishing House.

Yegar, Moshe. 2002. *Between Integration and Secession: The Muslim Communities of the Southern Philippines, Southern Thailand and Western Burma/Myanmar*. New York: Lexington Books.

———. 1982. 'The Muslims of Burma.' In Israeli Raphael (ed.), *The Crescent in the East: Islam in Asia Minor*. Curzon Press: Great Britain, 102–39.

———. 1972. *The Muslims of Burma*. Germany: Otto Harrassowitz.

———. 1966. 'The Panthay (Chinese Muslims) of Burma and Yunnan'. *Journal of Southeast Asian History* 7(1): 73–85.

Yin May. 1962. *Greater Rangoon. A Study in Urban Geography*. Unpublished Master's Thesis, Dept. of Geography, University of Rangoon.

Zainuddin, A. Rahman. 2000. 'Sejarah Minoritas Muslim Di Filipina, Thailand, dan Myanmar' [History of Muslim Minorities in the Philippines, Thailand and Myanmar]. In M. Riza Sihbudi (ed.), *Problematika Minoritas Muslim di Asia Tenggara: Kasus Moro, Pattani, dan Rohingya* (Problems of

Muslim Minorities in Southeast Asia: The Cases of Moro, Pattani and the Rohingya). Jakarta: Puslitbang Politik dan Kewilayahan, Lembaga Ilmu Pengetahuan Indonesia.

Zan, Myint. 2004. 'A Comparison of the First and Fiftieth Year of Independent Burma's Law Reports', *Victoria University of Wellington Law Review*, 35(2): 385–426.

———. 2010. 'Judicial Independence in Burma: No March Backwards Towards the Past', *Asian Pacific Law and Policy Journal*, 5: 1–36.

Zawacki, Benjamin. 2013. 'Defining Myanmar's 'Rohingya Problem''. *Human Rights Brief* 20(2): 18–25.

Zin Nwe Myint. 1998. *Geographical Study of the Urban Growth of Yangon City.* Unpublished Master's Thesis, Department of Geography, University of Yangon.

Laws

Myanmar

Buddhist Women's Special Marriage and Succession Act 1954
Burma Laws Act 1898 (Burma Code, Vol. I)
Burma Dissolution of Muslim Marriages Act 1953
Caste Disabilities Removal Act 1850 (Burma Code, Vol. XI)
Citizenship Act No. 4/1982 (Pyithu Hluttaw Law)
Condominium Law No 20/2012 (Pyidaungsu Hluttaw Law)
Constitution of the Republic of the Union of Myanmar 2008
Constitution of the Socialist Republic of the Union of Burma 1974
Constitution of the Union of Burma 1947
Foreign Investment Law No 21/2012 (Pyidaungsu Hluttaw Law)
Foreign Investment Rules Notification No 11/2013, 31 January 2013
Guardianship and Wards Act 1890 (Burma Code, Vol. XI)
Kazis Act 1880 (Burma Code, Vol. XI)
Lower Burma Land Revenue Manual, containing the Land and Revenue Act; the Rules; Notifications; Directions and Forms in Force Thereunder and Certain Acts and Orders Supplementary to Them. 15 June 1945.
Mussalman Wakf Validating Act 1913 (Burma Code, Vol. XI)
Mussalman Wakf Act 1924 (Burma Code, Vol. IX)
Myanmar Buddhist Women's Special Marriage Act 50/2015
The Constitution (Third Amendment) Act 1961
The Courts Manual, Part III: Civil Procedure

The Muslim Divorce Act (Vol. XI, Act XVI, 1953)
The State Religion Promotion Act 1961
Union Citizenship Act No. 66/1948 (Pyithu Hluttaw Law)

Sri Lanka

Constitution of The Democratic Socialist Republic of Sri Lanka 1978
Muslim Intestate Succession Ordinance No. 10 of 1931
Muslim Marriage and Divorce Act No. 22 of 1955
Muslim Mosques and Charitable Trusts or Wakfs Act No. 51 of 1956
Muslim Personal Law (Shariat) Application Act 1937

Court Cases

Myanmar

Ahmed and another v Ma Pwa [1895] UBR 529
Ali Asghar v Mi Kra Hla U [1916] LBR 461
Asha Bibi v Ma Kyaw Yin and others (1920) BLT 217
Daw Ma La pa nga hnin Daw Myin Myin Kain pa le (2005) MLR (CI) 1–12
Daw Rahema hnin Daw Thi pa hnit (1975) BLR (CeC) 79–83
Daw Than Myin hnin Daw Tin Myin (ka) Daw Cho Tu (1993) MLR 66–72
Ma ôn Than ba ku-hnit-se hnin Ma Hla Hla Than pa le (2001) MLR (CI) 493–504
Mahmut Yakut Mansa hnin Ayut Itsamel Atiya (1973) BLR (CC) 15–17
Mahomed Ismail Ariff and others v Hajee Hamed Moolla Dawood and another; Mahomed Ismail Ariff and others v Mahomed Suleiman Ismail Jee and others [1916] The Burma Law Times 141
Ma Pwe v Ma Hla Win [1894] UBR 536
Mohamed Khan v Damayanthi Parekh and two others [1952] BLR (HC) 356
Rahima Bi alias Ma Ta v Mahomed Saleh [1914] LBR 54
Saya Chè hnin Daw Tin Tin pa shi (1994) MLR 45–55
Shahar Banoo v Aga Mahomed Jaffer Bindaneem and others [1904] LBR 66
U Ahmed Ebrahem Madar v M Chella Sarmi Swar bir & 10 others (1966) BLR 15
U Aung Nyun hnin Maung Ohn Myin (1981) MLR (CI) 1231
U Ba Min hnin Daw Mya Mya pa hnit (2007) MLR (CI) 75–89
U Bo Gyi hnin U Ko Gyi (1985) BLR (CeC) 6–8
U Chit Pe v Daw Mya May (1966) BLR 710

India

Hirabai v Sonabai. 1847. Perry's Oriental Cases, no. 110

Other Court Documents

Circular Memorandum No. 5 of 1910, The Registrar, Court of the Judicial Commissioner of Upper Burma to the Divisional and District Judges, 12 March 1910, in Upper Burma Rulings 1910-1913 vol. 1.

Circular Memorandum No. 13 of 1913, From The Registrar, Court of the Judicial Commissioner of Upper Burma to All Judges and Magistrates, 19 November 1913, in Upper Burma Rulings 1910–1913 vol. 1.

Circular of Memorandum No. 15 of 1913 From The Registrar, Court of the Judicial Commissioner of Upper Burma to All Magistrates and Judges, 27 November 1913, in Upper Burma Rulings, 1910–1913 vol. 1.

High Court Office Manual 1959 (2nd edition, first published 15 March 1930). Rangoon: Government Printing and Stationary.

High Court Office Manual 1930. High Court of Judicature. Rangoon, Burma: Supdt., Govt. Print and Stationery.

Index*

---

* In this index, Burmese names have been listed according to the first letter of their names, given that they do not have surnames.

Editor and Contributors

Judith Beyer is Junior Professor of Anthropology at the University of Konstanz in Germany. She holds a PhD in Anthropology from the Martin Luther University, Halle/Wittenberg, as well as an MA in Anthropology, Public and International Law, and Slavonic Studies from the Eberhard Karls University, Tübingen. Her current research project investigates land and property regimes, investments, and belongings of non-Buddhist religious communities in Yangon, Myanmar. In addition to her research in Myanmar, she works on Kyrgyzstan in Central Asia, where she has conducted fieldwork since 2003. She has published on legal pluralism, the State, constitutional politics, authority, descent and well-being.

Alistair D.B. Cook is Coordinator of the Humanitarian Assistance and Disaster Relief Programme, and Research Fellow at the Centre for Non-Traditional Security Studies, S. Rajaratnam School of International Studies, Nanyang Technological University, Singapore. He holds an undergraduate degree from the University of St Andrews, Master of Arts from Purdue University and a PhD from the University of Melbourne. His research interests are geographically focused on the Asia-Pacific, Myanmar in particular, and thematically focused on non-traditional security issues; notably the root causes of internal conflict and international responses. His most recent publication, as a co-editor, is *Irregular Migration and Human Security in East Asia* (Routledge, 2015). He teaches a masters level course on governance and security in Myanmar.

Melissa Crouch teaches in the Law Faculty with the University of New South Wales, Sydney, Australia. She is the author of *Law and Religion in Indonesia: Conflict and the Courts in West Java* (Routledge, 2014). She is the co-editor of *Law, Society and Transition in Myanmar* (Hart Publishing, 2014) with Tim Lindsey. She teaches in the areas of constitutional and administrative law, comparative law, Islamic law and the legal traditions of Southeast Asia. Previously she has held positions as a Research Fellow at the National University of Singapore; the International Institute of Asian Studies; and the Melbourne Law School at the University of Melbourne.

Nicholas Farrelly is Research Fellow at the College of Asia and the Pacific at Australian National University (ANU), Canberra, where he is also the Director of the ANU Myanmar Research Centre. After graduating from the ANU with First Class Honours and the University Medal, he completed Masters and Doctoral theses at Balliol College, University of Oxford, where he was a Rhodes Scholar. In 2006, he co-founded an academic website called New Mandala. Based at the ANU, it provides daily analysis of social, cultural and political issues in the Southeast Asian region, with particular attention to Thailand, Malaysia and Myanmar. In June 2013, Nicholas commenced an Australian Research Council fellowship for a three–year study of Myanmar's political cultures 'in transition'.

Abdul Ghafur Hamid (U Khin Maung Sein) is Professor of Law at the International Islamic University Malaysia, Kuala Lumpur. He obtained his LL.B. and LL.M. in International Law from the University of Yangon, Myanmar, and his Ph.D. in Law from the International Islamic University Malaysia. With nearly 40 years of teaching and research experience, he has authored or edited 15 books and published numerous articles in international and refereed journals. He is the author of the leading book published in Burmese on Islamic law in Myanmar (1984, revised 2014).

Stephen Keck is Academic Director and Professor of History at Emirates Diplomatic Academy in the United Arab Emirates. Before assuming the position of Academic Director he taught at the American University of Sharjah, the National University of Singapore and the

College of Charleston. Keck has just published *British Burma in the New Century, 1895–1918* (2015) and *Sir Arthur Helps and the Making of Victorianism* (2013). He is currently working on a study of John Ruskin's historical thought and his other research interests are focused upon Britain's engagement with Southeast Asia, the emergence of global education, and Victorian and Edwardian encounters with the Ottoman Empire. Beyond the classroom, Stephen Keck enjoys co-hosting programs about history as a guest on Dubai Eye 103.8.

Nyi Nyi Kyaw completed his PhD thesis in politics at the University of New South Wales in Canberra, Australia. He also has two Master's degrees in international political economy and in human rights and democratization (Asia Pacific) awarded by Nanyang Technological University and Sydney University, respectively.

Clark B. Lombardi is Professor of Law at the University of Washington Law School, Seattle, United States. A specialist in Islamic law and constitutional law, he also teaches courses in federalism, comparative law, and development law. Professor Lombardi has a Ph.D. in Religion from Columbia University, where he focused on Islamic law. He has lived, worked or studied in Indonesia, Yemen, Egypt, and Afghanistan. He is the author of *State Law as Islamic Law in Modern Egypt: The Incorporation of the Shari`a into Egyptian Constitutional Law* (Brill, 2006). Professor Lombardi has also been involved in projects advising on constitutional or legal reform in the Muslim world, including Iraq and Afghanistan.

Phyu Phyu Oo is currently working with UNAIDS, the Joint United Nations Programme on HIV/AIDS, Myanmar as an Institutional Development Consultant. She received her Masters in Public Health from Johns Hopkins Bloomberg School of Public Health in the United States. In 2005, she earned her bachelor degree from the University of Pharmacy, Yangon. She worked with the United Nations and other International NGOs as a medical supply chain specialist for about nine years, providing technical support to National Disease Control Programs for Myanmar. She also studied Chartered Institute of Procurement and Supply (CIPS) Level 4 and possesses extensive experience in procuring medical commodities and managing supply chains of Public Health Programs. While in Yangon, she has been active in organizing seminars for Muslim students to expand their knowledge and awareness of educational and job opportunities both within and outside Myanmar.

Matt Schissler is a doctoral student in the Department of Anthropology at the University of Michigan and a graduate fellow at the Weiser Center for Emerging Democracies. From 2007 to 2015, he lived and worked in Myanmar and Thailand, supporting local efforts to document human rights violations, work as independent journalists and community organizers, and prevent religious violence. In January 2015, he co-founded the Myanmar Media and Society Research Project, a partnership between the University of Oxford and the Myanmar ICT for Development Organization. His current research focuses on the mobilization of religious violence and telecommunications infrastructure. He speaks Burmese and holds an MSt in international human rights law from Oxford and BAs in politics and in rhetoric/ film studies from Whitman College.

Benjamin Schonthal is Senior Lecturer in Asian Religions at the University of Otago, New Zealand. He received his PhD in the field of History of Religions at the University of Chicago. His research examines the intersections of law, politics and religion in late-colonial and contemporary Southern Asia, with a particular focus on Sri Lanka. Ben is the author of *Buddhism, Politics and the Limits of Law: The Pyrrhic Constitutionalism of Sri Lanka*, forthcoming with Cambridge University Press.